Lecture Notes in Computer Science 9962

Commenced Publication in 1973
Founding and Former Series Editors:
Gerhard Goos, Juris Hartmanis, and Jan van Leeuwen

More information about this series at http://www.springer.com/series/7408

Federica Sarro · Kalyanmoy Deb (Eds.)

Search Based
Software Engineering

8th International Symposium, SSBSE 2016
Raleigh, NC, USA, October 8–10, 2016
Proceedings

 Springer

Editors
Federica Sarro
University College London
London
UK

Kalyanmoy Deb
Michigan State University
East Lansing, MI
USA

ISSN 0302-9743   ISSN 1611-3349 (electronic)
Lecture Notes in Computer Science
ISBN 978-3-319-47105-1   ISBN 978-3-319-47106-8 (eBook)
DOI 10.1007/978-3-319-47106-8

Library of Congress Control Number: 2016952530

LNCS Sublibrary: SL2 – Programming and Software Engineering

Printed on acid-free paper

This Springer imprint is published by Springer Nature
The registered company is Springer International Publishing AG
The registered company address is: Gewerbestrasse 11, 6330 Cham, Switzerland

Preface

Message from the SSBSE 2016 General Chair

In its eight edition, the conference was organized, for the first time, in North America. USA was proudly selected to host the event at Raleigh in North Carolina as a co-located event with ICMSE 2016. The decision to organize the event in USA was based on the great success of the first North American SBSE symposium (NasBASE15) organized by my research group in Detroit and mainly in recognition of the growing SBSE community in North America and different other locations around the world. SSBSE emphasized and introduced different originalities to the event. We organized, for the first time, a panel about SBSE support for blind and visually impaired programmers. We used a double-blind submission and review process providing a fair and relevant evaluation of the papers submitted to the conference. We attracted several sponsorship grants to support the conference from the National Science Foundation, the University of Michigan-Dearborn, etc. The program of the conference included full and short papers for the different tracks (technical, challenge, graduate students). The conference also attracted top keynote speakers from the computational search area including Carlos Coello Coello, Yew-Soon Ong, and Patrick Reed.

This great event would not have been possible without the tremndous help of many people, to whom I would like to express my gratitude. First, I would like to thank our program chairs, Federica Sarro (University College London, UK) and Kalyanmoy Deb (Michigan State University, USA). They led the review process with great dedication to every detail and made a huge effort to provide an outstanding and very high quality scientific program. I extend this recognition to all members of our Program Committee, for the dedicated work in the review and selection process of our papers. Next, I thank our graduate student track chairs, Ali Ouni (Osaka University, Japan) and Thelma Elita Colanzi Lopes (State University of Maringa, Brazil), and our SBSE challenge track chairs, Leandro Minku (University of Leicester, UK) and Tanja Vos (Polytechnical University of Valencia, Spain), for their hard work in organizing these two special tracks. I would also like to give special thanks to Wiem Mkaouer (University of Michigan, USA), our Web chair, for accepting the important challenge of creating and maintaining our website. Also, I thank our publicity chair, Yuanyuan Zhang (University College London, UK), for the important job of advertising our event. Finally, I also thank the SSBSE Steering Committee, chaired by Gordon Fraser (University of Sheffield, UK), for their vote of confidence in giving us the privilege of organizing SSBSE 2016. I must also mention and thank our long list of sponsors, who believed in our proposal and had confidence in me and in the field of SBSE. Without their support, SSBSE 2016 would not have been nearly so special. I hope you enjoy reading these proceedings as much as I enjoyed organizing the event.

August 2016

Marouane Kessentini

Message from the SSBSE 2016 Program Chairs

On behalf of the SSBSE 2016 Program Committee, we are pleased to present the proceedings of the 8th International Symposium on Search Based Software Engineering.

This year SSBSE was hosted in North America for the first time, continuing to bring together international researchers to exchange and discuss ideas and to celebrate the latest progress in this rapidly advancing field.

It was a privilege for us to serve as program chairs and we believe that the quality of the program reflects the excellent efforts of the authors, reviewers, keynote speakers, panel presenters, and organizers.

First and foremost we are grateful for the widespread participation and support from the SBSE community. This year, SSBSE attracted a high number of submissions (48 for all tracks) from 20 different countries, namely: UK (25 authors), Brazil (23 authors), USA (14 authors), Italy (11 authors), China (9 authors), India (6 authors), Spain (5 authors), Germany, Iran, Ireland, and Korea (4 authors), Austria (3 authors), Belgium, Canada, France, and Lebanon (2 authors), as well as Algeria, Denmark, Norway, and Poland (1 author).

We would like to thank all the authors for their high-quality contributions. Specifically, we received: 25 research papers, nine short papers, seven graduate student papers, and seven challenge papers. Given the success of the double-blind review procedure introduced for the first time in 2014 for the research track, this year we maintained it for all the tracks but the challenge track. Each submission was reviewed by at least three Program Committee members and followed by an on-line discussion. At the end of the review process, 13 papers were accepted to the research track, four papers were accepted to both the short paper and the graduate student tracks, and seven papers were accepted to the challenge track.

We would like to thank the Program Committee members and the additional reviewers for providing timely, detailed and constructive feedback, and for actively participating in the on-line discussions. To acknowledge their precious effort we decided to introduce in this edition an award for the best reviewer.

We also wish to thank the general chair, Marouane Kessentini, who brought SSBSE to North America and put on, together with his team, such an enjoyable event. We are grateful to Leandro Minku and Tanja Vos for organizing an exciting challenge track, and to Ali Ouni and Thelma Elita Colanzi Lopes for chairing the graduate student track, which attracted twice as many papers as in the previous year: Graduate students are a vital part of any research field. Last but not least, we thank Wiem Mkaouer (Web chair) and Yuanyuan Zhang (publicity chair), for their precious help in reaching out the community.

In addition to the eight technical sessions, covering a wide range of topics, SSBSE 2016 attendees had the opportunity to hear on advanced topics from three esteemed keynote speakers: Carlos Coello Coello, (hybrid multi-objective approaches), Yew-Soon

Ong (evolutionary multitasking), and Patrick Reed (many-objective visual analytics). We were also very pleased to feature a panel and tool demo session where we explored how SBSE can support blind and visually impaired programmers.

We hope that, with these proceedings, anyone who did not have the chance to be with us in Railegh, will have the opportunity to follow the latest advances of the SBSE community.

August 2016   Federica Sarro
                                                                              Kalyanmoy Deb

Organizing Committee

General Chair

Marouane Kessentini   University of Michigan, USA

Program Chairs

Federica Sarro   University College London, UK
Kalyanmoy Deb   Michigan State University, USA

Graduate Student Track Chairs

Thelma Elita Colanzi Lopes   State University of Maringa, Brazil
Ali Ouni   Osaka University, Japan

SBSE Challenge Track Chairs

Leandro L. Minku   University of Leicester, UK
Tanja E.J. Vos   Polytechnical University of Valencia, Spain

Publicity Chair

Yuanyuan Zhang   University College London, UK

Web Chair

Wiem Mkaouer   University of Michigan, USA

Steering Committee

Mark Harman   University College London, UK
Andrea Arcuri   Scienta, Norway, and University of Luxembourg, Luxembourg
Marcio Barros   Federal University of the state of Rio de Janeiro, Brazil
Gordon Fraser (Chair)   University of Sheffield, UK
Claire Le Goues   Carnegie Mellon University, USA
Federica Sarro   University College London, UK
Jerffeson Souza   University of the State of Ceara, Brazil
David White   University College London, UK

Shin Yoo   Korea Advanced Institute of Science and Technology,
                               Korea
Yuanyuan Zhang   University College London, UK

Program Committee

Shaukat Ali   Simula Research Laboratory, Norway
Nadia Alshahwan   JP Morgan Chase, UK
Giuliano Antoniol   Ecole Polytechnique de Montréal, Canada
Andrea Arcuri   Scienta, Norway, and University of Luxembourg,
                               Luxembourg
Marcio Barros   Federal University of the State of Rio de Janeiro, Brazil
Francisco Chicano   University of Málaga, Spain
John Clark   University of York, UK
Myra Cohen   University of Nebraska-Lincoln, USA
Arilo Claudio Dias-Neto   Federal University of Amazonas, Brazil
Gordon Fraser   University of Sheffield, UK
Juan Pablo Galeotti   University of Buenos Aires, Argentina
Gregory Gay   University of South Carolina, USA
Alessandra Gorla   IMDEA Software Institute, Spain
Mark Harman   University College London, UK
Dongsun Kim   Sogang University, Seoul, Korea
Claire Le Goues   Carnegie Mellon University, USA
Raluca Lefticaru   University of Bucharest, Romania
Zheng Li   Beijing University of Chemical Technology, China
Phil McMinn   University of Sheffield, UK
Tim Menzies   NC State University, USA
Justyna Petke   University College London, UK
Marc Roper   University of Strathclyde, UK
Houari Sahraoui   Université De Montréal, Canada
Christopher Simons   University of the West of England, UK
Jerffeson Souza   State University of Ceara, Brazil
Jerry Swan   University of Stirling, UK
Paolo Tonella   Fondazione Bruno Kessler, Italy
Shin Yoo   Korea Advanced Institute of Science and Technology,
                               Korea
Yuanyuan Zhang   University College London, UK

Additional Reviewers

Edouard Batot   Université de Montréal, Canada
Bobby Bruce   University College London, UK
Jacques Klein   University of Luxembourg, Luxembourg
Hong Lu   University of Dartmouth, USA
Jaechang Nam   University of Waterloo, USA
Dipesh Pradhan   Simula Research Laboratory, Norway

Sponsors

Keynotes

Evolutionary Multi-objective Optimization Using Hybrid Approaches

Carlos Artemio Coello Coello

CINVESTAV-IPN,
Mexico City, Mexico

Abstract. The use of evolutionary algorithms for solving multi-objective optimization problems has become increasingly popular, mainly within the last 15 years. From among the several research trends that have originated in recent years, one of the most promising is the use of hybrid approaches that allow to improve the performance of multi-objective evolutionary algorithms (MOEAs). In this talk, some of the most representative research on the use of hybrid approaches in evolutionary multi-objective optimization will be discussed. The topics discussed will include multi-objective memetic algorithms, hybridization of MOEAs with gradient-based methods and with direct search methods, as well as multi-objective hyperheuristics. Some applications of these approaches as well as some potential paths for future research in this area will also be briefly discussed.

Towards Evolutionary Multitasking: A New Paradigm

Yew-Soon Ong

Nanyang Technological University,
Singapore, Singapore

Abstract. We are in an era where a plethora of computational problem-solving methodologies are being invented to tackle the diverse problems that are of interest to researchers. Some of these problems have emerged from real-life scenarios while some are theoretically motivated and created to stretch the bounds of current computational algorithms. Regardless, it is clear that in this new millennium a unifying concept to dissolve the barriers among these techniques will help to advance the course of algorithmic research. Interestingly, there is a parallel that can be drawn in memes from both socio-cultural and computational perspectives. The platform for memes in the former is the human minds while in the latter, the platform for memes is algorithms for problem-solving. In this context, memes can culminate into representations that enhance the problem-solving capability of algorithms. The phrase Memetic Computing has surfaced in recent years; emerging as a discipline of research that focuses on the use of memes as units of information which is analogous to memes in a social and cultural context. Memetic computing offers a broad scope, perpetuating the idea of memes into concepts that capture the richness of algorithms that defines a new generation of computational methodologies. It is defined as a paradigm that uses the notion of meme(s) as units of information encoded in computational representations for the purpose of problem solving. In this talk, we take a peek into some state-of-the-art memetic algorithms and frameworks of memetic computation. In particular, the new paradigm of multitasking optimization, which was recently proposed and published online in the IEEE Transactions on Evolutionary Computation journal in 2015, is introduced. It was noted that traditional methods for optimization, including the population-based search algorithms of Evolutionary Computation (EC), have generally been focused on efficiently solving only a single optimization task at a time. It is only very recently that Multifactorial Optimization (MFO) has been developed to explore the potential for evolutionary multitasking. MFO is found to leverage the scope for implicit genetic transfer across problems in a simple and elegant manner, thereby, opening doors to a plethora of new research opportunities in EC, dealing, in particular, with the exploitation of underlying synergies between seemingly distinct tasks. Last but not least, some applications of evolutionary multitasking in Software Engineering is showcased.

Discovering Tradeoffs, Vulnerabilities, and Stakeholder Dependencies in a Changing World

Patrick M. Reed

Cornell University, Ithaca, USA

Abstract. Over the past decade my research group has worked to operationalize our many-objective visual analytics (MOVA) framework for the design and management of complex engineered systems. The MOVA framework has four core components: (1) elicited problem conception and formulation, (2) massively parallel many-objective search, (3) interactive visual analytics, and (4) negotiated design selection. Problem conception and formulation is the process of abstracting a practical design problem into a mathematical representation. We build on the emerging work in visual analytics to exploit interactive visualization of both the design space and the objective space in multiple heterogeneous linked views that permit exploration and discovery. Negotiated design selection uses interactive visualization, reformulation, and optimization to discover desirable designs for implementation. Each of the activities in the framework is subject to feedback, both within the activity itself and from the other activities in the framework. These feedback processes transition formerly marginalized constructive learning activities of reformulating the problem, refining the conceptual model of the problem, and refining the optimization, to represent the most critical process for innovating real world systems (i.e., learning how to frame the problems themselves). My presentation will use our recent successful applications in urban water portfolio planning and satellite constellation design to demonstrate the key computational innovations in our MOVA framework.

Contents

Research Papers

Java Enterprise Edition Support in Search-Based JUnit Test Generation   3
  Andrea Arcuri and Gordon Fraser

HOMI: Searching Higher Order Mutants for Software Improvement   18
  Fan Wu, Mark Harman, Yue Jia, and Jens Krinke

Search Based Test Suite Minimization for Fault Detection and Localization:
A Co-driven Method   34
  Jingyao Geng, Zheng Li, Ruilian Zhao, and Junxia Guo

Validation of Constraints Among Configuration Parameters
Using Search-Based Combinatorial Interaction Testing   49
  Angelo Gargantini, Justyna Petke, Marco Radavelli,
  and Paolo Vavassori

Search-Based Testing of Procedural Programs: Iterative Single-Target
or Multi-target Approach?   64
  Simone Scalabrino, Giovanni Grano, Dario Di Nucci, Rocco Oliveto,
  and Andrea De Lucia

A Search Based Approach for Stress-Testing Integrated Circuits   80
  Basil Eljuse and Neil Walkinshaw

An (Accidental) Exploration of Alternatives to Evolutionary Algorithms
for SBSE   96
  Vivek Nair, Tim Menzies, and Jianfeng Chen

Improved Crossover Operators for Genetic Programming
for Program Repair   112
  Vinicius Paulo L. Oliveira, Eduardo F.D. Souza, Claire Le Goues,
  and Celso G. Camilo-Junior

Scaling up the Fitness Function for Reverse Engineering Feature Models   128
  Thammasak Thianniwet and Myra B. Cohen

A Multi-objective Approach to Prioritize and Recommend Bugs in Open
Source Repositories   143
  Duany Dreyton, Allysson Allex Araújo, Altino Dantas, Raphael Saraiva,
  and Jerffeson Souza

Search Based Clustering for Protecting Software with Diversified Updates . . .   159
    Mariano Ceccato, Paolo Falcarin, Alessandro Cabutto,
    Yosief Weldezghi Frezghi, and Cristian-Alexandru Staicu

Test Data Generation Efficiency Prediction Model for EFSM Based
on MGGP   176
    Weiwei Wang, Ruilian Zhao, Ying Shang, and Yong Liu

Search-Based Generalization and Refinement of Code Templates   192
    Tim Molderez and Coen De Roover

SBSE Challenge Papers

Amortised Deep Parameter Optimisation of GPGPU Work Group Size
for OpenCV   211
    Jeongju Sohn, Seongmin Lee, and Shin Yoo

Automated Testing of Web Applications with TESTAR: Lessons
Learned Testing the Odoo Tool   218
    Francisco Almenar, Anna I. Esparcia-Alcázar, Mirella Martínez,
    and Urko Rueda

API-Constrained Genetic Improvement   224
    William B. Langdon, David R. White, Mark Harman, Yue Jia,
    and Justyna Petke

Challenges in Using Search-Based Test Generation to Identify Real
Faults in Mockito   231
    Gregory Gay

Deep Parameter Optimisation for Face Detection Using the Viola-Jones
Algorithm in OpenCV   238
    Bobby R. Bruce, Jonathan M. Aitken, and Justyna Petke

Multi-objective Regression Test Suite Minimisation for Mockito   244
    Andrew J. Turner, David R. White, and John H. Drake

Searching for Configurations in Clone Evaluation – A Replication Study   250
    Chaiyong Ragkhitwetsagul, Matheus Paixao, Manal Adham,
    Saheed Busari, Jens Krinke, and John H. Drake

Short Papers

AVM*f*: An Open-Source Framework and Implementation of the Alternating
Variable Method   259
    Phil McMinn and Gregory M. Kapfhammer

A Method Dependence Relations Guided Genetic Algorithm   267
   Ali Aburas and Alex Groce

Preliminary Study of Multi-objective Features Selection for Evolving
Software Product Lines   274
   David Brevet, Takfarinas Saber, Goetz Botterweck,
   and Anthony Ventresque

Interactive Code Smells Detection: An Initial Investigation.   281
   Mohamed Wiem Mkaouer

Graduate Student Papers

Human Resource Allocation in Agile Software Projects Based
on Task Similarities.   291
   Lucas Roque, Allysson Allex Araújo, Altino Dantas, Raphael Saraiva,
   and Jerffeson Souza

Improving the Performance of Many-Objective Software Refactoring
Technique Using Dimensionality Reduction   298
   Troh Josselin Dea

Field Report: Applying Monte Carlo Tree Search for Program Synthesis   304
   Jinsuk Lim and Shin Yoo

Dynamic Bugs Prioritization in Open Source Repositories
with Evolutionary Techniques.   311
   Vanessa Veloso, Thiago Oliveira, Altino Dantas, and Jerffeson Souza

Author Index   317

Research Papers

Java Enterprise Edition Support in Search-Based JUnit Test Generation

Andrea Arcuri[1,2](✉) and Gordon Fraser[3]

[1] Westerdals Oslo ACT, Faculty of Technology, Oslo, Norway
arcand@westerdals.no
[2] University of Luxembourg, Luxembourg, Luxembourg
[3] Department of Computer Science, The University of Sheffield,
Sheffield, UK

Abstract. Many different techniques and tools for automated unit test generation target the Java programming languages due to its popularity. However, a lot of Java's popularity is due to its usage to develop enterprise applications with frameworks such as Java Enterprise Edition (JEE) or Spring. These frameworks pose challenges to the automatic generation of JUnit tests. In particular, code units ("beans") are handled by external web containers (e.g., WildFly and GlassFish). Without considering how web containers initialize these beans, automatically generated unit tests would not represent valid scenarios and would be of little use. For example, common issues of bean initialization are dependency injection, database connection, and JNDI bean lookup. In this paper, we extend the EvoSuite search-based JUnit test generation tool to provide initial support for JEE applications. Experiments on 247 classes (the JBoss EAP tutorial examples) reveal an increase in code coverage, and demonstrate that our techniques prevent the generation of useless tests (e.g., tests where dependencies are not injected).

Keywords: Java Enterprise Edition (JEE) · Search-based testing · Automated unit test generation · Database

1 Introduction

As the Java programming language remains one of the most popular programming languages, it is one of the dominant languages for research on software engineering and automated unit test generation. However, there are two main versions of Java: the Standard Edition (SE), and the one tailored for enterprise needs, i.e., the so called Java Enterprise Edition (JEE) [8]. JEE extends SE in various ways, for example by providing APIs for databases, distributed and multi-tier architectures, web applications (e.g., using servlets) and services (e.g., REST and SOAP). The popularity of the Java programming language is in part due to the use of the latter version of Java. However, there are large differences between SE and JEE programs.

In a typical Java SE application, there is an entry point class that has a `main` method with an array of strings as parameters, which represent the command line

© Springer International Publishing AG 2016
F. Sarro and K. Deb (Eds.): SSBSE 2016, LNCS 9962, pp. 3–17, 2016.
DOI: 10.1007/978-3-319-47106-8_1

arguments. This main method then typically calls methods from other classes in the application, and new object instances are created with the new keyword. Once the application is started, it then interacts with its *environment*, for example using a GUI, accessing the network, file system, console, etc. Writing a unit test for a class in this context usually means to instantiate it, call its methods with some input parameters, and to mock or simulate its interactions with the environment.

In JEE, in contrast to SE, the developed applications are not standalone: they need to be run in a container, like for example WildFly[1] or GlassFish[2]. These containers scan deployed applications for XML configurations or annotations directly in the Java classes. Object instances of the applications are created via reflection, and possibly augmented/extended (e.g., using proxy classes) based on the container's configurations. A typical case is access to databases: a Java class that needs to access the application's database will not need to have code to deal directly with all the low level details of accessing databases (e.g., handling of transactions), or configure it explicitly. In fact, a reference to a handler for the database can be automatically *injected* in a class by the container, and each of its method would be automatically marked for transaction delimiters (e.g., create a new transaction when a method is called, commit it once the method is finished, or rollback if any exceptions are thrown).

All these JEE functionalities make the development of enterprise applications much easier: engineers just need to focus on the business logic, where many complex tasks like handling databases and web connections are transparently delegated to the containers. However, these features make unit testing JEE classes more complicated. Given a class X, one cannot simply create an instance using new X() in a unit test, as that way all the dependencies injected by the container would be missing. This is a challenge for automated unit test generation: There has been a lot of research on how to automatically generate unit tests for Java software, and practitioners can freely download research prototypes like for example T3 [11], JTExpert [12], Randoop [9], or EvoSuite [7]. These tools, however, all target Java SE, and not JEE software.

To illustrate the effects of this, consider the example class JeeExample in Fig. 1a, which contains a number of JEE features. JeeExample is an Enterprise Java Bean, as it is annotated with @javax.ejb.Stateless. It has a reference to an EntityManager, which is used to access the application's database. This reference is expected to be injected by the container, because the field em is annotated with @PersistenceContext. The class has two methods: persist() to save data, and a boolean checkForMatch() which just does some checking on the existing state of the database. KeyValuePair is an auxiliary class shown in Fig. 1b.

Unit test generation tools intended for Java SE cannot cover any of the branches in this class. The reason is that the field em is not injected, and so all calls on it result in a null pointer exception. For example, Fig. 2 shows a test

---

[1] http://wildfly.org, accessed April 2016.
[2] https://glassfish.java.net, accessed April 2016.

```
import javax.ejb.Stateless;                    import javax.persistence.Entity;
import javax.persistence.EntityManager;        import javax.persistence.Id;
import javax.persistence.PersistenceContext;

@Stateless                                     @Entity
public class JeeExample {                      public class KeyValuePair {
                                                 @Id
  @PersistenceContext                            private String key;
  private EntityManager em;                       private String value;

  public void persist(String key, String value) {    public KeyValuePair(){}
    KeyValuePair pair = new KeyValuePair(key, value);
    em.persist(pair);                            public KeyValuePair(String key,
  }                                                                 String value) {
                                                   this.key = key;
  public boolean checkForMatch(String key,        this.value = value;
                      String value) {            }

    KeyValuePair pair = em.find(KeyValuePair.class,  public String getKey() { return key; }
                      key);
                                                 public void setKey(String key) {
    if(pair == null)                               this.key = key;
      return false;                              }

    if(pair.getValue().equals(value))            public String getValue() { return value; }
      return true;
    else                                         public void setValue(String value) {
      return false;                                this.value = value;
  }                                              }
}                                              }
```

(a) Class under test.   (b) Dependency entity class.

Fig. 1. Code example showing a stateless enterprise Java bean accessing a database.

```
@Test(timeout = 4000)
public void test0() throws Throwable {
  JeeExample jeeExample0 = new JeeExample();
  try {
    jeeExample0.checkForMatch("z", "]#");
    fail("Expecting exception: NullPointerException");
  } catch(NullPointerException e) {
    verifyException("JeeExample", e);
  }
}
```

Fig. 2. Example test generated by the standard version of EvoSuite on the example class from Fig. 1a.

generated by EvoSuite and Fig. 3 shows one generated by Randoop. Without handling dependency injection and database initialization, all tests result in null pointer exceptions. These tests are not particularly useful, as they test the class under test (CUT) only when it is not in an initialized, meaningful state.

In this paper, we describe and evaluate an approach to include JEE features in the search space of the search-based test data generation tool EvoSuite [7]. In particular, in this paper we provide the following contributions:

– Handling of dependency injection, which requires special care on how the tests are mutated and evolved. By construction, appropriate handling of dependency injection avoids that useless tests, like the one in Fig. 2, are generated.
– Automated initialization of in memory, embedded databases.

```
@Test
public void test1() throws Throwable {
    if (debug) { System.out.format("%n%s%n","ErrorTest0.test1"); }

    JeeExample jeeExample0 = new JeeExample();
    // during test generation this statement threw an exception of
    // type java.lang.NullPointerException in error
    jeeExample0.persist("hi!", "");
}
```

Fig. 3. Example test generated by Randoop on the example class from Fig. 1a.

- Handling of some JEE functionalities through environment mocks [3,4], like for example bean lookup resolution.
- An empirical study on 247 JEE classes, which shows that code coverage increases.

Using the JEE extension presented in this paper, EVOSUITE generates the tests shown in Fig. 4 when applied on the class JeeExample from Fig. 1a (note that further initialization is done in the @Before and @After methods, but these are not shown due to space limitations). Seven tests are generated, which achieve full code coverage. Furthermore, those tests even point to bugs in the class JeeExample, for example by throwing exceptions like PersistenceException, IllegalArgumentException, NullPointerException and EntityExistsException. In particular, test0 leads to a PersistenceException because it tries to persist to the database an entity with null id. test1 leads to an IllegalArgumentException because the method EntityManager#find cannot be called with a null key. test5 shows a null pointer exception due to the statement if(pair.getValue().equals(...)) in the method checkForMatch, where getValue() returns null. Finally, test6 tries to insert a new entity that already exists (same id) into the database, leading to a EntityExistsException. Note that no test was generated in which the field *em* was not injected (i.e., left null).

2   Background

2.1   Java Enterprise Edition

JEE aims at fulfilling enterprise needs by making it easier to develop distributed, multi-tier applications, such as web applications and web services. In this section, we briefly describe the main features of Java Enterprise Edition (JEE), in particular version 7. As this is a very large topic, here we only provide a high level overview to make the rest of the paper more accessible for readers not familiar with JEE. For further JEE details and links, we refer to [8].

JEE functionalities. JEE can be seen as a series of packages providing different functionalities, from database access to web communication handling. Among the main functionalities of JEE, some important examples are the following:

```java
@Test(timeout = 4000) public void test0() throws Throwable {
    JeeExample jeeExample0 = new JeeExample();
    Injector.injectEntityManager(jeeExample0, (Class<?>) JeeExample.class);
    Injector.validateBean(jeeExample0, (Class<?>) JeeExample.class);
    try {
        jeeExample0.persist((String) null, (String) null);
        fail("Expecting exception: PersistenceException");
    } catch(PersistenceException e) {}
}
@Test(timeout = 4000) public void test1() throws Throwable {
    JeeExample jeeExample0 = new JeeExample();
    Injector.injectEntityManager(jeeExample0, (Class<?>) JeeExample.class);
    Injector.validateBean(jeeExample0, (Class<?>) JeeExample.class);
    try {
        jeeExample0.checkForMatch((String) null, (String) null);
        fail("Expecting exception: IllegalArgumentException");
    } catch(IllegalArgumentException e) {}
}
@Test(timeout = 4000) public void test2() throws Throwable {
    JeeExample jeeExample0 = new JeeExample();
    Injector.injectEntityManager(jeeExample0, (Class<?>) JeeExample.class);
    Injector.validateBean(jeeExample0, (Class<?>) JeeExample.class);
    jeeExample0.persist("#", "#");
    boolean boolean0 = jeeExample0.checkForMatch("#", "#");
    assertTrue(boolean0);
}
@Test(timeout = 4000) public void test3() throws Throwable {
    JeeExample jeeExample0 = new JeeExample();
    Injector.injectEntityManager(jeeExample0, (Class<?>) JeeExample.class);
    Injector.validateBean(jeeExample0, (Class<?>) JeeExample.class);
    jeeExample0.persist("#", "#");
    boolean boolean0 = jeeExample0.checkForMatch("#", "\"");
    assertFalse(boolean0);
}
@Test(timeout = 4000) public void test4() throws Throwable {
    JeeExample jeeExample0 = new JeeExample();
    Injector.injectEntityManager(jeeExample0, (Class<?>) JeeExample.class);
    Injector.validateBean(jeeExample0, (Class<?>) JeeExample.class);
    boolean boolean0 = jeeExample0.checkForMatch("\"", "#");
    assertFalse(boolean0);
}
@Test(timeout = 4000) public void test5() throws Throwable {
    JeeExample jeeExample0 = new JeeExample();
    Injector.injectEntityManager(jeeExample0, (Class<?>) JeeExample.class);
    Injector.validateBean(jeeExample0, (Class<?>) JeeExample.class);
    jeeExample0.persist("", (String) null);
    try {
        jeeExample0.checkForMatch("", "");
        fail("Expecting exception: NullPointerException");
    } catch(NullPointerException e) {}
}
@Test(timeout = 4000) public void test6() throws Throwable {
    JeeExample jeeExample0 = new JeeExample();
    Injector.injectEntityManager(jeeExample0, (Class<?>) JeeExample.class);
    Injector.validateBean(jeeExample0, (Class<?>) JeeExample.class);
    jeeExample0.persist("", "");
    try {
        jeeExample0.persist("", "ZuWxZ_0hnf[");
        fail("Expecting exception: EntityExistsException");
    } catch(EntityExistsException e) {}
}
```

Fig. 4. Example test suite generated by EVOSUITE on the example class from Fig. 1a, when using the JEE improvements presented in this paper.

- Java Persistence API (JPA): This is used to automatically map Java classes to tables in databases, and to read/write those objects. To achieve this, these classes need to be annotated with the `@Entity` annotation (see the example in Fig. 1b). Read/write operations are done through an `EntityManager` provided by the container.
- Enterprise Java Bean (EJB): These are objects responsible for the business logic of the application. *Beans* are instantiated and managed by the container. A Java object is made into an EJB by using annotations like `@Stateless`, `@Stateful` and `@Singleton` (see example in Fig. 1a).
- Java Transaction API (JTA): This is used to handle the transactions with the databases. By default, each call to an EJB method will be in a transaction, which will be rolled back if any exceptions are thrown in the EJB code.
- Java Naming and Directory Interface (JNDI): This is used to find objects that were bound by name in the current application or remote servers.
- JavaServer Faces (JSF): This is used to create component-based user interfaces for web applications. A web page would be developed in the `xhtml` format, mixing together Html/CSS/JS elements with calls to the backend Java beans.
- Java Message Service (JMS): This is used to make asynchronous point-to-point and publish-subscribe communications between distributed components.
- Web Services: These are used to develop and query web services like REST and SOAP.

Convention over configuration. To simplify development, JEE follows the *convention over configuration* approach: A typical JEE application is not a stand-alone process packaged as a `jar` (Java Archive) file, but rather as a `war` (Web Application Archive) file that has to be deployed on a server container (e.g., WildFly or GlassFish). When such a `war` file is deployed on a server, the server will do a series of operations and initialization based on the `war`'s content. The developers do not need to configure them, unless they want to do something different from the standard convention.

For example, an entity Java class will be mapped to a database table with the same name as the Java class. The developers just need to use the annotation `@Entity`, and the server will take care of rest. However, if, for example, a given entity class needs to be mapped to a table with a different name (e.g., when using JPA on a legacy database that cannot be changed), further annotations/settings can be added to change that default naming convention. Similarly, all methods in an EJB are automatically marked for required transactions: the container will create a new transaction if the method is called from a non-transactional client. If this default behavior is not the desired one, JTA annotations (e.g., `@TransactionAttribute`) can be added to the EJB methods to achieve a different behavior.

On one hand, the use of convention over configuration makes development easier and quicker, as the engineers need to specify only the non-conventional cases. On the other hand, debugging and code understanding might become more difficult, as the container might do a lot of hidden operations behind the scenes that are not obvious for a non-expert in JEE.

Dependency Injection. One of the main characteristics that distinguish JEE from SE is *Dependency Injection.* If an object X needs to use Y, instead of instantiating Y directly (or calling an external method to get an instance of it), it will delegate the container to provide an instance of Y. This is particularly useful to decouple components, as an enterprise application could be deployed on different containers (e.g., WildFly and GlassFish) that have different implementations for resources like database management. Furthermore, dependency injection entails different wiring of the application based on different contexts without the need of recompilation. For example, in a testing scenario a container could rather inject a mocked bean instead of a production one. In JEE, there are different ways to do dependency injection. A typical case is to use annotations on private fields. See for example the `em` field in Fig. 1a, which is automatically injected by the container because it is annotated with `@PersistenceContext`.

2.2   JUnit Test Generation with EvoSuite

The EvoSuite tool [7] automatically generates JUnit test suites optimized to achieve high code coverage. Test generation uses a search-based approach, where a genetic algorithm evolves a population of candidate solutions (test suites), guided by a fitness function that captures the target coverage criteria. A test suite in EvoSuite is a variable size set of test cases, and a test case, in turn, is a sequence of statements that instantiate or manipulate objects. The initial population consists of randomly generated tests, and then search operators are applied throughout the search. First, the fitness value for each candidate test suite is calculated. Then, individuals are selected for reproduction based on their fitness value; fitter individuals are more likely to be selected. With a certain probability, crossover is applied to the selected individuals, and then, with a certain probability, mutation is applied. Mutation consists of adding new (random) test cases to a test suite, and modifying existing tests (e.g., by adding, removing, or changing some of the statements). The search operators are applied until a new generation of individuals has been produced, and this then becomes the next generation. At the end of the search (e.g., when the allocated time has been used up), the resulting test suite goes through several post-processing steps such as minimization (i.e., removal of redundant statements) or assertion generation (i.e., addition of JUnit assert statements to check the observed behavior).

The search algorithm and the post-processing steps are both applicable regardless of whether the underlying Java class under test is Java SE or JEE code. Nevertheless, EvoSuite up to now was not able to generate tests for JEE specific code; the main reason for this lies in restrictions to EvoSuite's search space that result from the design of the mutation operators for the test cases. In particular, consider the insertion of statements (which is also used to generate random test cases): EvoSuite either inserts a randomly selected method call of the class under test, or inserts a random method call to a randomly chosen object generated in the current sequence of calls. If the method takes parameters, these are either satisfied with existing objects in the test, or EvoSuite will recursively insert statements that generate the required objects.

Consider class `JeeExample` from Fig. 1a: The candidate methods of the class under test are `persist`, `checkForMatch`, and the implicitly defined default constructor. All parameters are of type `String`, and EVOSUITE will generate random or seeded strings. Although EVOSUITE can also read from and write to public fields, the standard operators will not access the private field `em`, and thus EVOSUITE has no means of initializing the `EntityManager`. Note that, if `JeeExample` would do dependency injection by providing a constructor with an `EntityManager`, then EVOSUITE would attempt to explicitly instantiate one. However, this does not guarantee that EVOSUITE would be able to create and configure a valid instance.

3 JEE Support in EvoSuite

In this section, we describe an approach to enable search-based tools like EVO-SUITE to generate unit tests for JEE software. We do not cover the whole JEE specification, as that is simply too large to cover in a single study, but rather focus on some of the most common features, in particular dependency injection, JPA and JNDI.

Support for these features is added via two techniques: First, the search space of call sequences is modified to include relevant JEE calls, for example to handle injection. The challenge lies in constraining these calls to result in valid JEE scenarios. Second, the code under test is instrumented to ensure that the JEE environment set up by EVOSUITE is used, for example by directing all database accesses to an in-memory database automatically initialized by EVOSUITE.

3.1 Dependency Injection

If dependency injection is not handled, then the tests generated by automated tools will just throw useless null pointer exceptions (recall Figs. 2 and 3).

One possibility would be to use an embedded container running on the same JVM of the tests, and to delegate all the dependency injections to it. However, such an embedded container would still need to be configured, e.g., to specify which beans should be used for injection when there is more than one alternative, and it would be difficult to customize for unit testing purposes (e.g., replace with mocks some beans using external resources). A simpler alternative, which we implemented, is to do the injection directly in the unit tests using support methods we developed. For example, in every test in Fig. 4 the instantiation of the class `JeeExample` is followed by calls to `Injector#injectEntityManager`, which is a helper method that sets the entity manager.

Every time a new object is created as part of the search, EVOSUITE checks if it, or any of its superclasses, has fields that should be injected. To check for injection, we look at JEE annotations like `@Inject`, `@PersistenceContext`, `@PersistenceUnit`, `@Resource`, `@EJB`, `@WebServiceRef`, `@ManagedProperty`, and `@Context`. We also look at annotations used in popular frameworks like

@Autowired in Spring[3]. For each of these types of injections, the helper class Injector provides helper methods. For each injectable field, the corresponding helper methods are inserted in the test.

We distinguish between two kinds of injected objects: *pre-defined* and *new*. For some types of objects, EVOSUITE defines specific, pre-defined instances that can be injected inject. These are, for example, customized entity managers, as done with Injector#injectEntityManager. The use of these pre-defined instances allows EVOSUITE to more easily explore complex scenarios, where the random object initialization is unlikely to lead to interesting scenarios.

If for an injectable field f, of type F in a class X, we have no pre-defined instance in EVOSUITE, we add a call to a more generic Injector#inject. This method takes not only X as input, but also an object i of type F, i.e., this new object i will be injected in the field f of object X. The new object i will be created as part of the search, just like standard method parameters, and will evolved like any other objects (e.g., mutation operators might add new calls on it). Note that this new object i might itself need injection for some of its fields, and this will be handled recursively.

After a class X has all of its injectable fields injected, EVOSUITE checks for methods marked with @PostConstruct in the class hierarchy of X, and also add calls to Injector#executePostConstruct.

Adding Injector methods in the tests has major consequences their evolution during the search. Recall from Sect. 2.2 that EVOSUITE performs several kinds of operations to evolve tests, such as deleting statements, changing function calls, creating new statements at any position in the test, etc. These can change the tests to an inconsistent state, e.g., EVOSUITE could delete all calls to Injector methods. To avoid this issue, we defined *constraints* on the test statements, and modified all EVOSUITE search operators to enforce these constraints. Given a class X with injectable fields, these constraints are for example:

- No call to Injector can be deleted until X is in the test.
- If X is deleted, then delete all its calls to Injector.
- Fields cannot be injected more than once.
- Calls to Injector should be automatically added when a new object is instantiated. Search operators should not add new unnecessary calls to Injector, or modify existing ones.
- Calls to Injector methods cannot take null as input. This might prevent the deletion of objects that are used as input.
- Between the statement where X is instantiated and its last call on Injector, X cannot be used as input in any method that is not an injector, and no call can be added on X (as X is not fully initialized yet).

One drawback of injecting fields directly in the unit tests is test maintenance. Assume tests are generated for a class X with some injected fields. Assume also that, in a future release of X, a new injected field is added, although the external behavior (i.e., its semantics) of X has not been changed. Now, it might well

---

[3] https://spring.io, accessed April 2016.

be that the previously generated tests for X will now fail due to null pointer exceptions on this new field, although no regression bugs were introduced. To avoid this kind of *false positives*, after each bean initialization we add a call to `Injector#validateBean` (recall Fig. 4). This method checks if all injectable fields have indeed been injected. If not, an `AssumptionViolatedException` is thrown, which prevents the tests from failing (JUnit will consider a test throwing this exception as ignored, as if it was marked with `@Ignore`).

3.2   Database Handling

JEE applications tend to depend on databases. To test applications that access a database, a database needs to be configured and running. As this is typically not within the scope of capabilities of a unit test generation tool, this configuration would typically need to be done manually. To avoid this issue, we extended EVOSUITE to be able to perform the initialization automatically. In particular, we use the Spring framework to scan the classpath for `@Entity` classes, and automatically start an embedded database (HyperSQL[4].) for those entities, using Hibernate[5] as JPA implementation.

When beans need entity managers, we inject custom ones that are configured for this embedded database. Furthermore, we mock `javax.persistence.Persistence`, which consists of only static methods to access entity managers, to return our custom entity manager.

The embedded database is cleaned up after each test execution, in order to avoid dependencies among tests. Starting/resetting the database is done in the `@Before` and `@After` methods in the tests. However, initializing a database is time consuming, and may potentially take several seconds to complete. Therefore, it is not initialized by default, but only if the CUT really uses the database.

3.3   JNDI Mocking

When unit testing a class, the CUT might use JNDI to access objects that have been initialized in other classes since the application was started, or remote ones outside the running JVM. This is a problem for unit testing, as JNDI lookups might fail. To avoid this issue, we mock JNDI, similarly to how EVOSUITE already mocks environment interactions with the file system [3] and the network [4]. In particular, we provide a mock version of the class `javax.naming.InitialContext`. During EVOSUITE's bytecode instrumentation phase, all calls to the original class are automatically replaced with calls to the mocked version. Furthermore, EVOSUITE maintains information about the known classes, their methods, and how to generate them (referred to as *test cluster*). This information is derived statically during initialization, and all references to the original class are replaced with references to the mock class.

---

[4] http://hsqldb.org, accessed April 2016.
[5] http://hibernate.org, accessed April 2016.

By default, the mock class for `InitialContext` will fail to resolve any object lookups, i.e., it will return null. However, it also keeps track of all objects that have been requested during the search. If any objects were requested, then EVO-SUITE's test cluster is extended with additional methods to instantiate these objects and to make them accessible through JNDI. The mocked JNDI resolution is re-initialized at each new test execution, in order to avoid dependencies among tests.

4   Empirical Study

The techniques presented in this paper enable tools like EVOSUITE to be applied on JEE software. By construction, tests with non-initialized beans (which are not useful; recall Figs. 2 and 3) are no longer generated. However, in order to understand the effects of this change, it is also important to see what is the impact on code coverage. In particular, in this paper we address the following research question:

RQ: What is the effect of the JEE extensions on branch coverage?

Note that looking at fault detection (e.g., the throwing of undeclared exceptions) is not trivial to do automatically, as the lack of dependency injection might lead to many failing tests that are just false positives (recall Figs. 2 and 3), because they would throw exceptions when non-injected fields are accessed. However, even when injection is handled, the CUT could lead to null pointer exceptions that show actual bugs (e.g., recall `test5` in Fig. 4).

4.1   Experimental Setup

Open-source repositories like GitHub[6]. and SourceForge[7]. host a large amount of Java SE software, like libraries and applications. However, as JEE is targeted at enterprises, the amount of JEE software on open-source repositories is obviously lower. Furthermore, a JEE project might be simply marked as "Java", and so a systematic search for JEE projects is not necessarily trivial.

As JEE specifications are very large, and we are only interested in classes that use JEE features, we chose the set of JEE examples used to demonstrate JBoss EAP/WildFly application servers as case study. These consist of a total of 247 Java classes, hosted on GitHub[8].

On each of these 247 classes, we ran EVOSUITE with and without our JEE extension, 30 times per CUT, for a total of $247 \times 2 \times 30 = 14,820$ runs. For the experiments, we used the default configuration of EVOSUITE, which is assumed to show good results on average [2]. In each experiment, the search phase for EVOSUITE was executed until either 100 % branch coverage was achieved, or a

---

[6] https://github.com, accessed April 2016.
[7] https://sourceforge.net, accessed April 2016.
[8] https://github.com/jboss-developer/jboss-eap-quickstarts, accessed April 2016.

timeout of two minutes was reached. For each run we collected data on the achieved branch coverage as reported by EvoSuite. Results were analyzed based on standard guidelines [1]. In particular, to assess statistical difference we used the non-parametric Mann-Whitney-Wilcoxon U-test, whereas we used the Vargha-Delaney $\hat{A}_{12}$ as effect size.

4.2   Results

Without JEE support, the default version of EvoSuite achieves an average of 77 % branch coverage on these 247 classes. When using the techniques presented in this paper, branch coverage increases to 80 %.

This modest +3 % increase warrants closer inspection: Only 102 out of the 247 classes have some kind of JEE annotation for dependency injection. In contrast, many classes are trivial (e.g., skeletons with empty bodies representing some business logic), and might only be needed to compile other classes in which the JEE features are really used. In particular, @Entity classes (e.g., recall Fig. 1b) usually have just basic setters and getters, and pose no challenge for unit test generation. This explains the already high coverage of 77 % that EvoSuite can achieve even without any JEE support.

If we assume that a class, on which EvoSuite can achieve 90 % or more branch coverage even without JEE support, does not depend on JEE, then the average coverage on the remaining 88 classes increases from 37.7 % to 46.0 %, i.e., a 8.3 % improvement.

To get a better picture of the importance of handling JEE features, Table 1 shows detailed data on the 25 challenging classes where JEE handling had most effect: On these classes, the average branch coverage nearly doubles from 43.8 % to 74.6 %. All comparisons are statistically valid (p-values very close to zero), and the average effect size for $\hat{A}_{12}$ is nearly maximal, i.e., 0.98.

RQ: *JEE support significantly increases branch coverage (average +3 %), with substantial increases in JEE relevant classes.*

---

5   Threats to Validity

Threats to *internal* validity result from how the experiments were carried out. The techniques presented in this paper have all been implemented as part of the EvoSuite tool. Although EvoSuite is a mature tool used by practitioners, no system is guaranteed to be error free. Furthermore, because EvoSuite is based on randomized algorithms, each experiment has been repeated several times, and the results have been evaluated with rigorous statistical methods.

To avoid disseminating flawed results, repeatability and reproducibility are cornerstones of the scientific process [5]. To address this issue, we released the implementation of all the techniques presented in this paper as open-source (LGPL license), and we made it available on a public repository[9].

---

[9] www.github.com/EvoSuite/evosuite

Table 1. Branch coverage comparison of EvoSuite with (JEE) and without (Base) support for JEE, on the 25 classes with the largest increase. Note, some classes have the same name, but they are from different packages.

Class	Base	JEE	$\hat{A}_{12}$	p-value
ManagedComponent	14.3%	41.2%	**0.96**	≤ 0.001
UnManagedComponent	47.0%	51.6%	**0.80**	≤ 0.001
ItemBean	89.7%	100.0%	**1.00**	≤ 0.001
HATimerService	57.1%	93.3%	**1.00**	≤ 0.001
SchedulerBean	60.0%	97.3%	**0.98**	≤ 0.001
IntermediateEJB	33.3%	66.7%	**1.00**	≤ 0.001
SecuredEJB	80.0%	98.7%	**0.97**	≤ 0.001
AsynchronousClient	20.0%	29.3%	**0.97**	≤ 0.001
RemoteEJBClient	25.0%	58.3%	**1.00**	≤ 0.001
TimeoutExample	60.0%	99.3%	**1.00**	≤ 0.001
GreetController	66.7%	100.0%	**1.00**	≤ 0.001
HelloWorldJMSClient	4.9%	23.1%	**1.00**	≤ 0.001
MemberResourceRESTService	19.1%	69.2%	**1.00**	≤ 0.001
MemberResourceRESTService	19.3%	67.7%	**0.96**	≤ 0.001
MemberRegistrationServlet	18.2%	87.1%	**1.00**	≤ 0.001
HelloWorldMDBServletClient	26.0%	61.3%	**0.99**	≤ 0.001
TaskDaoImpl	55.6%	77.8%	**1.00**	≤ 0.001
AuthController	30.0%	100.0%	**1.00**	≤ 0.001
TaskController	42.9%	100.0%	**1.00**	≤ 0.001
TaskDaoImpl	55.6%	75.0%	**0.96**	≤ 0.001
TaskListBean	75.0%	96.7%	**0.93**	≤ 0.001
TaskDaoImpl	55.6%	77.8%	**1.00**	≤ 0.001
TaskResource	55.4%	84.3%	**1.00**	≤ 0.001
Servlet	40.0%	60.9%	**0.92**	≤ 0.001
XAService	44.7%	49.3%	**0.96**	≤ 0.001
Average	43.8%	74.6%	0.98	

Threats to *construct* validity come from what measure we chose to evaluate the success of our techniques. We used branch coverage, which is a common coverage criterion in the software testing literature. However, it is hard to automatically quantify the negative effects of tests that do not handle dependency injection, as the presence of false positive tests on software maintenance is a little investigated topic in the literature.

Threats to *external* validity come from how well the results generalize to other case studies. To have a variegated set of classes showing different features of JEE, we chose the JEE examples used to demonstrate the JBoss EAP/WildFly application servers, which consist of 247 Java classes. Larger case studies on industrial systems will be needed to further generalize our results.

6   Related Work

While there are numerous tools and techniques to generate unit tests for Java classes and programs, we are not aware of any work targeting unit tests for JEE classes directly.

Some of the problems caused by JEE are related to its use of databases. Emmi et al. [6] use dynamic symbolic execution to collect constraints on database queries and populate a database with data to satisfy these queries. The MODA framework [13] instruments database-driven programs to interact with a mock database instead of a real database. A test generator based on dynamic symbolic execution is then applied to insert entries into the database. A refined version of this approach [10] correlates various constraints within a database application. The code coverage increase reported by these approaches is comparable to the increases we observed in our experiments in this paper.

Besides database applications, other external dependencies such as filesystem [3], networking [4], or cloud services [14] have been integrated into test generation, typically by making test generators configure mock objects. For some of the JEE features, the approach presented in this paper also follows this strategy.

7   Conclusions

Jave Enterprise Edition (JEE) applications pose challenges that have not previously been handled by Java unit test generation tools. In order to address this problem, we have extended the EVOSUITE unit test generation tool in order to support the core JEE features of (1) dependency injection, (2) database access, and (3) JNDI object lookups. This posed several technical challenges in order to ensure that several constraints on the validity of tests are maintained at all time during the search-based test generation. These techniques are fully automated, and require no human intervention (not even to initialize/run the databases). We are aware of no other tool that handles JEE specific functionalities.

An empirical study on 247 Java classes shows that, with high statistical confidence, our techniques improve branch coverage (+3 % on average), especially on challenging classes heavily dependent on JEE functionalities (increase from 43.8 % to 74.6 %). Importantly, this approach prevents, by construction, the generation of misleading tests that throw null pointer exceptions just because dependency injections are not handled.

JEE has a very large set of specifications, and what has been addressed in this paper is just a first step. Future work will focus on handling other JEE components, like for example JMS and REST/SOAP web services. Furthermore, there is large space for improving the handling of databases, like for example extending the search to directly create objects in the database based on the class under test's queries.

All techniques discussed in this paper have been implemented as part of the EvoSuite test data generation tool. EvoSuite is open-source (LGPL license) and freely available to download. To learn more about EvoSuite, please visit our website at: http://www.evosuite.org.

Acknowledgments. This work is supported by the EPSRC project (EP/N023978/1) and by the National Research Fund, Luxembourg (FNR/P10/03).

References

1. Arcuri, A., Briand, L.: A hitchhiker's guide to statistical tests for assessing randomized algorithms in software engineering. Softw. Test. Verification Reliab. **24**(3), 219–250 (2014)
2. Arcuri, A., Fraser, G.: Parameter tuning or default values? An empirical investigation in search-based software engineering. Empirical Softw. Eng. **18**(3), 594–623 (2013)
3. Arcuri, A., Fraser, G., Galeotti, J.P.: Automated unit test generation for classes with environment dependencies. In: IEEE/ACM International Conference on Automated Software Engineering (ASE), pp. 79–90 (2014)
4. Arcuri, A., Fraser, G., Galeotti, J.P.: Generating TCP/UDP network data for automated unit test generation. In: ACM SIGSOFT International Symposium on the Foundations of Software Engineering (FSE), pp. 155–165. ACM (2015)
5. Collberg, C., Proebsting, T.A.: Repeatability in computer systems research. Commun. ACM **59**(3), 62–69 (2016)
6. Emmi, M., Majumdar, R., Sen, K.: Dynamic test input generation for database applications. In: Proceedings of the 2007 International Symposium on Software Testing and Analysis, pp. 151–162. ACM (2007)
7. Fraser, G., Arcuri, A.: Evosuite: automatic test suite generation for object-oriented software. In: ACM SIGSOFT International Symposium on the Foundations of Software Engineering (FSE), pp. 416–419. ACM (2011)
8. Goncalves, A.: Beginning Java EE 7. Apress, New York (2013)
9. Pacheco, C., Lahiri, S.K., Ernst, M.D., Ball, T.: Feedback-directed random test generation. In: ACM/IEEE International Conference on Software Engineering (ICSE), pp. 75–84 (2007)
10. Pan, K., Wu, X., Xie, T.: Guided test generation for database applications via synthesized database interactions. ACM Trans. Softw. Eng. Methodol. (TOSEM) **23**(2), 12 (2014)
11. Prasetya, I.S.W.B.: T3i: A tool for generating and querying test suites for Java. In: ACM SIGSOFT International Symposium on the Foundations of Software Engineering (FSE) (2015)
12. Sakti, A., Pesant, G., Gueheneuc, Y.G.: Instance generator and problem representation to improve object oriented code coverage. IEEE Trans. Softw. Eng. (TSE) **41**, 294 (2015)
13. Taneja, K., Zhang, Y., Xie, T.: Moda: automated test generation for database applications via mock objects. In: IEEE/ACM International Conference on Automated Software Engineering (ASE), pp. 289–292. ACM (2010)
14. Zhang, L., Ma, X., Lu, J., Xie, T., Tillmann, N., De Halleux, P.: Environmental modeling for automated cloud application testing. IEEE Softw. **29**(2), 30–35 (2012)

HOMI: Searching Higher Order Mutants for Software Improvement

Fan Wu(✉), Mark Harman, Yue Jia, and Jens Krinke

Department of Computer Science, UCL,
Gower Street, London WC1E 6BT, UK
{fan.wu.12,mark.harman,yue.jia,j.krinke}@ucl.ac.uk

Abstract. This paper introduces HOMI, a Higher Order Mutation based approach for Genetic Improvement of software, in which the code modification granularity is finer than in previous work while scalability remains. HOMI applies the NSGAII algorithm to search for higher order mutants that improve the non-functional properties of a program while passing all its regression tests. Experimental results on four real-world C programs shows that up to 14.7% improvement on time and 19.7% on memory are found using only First Order Mutants. By combining these First Order Mutants, HOMI found further improvement in Higher Order Mutants, giving an 18.2% improvement on the time performance while keeping the memory improvement. A further manual analysis suggests that 88% of the mutation changes cannot be generated using line based 'plastic surgery' Genetic Improvement approaches.

1 Introduction

Optimising software for better performance such as speed and memory consumption can be demanding, especially when the resources in the running environment are limited. Manually optimising such non-functional properties while keeping or even improving the functional behaviour of softwasre is challenging. This becomes an even harder task if the properties considered are competing with each other [14]. Search-Based Software Engineering (SBSE) [13] has demonstrated many potential solutions, for example, to speed up software systems [21,28], or to reduce memory consumption [29] and energy usage [7].

Previous studies have applied different search-based techniques to automate the optimisation process [3,6,15,22]. However, scalability of these approaches remains a challenge. To scale up and optimise real world programs, recent studies use a so-called 'plastic surgery' Genetic Programming (GP) approach. To reduce the search space, it represents solutions as a list of edits to the subject program instead of the program itself [7,27]. Each sequence of edits consists of inserting, deleting or swapping pieces of code. To ensure scalability, this approach usually modifies programs at the 'line' level of granularity (the smallest atomic unit is a line of code). As a results, it is challenging for 'plastic surgery' to optimise subject programs in finer granularity.

Mutation Testing [9,16] is an effective testing technique to test software. It automatically inserts artificial faults in the programs under test, to create a set

© Springer International Publishing AG 2016
F. Sarro and K. Deb (Eds.): SSBSE 2016, LNCS 9962, pp. 18–33, 2016.
DOI: 10.1007/978-3-319-47106-8_2

of faulty programs that are called 'mutants'. These mutants are used to assess the quality of tests, to provide testing criteria for generating new tests [11], and to fix software bugs [22]. More recently they have also been suggested as a means to perform sensitivity analysis [29] and to optimise software [19].

We introduce the HOMI approach to improve non-functional properties of software while preserving the functionality. HOMI utilises search-based higher order mutation testing [12] to effectively explore the search space of varying versions of a program. Like other previous Genetic Improvement (GI) work [7,21,27], HOMI relies on high-quality regression tests to check the functionality of the program. Given a program p and its regression tests T. HOMI generates two types of mutants that can be used for performance improvement. A **GI-FOM** is constructed by making a single syntactic change to p, which improves some non-functional properties of p while passing all the regression tests T. Having the same characteristics as GI-FOMs, a **GI-HOM** is constructed from the combination of GI-FOMs.

By combining with Mutation Testing techniques, we specifically utilise equivalent mutants which are expressly avoided by mutation testers where possible [25]. We implemented a prototype tool to realise the HOMI approach. The tool is designed to focus on two aspects of software runtime performance: execution time and memory consumption. Time and space are important qualities for most software, especially on portable devices or embedded systems where the runtime resources are limited. Moreover, these two qualities are usually competing with each other, yielding an interesting multi-objective solution space. Our tool produces a set of non-dominated GI-HOMs (thus forming a Pareto front). We evaluate our tool using four open source benchmarks. Since the tool requires no prior knowledge about the subjects, it can be easily applied to other programs.

The paper presents evidence that using Higher Order Mutation is an effective, easy to adopt way to improve existing programs. The experimental results suggest that equivalent First Order Mutants (FOMs) can improve the subject programs by 14.7 % on execution time or 19.7 % on memory consumption. Further results show that by searching for GI-HOMs, we can achieve up to 18.2 % time reduction on extreme cases. Our static analysis suggests that 88 % of the changes in GI-HOMs cannot be achieved by 'plastic surgery' based approaches. The contributions of the paper are as follows:

1. We introduce an automatic approach to improve programs via Higher Order Mutation, which explores program search space at a fine granularity while maintaining good scalability.
2. We evaluate our approach on four open source programs with different sizes. We report the results and demonstrate that our approach is able to reduce the execution time by up to 18.2 % or to save the memory consumption by up to 19.7 %.
3. The results of a manual analysis are reported to show that our approach works on a smaller granularity, such that 88 % of the changes found by our approach cannot be achieved by line based 'plastic surgery' approaches.

4. We also show evidence that it is possible to combine the HOMI approach with Deep-Parameter-optimisation approach to further improve the performance.

2   The HOMI Approach

We propose the HOMI approach, a higher order mutation based solution to GI. Figure 1 shows the overall architecture of the HOMI approach. Given a subject program with a set of regression tests, and some optimisation goals, HOMI applies SBSE to evolve a set of GI-HOMs that improve the properties of interest while passing all the regression tests. To explore the search space efficiently, we follow the current practice of GI in separating our approach into two stages [20]. In the first stage, we apply first order mutation to find locations in the program at which making changes will lead to significant impact on the optimisation goals. In the second stage, we apply a multi-objective search algorithm at these program locations to construct a Pareto front of GI-HOMs.

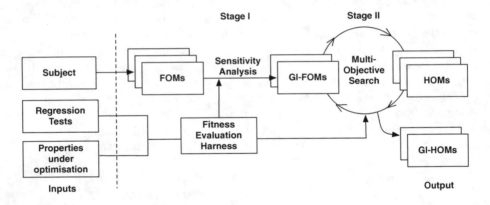

Fig. 1. The overall architecture of the HOMI approach.

2.1   Stage I: Sensitivity Analysis

Sensitivity analysis has been shown to be an effective way to reduce the search space in previous GI work [7,20,22]. Given a subject program under optimisation, some code pieces may have a greater impact on the properties of interest than others. Sensitivity analysis seeks to find small portions of code that have the greatest impact on the properties of interest. Thus, the subsequent optimisation can focus on a manageable amount of code, effectively reducing the search space. We use a first order mutation based sensitivity analysis approach to gather sensitivity information (See Sect. 2.3 for more details); this approach was introduced by Wu et al. [29]. We use this form of sensitivity analysis because it provides finer granularity than traditional statement or line-based sensitivity analysis.

As shown in Fig. 1, HOMI first generates a set of FOMs of the subject program and then evaluates them using a fitness evaluation harness. The evaluation harness is composed of regression tests and the measurement components for optimisation goals. It runs each FOM on all the tests and outputs the measurements of the optimisation goals as fitness values. After the fitness evaluation, HOMI removes FOMs that fail any regression tests and keeps only the survived ones. We do this because any mutants that pass all the regression tests are more likely to preserve the correctness of the subject. Finally, HOMI applies a non-dominated sorting [8] to rank all the survived FOMs by their fitness values.

The sensitivity analysis stage outputs a set of GI-FOMs. These FOMs are "potentially equivalent mutants" with respect to the regression test suites and have a positive impact on the properties of interest. We measure the sensitivity of code based on the FOMs' fitness values. A piece of code A is said to be more sensitive than another piece B, if a FOM generated from A dominates the FOM generated from B on the Pareto front. The range of a code piece can be measured at different granularity levels by aggregating the results of FOMs, such as at the syntactic symbol, the statement level, or the nesting code block level. The GI-FOMs generated and their sensitive information are passed to the next search stage as inputs.

2.2 Stage II: Searching for GI-HOMs

In the second stage, HOMI applies a multi-objective algorithm to search for a set of improved versions of the original program in the form of HOMs. We use an integer vector to represent HOMs, which is a commonly used data representation in search-based Higher Order Mutation Testing [18]. Each integer value in the vector encodes whether a mutable symbol is mutated and how it is mutated. For example, given a mutant generated from the arithmetic operator '+', a negative integer value means it is not mutated while the integer 0, 1, 2, 3 indicate that the code is mutated to '-', '*', '/', '%' respectively. In this way, each FOM is represented as a vector with only one non-negative number and HOMs can be easily constructed by the standard crossover and mutation search operators.

The algorithm takes the GI-FOMs as input and repeatedly evolves HOMs that inherit the strengths of the GI-FOMs from which they are constructed and yield better performance than any GI-FOMs alone. The fitness function that guides the search is defined as the sum of the measurement of each optimisation property over a given test suite. Given a set of N optimisation goals, for each mutant M, the fitness function $f_n(M)$ for the nth optimisation goal is formulated as follow:

$$Minimisation \quad f_n(M) = \begin{cases} \sum C_i(M) & \text{if } M \text{ passes all test cases} \\ C_{\text{MAX}} & \text{if } M \text{ fails any test case} \end{cases}$$

The fitness function is a minimisation function where $C_i(M)$ is the measurement of the optimisation goal n when executing the test i. If the mutant M fails any regression tests, we consider it as a bad candidate and assign it with the worst fitness values C_{MAX}. The algorithm produces a Pareto front of GI-HOMs. Each HOM on the front represents a modified version of the original program that passes all the regression tests while no property of interest can be further improved without compromising at least one other optimising goal.

2.3   Implementation

We implemented a prototype tool to realise the HOMI approach. The HOMI tool is designed to optimise two non-functional properties (running time and memory consumption) for C programs. In the fitness evaluation harness, we use *Glibc*'s *wait* system calls to gather the CPU time, and we instrument the memory management library to measure the 'high-water' mark of the memory consumption. We choose to measure virtual instead of physical memory consumption because the physical memory consumption is non-deterministic. This means it depends on the workload of the machine. By contrast, the virtual memory used is always an upper bound of the physical memory actually used.

HOMI uses the open source C mutation testing tool, Milu [17] to generate mutants. We chose Milu because it features search-based higher order mutation and can be used as an external mutant generator. By default, Milu supports only the traditional C mutation operators [1]. As memory consumption is one of the optimisation goals, we extended the original version of Milu to support Memory Mutation Operators proposed by Nanavati et al. [23]. Table 1 lists the Mutation Operators used in HOMI and their brief descriptions. During the search stage, HOMI transforms the internal integer vector representation of the candidate HOM to the data format recognisable by Milu, then invokes Milu to generate the HOM.

Table 1. Mutation Operators used by HOMI

Category	Name	Description
Selective	ABS	Change an expression `expr` to `ABS(expr)` or `-ABS(expr)`
Operators	OAAN	Change between `+`, `-`, `*`, `/`, `%`
Mutation	OLLN	Change between `&&`, `||`
	ORRN	Change between `>`, `>=`, `<`, `<=`, `==`
	OIDO	Change between `++x`, `--x`, `x++`, `x--`
	CRCR	Change a constant c to `0`, `1`, `-1`, `c+1`, `c-1`, `c*2`, `c/2`
Memory	REC2M	Replace `malloc()` with `calloc()`
Mutation	RMNA	Remove `NULL` assignment
Operators	REDAWN	Replace memory allocation calls to `NULL`
	REDAWZ	Replace allocation size with `0`
	RESOTPE	Replace `sizeof(T)` with `sizeof(*T)`
	REMSOTP	Replace `sizeof(*T)` with `sizeof(T)`
	REM2A	Replace `malloc()` with `alloca()`
	REC2A	Replace `calloc()` with `alloca()`
	RMFS	Remove `free()` statement

The HOMI tool employs a customised NSGA-II [8] to evolve GI-HOMs. During the search process, HOMI maintains a population of candidate HOMs. For each generation, the uniform crossover and mutation are performed to parent HOMs, generating offspring HOMs that are later evaluated using the fitness functions mentioned. A tournament selection is then performed to form the next generation. This process is repeated until a given budget of evaluation times is reached. Finally HOMI will generate a set of non-dominating GI-HOMs that perform better than the original program on time and/or memory consumption.

3   Empirical Study

This section first discusses the research questions we address in our empirical evaluation of the HOMI tool, followed by an explanation of the chosen subjects, tests and experiment settings.

3.1   Research Questions

Since the HOMI approach generates GI-HOMs from the combination of FOMs, a natural first question to ask is 'whether existing FOMs can be used to improve software'. This motivates our first research question.

RQ1: Can GI-FOMs improve program performance while passing all of its regression tests?

To answer this question, we run HOMI for sensitivity analysis only and report how much running time and memory can be saved by GI-FOMs. Of course, the answer also depends on the quality of the regression tests. All the tests used in our evaluation are regression tests generated by developers for real world systems. However, they may still not be sufficient to reveal the faults introduced by mutation. To make our experiment more rigorous and efficient, we carried out a pre-analysis in our evaluation. We analyse the function coverage of each subject using the GNU application *Gcov* and HOMI is set only to mutate the functions that are covered by regression tests.

RQ2: How much improvement can be achieved by GI-HOM in comparison with GI-FOMs?

If GI-FOMs alone can improve performance, we expect that GI-HOMs will inherit some strengths from the GI-FOMs and improve the performance further. To answer this question, we use HOMI to generate a GI-HOM Pareto front and investigate whether the GI-FOM solutions generated are on the Pareto front. Furthermore, it is interesting to see whether the new memory mutation operators help to improve the performance. This motivates our sub-question which studies the effect on mutation operators used.

RQ 2.1 How does the improvement achieved by applying the traditional mutation operators only compare to applying both of the traditional and memory mutation operators?

We answer this question by comparing the HyperVolume quality indicator of the Pareto fronts generated from HOMI using both sets of mutation operators. Given a Pareto front A and a reference Pareto front R, HyperVolume is the volume of objective space dominated by solutions in A. To take into account the stochastic nature of the search algorithms, we repeat both experiments 30 times. We use the non-parametric Mann-Whitney-Wilcoxon-signed rank tests to assess the statistical significance of the HyperVolume and untransformed [24] Vargha-Delaney effect size to further assess the magnitude of the differences [2].

RQ3: Can 'plastic surgery' GP based GI approach find edit sequences to construct the GI-HOMs found by HOMI?

We ask this question because we want to understand whether the granularity of mutation changes can be produced by the 'plastic surgery' GP approach. The 'plastic surgery' GP approach is a popular GI approach which searches for a list of edits from the existing source code. Typical changes generated by the GP approach are movements or replacements of different lines of code [20, 26]. To answer this question, we carried out a sanity-check experiment manually using all the GI-HOMs found. For each GI-HOM, we search the entire program to see if the mutated statement exists in the program. If it does, the GI-HOM can be constructed by the patches generated from the GP approach easily. Otherwise, we consider the line/statement based 'plastic surgery' GP might not able to generate the GI-HOM directly.

RQ4 Can HOMI be combined with Deep Parameter Optimisation to achieve further improvement?

Finally, we want to investigate whether the HOMI approach can be combined with other types of GI techniques. Deep Parameter Optimisation is one of the state-of-the-art parameter tuning based GI techniques. It seeks to optimise library code used instead of the source code of the subjects [29]. We answer this research question by evaluating the GI-HOMs after linking them to Deep-Parameter-optimised libraries, then comparing them with their performance before the linking, and with the performance of the original program after linking to Deep-Parameter-optimised libraries.

3.2   Subject Programs and Tests

We optimise four subjects in our evaluation. Table 2 lists the subjects and their brief description. All tests used are regression tests, deemed to be useful and practical by their developers. *Espresso* is a fast application for simplifying complex digital electronic gate circuits. *Gawk* is the GNU *awk* implementation for string processing. *Flex* is a tool for generating scanners, programs which recognise

Table 2. Subject programs

Name	LoC	# of Tests	Description
espresso	13,256	19	Digital circuit simplification
gawk	45,241	334	String processing
flex	9,597	62	Fast lexical analyzer generator
sed	5,720	362	Special file editor

lexical patterns in text, and *sed* is an editor that automatically modifies files given a set of rules. We use the *espresso* version as well as its test cases from *DieHard* project [5]. Version 4.1.0 of *gawk* is used in this work. The source code and the test cases can be found in the GNU archives. We obtain the last two programs and corresponding test suites from the SIR repository [10].

3.3 Search Settings

In the sensitivity analysis stage, we pick the top 10 % most sensitive locations of the GI-FOMs and only search for GI-HOMs from these locations. We use a relative ratio instead of an absolute number because the search space can be adapted to the size of the subject. The choice of 10 % is based on our observation that the locations in the first 10 % are usually much more sensitive than the remaining locations since sensitivity seems to follow a power law, according to our informal observation. However, the ratio can be easily adapted as a parameter to our approach accordingly.

We repeat all HOMI experiments 30 times to cope with the non-deterministic nature of NSGAII and to facilitate inferential statistical analysis. The NSGAII performs a tournament selection of size 2 and uniform crossover with a probability of 0.8. There are 50 HOMs in each generation and the algorithm stops at 100th generation. These numbers were chosen after initial calibration experimentation to determine suitable parameters for our search process. All of the experiments are carried out on a desktop machine with a quad-core CPU and 7.7 GB RAM running 64-bit Ubuntu version 14.04. *Gcc* 4.8.4 with optimisation option -O3 was used to compile all the mutants. The source of this project is publicly available at https://github.com/FanWuUCL/HOMI.

4 Results and Discussion

4.1 Improvement by GI-FOMs

We begin by looking at the time and memory performance of the GI-FOMs generated from the sensitivity analysis stage to answer the RQ1. We calculated the improvement of GI-FOMs relative to the original program, and reported them in Columns 2 and 5 in Table 3. These values are averaged from 10 repeated evaluations. By applying selective and memory mutation operators to generate

FOMs, we found the improved versions of all four subjects, both on time and memory performance. More specifically, the improvement ranges from 0.9 % to 14.7 % on time and from 0.5 % to 19.7 % on memory performance. However, there might be a large gap between the memory and time improvement for some subject, for example, the GI-FOM of *sed* can run up to 14.7 % faster to only save 0.5 % memory. We conclude that even with the simplest changes introduced by first order mutation, the HOMI approach is able to improve the execution time and memory consumption.

4.2   Improvement by GI-HOMs

We now turn to the improvement found by GI-HOMs. Since improvement was found on GI-FOMs, it is interesting to investigate whether we can improve the performance further by combining them to form GI-HOMs. We applied NSGA-II [8] to search for better performance in HOMs using Selective Mutation Operators (GI-HOMs-Sel) and using both Selective and Memory Mutation Operators (GI-HOMs-All) respectively. Each experiment was repeated for 30 times and the best time/memory performance found for each subject is reported in Table 3.

Table 3. Improvement on time and memory by GI-FOMs and GI-HOMs. GI-HOMs-Sel are found using only Selective Mutation Operators while GI-HOMs-All and GI-FOMs are found using both Selective and Memory Mutation Operators

Subject	Time (%)			Memory (%)		
	GI-FOMs	GI-HOMs-Sel	GI-HOMs-All	GI-FOMs	GI-HOMs-Sel	GI-HOMs-All
espresso	5.2	6.5	**6.9**	1.6	**1.7**	**1.7**
gawk	2.3	6.7	**9.8**	2.5	1.9	**4.3**
flex	0.9	**2.3**	**2.3**	**19.7**	**19.7**	**19.7**
sed	14.7	**18.2**	**18.2**	**0.5**	**0.5**	**0.5**

The results of GI-HOMs-Sel are reported in Columns 3 and 6, and those of GI-HOMs-All are reported in Columns 4 and 7. We immediately observe that GI-HOMs achieve greater improvement than GI-FOMs on execution time for all subjects, also on memory consumption for two out of four subjects. The greatest time improvement found by GI-HOMs can be promoted to 18.2 %, while the improvement can be up to four times better (on *gawk*) than the improvement yielded from GI-FOMs. We also observe one case *gawk*), on which the GI-HOMs-Sel achieve less memory improvement compared with GI-FOMs, because they are lack of some memory-related changes that can only be achieved by Memory Mutation Operators.

We combine the results of 30 runs for each experiment and plot the Pareto fronts of GI-HOMs using all Mutation Operators, GI-HOMs using Selective Mutation Operators and GI-FOMs in Fig. 2. In the figure, time (x-axis) and memory (y-axis) are both normalised to the original performance. On all four

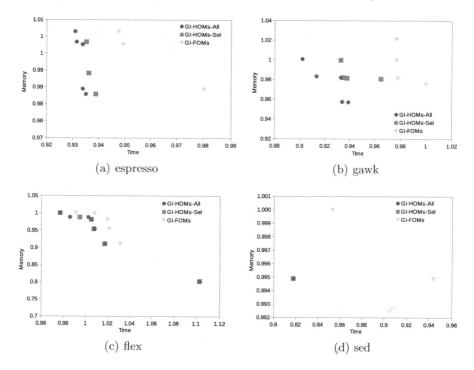

Fig. 2. Pareto fronts of GI-HOMs and GI-FOMs for each subject. Lower and lefthand solutions dominate high and righthand solutions.

subjects, we can see there is always an improvement from GI-FOMs to GI-HOMs, while the differences between GI-HOMs-Sel and GI-HOMs-All are less clear. To statistically demonstrate the difference, we calculated the HyperVolume [30] of the Pareto fronts of GI-HOMs-All and GI-HOMs-Sel over 30 runs, and applied Mann-Whitney-Wilcoxon U-test on the HyperVolume metric for these Pareto fronts. For subject *espresso* and *gawk*, the difference between HOMs (all) and HOMs (Selective) are significant ($p < 0.01$) with a large effect size ($A_{12} > 0.9$), while for the other two subjects, the difference is not significant.

In summary, the answer to RQ2 is that GI-HOMs can improve the time performance by up to 18.2 % or the memory performance by up to 19.7 %, compared with 14.7 % and 19.7 % in GI-FOMs. For the GI-HOMs using Selective Mutation Operators only, we found the same upper bound of the improvement, but only achieved sub-optimal solutions on two subjects. By including Memory Mutation Operators, further improvement on these subjects were found. Therefore, we can conclude that Memory Mutation Operators provide further improvement potentials for both time and memory optimisation.

4.3   HOMI vs 'Plastic Surgery' GP Based GI

This RQ investigates whether the granularity of mutation changes can also be generated by the 'plastic surgery' GP approach. To answer this question,

we investigated the GI-HOMs found in all experiments and manually reproduce them following the evolution rules used in the line/statement based 'plastic
surgery' GP approach [20,26]. All together HOMI found 273 mutations in the
improved GI-HOMs across all subjects. We first applied a simple hill-climbing
algorithm to clean up the mutations that do not contribute to the improvement.
This step narrowed the number of mutations down to 141. In total, there are
108 unique mutations identified (the same mutations may be found in several
GI-HOMs).

For each of the unique mutation changes, we search the entire program to see
if the mutated line/statement exists in the program. Because the typical changes
generated by the 'plastic surgery' GP approach are movements or replacements
of different lines of code [20,26], if a mutation does not appear somewhere else
in the original source code, it cannot be generated directly from this form of
GP approaches. The result shows that 95 (88 %) out of 108 mutations cannot
be found in the original source code. Therefore, the answer to RQ3 is, there are
108 unique mutational changes found in the GI-HOMs, 88 % of which cannot be
generated from the line-based 'plastic surgery' GP approach directly.

4.4   HOMI Combines with Deep Parameter Optimisation

In the last Research Question, we want to understand whether the improvement can be preserved or even promoted if we combine GI-HOMs with Deep-
Parameter-optimised memory management library. To answer this question, we
obtained a set of memory allocation libraries that were optimised for the time
and memory performance for each subject from the authors of the Deep Parameter Optimisation work. We created four new optimised version of each subject
by linking the most time/memory-saving GI-HOMs and libraries in pairwise.

The results are reported in Table 4. In the table, rows represent HOMI-
improved programs and columns represent Deep-Parameter-optimised libraries,
where 'Original' indicates the original program or library, 'T' indicates it is the
most time-saving ones and 'M' indicates the most memory-saving ones. All of the
numbers are the improvement in percentage compared with the original version.
If in a combination (that does not involve the Original program/library), the
time/memory performance is not worse than that of any of the 'ingredient' pro-
gram/library, it is highlighted in bold font. On the other hand, all the underlined
performances are the ones that are worse than both of the 'ingredient' program
and library. For subject *sed*, there is only one GI-HOM on the Pareto front, thus
it is both the most time and memory-saving program.

We observe that there are 10 out of 28 cases (bold numbers) when combining GI-HOMs with the Deep-Parameter-optimised library, the performance is at
least the same as the best performance of the GI-HOM or library it is combined
from, and is strictly better in four cases. However, there are three cases (underlined) that the combination makes their performance worse. In most of the cases,
the performance lies between the performance of the GI-HOM and the library
that it is combined from. In one extreme case (*flex*), we found that the most
memory-saving library breaks the functionality of HOMs (indicated by '-Inf' in

Table 4. HOMI combines with Deep Parameter Optimisation. Each cell reports the time improvement followed by memory improvement in percentage. 'T' or 'M' indicates it is most time-saving or memory-saving GI-HOM/optimised library.

		Memory Management Library					Memory Management Library		
		Original	Deep(T)	Deep(M)			Original	Deep(T)	Deep(M)
espresso	Original	0/0	0.8/0.1	0.7/0.2	*gawk*	Original	0/0	5.4/1.6	-0.2/2.3
	GI-HOM(T)	6.9/-0.2	4.8/**0.1**	4.7/**0.2**		GI-HOM(T)	9.8/-0.1	5.6/**1.6**	5.4/**2.3**
	GI-HOM(M)	6.5/1.7	4.7/**1.8**	**6.7**/1.7		GI-HOM(M)	6.1/4.3	<u>4.1</u>/**5.8**	4.8/**5.5**
flex	Original	0/0	15.7/-2.6	-1.1/0.6	*sed*	Original	0/0	7.9/-1208	5.6/2.0
	GI-HOM(T)	2.3/0	14.4/-2.6	-Inf/-Inf		GI-HOM(TM)	18.2/0.5	<u>5.8</u>/-1208	<u>4.1</u>/0.9
	GI-HOM(M)	-10.3/19.7	-3.5/**19.7**	-Inf/-Inf					

the table). Therefore, the answer to RQ4 is, when combining the HOMI approach with Deep Parameter optimisation, the GI-HOM programs can be either improved or jeopardised. This result motivates a future study that searches and optimises HOMI and Deep Parameters altogether.

5   Threats to Validity

We discuss the threats to validity in this sections, where the threats to internal validity are discussed in Sect. 5.1 and those to external validity are discussed in Sect. 5.2.

5.1   Internal Validity

We used the regression tests that come with the subjects to evaluate the correctness of mutants. All the subject programs used in this paper were well tested in established works, and their tests used are regression tests, deemed to be useful and practical by their developers. However, passing the regression tests does not necessarily mean the semantics of the mutant is the same as the original program. This may pose a threat to the correctness of the GI-HOMs. To mitigated this threat, we set HOMI to apply mutation changes at the code that is covered by the regression tests.

After the sensitivity information is collected, we focus on 10 % most sensitive locations only. This is based on an assumption that less sensitive code is less likely to affect the performance of the program. However, there are still chances that the interactions between multiple less sensitive code may lead to some significant improvement. This possible synergy, if there is any, requires a much larger search space, thus, will make the approach much less scalable. To make the HOMI approach scalable, we confine the search on the most sensitive locations, making the search more effective. Furthermore, we make the ratio of sensitive locations a parameter of our approach, such that it can be adapted to trade between exploration and exploitation.

Another threat to validity comes from the measurement of time and memory performance. We applied the measurement approach proposed by Wu et al. [29]. To make the measurement accurate, we use CPU time and use the mean of 10 measurements to minimise the noise. For memory consumption, we instrument the memory management library to calculate the exact use of virtual memory. Therefore, the measurement noise is minimised.

5.2   External Validity

The approach can be easily applied to other subjects, but the conclusion may not generalise to larger scale systems. We use four subjects with varying sizes from 5,000 to 45,000 lines of code, and the results are consistent across all subjects. Therefore, we have confidence that the results may likely be generalised to larger scale systems, and the threat is thereby ameliorated.

We adopt Memory Mutation Operators in our approach because we are interested in time and memory performance. However, the same set of Mutation Operators does not necessarily lead to similar results when other software qualities are concerned. Since the selection of Mutation Operators is independent of the other parts of the approach, the choices of Mutation Operators can be easily adapted accordingly, thereby minimising this threat.

6   Related Work

One of the closely related GI work is the 'plastic surgery' GP approach proposed by Langdon et al. [20,21]. Their approach searches for sequences of edits at the granularity of statements. Due to the operations of statement swapping, the optimised code is hard for human developers to understand. Our approach uses simple syntactic mutations to improve the code, therefore the structure of the original code is always preserved. Since mutations can happen at the expression level, our approach works on a finer granularity.

Deep Parameter Optimisation is a similar work that also used First Order Mutants for sensitivity analysis [29]. After sensitivity analysis, they inserted and exposed additional parameters at most sensitive locations, which were later optimised using multi-objective search algorithms. Our approach follows a simpler procedure, combining FOMs to achieve better performance. Furthermore, our approach searches for code changes that happen at much more locations at the same time than the Deep Parameter approach does, while the scalability of the approach remains.

Other Genetic Improvement (GI) works also consider other qualities of software, such the correctness [22] or energy consumption [7]. In our work, execution time and memory consumption are concerned not only because they are important qualities to many benchmark programs, but also because unlike other software qualities, they are known to compete with each other. Therefore, it is interesting to study the trade-off between these two software qualities.

Barr et al. investigated the plastic surgery hypothesis: the content of new code can often be assembled from existing code base [4]. They found that 43 % of the code changes could be composed of the same software program at the line level. While they focused on human-written patches, we investigated how likely a machine-generated mutational change can be found somewhere else in the source code. Our result suggests that 88 % of those mutational changes cannot be composed of the same code base at the line level.

7   Conclusion

In this paper, we have introduced, HOMI, a search-based higher order mutation approach to GI. HOMI uses mutation operators to automatically modify subject programs at a finer granularity. Using a multi-objective search algorithm, HOMI found GI-HOMs that improve subject programs by 18.2 % on time performance or 19.7 % on memory consumption without breaking any regression tests. In our empirical study, we also find that by including Memory Mutation Operators, HOMI can find GI-HOMs that achieve better performance than using just traditional Selective Mutation Operators on two subjects. Furthermore, we find that 88 % of the mutational changes in our GI-HOMs cannot be generated from the currently widely-used line based 'plastic surgery' GP approach. Finally, by combining GI-HOMs with Deep-Parameter-optimised memory management libraries, we found further improvement than GI-HOMs or optimised libraries alone could achieve, which motivates a future research direction that searches and optimises GI-HOMs and Deep Parameters altogether.

References

1. Agrawal, H., DeMillo, R.A., Hathaway, B., Hsu, W., Hsu, W., Krauser, E.W., Martin, R.J., Mathur, A.P., Spafford, E.: Design of mutant operators for the C programming language. techreport SERC-TR-41-P, Purdue University, West Lafayette, Indiana, March 1989
2. Arcuri, A., Briand, L.: A hitchhiker's guide to statistical tests for assessing randomized algorithms in software engineering. Softw. Test. Verif. Reliab. **24**(3), 219–250 (2014)
3. Arcuri, A., Fraser, G.: On parameter tuning in search based software engineering. In: Cohen, M.B., Ó Cinnéide, M. (eds.) SSBSE 2011. LNCS, vol. 6956, pp. 33–47. Springer, Heidelberg (2011)
4. Barr, E.T., Brun, Y., Devanbu, P., Harman, M., Sarro, F.: The plastic surgery hypothesis. In: Proceedings of the 22nd ACM SIGSOFT International Symposium on Foundations of Software Engineering, FSE 2014, pp. 306–317. ACM, New York (2014)
5. Berger, E.D., Zorn, B.G.: Diehard: probabilistic memory safety for unsafe languages. In: Programming Language Design and Implementation, PLDI 2006 (2006)
6. Brake, N., Cordy, J.R., Dan, Y.E., Litoiu, M., Popes U, V.: Automating discovery of software tuning parameters. In: Workshop on Software Engineering for Adaptive and Self-managing Systems, SEAMS 2008 (2008)

7. Bruce, B.R., Petke, J., Harman, M.: Reducing energy consumption using genetic improvement. In: Proceedings of the 2015 Annual Conference on Genetic and Evolutionary Computation, GECCO 2015, pp. 1327–1334. ACM, New York (2015)
8. Deb, K., Pratap, A., Agarwal, S., Meyarivan, T.: A fast and elitist multiobjective genetic algorithm: NSGA-II. IEEE Trans. Evol. Comput. **6**(2) (2002)
9. DeMillo, R.A., Lipton, R.J., Sayward, F.G.: Hints on test data selection: Help for the practicing programmer. Computer (4), 34–41 (1978)
10. Do, H., Elbaum, S., Rothermel, G.: Supporting controlled experimentation with testing techniques: an infrastructure and its potential impact. Empirical Softw. Eng. **10**(4), 405–435 (2005)
11. Harman, M., Jia, Y., Langdon, W.B.: Strong higher order mutation-based test data generation. In: Proceedings of the 19th ACM SIGSOFT Symposium and the 13th European Conference on Foundations of Software Engineering, ESEC/FSE 2011, pp. 212–222 (2011)
12. Harman, M., Jia, Y., Reales Mateo, P., Polo, M.: Angels and monsters: an empirical investigation of potential test effectiveness and efficiency improvement from strongly subsuming higher order mutation. In: Proceedings of the 29th ACM/IEEE International Conference on Automated Software Engineering, ASE 2014, pp. 397–408. ACM, New York (2014)
13. Harman, M., Jones, B.F.: Search-based software engineering. Inf. Softw. Technol. **43**(14), 833–839 (2001)
14. Harman, M., Langdon, W.B., Jia, Y., White, D.R., Arcuri, A., Clark, J.A.: The gismoe challenge: Constructing the pareto program surface using genetic programming to find better programs (keynote paper). In: Proceedings of the 27th IEEE/ACM International Conference on Automated Software Engineering, ASE 2012, pp. 1–14. ACM, New York (2012)
15. Hutter, F., Hoos, H.H., Leyton-Brown, K., Stützle, T.: ParamILS: an automatic algorithm configuration framework. J. Artif. Intell. Res. **36**(1), 267–306 (2009)
16. Jia, Y., Harman, M.: An analysis and survey of the development of mutation testing. IEEE Trans. Softw. Eng. **37**(5), 649–678 (2011)
17. Jia, Y., Harman, M.: MILU: a customizable, runtime-optimized higher order mutation testing tool for the full C language. In: Proceedings of the TAIC PART 2008, Windsor, UK, pp. 94–98, 29–31 August 2008
18. Jia, Y., Harman, M.: Higher order mutation testing. Inf. Softw. Technol. **51**(10), 1379–1393 (2009). Source Code Analysis and Manipulation
19. Jia, Y., Wu, F., Harman, M., Krinke, J.: Genetic improvement using higher order mutation. In: Proceedings of the Companion Publication of the 2015 Annual Conference on Genetic and Evolutionary Computation, GECCO Companion 2015, pp. 803–804. ACM, New York (2015)
20. Langdon, W., Harman, M.: Optimizing existing software with genetic programming. IEEE Trans. Evol. Comput. **19**(1), 118–135 (2015)
21. Langdon, W.B., Modat, M., Petke, J., Harman, M.: Improving 3D medical image registration CUDA software with genetic programming. In: Conference on Genetic and Evolutionary Computation, GECCO 2014 (2014)
22. Le Goues, C., Nguyen, T., Forrest, S., Weimer, W.: Genprog: a generic method for automatic software repair. IEEE Trans. Softw. Eng. **38**(1), 54–72 (2012)
23. Nanavati, J., Wu, F., Harman, M., Jia, Y., Krinke, J.: Mutation testing of memory-related operators. In: 2015 IEEE Eighth International Conference on Software Testing, Verification and Validation Workshops (ICSTW), pp. 1–10, April 2015

24. Neumann, G., Harman, M., Poulding, S.: Transformed Vargha-Delaney effect size. In: Barros, M., Labiche, Y. (eds.) SSBSE 2015. LNCS, vol. 9275, pp. 318–324. Springer, Heidelberg (2015)
25. Papadakis, M., Jia, Y., Harman, M., Traon, Y.L.: Trivial compiler equivalence: a large scale empirical study of a simple, fast and effective equivalent mutant detection technique. In: 2015 IEEE/ACM 37th IEEE International Conference on Software Engineering, vol. 1, pp. 936–946, May 2015
26. Petke, J., Harman, M., Langdon, W.B., Weimer, W.: Using genetic improvement and code transplants to specialise a C++ program to a problem class. In: Nicolau, M., Krawiec, K., Heywood, M.I., Castelli, M., García-Sánchez, P., Merelo, J.J., Rivas Santos, V.M., Sim, K. (eds.) EuroGP 2014. LNCS, vol. 8599, pp. 137–149. Springer, Heidelberg (2014)
27. Petke, J., Langdon, W.B., Harman, M.: Applying genetic improvement to MiniSAT. In: Ruhe, G., Zhang, Y. (eds.) SSBSE 2013. LNCS, vol. 8084, pp. 257–262. Springer, Heidelberg (2013)
28. White, D.R., Arcuri, A., Clark, J.A.: Evolutionary improvement of programs. IEEE Trans. Evol. Comput. 15(4), 515–538 (2011)
29. Wu, F., Weimer, W., Harman, M., Jia, Y., Krinke, J.: Deep parameter optimisation. In: Proceedings of the 2015 Annual Conference on Genetic and Evolutionary Computation, GECCO 2015, pp. 1375–1382. ACM, New York (2015)
30. Zitzler, E., Thiele, L.: Multiobjective evolutionary algorithms: a comparative case study and the strength pareto approach. IEEE Trans. Evol. Comput. 3(4), 257–271 (1999)

Search Based Test Suite Minimization for Fault Detection and Localization: A Co-driven Method

Jingyao Geng, Zheng Li[⊠], Ruilian Zhao, and Junxia Guo

College of Information Science and Technology, Beijing University
of Chemical Technology, Beijing 100029, People's Republic of China
lizheng@mail.buct.edu.cn

Abstract. Fault detection and fault localization are two independent but important processes in software testing, in which test cases and associated information are usually used. As there are different goals of the two processes, i.e., detect faults early and locate faults accurately, different information of test cases are required and thus different subsets of test cases are selected to achieve the goals. In general, fault localization is adjacent to fault detection. However, independence of these two processes will restrict the automatic process of software testing. This paper proposes an automatic approach to combining fault detection and fault localization, where a multi-objective optimization for test suite minimization is presented to balance and achieve the both goals. Empirical studies show the proposed method can give consideration to both fault detection and fault localization with a high test suite reduction ratio.

Keywords: Multi-objective · Test Suite Minimization · Fault Localization · Fault detection · Combination

1 Introduction

Fault detection and fault localization are two important phases in software testing. Fault detection aims at finding bugs while fault localization aims at locating where the bugs are [16]. Usually, fault detection and fault localization are independent of another.

High speed iterations of software development demand efficient automatic testing. Many automatic techniques for a specific process had been proposed to replace manual work, in which search based technique is widely used. Automatically and continuously implementing processes can highly improve the efficiency of software testing. It has become possible to combine two adjacent processes together with the increasing degree of automation in single process.

Fault localization is adjacent to fault detection. At fault detection process, designed test cases are executed to detect fault. If an executed test case has inconsistent output with expectant output, which is usually called a failed test case, the program under test is considered to have fault. Fault localization techniques are proposed to help programmers to locate the bugs. Spectrum-based Fault Localization (SBFL) [20] is one of the most popular automatic techniques,

© Springer International Publishing AG 2016
F. Sarro and K. Deb (Eds.): SSBSE 2016, LNCS 9962, pp. 34–48, 2016.
DOI: 10.1007/978-3-319-47106-8_3

in which the execution information of test cases is used to calculate the suspiciousness for each program element according to certain specific statistical methods. The suspiciousness that indicates the probability of a program element being faulty is provided for developers to identify bugs [19].

Many search based optimization techniques had been proposed for both fault detection and fault localization. It has been observed that test cases and associated information are used in the optimization. Thus it is possible to merge these two processes together to improve the efficiency of testing process. A few investigations had been conducted. Unfortunately, it had been presented that the two goals for each single process cannot substitute each other. Vidács found that test cases selected by fault detection driven metric behaves worse at fault localization than those selected by fault localization driven metric, and vice versa [16]. Gonzalez et al. implemented test case prioritization for fault localization, and found that executing test case according to fault localization driven prioritizing method behaves worse at fault detection than those ordered by fault detection driven metric [5], and vice versa [6]. Thus test cases cannot be selected according to one of these two metric to achieve both fault detection and localization goals.

Recently, fault localization prioritization (FLP) is proposed that test cases are ordered according to fault detection driven metric first, until there is a test case failed in the process, the rest test cases are reordered by fault localization driven metric to get the best fault localization effectiveness as soon as possible [25]. It has been realized that the increasing of software size and test suite size are key factors that affecting the efficiency of regression testing. This paper focuses on test suite minimization, and a multi-objective test suite minimization (MoTSM) technique with three objects (described in Sect. 3) is proposed to reduce the size of test suites and select a test case subset with consideration to optimize both fault detection and fault localization simultaneously. Both the merge of two adjacent processes and test suite size reduction can highly improve the efficiency of regression testing.

Test suite minimization for fault detection is a NP-complete problem [24], and we further explain that test suite minimization for fault localization is also a NP-hard problem (Sect. 3.1). Thus metaheuristic search algorithm, NSGA-II, is employed in MoTSM for fault detection and fault localization.

The primary contributions of this paper are:

1. This paper discussed the pre-condition of combination of two adjacent processes of software testing by using multi-objective optimization techniques.
2. This paper proposed a multi-objective test suites minimization approach aiming at combining two adjacent processes rather than the optimization for single process.
3. Empirical results showed that the proposed multi-objective test suites minimization can highly reduce the test suite size while with high fault detection rate and fault localization accuracy.

The rest of this paper is organized as follows. Section 2 presents the background of the proposed MoTSM and related work. Section 3 describes the details of our method and its validity assessment. Section 4 includes the experiments design and results analyses. Section 5 shows the limits of our experiments and Sect. 6 concludes this paper and presents research directions for future work.

2   Background and Related Work

2.1   Test Case and Program Spectra

A program spectrum is a collection of data that provides a specific view of the dynamic behaviour of software [14]. Two kinds of program spectra are widely used at fault detection and localization. Executable Statement Hit Spectrum (ESHS) records executable statements that are executed [18], and Output Spectrum (OPS) records the output produced by program when it executes [10]. If a test case output is different from the expected output, it is a failed test case.

Table 1 presents an example of program spectra that includes the source code and its ESHS and OPS. Black bullets are used to indicate that statements have been covered by test cases, and the execution results are represented by P/F ($Passed/Failed$). For example, t_7 is a failed test case that covers statements $s_1, s_2, s_3, s_4, s_6, s_7, s_{13}$.

2.2   Test Suite Reduction

An increasing number of test cases is designed and added to test suites in software development. How to optimize test suites to improve the efficiency of software

Table 1. Example of a program fragment with test suite execution information

int x,y,z,m;	test case							
mid() {	t_1	t_2	t_3	t_4	t_5	t_6	t_7	t_8
1: read("Enter 3 numbers:", x,y,z);	●	●	●	●	●	●	●	●
2: m = z;	●	●	●	●	●	●	●	●
3: if (y<z)	●	●	●	●	●	●	●	●
4: if (x<y)	●	●			●		●	●
5: m = y;		●						
6: else if (x<z)	●				●		●	●
7: m = y; // *** bug ***	●						●	●
8: else			●	●		●		
9: if (x>y)			●	●		●		
10: m = y;			●			●		
11: else if (x>z)				●				
12: m = x;								
13: print("Middle number is:", m);	●	●	●	●	●	●	●	●
}								
Pass/Fail Status	P	P	P	P	P	P	F	F

testing is widely researched in recent years. Test case selection and test suite minimization are two major research areas. Test case selection focuses on the identification of the modified parts of the program, while test case minimization aims at using least test cases to satisfy all test requirements [24]. This paper focuses on combination of fault localization and fault detection, and test suite minimization is chosen to be a bridge and to improve the efficiency of the whole process. In this section, test suite minimization for fault detection and fault localization are introduced.

Test Suite Minimization for Fault Detection. Fault detection aims at finding bugs in programs. In this phase, test cases are executed as input of the program. Once a test case failed, the program is judged to contain bugs. The more failures a test suite found, the higher quality of the test suite in terms of fault detection.

Test suite minimization for fault detection aims at identifying bugs with least test cases. Although there is a debate about the relation between code coverage and fault detection ratio, code coverage had been widely used as one of optimization object in test suite minimization for fault detection [6]. Vidács et al. proposed a metric to measure the covering power of a test case subset T [16].

$$FD = \frac{|\{p \in P \mid p \ covered \ by \ T\}|}{|P|} \tag{1}$$

FD measures the percentage of statement covered by test suite T, as shown in Formula (1), where $|P|$ means the statement number of program P. The higher metric value, the stronger covering power of T. For example, the program in Table 1, suppose $T = (t_1, t_2, ..., t_8)$, FD of T is $\frac{12}{13}$ since no test case covers statement 12.

Yoo did a survey on regression testing minimization, selection and prioritization [24], and proved regression testing minimization is NP-complete problem. They also used multi-objective search based method to do test case selection for fault detection [22], in which objects are code coverage and test case execution time.

Test Suite Minimization for Fault Localization. Fault localization helps programmers to locate bugs in program debugging. Spectrum-Based Fault Localization (SBFL) is one of the most popular fault localization techniques, in which suspiciousness is calculated to evaluate probability of a program element being faulty. The higher *suspiciousness* indicates that a statement appears higher suspicious to be faulty. Tarantula [11] and Op2 [14] are two popular SBFL suspiciousness calculating methods that are described as follows.

$$suspiciousness_T(s) = \frac{\frac{fail(s)}{total\,fail}}{\frac{fail(s)}{total\,fail} + \frac{pass(s)}{total\,pass}} \tag{2}$$

$$suspiciousness_O(s) = fail(s) - \frac{pass(s)}{total\,pass + 1} \tag{3}$$

In Formula (2) and (3), $fail(s)$ is the number of failed test cases that cover the statement s, and $total\,fail$ is the total number of failed test cases. $pass(s)$, likewise, is the number of passed test cases that cover the statement s, and $totalpass$ is the total number of passed test cases. Consider the example in Table 1, if all the eight test cases are used to calculating suspiciousness of fault statement s_7, $fail(s_7) = 2, total\,fail = 2, pass(s_7) = 1, totalpass = 6$. Calculating by tarantula, $suspiciousness_T(s_7) = \frac{6}{7}$, while its suspiciousness is $suspiciousness_O(s_7) = \frac{15}{8}$ when using Op2.

Test suite minimization for fault localization aims at using least test case to achieve the most precise fault localization effect. It has been investigated that statements covered by same test cases have the same suspiciousness according to Formula (2) and (3), which leads to a low precision of SBFL. Thus, test case optimization is to reduce the number of statements covered by same test cases. Based on previous research, statement partition is defined as follows.

Definition 1. *(statement partition) Given: a test suite T, a testing program P, the executable statements set of the testing program S, T_i is a subset of T, $\forall t \in T_i$, if t covers $s_i \leftrightarrow t$ covers s_j, it is called that s_i and s_j belong to the same statement partition under T_i.*

In order to distinguish fault statement from others for a program under test, the average size of statement partitions should be as small as possible while the number of statement partitions should be as large as possible [16].

Hao et al. [7] proposed a strategy to select test cases which can divide the statements covered by more fault test cases into more evenly partition. Dandan Gong et al. [2] used a failed test case set to select passed test cases instead of using one specific failed test case. They also used path vector to replace statement coverage information. Statement partition methods are widely used because of its high efficiency and effectiveness.

Gap Between Fault Detection and Fault Localization. There is a growing tendency toward automatic software testing. Harman proposed a hypothetical tool that can automatically detect programs, localize bugs and finally fix bugs [8]. In recent years, researchers start to research the relationship between fault detection and fault localization. Search based test case prioritization(TCP) has been used to reduce the cost during fault detection phase [12]. But if fault detection test case prioritization are continuously used for fault localization, a large number of test cases will be required [6]. For better automatically executing these two processes, researchers proposed Fault Localization Prioritization (FLP) method, to reorder test cases for fault localization [25]. Shin proposed an information theory based test case prioritization method for fault localization, namely FLINT [25], where the fault localization effect can reach the highest as soon as possible.

Vidács [16] firstly proposed a combined test suite reduction method for both fault detection and fault localization. They selected a fixed size test suite by mixing two different test suites, one of which is selected according to fault detection goal and the other is selected according to fault localization goal. However, this combination method is not so flexible and may have negative influence on both fault detection and fault localization phase. In addition, The two test suites are selected by greedy strategy, which cannot find the optimal solutions for NP-hard problems.

2.3   Multi-objective Optimization in SBSE

Many software engineering problems can be transformed into optimization problems that can be effectively solved using search algorithms, namely Search Based Software Engineering (SBSE) [9]. Multi-objective search based algorithms have been successfully used in SBSE, because most software engineering issues have more than one objective or constrain.

Since objectives are usually irrelevant or interact with each other, the outcome of multi-objective optimization process is usually a set of non-dominated solutions, namely Parato Front [23]. To explain more formally, for fitness functions f_i and f_j, A, B are two decision vectors which contain the values $f_i(A)$, $f_i(B)$, $f_j(A)$ and $f_j(B)$. A and B are said to non-dominated if and only if they satisfy the following relation [23]:

$$(\exists i \in \{1, 2, \cdots, m\}, f_i(A) > f_i(B)) \ \wedge \ (\exists j \in \{1, 2, \cdots, m\}, f_j(B) > f_j(A))$$

Decision makers usually pick up a suitable individual in Pareto Front as the final solution according to the importance of different objectives.

Most of the multi-objective optimization problems are NP-completeness, and search based methods are recommended to avoiding state explosion. For example, test suite minimization problem is one of the classical multi-objective optimization problem that hopes to use least test cases to cover most requirements. Shin proved that test suite minimization problem is NP-complete problem [24] which they recommend being solved by multi-objective search based method.

Non-dominated Sorting Genetic Algorithm (NSGA-II) [3] is a fast and elitist multi-objective genetic algorithm [3] that is suitable for optimization problem with two or three optimal objects. A NSGA-II procedure is similar to the genetic algorithm, including initializing population, evaluating individuals, selecting individuals to generate new individuals by crossover and mutation operators. The search process is iterated through a number of generations until the termination condition is satisfied.

In NSGA-II, an initial population is a set of individuals which are randomly generated. An individual is a solution which is usually presented in binary as strings of 0 and 1 or other encoding schemes. Genetic operators such as crossover and mutation are used to iterate new individuals. Fitness is calculated on the basis of different kinds of objectives to evaluate whether an individual is a good solution. Some of the individuals are selected to construct new generation by using elitist strategies. The algorithm is terminated once the fitness functions of all objectives are satisfied or a prefixed number of generations is reached.

3 Co-driven Multi-objective Test Suite Minimization for Fault Detection and Fault Localization

To apply multi-objective optimization techniques to combine two adjacent processes, pre-conditions are usually demanded. The first one is for all objects of both processes, the computation information should be based on the same source. For example, fault detection and fault localization, they both need information related test cases, although one is code coverage by test cases and the other is the number of code segments distinguished by test cases. The other is their object need to be relevant to each other. Usually the objects are conflicting each other. Recent researches suggest that there could be correlated objects in multi-objective optimization where the search space may be changed to improve the search process [15].

This section analyses the relationship between test suite minimization for fault detection and fault localization in Sect. 3.1. The necessity of using search based method and the details especially for objectives of the proposed method MoTSM (Sect. 3.2) are presents in the following part. In addition, validity assessment of our method is displayed in Sect. 3.3.

3.1 Relationship Between TSM for Fault Detection and Localization

To the best of our knowledge, test suite minimization for fault localization is harder to verified than test suite minimization for fault detection. To distinguish the two test suite minimization problems, we call the former code coverage maximization problem and the latter partition number maximization problem. They can be reformulated into the following form.

Definition 2. *(code coverage maximization) Given: a code coverage matrix C with n test cases and m statements which is denoted as $C = (S_1, S_2, ..., S_m)$ where $S_i = (a_{1i}, a_{2i}, ..., a_{ni})$. If $a_{ij} = 1$, test case i covers statement j, otherwise test case i doesn't cover statement j. There's a code coverage vector $P = (c_1, c_2, ...c_m)$. If $\exists a_{ij} \in S_j, a_{ij} = 1$, then $c_j = 1$. the covered code number of C is $Cov(C) = |P|$. $|P|$ means the number of 1 in P. Code coverage maximization problem aims to use least test cases to achieve the biggest $Cov(C)$ value.*

Similar to coverage maximization problem, we formally describe partition number maximization problem as follows:

Definition 3. *(partition number maximization) Given: a code coverage matrix with n test cases and m statements $C = (S_1, S_2, ..., S_m)$ where $S_i = (a_{1i}, a_{2i}, ..., a_{ni})$. If $a_{ij} = 1$, test case i covered statement j, otherwise test case i doesn't covered statement j. the statement partition number of C is $P(C) = |S|$. $|S|$ means the number of different rows in C.*

Now we construct another matrix $C' = (S_{11}, S_{12}, ..., S_{(m-1)m})$, where $S_{ij} = S_i \otimes S_j$. Obviously, for one row S_i in original matrix C, the new matrix C' corresponds $m - i$ rows. We also need to construct a vector $P' = (c'_1, c'_2, ...c'_m)$, where $c_1' = 1$ if and only if for $m - i$ rows of S_i, there's no null vector there. Statement partition number $P(C) = |P'|.|P'|$ means the number of 1 in P' Statement partition maximization problem aims to use least test case to achieve the biggest $P(C)$ value.

In this way, partition number maximization problem can be reduced to coverage maximization problem. Since coverage maximization problem is NP-complete problem and partition number maximization problem is at least as hard as coverage maximization problem, so the partition number maximization problem is an NP-hard problem. So we recommend to using search based method to solve this problem. In this paper, we firstly use search based algorithm to solve this problem.

Since both coverage maximization problem and partition number maximization problem are needed to be solved by search based method, to combine fault detection and localization by using this two metrics, search algorithm NSGA-II is selected in the experiment.

3.2   Three Objects in MoTSM

Since partition maximization problem can be reduced to coverage maximization problem, they are "helper objectives" [15]. Since we hope to use "helper objectives" to improve the search process, the two objects are both used in our search based method. Three objects in all are used in multi-objective test suite minimization for fault localization and fault detection.

Object 1: test suite reduction ratio. The size of test suites can affect the efficiency of both fault detection and fault localization. In case that two test suites have the same fault detection and fault localization effectiveness, it is apparent that the smaller one is better since fewer test cases is needed. Test suite reduction ratio is defined as the ratio of the test cases that not selected. Suppose T' is the subset of the original test suite T, the ratio of test suite reduction can be calculated by Formula (4). Higher *Reduction* is expected obviously.

$$R(T') = (1 - \frac{|T'|}{|T|}) * 100\% \tag{4}$$

Object 2: code coverage ratio. This object aims at improving fault detection. As described in Sect. 2.2, MoTSM reduces the size of test suite, but without losing fault detection ratio ideally. The metric of code coverage, i.e., the percentage of statements covered, is used as the second object in the proposed MoTSM. The coverage ability of a test suite T can be donated as $C(T)$ and a higher $C(T)$ is expected in MoTSM.

Object 3: the number of statement partitions. This object aims at improving fault localization. As described in Sect. 2.2, test suite reduction needs to guarantee the number of statement partitions not declining so that the fault localization effectiveness can be kept in a high level. So the third object of the proposed method is the number of statement partitions. Suppose test suite T can divide a program into n statement partitions, we donate this as $P(T) = n$. As far as this object, the more statement partitions a test suite can divide testing program into, the better it is.

3.3 Validity Assessment

Since the final destination is to combine fault detection and fault localization, we use validity assessment method at fault detection and spectrum based fault localization to assess our method. Considering fault localization, we do experiment on single-fault programs. We verify FD $score$ in [16] to assess the fault detection ability of selected test subset which is:

$$FD\ score = \frac{|versions_f|}{|total\ versions|} * 100\,\%$$ (5)

where $|versions_f|$ means the number of versions which is found to be faulty, which means corresponding selected test suites contains at least one failed test and $|total\ versions|$ means total number of fault versions we use in our experiments.

We use traditional fault localization assessment criteria $rank$ [16] to be our FL $score$ to assess our method which is described as follows. For a program and a statement s in this program, suppose that there are n statements that have same suspiciousness higher than s and m statements else which suspiciousness are equal to s, then the $rank$ of statement s is:

$$rank(s) = n + (m/2)$$ (6)

It means that $n+(m/2)$ statements need to be checked on average before developers check statement s. Suppose s_f is fault statement, then FL $score = rank(s_f)$, which is best with value 0 means that developers don't need to check extra statement before finding fault.

The reason using absolute rank rather than traditional relative proportions is that absolute rank makes more sense in terms of helping developing to narrow down the search space [17].

4 Empirical Study

Since multi-objective techniques usually get non-dominated solutions (described in Sect. 2.3), which means goals in different dimension usually cannot reach optimal simultaneously. For this reason we design a method to pick up test case subset in the set of non-dominated solutions. The ultimate goal of our combination is to omit fault detection and do fault localization directly, so effectiveness and efficiency of fault detection and fault localization need to be verified. The empirical study is conducted to address the following questions:

RQ1: How much can the reduced test suite by MoTSM effectively detect faults?

RQ2: Comparing with the original test suite, can the reduced test suite by MoTSM effectively locate faults?

RQ3: On the premise of guaranteeing high code coverage and statement partition number, how well the MoTSM can reduce test suite?

4.1 Experimental Settings and Subjects

NSGA-II is used to implement the multi-objective optimization process. One gene represents whether a test case is selected, 1 for selected and 0 for not selected. Each individual express a test case subset and the population number is set into 50. Single points crossover and single base substitution are used in multi-objective genetic algorithm and their rates are both 1.0. The termination is fixed at 200 iterations in the experiments.

In order to verify our method, 6 C/C++ programs have been employed, and the detail information is in Table 2. The software artifacts are available from Software-artifact Infrastructure Repository SIR [4]. Single-fault versions are used in the experiments.

In Table 2, *#versions* means the number of fault versions used in the experiments. *LOC* means lines of code. *sLOC* represents the number of executable source codes. The column *#test pool* shows the number of test cases of test pool. *#test suite* means the size range of test suites we use. In our experiments, different scales of *test suite* are used to instead of *test pool*, because researches at fault detection usually uses test suites to be close to practical testing process while researches at fault localization usually use test pool to get better fault localization effectiveness, and our goal is to combine fault detection and localization, using fault detection's input and fault localization's output seems more reasonable. We use 100 test suites whose test case is randomly selected until achieving maximum code coverage. For accuracy and without loss of generality, Each experiment has been repeated for 10 times.

4.2 Optimal Selection in Pareto Front

In general, there usually exists knee regions in Pareto Front where a small improvement in one objective would lead to a large deterioration in at least

Table 2. Subjects

program	#versions	LOC	sLOC	#test pool	#test suite
tcas	27	173	65	1608	15–463
totinfo	17	565	122	1052	6–637
schedule	5	412	149	2650	82–479
printtokens	2	726	195	4130	36–1685
printtokens2	6	570	199	4055	14–598
space	13	6199	3657	13585	600–3400

one other objective [1]. Obviously, such knee regions are potential parts of the Pareto Front presenting the maximal trade-offs between different objectives.

However, considering the specific multi-objective test suite minimization problem, different objectives have affected different aspect of test suite performance. For example, test suite reduction may improve the efficiency to the fault detection and localization, but may have no significant effect to effectiveness. We certainly hope that selected test suite subset T can achieve high value in both $C(T)$(object 2) and $P(T)$(object 3), and give less concentrations on $R(T)$(object 1). Considering fault localization succeed fault detection in regression testing, so statement partition number is firstly considered and then the code coverage, and test suite reduction ratio has been put into the last. So it seems for two test subset T_1, T_2, we select T_1 rather than T_2 if and only if one of the following conditions is true:

1. $P(T_1) > P(T_2)$
2. $(P(T_1) = P(T_2)) \wedge (C(T_1) > C(T_2))$
3. $(P(T_1) = P(T_2)) \wedge (C(T_1) = C(T_2)) \wedge (R(T_1) \geqslant R(T_2))$

4.3   Fault Detection Effectiveness

The optimals in both fault detection and fault localization are expected. If a test suite can't detect bugs in programs, it seems there's no failed test cases in test suite. According to fault metrics in Sect. 2.2, if $fail(s) = 0$ and $total\,fail = 0$, all covered statements will possess the same suspiciousness. So by using this significance, we can confirm that whether a test suite can detect fault.

All subjects used in experiments contain 70 fault versions, and for each fault version, we do experiment with 100 test suites and repeat 10 times, thus there are $70 * 100 * 10 = 70000$ test case subsets in all. To our surprise that 69750 in 70000 test subsets can exactly detect faults. According to the description of $FD\,score$ in Sect. 3.3, the $FD\,score \approx 99.65\,\%$. The high $FD\,score$ means that our test suite minimization method can successfully select failed test cases without knowing tests' results in advance. That is to say, our test suite minimization method can effectively detect fault in single-fault programs.

4.4   Fault Localization Effectiveness

Since Tarantula is one of the most popular SBFL methods while Op2 is one of the best methods in over 50 methods under Xie's theoretical framework [21], these two methods are used as evaluation metrics in our fault localization experiments. For all the 100 test suites with 10 times repeated experiments in each fault version, a *rank* value has been calculated and we use the average *rank* of 1000 times experiments to be the *rank* of each fault version and the results are shown in Fig. 1. Since space possesses much more lines of code than other programs, we draw figures of space and other small programs separately.

Figure 1a shows all subjects' rank distribution except space's and Fig. 1(b) shows the *rank* distribution of space. *MoTSM/base* in x-ray represents doing fault localization with selected test case subsets by our MoTSM method or whole test suite (Baseline), while *Op2/tarantula* means using Op2 or Tarantula. The breadth of each block presents data density of a special *rank*, and there's one box plot in each violin plot, in which the white dot represents median while upper and under edge of black box represent upper and lower quartiles.

Comparing Tarantula and Op2, Op2 performs better in both whole test suite and MoTSM method since the plots of Op2 are overall lower. But comparing our minimization method and using whole test suites, our method performs worse in fault localization which is similar to many test suite reduction methods. It is because that test suite reduction can't provide more useful information to fault localization than whole test suite as long as there's no noise in test suites. Noise such as coincidental correctness [13] can decrease effectiveness of fault localization, but test suite minimization method can decrease these disadvantages in a certain chance, this is why some of the fault versions' localization results behaves better in MoTSM.

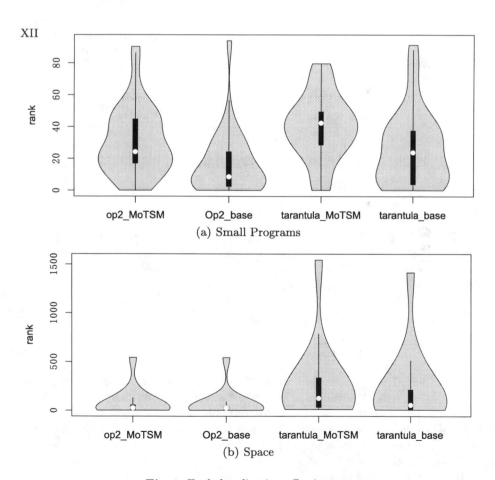

(a) Small Programs

(b) Space

Fig. 1. Fault localization effectiveness

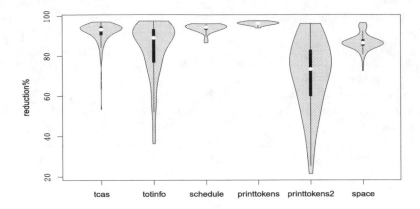

Fig. 2. Test Suite Reduction Ratio of six programs

There is another interesting phenomenon in Fig. 1(b) that violin's shape between MoTSM and using whole test suites are almost same, which means the effectiveness in space between our methods and whole test suite may too small to come into notice. To analysis more precisely, we use Mann-Whitney U test to do an significance testing on rank value got by MoTSM and base. We assume null hypothesis is that there's no significant difference on fault localization effects between minimization method and baseline. After using two groups rank data of space(fault localization by using Op2 and Tarantula), null hypothesis is kept up under *significant level* = 0.05. That means, our minimization method can almost keep same localization effects with that by using whole test suites under big programs.

4.5   Reduction Ratio

We also analysis the test suite reduction ratio of MoTSM method. Figure 2 shows test suite reduction ratio's distribution of all 70 fault versions. We found that all programs can keep at least 70 % reduction in general though we use test suite rather than test pool to do test suite minimization.

Though our test suite minimization methods give consideration to both fault detection and localization, it can still keep a high test suite reduction ratio.

5   Threats to Validity

We use the Simens programs as subjects in the study. All but space are small-sized programs with seeded faults. To simplify the experiment's process, we only use single fault versions. Further empirical studies on larger programs with multiple faults may further to strengthen the external validity of our conclusions. Although we observe that the outcome of different repetitions is very close to each other in the process of experiment, the repetitions of our experiments need to be further strengthen to verify our conclusions since it is truly affecting the accuracy of experiment.

6 Conclusion and Future Work

In this paper, we propose a search based test suite minimization method to tentatively combine fault detection and fault localization, in order to improve the regression testing efficiency by merging two adjacent processes into one. A pre-condition of combination using multi-objective optimization technique is discussed and three objects are proposed to balance the goals of fault detection and fault localization. We explain that test suite minimization for fault detection and fault localization is NP-hard problem that search based techniques is required to solve the problem. The results show our method can obtain a high reduction ratio while detecting fault effectively and locating faults effectively.

The future work will consider more objects to improve fault localization effectiveness and provide additional information to help developers understanding faults. A general approach will be discussed and studied to combine more processes together with automatic implementation in software testing.

Acknowledgment. The work described in this paper is supported by the National Natural Science Foundation of China under Grant No.61170082 and 61472025 and the Program for New Century Excellent Talents in University (NCET-12-0757).

References

1. Branke, J., Deb, K., Dierolf, H., Osswald, M.: Finding knees in multi-objective optimization. In: Yao, X., Burke, E.K., Lozano, J.A., Smith, J., Merelo-Guervós, J.J., Bullinaria, J.A., Rowe, J.E., Tiño, P., Kabán, A., Schwefel, H.-P. (eds.) PPSN 2004. LNCS, vol. 3242, pp. 722–731. Springer, Heidelberg (2004)
2. Dandan, G., Tiantian, W., Xiaohong, S., Peijun, M.: A test-suite reduction approach to improving fault-localization effectiveness. Comput. Lang. Syst. Struct. **39**(3), 95–108 (2013)
3. Deb, K., Pratap, A., Agarwal, S., Meyarivan, T.: A fast and elitist multiobjective genetic algorithm: NSGA-II. IEEE Trans. Evol. Comput. **6**(2), 182–197 (2002)
4. Do, H., Elbaum, S.G., Rothermel, G.: Supporting controlled experimentation with testing techniques: an infrastructure and its potential impact. Empirical Softw. Eng. Int. J. **10**(4), 405–435 (2005)
5. Gonzalez-Sanchez, A., Abreu, R., Gross, H.G., van Gemund, A.J.: Prioritizing tests for fault localization through ambiguity group reduction. In: 2011 26th IEEE/ACM International Conference on Automated Software Engineering (ASE), pp. 83–92. IEEE (2011)
6. Gonzalez-Sanchez, A., Piel, É., Abreu, R., Gross, H.-G., van Gemund, A.J.C.: Prioritizing tests for fault localization. In: van de Laar, P., Tretmans, J., Borth, M. (eds.) Situation Awareness with Systems of Systems, pp. 247–257. Springer, New York (2013)
7. Hao, D., Xie, T., Zhang, L., Wang, X., Sun, J., Mei, H.: Test input reduction for result inspection to facilitate fault localization. Autom. Softw. Eng. **17**(1), 5–31 (2010)
8. Harman, M., Jia, Y., Zhang, Y.: Achievements, open problems and challenges for search based software testing. In: IEEE 8th International Conference on Software Testing, Verification and Validation (ICST), pp. 1–12 (2015)

9. Harman, M., Jones, B.F.: Search-based software engineering. Inf. Softw. Technol. **43**(14), 833–839 (2001)
10. Harrold, M.J., Rothermel, G., Wu, R., Yi, L.: An empirical investigation of program spectra. In: ACM SIGPLAN Notices, vol. 33, pp. 83–90. ACM (1998)
11. Jones, J.A., Harrold, M.J.: Empirical evaluation of the tarantula automatic fault-localization technique. In: Proceedings of the 20th IEEE/ACM International Conference on Automated Software Engineering, pp. 273–282. ACM (2005)
12. Li, Z., Harman, M., Hierons, R.: Search algorithms for regression test case prioritization. IEEE Trans. Softw. Eng. **33**(4), 225–237 (2007)
13. Masri, W., Assi, R.: Cleansing test suites from coincidental correctness to enhance fault-localization. In: Third International Conference on Software Testing, Verification and Validation (ICST), pp. 165–174 (2010)
14. Naish, L., Lee, H.J., Ramamohanarao, K.: A model for spectra-based software diagnosis. ACM Trans. Softw. Eng. Methodol. (TOSEM) **20**(3), 11 (2011)
15. Praditwong, K., Harman, M., Yao, X.: Software module clustering as a multi-objective search problem. IEEE Trans. Softw. Eng. **37**(2), 264–282 (2011)
16. Vidács, L., Beszédes, Á., Tengeri, D., Siket, I., Gyimóthy, T.: Test suite reduction for fault detection and localization: a combined approach. In: 2014 Software Evolution Week-IEEE Conference on Software Maintenance, Reengineering and Reverse Engineering (CSMR-WCRE), pp. 204–213. IEEE (2014)
17. Wang, Q., Parnin, C., Orso, A.: Evaluating the usefulness of IR-based fault localization techniques. In: Proceedings of the 2015 International Symposium on Software Testing and Analysis, pp. 1–11. ACM (2015)
18. Wong, W.E., Debroy, V.: A survey of software fault localization. Department of Computer Science, University of Texas at Dallas, Technical report UTDCS-45-09 (2009)
19. Wong, W.E., Qi, Y., Zhao, L., Cai, K.Y.: Effective fault localization using code coverage. In: 31st Annual International Computer Software and Applications Conference, COMPSAC 2007, vol. 1, pp. 449–456. IEEE (2007)
20. Xie, X., Chen, T.Y., Kuo, F.C., Xu, B.: A theoretical analysis of the risk evaluation formulas for spectrum-based fault localization. ACM Trans. Softw. Eng. Methodol. **22**(4), 31:1–31:40 (2013)
21. Xie, X., Kuo, F.-C., Chen, T.Y., Yoo, S., Harman, M.: Provably optimal and human-competitive results in SBSE for spectrum based fault localisation. In: Ruhe, G., Zhang, Y. (eds.) Search Based Software Engineering. LNCS, vol. 8084, pp. 224–238. Springer, Heidelberg (2013)
22. Yoo, S., Harman, M.: Pareto efficient multi-objective test case selection. In: Proceedings of the 2007 International Symposium on Software Testing and Analysis, ISSTA 2007, pp. 140–150. ACM, New York (2007)
23. Yoo, S., Harman, M.: Pareto efficient multi-objective test case selection. In: Proceedings of the 2007 International Symposium on Software Testing and Analysis, pp. 140–150. ACM (2007)
24. Yoo, S., Harman, M.: Regression testing minimization, selection and prioritization: a survey. Softw. Test. Verification Reliab. **22**(2), 67–120 (2012)
25. Yoo, S., Harman, M., Clark, D.: Fault localization prioritization: comparing information-theoretic and coverage-based approaches. ACM Trans. Softw. Eng. Methodol. **22**(3), 19:1–19:29 (2013)

Validation of Constraints Among Configuration Parameters Using Search-Based Combinatorial Interaction Testing

Angelo Gargantini[1], Justyna Petke[2], Marco Radavelli[1],
and Paolo Vavassori[1(✉)]

[1] University of Bergamo, Bergamo, Italy
{angelo.gargantini,marco.radavelli,paolo.vavassori}@unibg.it
[2] University College London, London, UK
j.petke@ucl.ac.uk

Abstract. The appeal of highly-configurable software systems lies in their adaptability to users' needs. Search-based Combinatorial Interaction Testing (CIT) techniques have been specifically developed to drive the systematic testing of such highly-configurable systems. In order to apply these, it is paramount to devise a model of parameter configurations which conforms to the software implementation. This is a non-trivial task. Therefore, we extend traditional search-based CIT by devising 4 new testing policies able to check if the model correctly identifies constraints among the various software parameters. Our experiments show that one of our new policies is able to detect faults both in the model and the software implementation that are missed by the standard approaches.

Keywords: Combinatorial testing · Feature models · Configurable systems · CIT

1 Introduction

Most software systems can be configured in order to improve their capability to address user's needs. Configuration of such systems is generally performed by setting certain parameters. These options, or *features*, can be created at the software design stage (e.g., for *software product lines*, the designer identifies the features unique to individual products and features common to all products in its category), during compilation (e.g., to improve the efficiency of the compiled code) or while the software is running (e.g., to allow the user to switch on/off a particular functionality). A configuration file can also be used to decide which features to load at startup.

Large configurable systems and software product lines can have hundreds of features. It is infeasible in practice to test all the possible configurations. Consider, for example, a system with only 20 Boolean parameters. One would have to check over one million configurations in order to test them all (2^{20} to be exact). Furthermore, the time cost of running one test could range from fraction of a second to hours if not days. In order to address this combinatorial explosion

© Springer International Publishing AG 2016
F. Sarro and K. Deb (Eds.): SSBSE 2016, LNCS 9962, pp. 49–63, 2016.
DOI: 10.1007/978-3-319-47106-8_4

problem, Combinatorial Interaction Testing (CIT) has been proposed for testing configurable systems [4]. It is a very popular black-box testing technique that tests all interactions between any set of t parameters. There have been several studies showing the successful efficacy and efficiency of the approach [13,14,21].

Furthermore, certain tests could prove to be infeasible to run, because the system being modelled can prohibit certain interactions between parameters. Designers, developers, and testers can greatly benefit from modelling parameters and constraints among them by significantly reducing modelling and testing effort [21] as well as identifying corner cases of the system under test. Constraints play a very important role, since they identify parameter interactions that need not be tested, hence they can significantly reduce the testing effort. Certain constraints are defined to prohibit generation of test configurations under which the system simply should not be able to run. Other constraints can prohibit system configurations that are valid, but need not be tested for other reasons. For example, there's no point in testing the *find* program on an empty file by supplying all possible strings.

Constructing a CIT model of a large software system is a hard, usually manual task. Therefore, discovering constraints among parameters is highly error prone. One might run into the problem of not only producing an incomplete CIT model, but also one that is over-constrained. Even if the CIT model only allows for valid configurations to be generated, it might miss important system faults if one of the constraints is over-restrictive. Moreover, even if the system is not *supposed* to run under certain configurations, if there's a fault, a test suite generated from a CIT model that correctly mimics only desired system behaviour will not find that error. In such situations tests that exercise those corner cases are desirable.

The objective of this work is to use CIT techniques to validate constraints of the model of the system under test (SUT). We extend traditional CIT by devising a set of six policies for generating tests that can be used to detect faults in the CIT model as well as the SUT.

2   Combinatorial Models of Configurable Systems

Combinatorial Interaction Testing (CIT), or simply combinatorial testing, aims to test the software or the system with selected combinations of parameter values. There exist several tools and techniques for CIT. Good surveys of ongoing research in CIT can be found in [9,19], while an introduction to CIT and its efficacy in practice can be found in [15,21].

A model for a combinatorial problem consists of several parameters which can take several domain values. In most configurable systems, dependencies exist between parameters. Such constraints may be introduced for several reasons, e.g., to model inconsistencies between certain hardware components, limitations of the possible system configurations, or simply design choices [4]. In our approach, tests that do not satisfy the constraints in the CIT model are considered *invalid*.

We assume that the models are specified using CITLAB [3, 7]. This is a framework for combinatorial testing which provides a rich abstract language with precise formal semantics for specifying combinatorial problems, and an eclipse-based editor with a rich set of features. CITLAB does not have its own test generators, but it can utilise, for example, the search-based combinatorial test generator CASA[1][8]. CIT problems can be formally defined as follows.

Definition 1. *Let $P = \{p_1, \ldots, p_m\}$ be the set of parameters. Every parameter p_i assumes values in the domain $D_i = \{v_1^i, \ldots, v_{o_i}^i\}$. Every parameter has its name (it can have also a type with its own name) and every enumerative value has an explicit name. We denote with $C = \{c_1, \ldots, c_n\}$ the set of constraints.*

Definition 2. *The objective of a CIT test suite is to cover all parameter interactions between any set of t parameters. t is called the strength of the CIT test suite. For example, a pairwise test suite covers all combinations of values between any 2 parameters.*

Constraints c_i are given in general form, using the language of propositional logic with equality and arithmetic. Figure 1a shows the CITLAB model of a simple washing machine consisting of 3 parameters. The user can select if the machine has `HalfLoad`, the desired `Rinse`, and the `Spin` cycle speed. There are two constraints, including, if `HalfLoad` is set then the speed of spin cycle cannot exceed `maxSpinHL`.

Software systems can be configured by setting specific parameter values at different stages of the software testing process.

Compile Time. Configurations can be set at compile time. An example is shown in Fig. 1b. Depending on the value settings of the Boolean variables `HELLO` and `BYE` different messages will be displayed when the program is run.

Design Time. Configurations can also be set at design time. For example, in case of a SPL, a configurability model is built during the design.

```
Model WashingMachine
  Definitions:
    Number maxSpinHL = 1400;
  end
  Parameters:
  Boolean HalfLoad;
  Enumerative Rinse {Delicate Drain Wool};
  Numbers Spin { 800 1200 1800 };
  end
  Constraints:
  # HalfLoad => Spin < maxSpinHL #
  # Rinse==Rinse.Delicate =>
    ( HalfLoad and Spin==800) #
end
```

(a) Washing Machine example

```
Model Greetings
  Parameters:
    Boolean HELLO;
    Boolean BYE;
  end
  Constraints:
    # HELLO != BYE#
  end
```

```
#ifdef HELLO
char* msg = "Hello!\n";
#endif
#ifdef BYE
char* msg = "Bye_bye!\n";
#endif

void main() {
    printf(msg);
}
```

(b) Compile time configurable example, its CIT model (left) and the source code (right)

Fig. 1. Combinatorial interaction CITLAB models

---

[1] http://cse.unl.edu/~citportal/.

Runtime. Another way of setting parameter configurations is at runtime. This can be usually done by means of a graphical user interface (GUI). In a chat client, e.g., you can change your availability status as the program is running.

Launch Time. We also differentiate the case where parameters are read from a separate configuration file or given as program arguments, *before* the system is run. We say that these parameters are set at launch time of the given application. They decide which features of the system should be activated at startup. Examples of such systems include chat clients, web browsers and others.

3 Basic Definitions

We assume that the combinatorial model represents the specification of the parameters and their constraints for a real system as it has been implemented. We are interested in checking whether this system specification correctly represents the software implementation. We assume that the parameters and their domains are correctly captured in the specification, while the constraints may contain some faults. Specification S belongs to the problem space while software implementation I belongs to the solution space [18].

Formally, given an assignment $\bar{p}$ that assigns a value to every parameter in P of the model S, we introduce two functions:

Definition 3. *Given a model S and its implementation I, val_S is the function that checks if assignment $\bar{p}$ satisfies the constraints in S, while $oracle_I(\bar{p})$ checks if $\bar{p}$ is a valid configuration according to implementation I.*

We assume that the oracle function $oracle_I$ exists. For instance, in case of a compile-time configurable system, we can assume that the compiler plays the role of an oracle: if and only if the parameters $\bar{p}$ allow the compilation of the product then we say that $oracle(\bar{p})$ holds. We may enhance the definition of oracle by considering also other factors, for example, if the execution of the test suite completes successfully. However, executing $oracle_I$ may be very time consuming and it may require, in some cases, human intervention.

On the model side, the evaluation of $val_S(P)$ is straightforward, that is, $val_S(\bar{p}) = c_{1[P \leftarrow \bar{p}]} \wedge \ldots \wedge c_{n[P \leftarrow \bar{p}]}$.

Definition 4. *We say that the Constrained CIT (CCIT) model is correct if, for every p, $val_S(p) = oracle_I(p)$. We say that a specification contains a conformance fault if there exists a $\bar{p}$ such that $val_S(\bar{p}) \neq oracle_I(\bar{p})$.*

3.1 Finding Faults by Combinatorial Testing

In order to find possible faults as defined in Definition 4, the exhaustive exploration of all the configurations of a large software system is usually impractical. In many cases, the evaluation of $oracle_I$ is time consuming and error prone, so the number of tests one can check on the implementation can be very limited.

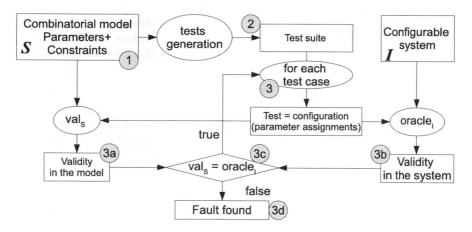

Fig. 2. Validating constraints by CIT

Instead, we can apply combinatorial testing in order to select the parameters values and check that for every generated CIT test $val_S(p) = oracle_I(p)$ holds. This approach does not guarantee, of course, finding all possible conformance faults, but we can assume that faults are due to the interaction of parameters and we can leverage the success of CIT in finding faults in real configurable systems [14,21].

We have devised a process that is able to find possible conformance faults. It is depicted in Fig. 2 and consists of the following steps:

1. Create a CIT model S that takes constraints into account.
2. Generate a CIT test suite according to one of the policies (see Sect. 4).
3. For every test in the test suite,
   (a) Compute its validity as specified by the constraints in the CIT model.
   (b) Compute $oracle_I$, by executing the software system under each configuration to check if it's acceptable.
   (c) Compare the validity, as defined by the model, with the actual result.
   (d) If $val_S \neq oracle_I$ a fault (either in the model or in the system) is found.

A discrepancy between the model and the real system means that a configuration is correct according to the model but rejected by the real system (or the other way around) and this means that the constraints in the model do not correctly describe constraints in the system under test.

Invalid Configuration Testing. In classical combinatorial interaction testing, only valid tests are generated, since the focus is on assessing if the system under test produces valid outputs. However, we believe that invalid tests are also useful. In particular, they address the following issues.

The CIT model should minimise the number of constraints and the invalid configuration set: invalid configurations, according to the model, should only be those that are actually invalid in the real system. This kind of test aims at discovering faults of over-constraining the model. This problem is a variant of the bigger problem of over-specification. Moreover, critical systems should be tested if they safely fail when the configuration is incorrect. This means that the system should check that the parameters are not acceptable (i.e. it must *fail*) and it should fail in a safe way, avoiding crashes and unrecoverable errors (it must fail *safely*). Furthermore, creation of a CIT model for a large real-world software system is usually a tedious, error-prone task. Therefore, invalid configurations generated by the model at hand can help reveal constraints within the system under test and help refine the CIT model. In line with the scientific epistemology, our research focuses on generating not only tests (i.e., valid configurations) that confirm our theory (i.e., the model), but also tests that can *refute* or *falsify* it. Since the number of invalid configurations might be huge, such configurations must be chosen in accordance with some criteria. We choose to use the same t-way interaction paradigm as in standard CIT.

4   Combinatorial Testing Policies

We propose to use search-based combinatorial interaction testing techniques to verify the validity of CIT models. In particular, given a CIT model, we modify it according to one of the policies introduced in this section. Next, we use CASA to generate the test suite satisfying the modified CIT model. We use the term "valid test" to denote the generated configuration that satisfies all the constraints of the original CIT model. Conversely, the term "invalid test" is used for a configuration that does not satisfy at least one of the constraints of the original CIT model. Words "test" and "configuration" are used interchangeably, though we note in real-world systems one configuration may lead to multiple tests.

UC: Unconstrained CIT. In unconstrained CIT, constraints are ignored during CIT test generation. They are used only to check the validity of the configuration selected during generation. The main advantage is that test generation is simplified and efficient methods that work without constraints can be used. Moreover, in principle, both valid and invalid configurations can be generated - there is no control over model validity. It may happen that the test generation algorithm generates only valid combinations (i.e., $val_S(t)$ for every t in the test suite). This may reduce the effectiveness of the test suite: if only valid tests are generated, one can miss faults only discoverable by invalid tests, as explained in Sect. 3.1. On the other hand, only invalid tests can be equally useless.

Example 1. In the washing machine example shown in Fig. 1a, UC policy will produce a pairwise test suite with at least 9 test cases, including an invalid test case where HalfLoad is set to true in combination with Spin equal to 1800.

Test Generation. UC can be applied by simply removing the constraints c_i from the original CIT model. The validity of each test can be later computed by checking if the generated configuration satisfies all the c_i. There are several CIT tools that do not handle constraints (for example, those that use algebraic methods for CIT test suite generation), hence can be used with this policy.

CC: Constrained CIT. In this classical approach, constraints are taken into account and only valid combinations among parameters are chosen. Among these parameters a certain level of desired strength is required. The rationale behind this policy is that one wants to test only valid combinations. If a certain interaction among parameters is not possible, then it is not considered even if it would be necessary in order to achieve the desired level of coverage. The main advantage is that no error should be generated by the system. However, this technique can only check one side of equation given in Definition 4, namely that $val_S(p) \rightarrow oracle_I(p)$, since val_S is always true. If the specification is too restrictive, no existing fault will be guaranteed to be found, if it refers to configurations that are invalid.

Example 2. In the washing machine example shown in Fig. 1a, the CC policy produces 7 tests for pairwise, all of which satisfy the constraints. Some pairs are not covered: for instance HalfLoad=true and Spin=1800 will not be covered.

Test Generation. CC is the classical constrained combinatorial testing (CCIT), and CASA can correctly deal with the constraints and generate only valid configurations. However, CASA requires the constraints in Conjunctive Normal Form (CNF), so CITLAB must convert the constraints from general form to CNF.

CV: Constraints Violating CIT. In case one wants to test the interactions of parameters that produce errors, only tests violating the constraints should be produced. This approach is complementary with respect to the CC in which only valid configurations are produced. In CV, we ask that the maximum possible CIT coverage for a given strength is achieved considering only tuples of parameter values that make at least one constraint false (i.e. each test violates the conjunction $c_1 \wedge \cdots \wedge c_n$).

Example 3. In the example presented in Fig. 1a, the CV policy produces 6 test cases, all of which violate some constraint of the model. For instance, a test has Rinse=Delicate, Spin =800, and HalfLoad=false.

Test Generation. CV can be applied by modifying the model by replacing all the constraints with $\neg(c_1 \wedge \cdots \wedge c_n)$ and then classical CC is applied.

CuCV: Combinatorial Union. One limitation of the CC technique is that with an over-constrained model, certain faults may not be discovered. On the other hand, by generating test cases violating constraints only, as in CV, certain parameter interactions may not be covered by the generated test suite. In order to overcome these limitations we propose the combination of CC and CV.

Test Generation. CuCV is achieved by generating tests using policy CC and policy CV and then by merging the two test suites. Since every test is either valid (in CC) or invalid (in CV), merging the test suites consists of simply making the union of the two test suites.

ValC: CIT of Constraint Validity. CuCV may produce rather big test suites, since it covers all the desired parameter interactions that produce valid configurations *and* all those that produce invalid ones according to the given CIT model. On the other hand, UC may be too weak since there is no control over the final constraint validity and therefore there is no guarantee that the parameter values will influence the final validity of the configuration. On one extreme, UC might produce a test suite without any test violating the constraints. We propose the ValC policy that tries to balance the validity of the tests without requiring the union of valid and invalid tests. ValC requires the interaction of each parameter with the validity of the whole CIT model. That is, both tests that satisfy all the constraints will be generated as well as those that don't satisfy any of the constraints in the given CIT model. Formally, ValC requires that the validity of each configuration $\bar{p}$ (i.e., $val_S(\bar{p})$) is covered in the same desired interaction strength (see Definition 2) among all the parameters.

Example 4. For the WashingMachine, CuCV generates 13 test cases (6+7). ValC requires only 11 test cases.

Test Generation. ValC requires to modify the original CIT model by introducing a new Boolean variable validity and replacing all the constraints with one constraint equal to validity $\leftrightarrow (c_1 \wedge \cdots \wedge c_n)$

CCi: CIT of the Constraints. Every constraint may represent a condition over the system state. For instance, the constraint HalfLoad => Spin < maxSpinHL identifies the critical states in which the designer wants a lower spin speed. One might consider each constraint as a property of the system and be interested in covering how these conditions interact with each other and with the other parameters. The goal is to make the constraints interact with the other system parameters.

Test Generation. CCi requires the introduction of a new Boolean variable validity$_i$ for every constraint, and replacing every constraint c_i with validity$_i \Leftrightarrow c_i$.

5   Experiments

In order to test our proposed approach we conducted the following experiments. We used 4 case studies to evaluate our proposed approach:

1. **Banking1** represents the testing problem for a configurable Banking application presented in [22].

2. **libssh** is a multi-platform library implementing SSHv1 and SSHv2 written in C[2]. The library consists of around 100 KLOC and can be configured by several options and several modules (like an SFTP server and so on) can be activated during compile time. We have analysed the cmake files and identified 16 parameters and the relations among them. We have built a feature model for it in [1] and we have derived from that a CITLAB model.

---

[2] https://www.libssh.org/.

Model Heartbeat
Parameters:
   Range REQ_Length [0 .. 65535] step 4369;
   Range REQ_PayloadData_length [0 .. 65535] step 4369;
   Range RES_Length [0 .. 65535] step 4369;
   Range REQ_PayloadData_length [0 .. 65535] step 4369;
end
Constraints:
// the declared length in the REQUEST is correct
REQ_Length==REQ_PayloadData_length
// the declared length in the RESPONSE is correct
RES_Length==RES_PayloadData_length
// the RESPONSE has the same length as the REQUEST
REQ_Length==RES_Length
end

Fig. 3. HeartbeatChecker CIT model

3. **HeartbeatChecker** is a small C program, written by us, that performs a Heartbeat test on a given TLS server. The Heartbeat Extension is a standard procedure (RFC 6520) that tests secure communication links by allowing a computer at one end of a connection to send a "Heartbeat Request" message. Such a message consists of a payload, typically a text string, along with the payload's length as a 16-bit integer. The receiving computer then must send exactly the same payload back to the sender. HeartbeatChecker reads the data to be used in the Heartbeat from a configuration file with the following schema:

```
TLSserver: <IP>
TLS1_REQUEST Length: <n1> PayloadData: <data1>
TLS1_RESPONSE Length: <n2> PayloadData: <data2>
```

Configuration messages with n1 equal to n2 and data1 equal to data2 represent a successful Heartbeat test (when the TLS-server has correctly responded to the request). HeartbeatChecker can be considered as an example of a _runtime_ configurable system, since thanks to the parameters one can perform different types of tests (with different lengths and payloads). We have written an abstract version of HeartbeatChecker in the combinatorial model shown in Fig. 3: we ignore the actual content of the PayloadData and we model only the lengths: Length represents the declared lengths and PayloadData_length is the actual length of the PayloadData. The constraints represent successful exchanges of messages in the Heartbeat test. The oracle is true if the Heartbeat test has been successfully performed with the specified parameters.

4. **Django** is a free and open source web application framework, written in Python, consisting of over 17 k lines of code, that supports the creation of complex, database-driven websites, emphasizing reusability of components[3]. Each

---

[3] https://www.djangoproject.com/.

Table 1. Benchmark data. *vr* is the validity ratio, defined as the percentage of configurations that are valid.

Name	#Var	#Constraints	#Configurations	vr	#Pairs
Banking1	5	112	324	65.43 %	102
Libssh	16	2	65536	50 %	480
HeartbeatChecker	4	3	65536	0.02 %	1536
Django	24	3	33554432	18.75 %	1196

Django project can have a configuration file, which is loaded every time the web server that executes the project (e.g. Apache) is started. Therefore, the configuration parameters are loaded at *launch time*. In the model we made, among all the possible configuration parameters, we selected and considered one Enumerative and 23 Boolean parameters. We elicited the constraints from the documentation, including several forum articles and from the code when necessary. We have also implemented the oracle, which is completely automated and returns true if and only if the HTTP response code of the project homepage is 200 (HTTP OK).

Table 1 presents various benchmark data: number of variables and constraints, size of the state space (the total number of possible configurations), the percentage of configurations that are valid (i.e. the ratio *vr*), the number of pairs that represent the pairwise testing requirements (ignoring constraints). Note that a low ratio indicates that there are only few valid configurations (see, for example, the HeartbeatChecker benchmark). We collected models of real-world systems from different domains, with a good level of diversity (in terms of size, constraints, etc.) in order to increase the validity of our findings.

Experiments were executed on a Linux PC with two Intel(R) i7-3930K CPU (3.2 GHz) and 16 GB of RAM. All reported results are the average of 10 runs with a timeout for a single model of 3600 s. Test suites were produced using the CASA CIT test suite generation tool according to the pairwise testing criterion.

5.1   Test Generation and Coverage

In our first experiment, we are interested in comparing the policies in terms of test *effort* measured by the number of tests and by the test suite generation time. Table 2 presents the following data:

- The *time* required to generate the tests and to evaluate their validity (it does not include the evaluation of the $oracle_I$) in seconds.
- The *size* in terms of the number of tests and how many of those are valid (#Val), i.e. val_S returns true.
- The percentage of parameter interactions (pairs) that are covered. In the count of the pairs to be covered, we ignore constraints as in Table 1.

From Table 2 we can draw the following observations:

- UC usually produces both valid and invalid tests. However, it may produce all invalid tests (especially if the constraints are strong - see HeartbeatChecker). Having all invalid tests may reduce test effectiveness.

Table 2. Valid pairwise parameter interactions covered by six test generation policies. (Shaded cells are covered in the prose.) Out of memory errors are due to constraint conversion into the CNF format required by CASA. In particular, as known in the literature, the size in CNF of the negation of a constraint can grow exponentially.

Pol	Banking1				Django				libssh				HeartbeatChecker			
	time	size	#Val	Cov	time	size	#Val	Cov	time	size	#Val	Cov	time	size	#Val	Cov
UC	0.22	12	11	100 %	0.65	10	2	100 %	0.25	8	4	100 %	447	267	0	100 %
CC	0.26	13	13	100 %	1.24	10	10	91.8 %	0.28	8	8	99.3 %	2.74	141	141	6.2 %
CV	Out of memory				0.32	11	0	100 %	0.25	8	0	99.3 %	Out of memory			
CuCV	Out of memory				1.58	21	10	100 %	0.52	16	8	100 %	Out of memory			
ValC	Out of memory				0.31	11	4	100 %	0.29	8	5	100 %	Out of memory			
CCi	6.22	12	9	100 %	0.58	13	3	100 %	0.30	8	2	100 %	460	268	0	100 %

- CC usually does not cover all the parameter interactions, since some of them are infeasible because they violate constraints in the original model. On the other hand, CC generally produces smaller test suites (as in the case of HeartbeatChecker). However, in some cases, CC is able to cover all the required tuples at the expense of larger test suites (as in the case of Banking1).
- CV generally does not cover all the parameter interactions, since it produces only invalid configurations. However, in one case (Django) CV covered all the interactions. This means that 100 % coverage of the tuples in some cases can be obtained with no valid configuration generated and this may reduce the effectiveness of testing. Sometimes CV is too expensive to perform.
- CuCV guarantees to cover all the interactions and it produces both valid and invalid configurations. However, it produces the bigger test suites and it may fail because it relies on CV.
- ValC covers all the interactions with both valid and invalid configurations. It produces test suites smaller than CuCV and it is generally faster, but as CuCV may not terminate.
- CCi covers all the interactions, it generally produces both valid and invalid test. However, it may produce all invalid tests (see HeartbeatChecker), and it produces a test suite comparable in size with UC. However, it guarantees an interaction among the constraint validity. It terminates, but it can be slightly more expensive than UC and CC. If the strength of combinatorial testing is greater or equal to the number of constraints, it guarantees also that valid and invalid configurations are generated.

5.2 Fault Detection Capability

We are interested in evaluating the fault detection capability of the tests generated by the policies presented above. We have applied mutation analysis [12] which consists of introducing artificial faults and checking if the proposed technique is able to find them. In our case, we have introduced the faults by hand and then we have applied our technique described in Sect. 3.1 in order to check if the fault is detected (or *killed*). Tables in Fig. 4 present a brief description of each introduced fault and if each policy was able to kill it.

libssh

L1 forgot all the constraints	S
L2 remove a constraint	S
L3 add a constraint	S
L5 remove a dependency	I
L6 add a dependency	I

HeartBeatChecker

H1 remove one constraint	S
H2 == to <=	S
H4 && to ||	I
H5 == to != (all)	I
H6 == to != (one)	I
H7 HeartBleed	I

Policy	Is the fault detected?													mut. score
	L1	L2	L3	L4	L5	L6	H1	H2	H3	H4	H5	H6	H7	
UC	✓	✓		✓	✓		✓	✓	✓	✓	✓	✓		10/13
CC	✓	✓				✓	✓	✓	✓		✓			7/13
CV	✓		✓	✓	✓		-	-	-	-	-	-	-	4/13
CuCV	✓	✓	✓	✓	✓	✓	-	-	-	-	-	-	-	6/13
ValC	✓	✓		✓	✓		-	-	-	-	-	-	-	4/13
CCi	✓	✓	✓	✓	✓		✓	✓	✓	✓	✓	✓	✓	12/13

(a) Seeded Faults (S: in Spec, I: in implementation)

(b) Fault detection capability of the policies (- means that the test suite was not generated.)

Fig. 4. Fault detection capability

In principle, our technique is able to find conformance faults both in the model and in the implementation. Indeed, when a fault is found, it is the designer's responsibility to decide what is the source of the fault. For libssh we have modified both the model and the code (the `cmake` script) (faults Lx). For the HeartbeatChecker we have modified the model and the source code (faults Hx). Table in Fig. 4a presents the details of each injected fault, including if it refers to the specification (S) or to the implementation (I).

Table in Fig. 4b reports which faults were killed by each policy. We can observe that the unconstrained CIT (UC) policy performs better than some policies that consider constraints (CC and CV) even if normally their test suites have the same dimensions. However, in some cases (L6) CC detected a fault where UC failed. For CV, CuCV, and ValC we can analyze only the results for libssh, since they did not complete the test generation for HeartbeatChecker. However, even if we restrict to libssh, CuCV has a very good fault detection capability (but it produces the biggest test suite) while ValC and CV scored as well as UC, although they are more expensive, so according to our studies there is no particular reason to justify the use of ValC and CV alone. However, in one case (L3) CV detected a fault that UC did not.

Overall CCi was the best in terms of fault detection, even with test suites as big as those for UC. However, it missed one of the injected faults (L6). CCi was the only one to find the fault H7 (*HeartBleed*). The HeartBleed fault simulates the famous Heartbleed security bug of the OpenSSH implementation of the TLS protocol. It results from improper input validation (due to a missing bounds check) in the implementation of the TLS Heartbeat extension. In detail, the implementation built the payload length of message to be returned based on the length field in the requesting message, without regard to the actual size of that message's payload. In our implementation, the faulty HeartbeatChecker missed to check that `REQ_Length==RES_Length`. This proves that testing how parameters can interact with single constraints increases the fault detection capability of combinatorial testing. Our new policies may thus prove useful in detecting faults missed by standard approaches due to the so-called *masking effects* [25].

6   Related Work

The problem of modelling and testing the configurability of complex systems is non-trivial. There has been much research done in extracting constraints among parameter configurations from real systems (problem space) and modelling system configurability [11, 23, 25]. For instance, the importance of having a model of variability and having the constraints in the model aligned with the implementation is discussed in [18]. However, in that paper, authors try to identify the sources of configuration constraints and to automatically extract the variability model. Our approach is oriented towards the validation of a variability model that already exists. Moreover, they target C-based systems that realise configurability with their build system and the C preprocessor. A similar approach is presented in [24], where authors extract the compile-time configurability from its various implementation sources and examine for inconsistencies (e.g., dead features and infeasible options). We believe that our approach is more general (not only compile-time and C-code) and can be complementary used to validate and improve automatically extracted models.

Testing configurable systems in the presence of constraints is tackled in [4] and [21]. In these papers, authors argue that CIT is a very efficient technique and that constraints among parameters should be taken into account in order to generate only valid configurations. This allows to reduce the cost of testing. Also in [2], authors have shown how to successfully deal with the constraints by solving them by using a constraint solver such as a Boolean satisfiability solver (SAT). However, the emphasis of that research is more on testing of the final system not its model of configurability. CIT is also widely used to test SPLs [20].

In SPL the validation and extraction of constraints between features is generally given in terms of feature models (FMs). Synthesis of FMs can be performed by identifying patterns among features in products and in invalid configurations and build hierarchies and constraints (in limited form) among them. For instance, Davril et al. apply feature mining and feature associations mining to informal product descriptions [5]. There exist several papers that apply search based techniques, which generally give better results [6, 10, 16, 17]. However, checking and maintaining the consistency between a SPL and its feature model is still an open problem. A preliminary proposal is presented in [1], which however does not use CIT but a more complex logic based approach. We plan to compare our approach with [1] in order to check if CIT can provide benefits in terms of easiness in test generation and shorter generation times.

7   Conclusions

We proposed a novel approach that extends CIT and aims to automatically check the validity of the configurability model of the system under test. In particular, we described how combinatorial interaction testing techniques can be utilised for this purpose. We devised four original policies that can help software testers discover faults in the model of system configurations as well as faults in the software implementation that the model describes. Several experiments conducted show the efficacy of our approach. We confirm that constraints play an important role in configurability testing, but the experiments show that also invalid configurations should be considered in order to avoid some problems (like over-specification) and to detect a wider range of faults. Our experiments suggest that techniques including both valid and invalid tests (as CuCV) have a better fault detection capability than techniques including only valid (as CC) or invalid tests (as CV). However, producing invalid tests may be not feasible. In these cases we would suggest the tester to use CCi instead of UC and CC. The experiments suggest that CCi is not very expensive and it offers a superior fault detection capability. The techniques presented should significantly help software developers in the modelling and testing process of software systems configurations.

References

1. Arcaini, P., Gargantini, A., Vavassori, P.: Automatic detection and removal of conformance faults in feature models. In: 2016 IEEE 9th International Conference on Software Testing, Verification and Validation (ICST), April 2016
2. Calvagna, A., Gargantini, A.: A formal logic approach to constrained combinatorial testing. J. Autom. Reason. **45**(4), 331–358 (2010). Springer
3. Calvagna, A., Gargantini, A., Vavassori, P.: Combinatorial interaction testing with CitLab. In: Sixth IEEE International Conference on Software Testing, Verification and Validation - Testing Tool Track (2013)
4. Cohen, M., Dwyer, M., Shi, J.: Constructing interaction test suites for highly-configurable systems in the presence of constraints: a greedy approach. IEEE Trans. Softw. Eng. **34**(5), 633–650 (2008)
5. Davril, J.-M., Delfosse, E., Hariri, N., Acher, M., Clelang-Huang, J., Heymans, P.: Feature model extraction from large collections of informal product descriptions, 22 Aug 2013
6. Ferreira, J.M., Vergilio, S.R., Quináiaferreia, M.A.: A mutation approach to feature testing of software product lines. In: The 25th International Conference on Software Engineering and Knowledge (SEKE) Engineering, Boston, MA, USA, 27–29 June, pp. 232–237 (2013)
7. Gargantini, A., Vavassori, P.: CitLab: a laboratory for combinatorial interaction testing. In: Workshop on Combinatorial Testing (CT) In conjunction with International Conference on Software Testing, ICST 2012, Montreal, Canada, 17–21 April, pp. 559–568 (2012)
8. Garvin, B.J., Cohen, M.B., Dwyer, M.B.: An improved meta-heuristic search for constrained interaction testing. In: 1st International Symposium on Search Based Software Engineering, pp. 13–22, May 2009
9. Grindal, M., Offutt, J., Andler, S.F.: Combination testing strategies: a survey. Softw. Test Verif. Reliab **15**(3), 167–199 (2005)
10. Harman, M., Jia, Y., Krinke, J., Langdon, W.B., Petke, J., Zhang, Y.: Search based software engineering for software product line engineering: a survey and directions for future work. In: Proceedings of the 18th International Software Product Line Conference (SPLC 2014), pp. 5–18. ACM (2014)

11. Henard, C., Papadakis, M., Perrouin, G., Klein, J., Traon, Y.L.: Towards auto-mated testing and fixing of re-engineered feature models. In: 35th International Conference on Software Engineering, ICSE 2013, San Francisco, CA, USA, 18–26 May, pp. 1245–1248 (2013)
12. Jia, Y., Harman, M.: An analysis and survey of the development of mutation testing. IEEE Trans. Softw. Eng. **37**(5), 649–678 (2011)
13. Kuhn, D.R., Okun, V.: Pseudo-exhaustive testing for software. In: 30th Annual IEEE/NASA Software Engineering Workshop (SEW-30 2006), 25–28 April 2006, Loyola College Graduate Center, Columbia, MD, USA, pp. 153–158 (2006)
14. Kuhn, D.R., Wallace, D.R., Gallo, A.M.: Software fault interactions and implica-tions for software testing. IEEE Trans. Softw. Eng **30**(6), 418–421 (2004)
15. Kuhn, R., Kacker, R., Lei, Y., Hunter, J.: Combinatorial software testing. Com-puter **42**(8), 94–96 (2009)
16. Lopez-Herrejon, R.E., Galindo, J.A., Benavides, D., Segura, S., Egyed, A.: Reverse engineering feature models with evolutionary algorithms: an exploratory study. In: Fraser, G., Teixeira de Souza, J. (eds.) SSBSE 2012. LNCS, vol. 7515, pp. 168–182. Springer, Heidelberg (2012)
17. Lopez-Herrejon, R.E., Linsbauer, L., Egyed, A.: A systematic mapping study of search-based software engineering for software product lines. Inf. Softw. Technol. **61**, 33–51 (2015)
18. Nadi, S., Berger, T., Kästner, C., Czarnecki, K.: Mining configuration constraints: static analyses and empirical results. In: Jalote, P., Briand, L.C., van der Hoek, A. (eds.) ICSE, pp. 140–151. ACM (2014)
19. Nie, C., Leung, H.: A survey of combinatorial testing. ACM Comput. Surv **43**(2), 11 (2011)
20. Perrouin, G., Sen, S., Klein, J., Baudry, B., Le Traon, Y.: Automated and scalable t-wise test case generation strategies for software product lines. In: Proceedings of the International Conference on Software Testing (ICST), Paris, France, pp. 459–468. IEEE, April 2010
21. Petke, J., Cohen, M.B., Harman, M., Yoo, S.: Practical combinatorial interaction testing: empirical findings on efficiency and early fault detection. IEEE Trans. Softw. Eng. **41**(9), 901–924 (2015)
22. Segall, I., Tzoref-Brill, R., Farchi, E.: Using binary decision diagrams for combi-natorial test design. In: Proceedings of the International Symposium on Software Testing and Analysis, ISSTA 2011, pp. 254–264. ACM (2011)
23. Shi, J., Cohen, M.B., Dwyer, M.B.: Integration testing of software product lines using compositional symbolic execution. In: de Lara, J., Zisman, A. (eds.) Fun-damental Approaches to Software Engineering. LNCS, vol. 7212, pp. 270–284. Springer, Heidelberg (2012)
24. Tartler, R., Lohmann, D., Sincero, J., Schröder-Preikschat, W.: Feature consistency in compile-time-configurable system software: facing the linux 10,000 feature prob-lem. In: Proceedings of the Sixth Conference on Computer Systems, EuroSys 2011, pp. 47–60. ACM, New York (2011)
25. Yilmaz, C., Dumlu, E., Cohen, M.B., Porter, A.A.: Reducing masking effects in combinatorial interaction testing: a feedback driven adaptive approach. IEEE Trans. Softw. Eng. **40**(1), 43–66 (2014)

Search-Based Testing of Procedural Programs: Iterative Single-Target or Multi-target Approach?

Simone Scalabrino[1]([✉]), Giovanni Grano[2], Dario Di Nucci[2], Rocco Oliveto[1], and Andrea De Lucia[2]

[1] University of Molise, Campobasso, Italy
{simone.scalabrino,rocco.oliveto}@unimol.it
[2] University of Salerno, Salerno, Italy
g.grano1@studenti.unisa.it, {ddinucci,adelucia}@unisa.it

Abstract. In the context of testing of Object-Oriented (OO) software systems, researchers have recently proposed search based approaches to automatically generate whole test suites by considering simultaneously all targets (*e.g.*, branches) defined by the coverage criterion (*multi-target approach*). The goal of whole suite approaches is to overcome the problem of wasting search budget that iterative single-target approaches (which iteratively generate test cases for each target) can encounter in case of infeasible targets. However, whole suite approaches have not been implemented and experimented in the context of procedural programs. In this paper we present OCELOT (Optimal Coverage sEarch-based tooL for sOftware Testing), a test data generation tool for C programs which implements both a state-of-the-art whole suite approach and an iterative single-target approach designed for a parsimonious use of the search budget. We also present an empirical study conducted on 35 open-source C programs to compare the two approaches implemented in OCELOT. The results indicate that the iterative single-target approach provides a higher efficiency while achieving the same or an even higher level of coverage than the whole suite approach.

Keywords: Test data generation · Search-based software testing · Genetic Algorithm

1 Introduction

Software testing is widely recognized as an essential part of any software development process, representing however an extremely expensive activity. The overall cost of testing has been estimated at being at least half of the entire development cost, if not more [5]. Generating good test cases represents probably the most expensive activity in the entire testing process. Hence, testing automation is receiving more and more attention by researchers and practitioners in order to increment the system reliability and to reduce testing costs. In this context, search-based algorithms have been efficiently used for the test data generation

© Springer International Publishing AG 2016
F. Sarro and K. Deb (Eds.): SSBSE 2016, LNCS 9962, pp. 64–79, 2016.
DOI: 10.1007/978-3-319-47106-8_5

problem [24]. Specifically, such approaches can be used to generate test data with respect to a coverage criterion (typically, branch coverage) aiming at covering a specific target at a time (typically, a branch). In order to obtain a complete test suite, the approach is executed multiple times, changing the target branch each time, until all branches are covered or the total search budget, *e.g.,* time available, is consumed (*iterative single-target test suite generation*).

The iterative single-target test suite generation has two important limitations [13]. First, in the program under test there might be branches that are more difficult to cover as compared to others or there might be infeasible branches. Thus, the search algorithm may be trapped on these branches wasting a significant amount of the search budget [13]. Second, the order in which target branches are selected can have a large impact on the final performance. In order to mitigate these limitations, Fraser and Arcuri [13] proposed the *whole test suite* approach, where instead of searching iteratively for tests that cover specific branches, the search algorithm searches for a set of tests (test suite) that covers all the branches at the same time. Following the same underlying idea, Panichella *et al.* [29] recently proposed MOSA (Many-Objective Sorting Algorithm), an algorithm where the *whole test suite* approach is re-formulated as a many-objective problem, where different branches are considered as different objectives to be optimized. MOSA is able to achieve higher coverage or a faster convergence at the same coverage level as compared to a single-objective whole test suite approach [29]. Nevertheless, whole suite approaches have been introduced in the context of Object-Oriented (OO) software systems and they have never been experimented and compared to iterative single-target approaches in the context of procedural programs.

In this paper we present a new test data generation tool for C programs named OCELOT (Optimal Coverage sEarch-based tooL for sOftware Testing) which implements both the many-objective whole suite approach MOSA [29] and a new iterative single-target approach named LIPS (Linearly Independent Path based Search) designed to efficiently use the search budget and re-use profitable information from previous iterations. We also conduct an empirical study on 35 open-source C programs to compare the two test data generation approaches. The results achieved indicate that, if targets are selected aiming at parsimoniously using the search budget, the iterative single target method provides comparable or better performance than the more sophisticated whole suite approach.

The remainder of this paper is organized as follows. Section 2 summarizes background information and presents the related literature. Section 3 presents OCELOT and the implemented test data generation approaches (MOSA and LIPS). The results of the empirical study are reported in Sect. 4, while Sect. 5 concludes the paper highlighting future research directions.

2   Background and Related Work

Search-based software testing approaches apply search-based algorithms—such as Hill Climbing [16], Simulated Annealing [32], Alternating Variable Method

(AVM) [19] and Genetic Algorithm (GA) [36]—to automatically generate test input data.

The design of any search algorithm for a specific optimization problem usually requires the definition of the solution representation and the fitness function. In the context of test data generation, a solution is represented by a set of test inputs [24]. The fitness function, instead, highly depends on the coverage criterion. Usually, branch coverage is used as code coverage criterion [18, 26, 30, 32, 35, 36]. Specifically, the fitness function is mainly based on two measures: *approach level* [30] and *branch distance* [18]. The *approach level* represents how far is the execution path of a given test case from covering the target branch, while the *branch distance* represents how far is the input data from changing the boolean value of the condition of the decision node nearest to the target branch. As the branch distance value could be arbitrarily greater than the approach level, it is common to normalize the value of the branch distance [1, 35].

The first search-based approaches for test data generation defined in the literature select the branches to covered incrementally (single-target strategy) [35]. A simple single-target strategy for branch coverage could be summarized as: (i) enumerate all targets (branches); (ii) perform a single-objective search, for each target, until all targets are covered or the total search budget is consumed; (iii) combine all generated test cases in a single test suite. Among the many tools, prototype tools and framework that implemented the early single-target approaches, we can mention *TESTGEN* [10], *QUEST* [6], *ADTEST* [14] and *GADGET* [27]. A typical problem of tools that generate test cases for programs developed in C is the handling of pointers. Lakhotia *et al.* [20] try to solve this problem introducing a new approach, named AVM+. Such an approach is implemented in *AUSTIN*, an open-source tool for automated test data generation in C [20].

It is worth noting that the generated test cases need to be manually refined to specify for each of them the oracle [4]. This means that the higher the number of generated test cases the higher the effort for the tester to generate the oracle [4]. Such a problem has recalled the need to consider the *oracle effort* when generating the test suite. A simple solution for solving this issue consists of reducing the size of the generated test suite. With this goal, Oster and Saglietti [28] introduced a technique, based on control and data flow graph criteria, aimed at maximizing the code coverage and minimize the number of test cases. Afterwards, Harman *et al.* [15] proposed three formulations of the test case generation problem aiming at reducing oracle effort: (i) the *Memory-Based Test Data Reduction* that maintains a set of not yet covered target branches during the iterations; (ii) a greedy set cover algorithm; and (iii) a *CDG-Based* algorithms. In the third formulation the fitness function is split in two parts: the first consisting in the sum of approach level and branch distance and the second considering the *collateral coverage* (serendipitously achieved). All such formulations were implemented in IGUANA [25], a tool designed to simplify the implementation of different single-target approaches and the comparison among them. Finally, Ferrer *et al.* [11] dealt with coverage and oracle cost as equally important targets.

Besides the aforementioned improvements, single target approaches still suffer of two important limitations: (i) they can waste a significant amount of the search budget trying to cover difficult or infeasible branches; (ii) the search for each target is typically independent, and potentially useful information is not shared between individual searches. In order to mitigate such problems, Fraser and Arcuri [13] proposed the *whole test suite generation* approach, implemented in the Evosuite tool [12]. This approach evolves testing goals simultaneously. A candidate solution is represented as a test suite and the fitness function is represented by the sum of all branch distances and approach levels of all the branches of the program under test. An experimentation conducted on 1,741 Java classes showed that the whole suite approach achieves higher coverage than single target approaches (on average 83 % vs 76 %) and produces smaller test suites in 62 % of the cases. Nonetheless the whole suite approach proposed by Fraser and Arcuri [13] has a drawback: it tends to reward the whole coverage more than the coverage of single branches [29]. Thus, in some cases, trivial branches are preferred to branches that are harder to cover, affecting the overall coverage. To mitigate such a problem, Panichella *et al.* [29] formulate the test data generation problem as a many-objective problem. In particular, the authors consider the branch distance and the approach level of each branch as a specific fitness function. In this reformulation, a test case is considered as a candidate solution, while fitness is evaluated according to all branches at the same time. Since the number of fitness functions could be very high, the authors introduced a novel many-objective GA, named *MOSA* (Many-Objective Sorting Algorithm), and integrated the new approach in Evosuite. The results of an empirical evaluation conducted on 64 Java classes indicated that MOSA produces better results compared to a single-objective whole test suite approach, *i.e.,* MOSA achieved a higher coverage or a faster convergence when the coverage level is comparable.

From the analysis of the state-of-the-art—to the best of our knowledge—emerges that whole test suite approaches have been never experimented and compared to single target approaches in the context of procedural programs. Moreover, none of the tools presented in this section implements both single-target and multiple-target approaches for procedural programs. In this paper we bridge this gap by introducing a new tool for search-based test data generation for C programs. The tool implements both a whole test suite approach and a novel iterative single-target approach, allowing to compare, for the first time, single-target and a multiple-target test data generation approaches in the context of procedural programs.

3   OCELOT in a Nutshell

OCELOT (**O**ptimal **C**overage s**E**arch-based too**L** for s**O**ftware **T**esting) is a new test suite generation for C programs implemented in Java. Unlike previous tools for C programs, OCELOT automatically detects the input types of a given C function without requiring any specification of parameters. In addition, the tool handles the different data types of C, including structs and pointers and it is able to produce test suites based on the Check unit testing framework[1]. As well as all the tools presented in Sect. 2, OCELOT is not able to generate oracles: such a task is delegated to a human expert.

OCELOT includes two different target selection strategies. The first strategy is represented by MOSA [29], while the second one is represented by LIPS (Linearly Independent Path based Search), a technique inspired by the baseline method proposed by McCabe *et al.* [34] and never used for search-based test data generation before. We define LIPS in the context of this study and we do not use a state-of-the-art technique in order to have a fair comparison between the two families of approaches, *i.e.,* iterative single-target and multi-target. Indeed, LIPS was properly customized to share with whole suite approaches the main goals of efficient use of the search budget and re-use of profitable information from previous iterations.

The proposed iterative single-target approach is independent of the search algorithm used to generate test data. However, we decided to use GA to have a fair comparison with MOSA that is based on a many-objective GA, using *JMetal* [9], a Java-based framework for multi-objective optimization with metaheuristics. We used the default GA configuration parameters, the *SBX-Crossover* for the crossing-over, the *Polynomial Mutation* for the mutation, and the *Binary Tournament* operator for selecting the fittest individuals. The GA configuration and the genetic operators are exactly the same for both the whole suite and the iterative single-target approach. It is worth noting that a solution in OCELOT is represented as a list of input data [19], differently from Evosuite [12]. Therefore, the version of MOSA implemented in OCELOT differs from the original one as for this aspect. In the following we provide more details on the two approaches.

Many-Objective Sorting Algorithm (MOSA). MOSA reformulates the test suite generation problem as a many-objective optimization problem [29]. A solution is a test case and each objective represents how far a test case is from covering a specific branch.

As first step MOSA randomly generates an initial set of test cases. Such test cases represent the starting population of the genetic algorithm. In the generic i^{th} iteration (*generation*) of the genetic algorithm, *offspring* solutions are created from the actual population and added to a set R_t, together with the population P_i. All such solutions are sorted in Pareto-fronts $\mathbb{F}$, each of which has a specific *rank*. If a solution belongs to a Pareto-front with rank a, it means that such a solution is better than all the solutions which belong to a Pareto-front with rank $b > a$. MOSA generates the population for the next generation P_{i+1} starting from the Pareto-front with rank 0, and adding whole fronts until a $\mathbb{F}_d$, so that the addition of such a front would make the population larger than maximum size, specified through the parameter PS. Anyhow, it may be necessary to add some of the solutions belonging to $\mathbb{F}_d$ to the next population P_{i+1} in order to reach the maximum population size. MOSA promotes diversity adding to P_i solutions from $\mathbb{F}_d$ that increase most the crowding distance.

---

[1] https://libcheck.github.io/check/.

In MOSA, the preference-sorting algorithm of Pareto-fronts has a key role. The main problem is that multi-objective algorithms, like Non-dominated Sorting Genetic Algorithm II (NSGA-II) [8], Strength Pareto Evolutionary Algorithm (SPEA2) [39] or Indicator Based Evolutionary Algorithm (IBEA) [38] do not scale efficiently and effectively for problems with more than 15 objectives (even less, in some cases) [22]. In the context of test suite generation, a program could have hundreds of branches. For this reason, MOSA introduces a novel sorting algorithm which is specific for the test case generation problem. F_0 will contain the solutions that minimize the objective function relative to branches not covered yet. Such an expedient allows to include solutions that could lead to a strong improvement of the coverage. The preference-sorting algorithm ranks other solutions using the non-dominated sorting algorithm used by NSGA-II [8]. Such an algorithm focuses only on objectives relative to uncovered branches, in order to concentrate the search in interesting areas of the search space. Test cases that cover specific branches are progressively saved in a separate data-structure: the *archive*. In each iteration of the genetic algorithm, the archive will be updated, so that if a solution is able to cover a previously uncovered branch, it is stored into the archive. At the end of the algorithm, the archive will contain the final test suite.

Whole test suite approaches, in general, and MOSA, in particular, have been designed to work on OO languages. Since in such a context unit testing is generally focused on classes, a test case is represented as a sequence of statements in order to handle many aspects such as instantiation, method calls and so on [31]. Conversely, in the context of procedural languages, a function can be considered as the unit to test. Thus, we properly customize MOSA in order to represent a test case as the input data (test data) of the function that has to be tested [24].

Linearly Independent Path based Search(LIPS). LIPS is an iterative single-target approach we designed with the goal of mitigating the main limitations of previous single-target approaches.

The target selection strategy exploited by LIPS takes inspiration from the baseline method proposed by McCabe *et al.* [34], which computes a maximal set of linearly independent paths of a program (a basis) [23]. This algorithm incrementally computes a basis, by adding at each step a path traversing an uncovered branch [34]. This means that executing all the paths in a basis implies the coverage of all branches in the control flow graph [23]. Similarly, LIPS incrementally builds a set of linearly independent paths by generating at each iteration a test case (and then a path) able to cover a still uncovered branch. It is worth noting that LISP does not need to generate test data for all linearly independent paths of a basis in case the maximal coverage is achieved in advance (due to collateral coverage).

The algorithm is partly inspired by Dynamic Symbolic Execution [21]. The first step is to randomly generate the first test case (t_0). For each decision node in the execution path of t_0 the uncovered branch of the decision is added to a worklist. A random population which includes t_0 is then generated to be used by the second iteration of the algorithm. At the generic iteration i, the last branch added to the worklist is removed and used as a target of the search algorithm. If the search algorithm is able to find a test case that covers the target, a new test case, t_i is added to the test suite and all the uncovered branches of decision nodes on the path covered by t_i are added to the worklist. This procedure is iterated until the worklist is empty (i.e. all the branches are covered) or until the search budget, measured as number of fitness evaluations, is entirely consumed. Note that at each iteration the last branch added to the worklist is used as target of the search algorithm and the final population of the previous iteration is reused (seeding), since it likely includes the test case covering the alternative branch. In this way, we expect that the search algorithm will take less time to generate a test case able to cover the target branch.

Sometimes, a test case can cover some branches that are already in the worklist (*collateral coverage*). These branches are removed from the worklist and marked as "covered". On the other hand, it could happen that, while searching for the test case which covers a certain branch, some of the partial solutions generated by the search algorithm are able to cover other branches in the worklist. Such test cases are added to the test suite and the covered branches are removed from the worklist. It is worth noting that while this approach improves the search efficiency (time) and effectiveness (coverage), it might result in adding redundancy to the test suite. This issue will be discussed in Sect. 4.2.

Handling the budget in single-target approaches can be tricky. Allocating the remaining budget to the search for covering a specific branch could be very damaging, because budget will be wasted in case the target branch is infeasible or difficult to cover. An alternative budget handling policy consists of distributing equally the budget over the branches. In other words, if the total budget is SB (*e.g.,* number of fitness function evaluation) and the program contains n branches, a budget of $\frac{SB}{n}$ will be available for such branch. LIPS uses a *dynamic* allocation of the search budget. Specifically, at the iteration i of the test generation process, the budget for the specific target to cover is computed as $\frac{SB_i}{n_i}$, where SB_i is the remaining budget and n_i is the estimated number of remaining targets to be covered. We estimate the number of targets to be covered by subtracting from the total number of branches of the Control-Flow Graph the number of branches already covered and/or used as targets (but not covered because they are infeasible or difficult to cover) at iteration i. Note that this is a conservative estimation, due to the possible collateral coverage of non target branches in the remaining iterations.

4   Empirical Evaluation of OCELOT

The *goal* of the study is to compare the two test case generation methods implemented in OCELOT, *i.e.,* MOSA, a whole suite approach, and LIPS, an iterative single target approach. The *quality focus* of the study is the effectiveness and the efficiency of the two test case generation approaches, as well as the effort required for the definition of oracle of the generated test cases. The *context*

Table 1. C functions used in the study

#	Function name	Program name	LOC	Branches	Cyclomatic complexity
1	check_ISBN	bibclean	85	29	21
2	cliparc	spice	136	64	32
3	clip_line	spice	85	56	28
4	clip_to_circle	spice	117	44	22
5	Csqrt		26	6	3
6	gimp_cmyk_to_rgb	gimp	28	2	1
7	gimp_cmyk_to_rgb_int	gimp	23	2	1
8	gimp_hsl_to_rgb	gimp	31	4	2
9	gimp_hsl_to_rgb_int	gimp	34	4	2
10	gimp_hsl_value	gimp	22	10	5
11	gimp_hsl_value_int	gimp	22	10	5
12	gimp_hsv_to_rgb	gimp	69	11	8
13	gimp_rgb_to_cmyk	gimp	36	8	4
14	gimp_rgb_to_hsl	gimp	51	14	7
15	gimp_rgb_to_hsl_int	gimp	58	14	7
16	gimp_rgb_to_hsv4	gimp	62	18	9
17	gimp_rgb_to_hsv_int	gimp	59	16	8
18	gimp_rgb_to_hwb	gimp	32	2	1
19	gimp_rgb_to_l_int	gimp	19	2	1
20	gradient_calc_bilinear_factor	gimp	30	6	3
21	gradient_calc_conical_asym_factor	gimp	35	6	3
22	gradient_calc_conical_sym_factor	gimp	43	8	4
23	gradient_calc_linear_factor	gimp	30	8	4
24	gradient_calc_radial_factor	gimp	29	6	3
25	gradient_calc_spiral_factor	gimp	37	8	4
26	gradient_calc_square_factor	gimp	29	6	3
27	triangle		21	14	7
28	gsl_poly_complex_solve_cubic	GLS	113	20	11
29	gsl_poly_complex_solve_quadratic	GLS	77	12	7
30	gsl_poly_eval_derivs	GLS	41	10	6
31	gsl_poly_solve_cubic	GLS	73	14	8
32	gsl_poly_solve_quadratic	GLS	60	12	7
33	sglib_int_array_binary_search	SGLIB	32	8	5
34	sglib_int_array_heap_sort	SGLIB	80	28	15
35	sglib_int_array_quick_sort	SGLIB	102	30	16

of the study consists of 35 open-source C functions, with a total of 605 branches, taken from different programs, in particular from `gimp`, an open source GNU image manipulation software, `GSL`, the GNU Scientific Library, `SGLIB`, a generic library for C, and `spice`, an analogue circuit simulator. We selected these functions since they have been used in previous work on test case generation for C language [20]. It is worth noting that, since the current implementation of OCELOT does not properly support the generation of test cases for functions having complex data types as input (e.g. pointers to struct), we selected only a subset of functions from the chosen programs. The main characteristics of the object programs are summarized in Table 1.

4.1   Research Questions and Analysis Method

The study is steered by the following research questions:

- **RQ$_1$ (Effectiveness)**: *Which is the coverage of MOSA as compared to LIPS when generating test cases for procedural code?*
- **RQ$_2$ (Efficiency)**: *Which is the execution time of MOSA as compared to LIPS when generating test cases for procedural code?*

– **RQ$_3$ (Oracle Cost**): *Which is the size of the test suite generated by MOSA as compared to the size of the test suite generated by LIPS?*

To address the three research questions we run the MOSA and LIPS 30 times for each object function and compute the average performance of the two approaches. Specifically:

– for **RQ$_1$** we compare the average percentage of branches covered by each approach for each function.
– for **RQ$_2$** we compare the average running time required by each approach for each function. The execution time was measured using a machine with Intel Core i7 processor running at 3.1 GHz with 4 GB RAM.
– for **RQ$_3$** we measure the average size of the test suite generated by each approach for each function.

We also statistically analyze the achieved results. Statistical significance is measured with the *Wilcoxon's test* [7], with a p-value threshold of 0.05. Significant p-values indicate that the corresponding null hypothesis can be rejected in favor of the alternative one, *i.e.,* one of the approaches reaches a higher coverage (**RQ$_1$**), it is faster in term of running time (**RQ$_2$**), or it generates smaller test suites (**RQ$_3$**). Other than testing the null hypothesis, we use the Vargha-Delaney ($\hat{A}_{12}$) statistical test [33] to measure the magnitude of difference between the results achieved by the two experimented approaches. Vargha-Delaney ($\hat{A}_{12}$) statistic also classifies the magnitude of the obtained effect size value into four different levels (*negligible, small, medium,* and *large*). It's important to note that in our experiments we setup the population size to 100 individuals and the search budget is 200.000 evaluations. Moreover the crossover probability is 0.90.

4.2   Analysis of the Results and Discussion

In this section we discuss the achieved results aiming at answering the research questions previously formulated. Table 2 shows the achieved results along with p-values obtained from Wilcoxon test [7]. The table also shows the effect size metric from Vargha-Delaney ($\hat{A}_{12}$) statistic [33], indicating also the magnitude of the difference.

RQ$_1$ (Effectiveness). The first part of Table 2 summarizes the results in term of coverage achieved by MOSA and LIPS. The overall average coverage was 84.73 % for MOSA and and 86.29 % for LIPS. Also, LIPS is significantly better in *10 out of 35 cases* with an effect size `large` or `medium` in *8 cases*. Instead, MOSA achieves a significantly higher coverage just in two cases: once with a `small` effect size and once with a `large` effect size. Moreover, we can notice that when LIPS outperforms MOSA, the coverage increases between 0.28 % and 15.83 %; on the other hand, in the only case where MOSA performs better with a `large` effect size, the difference in terms of coverage is of 8.6 % with respect to LIPS.

RQ$_2$ (Efficiency). The second part of Table 2 shows the results achieved in terms of *efficiency*, measured as time spent for the generation of the test suites.

Table 2. Comparison of results achieved by LIPS and MOSA.

#	Coverage					Execution time					Test suite size				
	LIPS	MOSA	p-value	$\hat{A}_{12}$	Magnitude	LIPS	MOSA	p-value	$\hat{A}_{12}$	Magnitude	LIPS	MOSA	p-value	$\hat{A}_{12}$	Magnitude
1	86.21%	86.21%	1.000	0.50	negligible	36.30	59.10	<0.001	1.00	large	9.37	7.43	<0.001	0.10	large
2	94.95%	95.00%	0.276	0.47	negligible	7.80	26.10	<0.001	1.00	large	18.67	15.67	<0.001	0.05	large
3	87.50%	85.00%	<0.001	1.00	large	15.00	37.00	<0.001	1.00	large	10.90	9.40	0.022	0.24	large
4	86.59%	87.05%	0.659	0.55	negligible	8.80	31.40	<0.001	1.00	large	16.10	14.40	0.125	0.35	small
5	83.33%	83.33%	1.000	0.50	negligible	6.87	9.13	<0.001	1.00	large	3.47	2.43	<0.001	0.12	large
6	100.00%	100.00%	1.000	0.50	negligible	0.00	7.53	<0.001	1.00	large	4.00	2.00	<0.001	0.00	large
7	88.33%	80.00%	0.086	0.58	small	1.53	7.53	<0.001	0.97	large	2.77	1.60	<0.001	0.07	large
8	91.67%	92.50%	0.395	0.48	negligible	2.43	8.70	<0.001	0.97	large	4.33	2.70	<0.001	0.12	large
9	93.33%	86.67%	0.019	0.63	small	1.93	9.50	<0.001	1.00	large	4.47	2.47	<0.001	0.06	large
10	100.00%	100.00%	1.000	0.50	negligible	0.00	10.23	<0.001	1.00	large	6.67	4.60	<0.001	0.00	large
11	100.00%	100.00%	1.000	0.50	negligible	0.00	10.60	<0.001	1.00	large	6.37	4.73	<0.001	0.05	large
12	87.27%	90.00%	0.004	0.35	small	4.93	12.47	<0.001	0.97	large	10.20	7.90	<0.001	0.00	large
13	100.00%	100.00%	1.000	0.50	negligible	0.00	10.67	<0.001	1.00	large	4.90	3.93	<0.001	0.14	large
14	85.00%	78.57%	<0.001	0.95	large	4.97	11.83	<0.001	1.00	large	5.97	3.60	<0.001	0.00	large
15	92.86%	89.05%	<0.001	0.77	large	7.07	12.03	<0.001	1.00	large	5.87	4.43	<0.001	0.09	large
16	83.33%	83.33%	1.000	0.50	negligible	7.53	15.23	<0.001	1.00	large	5.30	4.50	<0.001	0.17	large
17	86.67%	83.12%	<0.001	0.78	large	7.87	15.83	<0.001	1.00	large	6.37	5.20	<0.001	0.09	large
18	51.67%	50.00%	0.167	0.52	negligible	7.97	9.10	<0.001	0.98	large	2.07	1.00	<0.001	0.00	large
19	100.00%	100.00%	1.000	0.50	negligible	0.00	8.03	<0.001	1.00	large	3.00	2.00	<0.001	0.00	large
20	84.44%	83.33%	0.157	0.53	negligible	2.53	8.53	<0.001	1.00	large	5.17	3.00	<0.001	0.02	large
21	83.33%	83.33%	1.000	0.50	negligible	4.07	11.07	<0.001	1.00	large	5.00	3.00	<0.001	0.00	large
22	86.67%	87.50%	0.080	0.47	negligible	4.30	11.67	<0.001	1.00	large	5.87	4.00	<0.001	0.03	large
23	87.92%	87.50%	0.285	0.52	negligible	2.43	9.03	<0.001	1.00	large	6.13	4.00	<0.001	0.02	large
24	87.78%	83.33%	0.006	0.63	small	2.60	8.23	<0.001	1.00	large	5.53	3.00	<0.001	0.03	large
25	87.08%	87.50%	0.167	0.48	negligible	3.97	11.07	<0.001	1.00	large	5.33	3.50	<0.001	0.03	large
26	88.89%	83.33%	<0.001	0.67	medium	2.47	8.07	<0.001	1.00	large	5.70	3.00	<0.001	0.00	large
27	88.89%	88.89%	1.000	0.50	negligible	6.07	12.10	<0.001	1.00	large	12.13	7.80	<0.001	0.00	large
28	58.33%	52.73%	<0.001	0.79	large	4.10	16.33	<0.001	1.00	large	5.87	3.97	<0.001	0.03	large
29	58.33%	58.33%	1.000	0.50	negligible	3.50	10.50	<0.001	1.00	large	4.00	3.00	<0.001	0.00	large
30	100.00%	100.00%	1.000	0.50	negligible	0.00	24.27	<0.001	1.00	large	2.40	1.63	<0.001	0.19	large
31	55.00%	63.50%	<0.001	0.17	large	3.63	14.60	<0.001	1.00	large	5.00	5.03	0.400	0.52	negligible
32	58.33%	58.61%	0.167	0.48	negligible	3.23	10.40	<0.001	1.00	large	4.00	3.03	<0.001	0.02	large
33	100.00%	84.17%	<0.001	0.82	large	0.07	11.57	<0.001	1.00	large	4.37	1.43	<0.001	0.00	large
34	100.00%	100.00%	1.000	0.50	negligible	0.00	18.63	<0.001	1.00	large	3.17	2.20	<0.001	0.16	large
35	96.67%	93.89%	<0.001	0.83	large	12.17	20.10	<0.001	1.00	large	4.63	3.17	<0.001	0.18	large

Results are clearly in favor of LIPS. The overall average execution time for MOSA is 14.80 s, while LIPS spent, on average, 5.03 s for each function, with an improvement with respect to MOSA of about 66 %. The improvement in terms of execution time is also supported by statistical tests. Specifically, the execution time of LIPS is statistically lower than the execution time of MOSA in *all the cases*, with a *large* effect size. It is worth noting that LIPS is faster even when it is able to achieve a significantly higher coverage. The most evident difference in terms of execution time can be observed in the case of function gsl_poly_eval_derivs (#30): MOSA spent about 24.27 s for the overall test suite generation process, while LIPS always needed less than a second. On this function the two approaches achieve exactly the same level of coverage (100 %). In order to have more insights on why the iterative single target approach is faster than the whole test suite approach, we launched LIPS and MOSA on the function which requires the highest execution time for both the approaches (*i.e.*, cliparc) and used a Java profiler (VisualVM) to check at which step MOSA requires more time. We observed that the bottleneck in MOSA is represented by the algorithm used to compare the solutions, *i.e.*, ranking the solutions in different Pareto-fronts. LIPS does not need such an algorithm, thus saving execution time.

74   S. Scalabrino et al.

RQ₃ (Oracle cost). The third part of Table 2 shows the average size of the test suites generated by each approach for all the functions under test. The results show that, on average, MOSA generates about 4.4 test cases, compared to about 6.1 test cases of LIPS. This means that MOSA generates test suites that are 28.0 % smaller, on average. The differences between the size of the generated test suites is significant with a `large` effect size in almost all the cases. It is worth noting that, in one of the 3 cases where the effect size is not large, MOSA achieves a significantly higher level of coverage as compared to LIPS.

The results achieved are quite expected since LIPS has been defined to efficiently use the search budget and maximize the coverage through the inclusion in the test suite of test cases covering branches not selected as target. Thus, it does not take into account the size of the test suite explicitly, as done, for instance, by the approach proposed by Harman *et al.* [15], but rather the underlying strategy often results in the inclusion of redundant test cases.

We also implemented a revised version of LIPS (indicated as LIPS*) where we avoid the inclusion in the test suite of test cases covering branches not selected as target. Table 3 shows the comparison between LIPS* and MOSA. The two approaches attain levels of coverage and test suite size very similar. They both achieve a significantly higher coverage in only 3 cases. About test suite size, MOSA generates smaller test suites in 6 cases, while LIPS* in 7 cases. It is worth

Table 3. Comparison of the results achieved by LIPS* and MOSA.

#	Coverage					Execution time					Test suite size				
	LIPS*	MOSA	p-value	$\hat{A}_{12}$	Magnitude	LIPS*	MOSA	p-value	$\hat{A}_{12}$	Magnitude	LIPS*	MOSA	p-value	$\hat{A}_{12}$	Magnitude
1	85.29%	85.75%	0.285	0.48	negligible	33.37	55.63	<0.001	1.00	large	5.10	7.30	<0.001	0.94	large
2	94.79%	95.05%	0.063	0.41	small	4.57	26.27	<0.001	1.00	large	13.40	15.73	<0.001	0.94	large
3	85.18%	85.54%	0.228	0.59	small	14.20	36.80	<0.001	1.00	large	9.40	8.50	0.100	0.67	medium
4	85.91%	85.91%	0.562	0.52	negligible	6.30	32.50	<0.001	1.00	large	12.40	12.70	0.408	0.54	negligible
5	83.33%	83.33%	1.000	0.50	negligible	5.20	8.07	<0.001	1.00	large	2.47	2.53	0.307	0.53	negligible
6	100.00%	100.00%	1.000	0.50	negligible	0.00	6.03	<0.001	1.00	large	2.00	2.00	1.000	0.50	negligible
7	86.67%	85.00%	0.391	0.52	negligible	1.50	6.53	<0.001	0.95	large	1.73	1.70	0.392	0.48	negligible
8	91.67%	94.17%	0.200	0.45	negligible	1.67	6.77	<0.001	1.00	large	2.67	2.77	0.200	0.55	negligible
9	90.00%	91.67%	0.301	0.47	negligible	2.33	7.13	<0.001	1.00	large	2.60	2.67	0.301	0.53	negligible
10	100.00%	100.00%	1.000	0.50	negligible	0.00	8.30	<0.001	1.00	large	4.43	4.70	0.020	0.63	small
11	100.00%	100.00%	1.000	0.50	negligible	0.00	8.43	<0.001	1.00	large	4.60	4.57	0.446	0.49	negligible
12	88.18%	89.39%	0.115	0.43	negligible	3.43	10.63	<0.001	1.00	large	7.70	7.83	0.115	0.57	negligible
13	100.00%	100.00%	1.000	0.50	negligible	0.00	8.20	<0.001	1.00	large	3.77	3.73	0.414	0.48	negligible
14	83.81%	78.57%	<0.001	0.87	large	4.73	11.07	<0.001	1.00	large	4.07	3.67	0.012	0.35	small
15	89.29%	89.76%	0.307	0.47	negligible	0.90	12.00	<0.001	1.00	large	4.57	4.63	0.247	0.55	negligible
16	83.33%	83.15%	0.167	0.52	negligible	6.20	14.07	<0.001	1.00	large	4.20	4.57	0.002	0.68	medium
17	84.79%	83.96%	0.155	0.57	negligible	3.20	12.10	<0.001	1.00	large	5.10	5.23	0.252	0.54	negligible
18	53.33%	50.00%	0.080	0.53	negligible	5.23	7.03	<0.001	1.00	large	1.07	1.00	0.080	0.47	negligible
19	100.00%	100.00%	1.000	0.50	negligible	0.00	5.53	<0.001	1.00	large	2.00	2.00	1.000	0.50	negligible
20	82.22%	82.78%	0.322	0.48	negligible	2.50	8.10	<0.001	1.00	large	2.93	2.97	0.322	0.52	negligible
21	81.67%	83.33%	0.041	0.45	negligible	3.37	8.13	<0.001	1.00	large	2.90	3.00	0.041	0.55	negligible
22	87.50%	87.50%	1.000	0.50	negligible	3.00	9.07	<0.001	1.00	large	4.00	4.00	1.000	0.50	negligible
23	88.33%	87.92%	0.285	0.52	negligible	1.87	8.93	<0.001	1.00	large	4.07	4.03	0.285	0.48	negligible
24	90.56%	83.33%	<0.001	0.72	medium	1.53	7.70	<0.001	1.00	large	3.43	3.00	<0.001	0.28	medium
25	87.50%	87.50%	1.000	0.50	negligible	3.03	9.10	<0.001	1.00	large	3.33	3.53	0.062	0.60	small
26	86.11%	83.33%	0.010	0.58	small	2.03	7.77	<0.001	1.00	large	3.17	3.00	0.011	0.42	small
27	87.59%	88.89%	0.003	0.38	small	5.20	12.03	<0.001	1.00	large	7.43	7.77	0.013	0.64	small
28	45.45%	53.48%	<0.001	0.17	large	3.03	15.80	<0.001	1.00	large	3.00	4.10	<0.001	0.83	large
29	58.33%	58.33%	0.167	0.50	negligible	3.07	10.03	<0.001	1.00	large	3.00	3.00	1.000	0.50	negligible
30	100.00%	100.00%	1.000	0.50	negligible	0.00	25.17	<0.001	1.00	large	1.63	1.63	0.578	0.51	negligible
31	55.00%	58.50%	0.001	0.37	small	3.20	14.20	<0.001	1.00	large	4.00	4.43	0.001	0.63	small
32	58.33%	58.61%	0.167	0.48	negligible	3.10	10.13	<0.001	1.00	large	3.00	3.03	0.167	0.52	negligible
33	100.00%	82.50%	<0.001	0.85	large	0.43	11.23	<0.001	1.00	large	2.50	1.30	<0.001	0.09	large
34	100.00%	100.00%	1.000	0.50	negligible	0.00	18.77	<0.001	1.00	large	2.77	2.13	0.009	0.33	medium
35	94.67%	94.11%	0.173	0.56	negligible	11.63	20.77	<0.001	1.00	large	4.27	3.30	0.001	0.27	medium

Table 4. Test suite sizes after greedy minimization for LIPS and MOSA.

					Test suite sizes after greedy minimization												
#	LIPS	MOSA	p-value	$\hat{A}_{12}$	Magnitude	#	LIPS	MOSA	p-value	$\hat{A}_{12}$	Magnitude	#	LIPS	MOSA	p-value	$\hat{A}_{12}$	Magnitude
1	4.00	4.03	0.434	0.51	negligible	13	3.13	3.00	0.120	0.44	negligible	25	3.07	3.17	0.158	0.55	negligible
2	11.00	10.87	0.273	0.46	negligible	14	4.00	3.13	<0.001	0.11	large	26	3.33	3.00	<0.001	0.33	medium
3	5.70	5.40	0.289	0.42	small	15	4.10	4.17	0.230	0.53	negligible	27	6.00	6.03	0.167	0.52	negligible
4	7.30	8.00	0.220	0.60	small	16	4.00	4.00	1.000	0.50	negligible	28	4.87	3.97	<0.001	0.21	large
5	2.13	2.13	0.505	0.50	negligible	17	4.00	4.00	1.000	0.50	negligible	29	3.00	3.00	1.000	0.50	negligible
6	2.00	2.00	1.000	0.50	negligible	18	1.03	1.00	0.167	0.48	negligible	30	1.17	1.27	0.178	0.55	negligible
7	1.77	1.60	0.086	0.42	small	19	2.00	2.00	1.000	0.50	negligible	31	4.00	5.03	<0.001	0.83	large
8	2.67	2.70	0.395	0.52	negligible	20	3.07	3.00	0.157	0.47	negligible	32	3.00	3.03	0.167	0.52	negligible
9	2.73	2.47	0.019	0.37	small	21	3.00	3.00	1.000	0.50	negligible	33	2.00	1.37	<0.001	0.18	large
10	4.23	4.20	0.382	0.48	negligible	22	3.93	4.00	0.080	0.53	negligible	34	1.90	1.87	0.457	0.49	negligible
11	4.20	4.20	0.504	0.50	negligible	23	4.03	4.00	0.285	0.48	negligible	35	1.90	1.87	0.457	0.49	negligible
12	6.60	6.90	0.004	0.65	small	24	3.27	3.00	0.006	0.37	small						

noting that a difference in terms of coverage always implies a difference in terms of test suite size. Excluding such cases, only LIPS* achieves a *large* difference in terms of test suite size. Nevertheless, LIPS* still maintains a significantly higher efficiency in all the cases. This proves that LIPS privileges coverage as for test suite size. However, in our opinion this is not a limitation of the approach, as the size of the generated test suites can be easily reduced by using well-known minimization techniques [37].

To verify the effect of test suite minimization, Table 4 shows the comparison between the size of the test suites generated by MOSA and LIPS after minimizing the test suites using a greedy algorithm [17,37]. It is worth noting that in order to have a fair comparison, the test suite minimization was applied also on the test suites generated by MOSA (even if minimization is implicit in MOSA). As we can see, the differences in terms of test suite size are radically ironed out after the minimization. As expected, the only significant differences concern some of the functions for which the achieved coverage is significantly different. In addition, the average time spent for the minimization task is always less than a second (nearly 0 s), hence its effect on the execution time is negligible.

4.3   Threats to Validity

This section discusses the threats to the validity of our empirical evaluation.

Construct Validity. We used three metrics widely adopted in literature: branch coverage, execution time and number of generated test cases [24]. In the context of our study, these metrics provides a good estimation of effectiveness (code coverage), efficiency (execution time) and oracle effort (test suite size). Another threat consists of the methodology used to compare LIPS with MOSA. Considering that an implementation of MOSA for the C language is not publicly available, we had to implement the approach in our tool. However, we strictly followed the definition of the algorithm provided by Panichella *et al.* [29]. Since also LIPS has been implemented in the same tool, the comparison of the two approach is much fairer, since it is not influenced by the underlying technology. Another threat to the construct validity consists of the meta-heuristic used in the study. Considering that MOSA is strictly based on GAs, due to its multi-objectives nature, we decided to limit our study to this kind of algorithm. However, in the future we plan to integrate other search-based algorithms in LIPS.

Internal Validity. We ran test data generation techniques 30 times for each subject program and reported average results together with statistical evidence to address the random nature of the GAs themselves [2]. The tuning of the GA's parameters is another factor that could affect the internal validity of this work. However, in the context of test data generation it is not easy to find good settings that significantly outperform the default values suggested in the literature [3]. For this reason, we used the default values widely used in literature.

External Validity. We considered 35 open-source functions taken from different programs. We selected these functions since they have been used in previous work on test case generation [20] for C language. Functions were selected to have small and quite large samples, as well as samples with low and high cyclomatic complexity. Also, `triangle` and `bibclean` are used in search-based software testing [16,24], while `Csqrt` represents a valuable testing scenario since it contains a condition really hard to cover, namely a comparison between a double and a fixed number (0.0). Also, besides numerical input values, the considered functions take as input structures (`gimp_rgb_to_hsl`) and strings (`check_ISBN`) as well. However, in order to corroborate our findings, we plan to replicate the study on a wider range of programs. Our results are different than those achieved in the context of OO programming [13]. We cannot state if these differences are related to LIPS or concern the different characteristics between procedural and OO code. For this reason, in the future, we plan to implement LIPS in the context of Evosuite [12] and compare it with other whole suite approaches.

Conclusion Validity. We used appropriate statistical tests coupled with enough repetitions of the experiments. In particular, we used the Wilcoxon test [7] to test the significance of the differences and the Vargha-Delaney statistic [33] to estimate the magnitude and the effect size of the observed differences.

5   Conclusion and Future Work

We presented OCELOT, a tool for test case generation for C programs. OCELOT implements the most efficient and effective state-of-the-art whole suite approach MOSA [29], adapted for procedural test case representation, and a new iterative single-target approach named LIPS (Linearly Independent Path based Search), inspired by the baseline method for the construction of a maximal set of linearly independent paths [34] and designed to avoid search budget wasting. An empirical study conducted on 35 C functions was carried out to compare the two test data generations approaches implemented in OCELOT. The results indicate that the iterative approach provides a better or comparable level of coverage with respect to whole suite approach with a much lower execution time. The main weakness of LIPS with respect to MOSA is represented by the size of the generated test suites. However, after applying a test suite minimization approach based on greedy algorithm [17] the difference in terms of test suite size between the two techniques becomes negligible, without affecting execution time.

As future work, we plan to replicate the study on a larger dataset of programs and also in the context of OO programs. We also plan to implement in OCELOT different search algorithms and compare them with genetic algorithms.

References

1. Arcuri, A.: It does matter how you normalise the branch distance in search based software testing. In: International Conference on Software Testing, Verification and Validation, pp. 205–214. IEEE (2010)
2. Arcuri, A., Briand, L.: A practical guide for using statistical tests to assess randomized algorithms in software engineering. In: International Conference on Software Engineering, pp. 1–10. IEEE (2011)
3. Arcuri, A., Fraser, G.: Parameter tuning or default values? An empirical investigation in search-based software engineering. Empirical Softw. Eng. **18**(3), 594–623 (2013)
4. Barr, E.T., Harman, M., McMinn, P., Shahbaz, M., Yoo, S.: The oracle problem in software testing: a survey. IEEE Trans. Softw. Eng. **41**(5), 507–525 (2015)
5. Beizer, B.: Software Testing Techniques. Van Nostrand Reinhold Co., New York (1990)
6. Chang, K.H., Cross II, J.H., Carlisle, W.H., Liao, S.S.: A performance evaluation of heuristics-based test case generation methods for software branch coverage. Int. J. Softw. Eng. Knowl. Eng. **6**(04), 585–608 (1996)
7. Conover, W.J.: Practical Nonparametric Statistics (1980)
8. Deb, K., Pratap, A., Agarwal, S., Meyarivan, T.: A fast and elitist multiobjective genetic algorithm: NSGA-II. IEEE Trans. Evol. Comput. **6**(2), 182–197 (2002)
9. Durillo, J.J., Nebro, A.J.: JMetal: a java framework for multi-objective optimization. Adv. Eng. Softw. **42**(10), 760–771 (2011)
10. Ferguson, R., Korel, B.: The chaining approach for software test data generation. ACM Trans. Softw. Eng. Methodol. **5**(1), 63–86 (1996)
11. Ferrer, J., Chicano, F., Alba, E.: Evolutionary algorithms for the multi-objective test data generation problem. Softw. Pract. Experience **42**(11), 1331–1362 (2012)
12. Fraser, G., Arcuri, A.: Evosuite: automatic test suite generation for object-oriented software. In: Joint Meeting of the European Software Engineering Conference and the ACM SIGSOFT Symposium on the Foundations of Software Engineering, pp. 416–419. ACM (2011)
13. Fraser, G., Arcuri, A.: Whole test suite generation. IEEE Trans. Softw. Eng. **39**(2), 276–291 (2013)
14. Gallagher, M.J., Narasimhan, V.L.: ADTEST: a test data generation suite for Ada software systems. IEEE Trans. Softw. Eng. **23**(8), 473–484 (1997)
15. Harman, M., Kim, S.G., Lakhotia, K., McMinn, P., Yoo, S.: Optimizing for the number of tests generated in search based test data generation with an application to the oracle cost problem. In: International Conference on Software Testing, Verification, and Validation Workshops, pp. 182–191. IEEE (2010)

16. Harman, M., McMinn, P.: A theoretical & empirical analysis of evolutionary testing and hill climbing for structural test data generation. In: International Symposium on Software Testing and Analysis, pp. 73–83. ACM (2007)
17. Harrold, M.J., Gupta, R., Soffa, M.L.: A methodology for controlling the size of a test suite. ACM Trans. Softw. Eng. Methodol. **2**(3), 270–285 (1993)
18. Jones, B.F., Sthamer, H.H., Eyres, D.E.: Automatic structural testing using genetic algorithms. Softw. Eng. J. **11**(5), 299–306 (1996)
19. Korel, B.: Automated software test data generation. IEEE Trans. Softw. Eng. **16**(8), 870–879 (1990)
20. Lakhotia, K., Harman, M., Gross, H.: AUSTIN: an open source tool for search based software testing of C programs. Inf. Softw. Technol. **55**(1), 112–125 (2013)
21. Larson, E., Austin, T.: High coverage detection of input-related security faults. Ann Arbor **1001**(48105), 29 (2003)
22. Laumanns, M., Thiele, L., Deb, K., Zitzler, E.: Combining convergence and diversity in evolutionary multiobjective optimization. Evol. Comput. **10**(3), 263–282 (2002)
23. McCabe, T.J.: A complexity measure. IEEE Trans. Softw. Eng. **4**, 308–320 (1976)
24. McMinn, P.: Search-based software test data generation: a survey. Softw. Test. Verification Reliab. **14**(2), 105–156 (2004)
25. McMinn, P.: IGUANA: Input Generation Using Automated Novel Algorithms. a plug and play research tool. Technical report. CS-07-14, Department of Computer Science, University of Sheffield (2007)
26. Michael, C.C., McGraw, G., Schatz, M.A.: Generating software test data by evolution. IEEE Trans. Softw. Eng. **27**(12), 1085–1110 (2001)
27. Michael, C.C., McGraw, G.E., Schatz, M.A., Walton, C.C.: Genetic algorithms for dynamic test data generation. In: International Conference Automated Software Engineering, pp. 307–308. IEEE (1997)
28. Oster, N., Saglietti, F.: Automatic test data generation by multi-objective optimisation. In: Górski, J. (ed.) SAFECOMP 2006. LNCS, vol. 4166, pp. 426–438. Springer, Heidelberg (2006). doi:10.1007/11875567_32
29. Panichella, A., Kifetew, F.M., Tonella, P.: Reformulating branch coverage as a many-objective optimization problem. In: International Conference on Software Testing, Verification and Validation, pp. 1–10. IEEE (2015)
30. Pargas, R.P., Harrold, M.J., Peck, R.R.: Test-data generation using genetic algorithms. Softw. Test. Verification Reliab. **9**(4), 263–282 (1999)
31. Tonella, P.: Evolutionary testing of classes. In: ACM SIGSOFT Software Engineering Notes, vol. 29, pp. 119–128. ACM (2004)
32. Tracey, N., Clark, J., Mander, K., McDermid, J.: An automated framework for structural test-data generation. In: International Conference on Automated Software Engineering, pp. 285–288. IEEE (1998)
33. Vargha, A., Delaney, H.D.: A critique and improvement of the CL common language effect size statistics of McGraw and Wong. J. Educ. Behav. Stat. **25**(2), 101–132 (2000)
34. Watson, A.H., McCabe, T.J., Wallace, D.R.: Structured testing: a testing methodology using the cyclomatic complexity metric. NIST Spec. Publ. **500**(235), 1–114 (1996)
35. Wegener, J., Baresel, A., Sthamer, H.: Evolutionary test environment for automatic structural testing. Inf. Softw. Technol. **43**(14), 841–854 (2001)
36. Xanthakis, S., Ellis, C., Skourlas, C., Le Gall, A., Katsikas, S., Karapoulios, K.: Application of genetic algorithms to software testing. In: International Conference on Software Engineering and Its Applications, pp. 625–636 (1992)

37. Yoo, S., Harman, M.: Regression testing minimization, selection and prioritization: a survey. Softw. Test. Verification Reliab. **22**(2), 67–120 (2012)
38. Zitzler, E., Künzli, S.: Indicator-based selection in multiobjective search. In: Yao, X., Burke, E.K., Lozano, J.A., Smith, J., Merelo-Guervós, J.J., Bullinaria, J.A., Rowe, J.E., Tiňo, P., Kabán, A., Schwefel, H.-P. (eds.) PPSN 2004. LNCS, vol. 3242, pp. 832–842. Springer, Heidelberg (2004). doi:10.1007/978-3-540-30217-9_84
39. Zitzler, E., Laumanns, M., Thiele, L.: SPEA 2: Improving the strength pareto evolutionary algorithm. Technical report (2001)

A Search Based Approach for Stress-Testing Integrated Circuits

Basil Eljuse[✉] and Neil Walkinshaw

University of Leicester, Leicester, UK
be38@leicester.ac.uk, nw91@leicester.ac.uk

Abstract. In order to reduce software complexity and be power efficient, hardware platforms are increasingly incorporating functionality that was traditionally administered at a software-level (such as cache management). This functionality is often complex, incorporating multiple processors along with a multitude of design parameters. Such devices can only be reliably tested at a 'system' level, which presents various testing challenges; behaviour is often non-deterministic (from a software perspective), and finding suitable test sets to 'stress' the system adequately is often an inefficient, manual activity that yields fixed test sets that can rarely be reused. In this paper we investigate this problem with respect to ARM's Cache Coherent Interconnect (CCI) Unit. We present an automated search-based testing approach that combines a parameterised test-generation framework with the hill-climbing heuristic to find test sets that maximally 'stress' the CCI by producing much larger numbers of data stall cycles than the corresponding manual test sets.

Keywords: Automated search based testing · Cache Coherent Interconnect · System level stress testing

1   Introduction

Integrated Circuits (ICs) are commonly designed in a modular fashion. A developer will combine various subsystems into a comprehensive specification (often in the form of an RTL representation), which is then used to synthesise the hardware component. This can often require the setting of various parameters, with a view to optimising performance. When it comes to testing, this is commonly carried out at a 'system-level', i.e. by formulating and running software applications that are designed to exercise the ICs. Helper-applications can then be used to monitor the state of the underlying ICs, to ensure that its performance is as planned. Conventionally, these test suites are constructed by hand, often with the aim of 'stress-testing' various aspects of the ICs.

Hand-crafted tests are problematic for the conventional reasons that they require a significant amount of time and effort to formulate. In the context of ICs, which are often produced by combining a multitude of components, test cases can rarely be reused because, for a given system, it is often difficult to predict how different software parameters will interact and affect the underlying ICs.

© Springer International Publishing AG 2016
F. Sarro and K. Deb (Eds.): SSBSE 2016, LNCS 9962, pp. 80–95, 2016.
DOI: 10.1007/978-3-319-47106-8_6

Aside from these somewhat conventional software testing problems, ICs also suffer from significant testability problems. From a software standpoint, their behaviour is often highly non-deterministic, being subject to a large degree of interference from other routine operating-system processes that are difficult to control. In other words, the same test execution can lead to markedly different behaviours.

We highlight this testing challenge in the context of one of the hardware component - the ARM®CoreLink™Cache Coherent Interconnect (CCI). This is a component that seeks to maintain multi-level cache coherency support across multiple processor clusters, ensuring that each 'master' accessing the memory has the most up-to-date view of the data. The CCI provides developers with a host of parameters, and its performance and behaviour is highly affected by other processes run by an operating system (making it highly non-deterministic from a test-application standpoint).

The Search based software testing methodology have been successfully applied in testing embedded systems [1]. In this paper we describe a search-based approach to automatically produce test sets for the CCI that circumvents the above mentioned issues with non-determinism. The specific contribution are as follows:

- A brief description of our initial attempt, based upon conventional Genetic Algorithm-based test generation approaches, which used the search to directly identify potential combinations of memory configurations to stress the CCI.
- A higher-level test-input generation approach that uses hill-climbing, which was developed to circumvent the problems that had arisen with the non-determinism in our initial GA-based approach.
- An experiment that demonstrates that the hill-climbing approach manages to stress the CCI much more effectively than conventional hand-crafted test sets.

The rest of the paper is structured in the following fashion. Section 2 provides the essential details about one specific hardware cache coherency component, key aspects of cache operations in such a system and the configurability of this component which adds to the testing challenge, which underscores the research motivation. Section 3 provides the implementation details of the test framework implementing the search based algorithm and its key components. Section 4 discuss the results obtained from the application of this approach to a reference platform and the conclusions. The Sect. 5 outlines the related work that helped shape our approach and finally Sect. 6 outlines the future direction of this research.

2   Background

In this section we describe the underlying hardware testing problem. We introduce the typical industrial scenario, where ICs development involves the combination of multiple highly-configurable parameters, but where tests are commonly written by hand. We then cover the technical components of the test environment used in our experiments.

2.1   Motivating Scenario

The CCI is a hardware component that provides cache coherency management. It provides multiple levels of configurability specifically at (a) design time and (b) reset time. As outlined in [2] these configuration options include but not limited to transaction tracker size, QoS (Quality of Service) settings, address width, address striping size, snoop related configurations, and many more.

During system design a key consideration for the designer is to ensure the components are configured for optimal system behaviour. The design time parameters would have to be configured as a one-time setting. However the designer can vary the reset-time configurations during development to arrive at a configuration that produces 'optimal' behaviour – it should be as resource and time-efficient as possible. Configurations are evaluated for desired behaviour with specific test data sets.

Currently the test data design is hand-crafted. They take into account many platform attributes including but not limited to cache line size, page size, the number of memory banks etc. As these attributes do change across different configurations on a single platform (and certainly across multiple platforms), test sets cannot be readily reused.

2.2   The Cache Coherent Interconnect

The Cache Coherent Interconnect (CCI) is an infrastructure component in ARM® based systems that provides both interconnect and cache coherency functionality. It comprises a complex set of base-functionalities [2], and is delivered as a synthesisable Resistor-Transistor Logic (RTL) [3], which enables configurability of its behaviour at various phases during its design and operation.

The CCI product family includes many product versions and in our experiment we focused on CCI-400, which is a specific version of the component. It provides the interconnect and cache coherency functionality across 2 CPU clusters.

The CCI component allows various events to be monitored using its own internal counters. One such event is data stall cycle, which happens for both read and write operations, where a transaction is being stalled by CCI to cope with any issues arising. Such issues could be as a result of CCI's internal transaction tracker queues being full or any type of hazard being detected during operation. Transaction trackers can be full if there are differences in the throughput between components connected to the CCI, as typical of any producer-consumer scenario. Hazards occur in a multi-stage pipelined CPU architecture, when execution of an instruction in the pipeline could result in a wrong operation. Similar hazards are possible during CCI operations which will be handled by CCI by introducing stall cycles during its operation.

TC2 platform. The CCI [4] is designed to be deployed as part of a 'platform' – a collection of hardware and software components that are designed to underpin software applications. As such, it is one of the core infrastructure components of ARM's reference TestChip2 (TC2) [5] platform.

TC2 is an ARM development board implementing a big.LITTLE[TM] architecture. This architecture adds a degree of complexity to cache management because it consists of multiple clusters of CPUs, where the size of the L2 cache is based on the cluster composition. This variation in the L2 cache size is resulting from the heterogeneous nature of CPU Clusters - due to difference in both CPU type and in CPU topology - which make the data access operations across clusters different in nature. The TC2 platform has a big cluster made of dual-core Cortex-A15 MPCore[TM]CPU and a little cluster made of tri-core Cortex-A7 MPCore[TM]CPU. It has both level1 (L1) and level2 (L2) caches, with the CCI-400 providing the interconnect and hardware cache coherency across the 2 CPU clusters.

We used a full Android[TM1] software stack for TC2 in our experimentation. ARM provides the firmware and full Android software stack supported on this platform via the non-profit organisation called Linaro [6]. This provides a test environment representative of a real system from both hardware and software perspective.

Figure 1 outlines the cache configuration in the TC2 platform and various software components involved during the stress test execution flow at system level. In a TC2 platform all CPUs have 32 KB of L1 cache. While the little

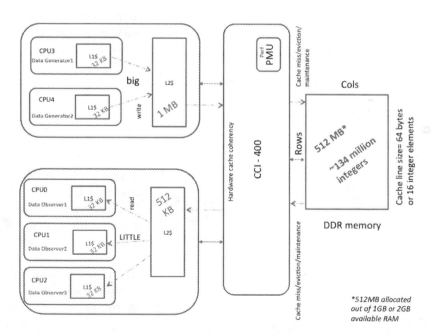

Fig. 1. TC2 platform with CCI-400. *Details the multi-level cache configuration and the various data actors.*

---

[1] Android is a registered trademark of Google.

cluster has a 512 KB L2 cache, the big cluster has a larger 1 MB L2 cache. More details of the various software components are explained in later sections.

Testability Challenge. The CCI has one feature (shared by most embedded systems) that is particularly challenging from a testing perspective: It is difficult to control externally. Since it is at the bottom of a relatively complex stack of hardware and software components (not least including the Android operating system) it is virtually impossible to reset to a fixed state. With the operating system continually manipulating the memory and catering for other routine OS processes, the behaviour of the CCI becomes effectively non-deterministic. Advanced features of CCI (like speculative data fetch) only adds to this level of non-determinism.

Performance Monitoring Unit. CCI includes a component called Performance Monitoring Unit (PMU) [2], which has the logic to gather various statistics about the operation of the interconnect at runtime and expose them through counters monitoring certain events. Typically there are multiple counters and different event types that could be monitored using this PMU logic. CCI-400 supports four 32-bit counters allowing one event per counter to be monitored in parallel. This means one can monitor up-to 4 events in parallel without incurring any penalty on accuracy.

The following is a non-exhaustive list of events which are of interest to this research

- Read data stall cycle
- Read request stall cycle due to transaction tracker full
- Write request stall cycle due to transaction tracker full
- Stall cycle because of an address hazard

As a general rule of thumb, the occurrence of stall cycles indicate that the CCI component is having to pause some of its operations to cope with the demand for ensuring coherency. Thus stall cycles can be used as a measure of stress in the system. Larger numbers of stall cycles observed can be an indication of stress in the platform leading to sub-optimal system performance. This can be used as an indication to conclude that the configurations evaluated by the system designer during design phase is sub-optimal.

3   Stress Test Data Generation Using Search Based Technique

In this paper we present a search-based technique that is designed to automatically generate the test sets for configurations of hardware components such as CCI. The aim of the technique is to 'stress-test' the component.

3.1   Test Case Representation

Input data. Ultimately, to test the CCI, the input consists of requests to write-to and read-from regions within memory. If we adopt a simplistic view of the problem, the testing challenge is to find a set of memory-addresses to write-to and read-from in such a way that the cache is 'stretched' – i.e. that we arrive at a situation where requests for data frequently cannot be met by the cache.

One issue with this 'simplistic' view of the problem is the lack of determinism in the CCI (as discussed in Sect. 2.2). A single memory configuration can on one occasion trigger a large number of data stall cycles, and on another run trigger very few. In our preliminary experiments, this severely hampered any search-based approaches we attempted.

As a consequence, we re-analysed the test case representation, with the goal of producing a representation that was more robust in the face of poor testability. Our solution was to step back, and to use our domain knowledge [2] to identify the key high-level factors that could influence the performance of the CCI, and to use these to encode the test cases instead of concrete address spaces. As a result, we now represent our test cases in three dimensions: payload size, sparsity and actor profile. These factors are elaborated below.

Payload size. We vary the amount of test data that is read and written. In practice, the size of the data is specified by two integers: x and y – representing the number of columns and rows required to contain the data. We limit this between 1 MB and 80 MB - i.e. $16 \leq x \leq 5120$ and $16 \leq y \leq 4096$. The number of columns and rows are determined based on the data size of individual data units (current experiment has this as 4 byte length).

Sparsity. We need to vary the range of locations that are available to us in memory. The behaviour of the cache will differ if all of the data is to be written and read from a single, contiguous zone of memory, as opposed to a range of non-contiguous, widely dispersed regions. This is based on the principles of locality of reference based on which memory systems work efficiently. Accordingly, we allow for four categories of data 'sparsity': (1) Unconstrained – the payload can be written-to or read-from anywhere in the 512 MB of available memory, (2) relatively sparse – the operational memory is limited to half of the available memory (256 MB). (3) dense – the operational memory is limited to a tenth of the memory (51.2 MB), or (4) very dense – the operational memory is limited to a hundredth of the total memory (5.1 MB).

We chose an upper limit of 512 MB because it is substantially larger than the L2 cache size for the largest cluster (which is 1 MB for the big cluster) in our reference platform, which means that with this setting there would invariably be a large number of cache misses which could lead to data stall cycles being generated. In the case where the payload size is high (i.e. 80 MB) and the sparsity is low (i.e. 5 MB), this would result in the 80 MBs of data being written-to and read-from the same set of memory locations (with high probability).

Actor profile. The number of actors (or processes) writing to and reading from memory can affect cache performance. The affinity of the actors of certain type (read or write) to the clusters were fixed for our experiment - read actors pinned to little cluster and write actors pinned to big cluster. However the number of actors were varied in 3 settings viz, (a) single read and write actors, (b) dual read and write actors and (c) 3 read and 2 write actors. The number of actors performing read and write operations in parallel do affect the level of stress on CCI's operations. Especially with cache sizes being different across clusters and multiple actors operating on memory, the cache miss rates at each of the L1 and L2 caches in the system will vary quite significantly, affecting the number of data stall cycle generated.

Monitoring outputs. To monitor the performance of the CCI in response to the test inputs, we use the event counters exposed by PMU (discussed above). Specifically, we use the PMU to record the number of data stall cycles for a given test. To address the problems posed by non-determinism, for each configuration of the above test case representation, we would record the average number of data stall cycle from 100 executions of a test. The decision of fixing the number of iterations to 100 was based on a very conservative approach adopted in our initial experiments.

3.2   The Search Algorithm

Our intuition was to start with a search strategy that is as simple as possible, for which the Hill-Climbing algorithm is an obvious choice. Hill-climbing algorithm starts from a random solution (in our case a random configuration of our test case representation) and navigates through the search space by continuously selecting a better solution from its 'neighbouring' solutions. The hill-climbing stops once the fitness function score is maximised - either finding a local or global maxima - or when a set amount of iterations is attempted.

The choice of hill-climbing is (at least to begin with) justified because it often performs surprisingly well for other search-based testing problems, often even outperforming more sophisticated evolutionary search techniques [7].

An overview of the approach is provided in Algorithm 1. The algorithm uses three auxiliary functions:

- $randomInteger(x)$ provides a random integer between 1 and (including) x.
- $fitnessfunction(x, y, sparsity, actors)$ evaluates the generated test cases that conform to the parameters, in terms of recorded data stall cycles. These test cases are run multiple times (we opt for 100 times) to account for any non-determinism, and the average number of data stall cycles is returned.
- $generateNeighbours(x, y, sparsity, actors)$ generates all of the possible configurations that are 'adjacent' to the given configuration. For each parameter a number of new test cases are generated. In case of payload size it generates two new test cases where we increase and decrease the size by a pre-defined step value, whilst keeping the other parameters fixed to their original values. In case of sparsity parameter we generate 3 new test cases and finally for actor

Output: The optimal configuration from the input set
begin

$maximum = 0$

$x \leftarrow$ randomInteger(5120)

$y \leftarrow$ randomInteger(4096)

$sparsity \leftarrow$ randomInteger(4)

$actors \leftarrow$ randomInteger(3)

while fitnessFunction$(x, y, sparsity, actors) > maximum$ **do**

$maximum \leftarrow$ fitnessFunction$(x, y, sparsity, actors)$

$Neighbours \leftarrow$ generateNeighbours$(x, y, sparsity, actors)$

forall the $(x', y', sparsity', actors') \in Neighbours$ **do**

/* Evaluate fitness of child testdata   */

if fitnessFunction$(x', y', sparsity', actors') > maximum$ **then**

$x \leftarrow x'$

$y \leftarrow y'$

$sparsity \leftarrow sparsity'$

$actors \leftarrow actors'$

end

end

end

return $(x, y, sparsity, actors)$

end

Algorithm 1: Dynamic Test Data Generation

profile we generate 2 new test cases. This produces, for a given test set, a total of 7 new configurations.

3.3   Implementation of the Software Test Execution Framework

One of the inherent challenges of testing ICs is that (unlike conventional software testing) there is a distance between the system being tested (in our case the CCI) and the mechanism that is carrying out the testing. Our automated software testing software is executed as a conventional software application in Android 'user-space'. In this subsection we describe how the high-level representation discussed above is mapped into concrete inputs to the CCI.

Test setup. As discussed previously, the contents of the memory and cache are routinely affected by many processes within the system that are difficult to control in the context of the test-application. Nonetheless, there are some steps that we carry out at each test to reduce this potential interference:

– We stop as many Android background tasks as is possible (some cannot be stopped).
– We perform an identical memory walk-through sequence between iterations to give better chances for an equivalent initial state.

– We use data barrier instructions - an ARM architecture specific instruction
[8] - to ensure all out-of-order data access is cleared before every test data is
evaluated.

Inputs

Payload: The payload holds information about the memory addresses from the
defined search area, which is represented as a 2 dimensional array. This 2 dimensional array of (x,y) coordinates are populated with random set of memory locations. The payload size control the number of such memory locations that are
involved during the test case execution.

Sparsity: The sparsity of the memory locations populated is controlled by limiting the range of values from which the individual (x,y) coordinates can be set.
By setting the maximum range from which both the x and y coordinates can
be picked during payload generation allows one to control the sparsity. If this
maximum range is set as a low value then that would force the payload to be
populated from memory address locations which are highly probable to be in
closer proximity. On the other hand, if the maximum range is set to the highest possible value, then the payload could be populated with memory locations
which are far from each other (non-contiguous).

Actors: The necessity for multiple actors to be reading from and writing to
the memory at the same time means that we execute tests as a multi-threaded
application. For our tests, an actor can either be a data-generator (which writes
data to memory) or data-observer (which reads data from memory). Each actor
is assigned (pinned) to its own CPU, where the CPU can belong to one of the
big.LITTLE™ clusters.

The hill climbing algorithm relies on this infrastructure while navigating the
search space. Once a test data is generated, using the Message Queue IPC (Inter
Process Communication) mechanism, the data operation is initiated using actors
running in a multi-threaded fashion, while the Linux Perf utility will capture the
monitored events as the fitness score. The hill climbing algorithm uses this fitness
score associated with each of the candidate test data and arrives at the maxima
as per the Algorithm 1 outlined in earlier section.

Outputs. The outputs (i.e. the number of data stall cycles on the CCI) are
read from the CCI's PMU by using the Linux Perf tool[2]. Perf is a user space
utility that provides a standard way of accessing performance measurement on
supported platforms. Linux Perf can be used to capture both software and hardware events and also other kernel supported events like tracepoint events. Perf
also provides the ability to perform counting of events on a per task or per CPU
or system wide basis. Perf counters can be configured to operate in either counting or sampling mode. In counting mode the Perf takes the running count of the

---

[2] https://perf.wiki.kernel.org/index.php/Main_Page.

monitored event which is more accurate, while in case of sampling mode it captures the monitored events at a pre-defined sampling rate, thus providing only an approximate event count. In our experiments we use Perf utility in counting mode and configured to capture system wide events.

4   Evaluation

In order to evaluate our testing technique, we carried out an experiment that was designed to compare the effectiveness of the test-sets generated by our approach against a set of hand-crafted test sets. Specifically, the experiment aims to answer the following research question:

- RQ1 - Does the test data generated with our search-based algorithm yield better results than hand-crafted test data?

4.1   Methodology

To answer the research question, we compare the data stall cycles produced by the test set that was generated by our search-based approach against similar random test sets, as well as a set of established, hand-crafted test sets, that are conventionally used to test the CCI component.

For the hand-crafted test cases we identified a series of test sets used for functional validation of CCI component within ARM. Some of the existing suite of tests did perform various operations like memory walk-through operations, circular memory copy operations, simultaneous memory operations, accessing random memory locations etc. A key focus for these tests were to check for the functional correctness and that involved performing data integrity checks as part of the test execution. We chose the random memory access operations to characterise our baseline test case in our experiments.

To generate the test sets the payload was populated with random memory location coordinates similar to the hill climbing methodology. We had a fixed configuration for each of the payload attributes - payload size, actor profile and sparsity. In our baseline tests we ran tests where we fixed two of the attributes and varied the remaining final attribute alone.

In case of the payload-size attribute we fixed the actor profile and sparsity attributes and kept varying the size from a minimum (1 MB) to a maximum (80 MB) value with a predefined step. In case of actor profile we fixed the other two attributes and varied the actor profile against the possible variations of single, dual and multi-actor configurations. Similarly for sparsity attribute we fixed the other 2 and varied the level of sparsity - unconstrained, relative sparse, dense and very dense - by setting the maximum value the x and y coordinates for the memory location addresses being populated.

As explained in earlier section, one of the measures we employed to overcome the issue with non determinism was to repeat each test for 100 iterations. This was consistently applied during the evaluation of baseline test and hill climbing methodology.

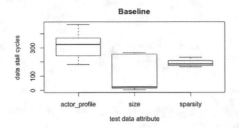

Fig. 2. Baseline scores. *Each payload attribute evaluated in isolation.*

Finally, in order to provide a further comparable baseline the same experiment, we produced random a test set by choosing random configurations of the parameters. Here we repeated the same number of iterations as that of the hill climbing experiments but randomly populating all the attributes across generations.

4.2   Results

Baseline test data. Figure 2 shows the distributions of scores for our manual baseline test data, considering each attribute in isolation. The plot shows how the three different attributes have varying effects on the number of data stall cycles. No baseline test data generated a score beyond 500 stall cycles. Comparing these we can observe that the actor profile seems to yield the best scores among the baseline candidates. However there is an overlap between the scores generated by each of these factors, which indicates that all of these factors are relevant to be considered in the search based test implementation.

Figure 3 shows the mean scores for our hill-climbing approach, compared with an equivalent random approach, and also alongside the manually generated test scores. The results indicate that the hill-climbing approach rapidly outperforms the other approaches, finishing off at a mean score of over 1000 stall cycles, whereas other approaches fail to improve beyond 600.

4.3   Discussion

The results from hill climbing algorithm captured in Fig. 3 show the typical plot where the later generations yielding better results than the initial ones. It starts with scores at a similar level as that of the baseline test data in the experiment and keeps improving over subsequent generations. In the final set of generations the results approach a maximum.

Comparing the scores achieved in hill climbing approach against the baseline it is clear that there is over 2 times improvement in the generated scores. In this experiment hill climbing yields almost 1100 data stall cycles. This is against the maximum value of up to 500 data stall cycles from baseline test data evaluation. The random search approach did not yield any scores better than 600 data

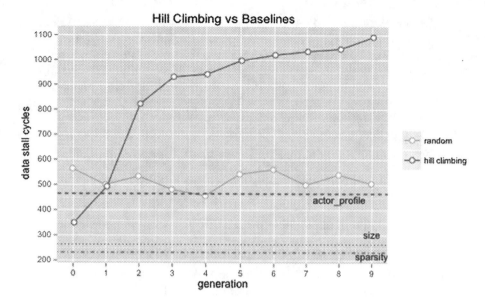

Fig. 3. Hill Climbing scores. *Final scores generated from hill climbing better than any of the baseline scores. Hill climbing scores also performed better than equivalent random test generation experiment*

stall cycles which is way below from what was achieved using the hill climbing approach.

The results from our experiments clearly shows the suitability of search based software testing techniques in stress testing of platforms with hardware coherency support. By exploiting the PMU counters as a fitness function, a rather straight forward application of search based technique is possible in this testing domain. Additional meta-heuristics in defining next generation nodes and fitness function evaluation could only improve the application of SBST methodology in this area.

We have successfully validated the research question by comparing the results from hill climbing implementation against the baseline test data, which shows a clear benefit with the search based test approach.

4.4 Threats to Validity

Hardware cache coherency components do provide additional hardware mechanisms like PMU that can be exploited by this methodology. In the absence of such hardware support, relevant meta-heuristics need to be defined to ensure the applicability of the proposed methodology. Although here we leveraged the hardware mechanisms to apply this technique, in situations where such mechanisms are not present can limit the easy application of this methodology. A large variation in the measure of data stall cycles could pose a threat to the validity of the results, unless controlled. We observed in our experimentation a large extent of variation in the PMU counter values even when same test data is executed repeatedly. The potential for additional variability can be introduced by the fact that the test framework is also running on the target. In absence of effective measures to reduce the variability of the measured scores, we could get unreliable results which may not necessarily lead to the global maxima. There is a possibility that more needs to be done beyond current measures to reduce the impact of variability in the scores.

We adopted hill climbing as it was a simpler form of search based algorithm to implement and to apply on the target domain. With the known limitations of hill climbing, we could be stuck at a local maxima and miss achieving the global maxima. This could reduce the effectiveness of the approach.

5   Related Work

The Search Based testing techniques are used for automated test data generation in various domains including black box testing [9]. The surveys as in [10] indicates that test data generation for non-functional testing of software using SBST techniques were initially focussed on execution time analysis. More work in [11] shows the use of SBST for worst case execution time analysis using multi-objective criteria. The possibility of automated test generation for testing non functional attributes of embedded systems is proven in [12], even though these don't seem to rely on search based techniques.

The application of SBST for non functional testing of systems recently have been wide and varied including performance analysis as explained in [13]. Automated test generation using search based testing techniques are described by [14] for testing worst case interrupt latencies in embedded systems. Further surveys in [15] confirms its application being extended to other non functional system attributes like safety [16], usability, quality of service [17] and security [18]. It has been successfully used in stress testing of real-time systems too as explained in [19].

While most of the above referenced work are focusing on testing software components, application of SBST to hardware component testing can also be seen. We found that the research into the application of SBST techniques with focus on hardware components were mostly in the context of hardware-in-the-loop systems as captured in [20,21].

All the prevalent research into cache testing are mostly focused on hardware self testing as explained in [22,23]. There are established methodologies for targeted testing of cache memory at very low level as found in [24]. More standard techniques are outlined in the work published in [25]. Successful application of search based software testing methodology in the area of memory system validation can be seen in the work using genetic algorithms with memory consistency model (MCM) verification as per [26].

Similar to the general approach to cache testing some of the L2 cache testing had been also using on-line testing, but looking from a functional testing perspective mostly, as outlined in [27]. Further we could see that in the area of testing cache coherency management, again the focus had been mostly on functional testing as explained in [28]. The work on improving coverage for cache coherency protocol verification can be seen in [29].

However Search Based software testing methodology being adopted for stress testing of L2 cache coherency component from a system perspective is not seen adopted so far. Our research establishes the successful extension of the use of search based software testing techniques for stress testing systems with hardware cache coherency support. Given the fact that this specific application of the technique in this area don't seemed to be attempted earlier, there are no direct comparisons available. Nonetheless this study establishes the benefits of using this technique and provides wider possibilities to make stress testing of systems with complex hardware components more efficient in future with SBST.

6   Conclusions and Future Work

In this study we have investigated the possibility of applying search based software testing techniques in stress testing systems with hardware cache coherency support. Based on the results we have from the selected hardware platform it is evident that the proposed methodology is applicable and more over provides benefits over the traditional approach. We are confident this will improve the adoption of SBST techniques in the related field.

In the current evaluation we focused on using a single objective fitness function targeting a single PMU event. Since the hardware we used supports multiple counters and can monitor up to 4 events in parallel, there is a possibility of extending the methodology to be used in a multi-objective manner. This is an area to be evaluated in future.

Suitability of advanced search based algorithms needs to be evaluated which could potentially avoid the issue of being stuck at a local maxima. However this is a wider problem with any search based algorithm implementation and various strategies are devised in the academic research arena which could be found useful in this specific testing domain. This is another area that needs to be looked into in future.

References

1. Arcuri, A., Iqbal, M.Z., Briand, L.: Black-box system testing of real-time embedded systems using random and search-based testing. In: Petrenko, A., Simão, A., Maldonado, J.C. (eds.) ICTSS 2010. LNCS, vol. 6435, pp. 95–110. Springer, Heidelberg (2010)
2. ARM CoreLink CCI-400 Cache Coherent Interconnect - Technical Reference Manual.   http://infocenter.arm.com/help/topic/com.arm.doc.ddi0470k/DDI0470K_cci400_r1p5_trm.pdf
3. IEC 62142–2005 First 2005th edn. –06 IEEE Std 1364.1 - Verilog Register Transfer Level Synthesis
4. White paper on big.LITTLE^{TM} processing Technology. http://www.arm.com/files/pdf/CacheCoherencyWhitepaper_6June2011.pdf

5. TestChip2 - part of ARM Versatile Express product family. http://www.arm.com/products/tools/development-boards/versatile-express/index.php
6. Linaro - A non-profit organisation working on open source software for ARM based platforms. http://www.linaro.org
7. Harman, M., McMinn, P.: A theoretical & empirical analysis of evolutionary testing and hill climbing for structural test data generation. In: International Symposium on Software Testing and Analysis (2007)
8. When to use Barrier instructions? http://infocenter.arm.com/help/index.jsp?topic=/com.arm.doc.faqs/ka14041.html
9. Fischer, M., Tonjes, R.: Generating test data for black-box testing using genetic algorithms. In: IEEE 17th International Conference on Emerging Technologies and Factory Automation (2012)
10. McMinn, P.: Search based software test data generation: a survey. Softw. Test. Verification Reliab. (2004). Wiley
11. Khan, U., Bate, I.: WCET analysis of modern processors using multi-criteria optimisation. In: First Symposium on Search Based Software Engineering (2009)
12. Chattopadhyay, S., Eles, P., Peng, Z.: Automated software testing of memory performance in embedded GPUs. In: International Conference on Embedded Software (2014)
13. Shen, D., Luo, Q., Poshyvanyk, D., Grechanik, M.: Automating performance bottleneck detection using search-based application profiling. In: International Symposium on Software Testing and Analysis (2015)
14. Yu, T., Srisa-an, W., Cohen, M., Rothermel, G.: SimLatte: a framework to support testing for worst-case interrupt latencies in embedded software. In: International Conference on Software Testing, Verification and Validation (2014)
15. Afzal, W., Torkar, R., Feldt, R.: A systematic review of search-based testing for non-functional system properties. Inf. Softw. Technol. (2009)
16. Baresel, A., Pohlheim, H., Sadeghipour, S.: Structural and functional sequence test of dynamic and state-based software with evolutionary algorithms. In: Genetic and Evolutionary Computation Conference (2003)
17. Canfora, G., Penta, M.D., Esposito, R., Villani, M.L.: An approach for QoS-aware service composition based on genetic algorithms. In: Conference on Genetic and Evolutionary Computation (2005)
18. Grosso, C., Antoniol, G., Penta, M.D., Galinier, P., Merlo, E.: Security, improving network applications: a new heuristic to generate stress testing data. In: Annual Conference on Genetic and Evolutionary Computation (2005)
19. Briand, L.C., Labiche, Y., Shousha, M.: Stress testing real-time systems with genetic algorithms. In: 7th Annual Conference on Genetic and Evolutionary Computation (2005)
20. Wegener, J., Kruse, P.M.: Search-based testing with in-the-loop systems. In: First International Symposium on Search Based Software Engineering (2009)
21. Lindlar, F., Windisch, A.: A search-based approach to functional hardware-in-the-loop testing. In: Second International Symposium on Search Based Software Engineering (2010)
22. Theodorou, G., Kranitis, N., Paschalis, A., Gizopoulos, D.: Software-based self test methodology for on-line testing of L1 caches in multithreaded multicore architectures. IEEE Trans. Very Large Scale Integr. Syst.(VLSI) (2013)
23. Theodorou, G., Kranitis, N., Paschalis, A., Gizopoulos, D.: Software-based self-test for small caches in microprocessors. IEEE Trans. Comput. Aided Des. Integr. Circ. Syst. (2014)

24. Al-Ars, Z., Hamdioui, S., Gaydadjiev, G., Vassiliadis, S.: Test set development for cache memory in modern microprocessors. IEEE Trans. Very Large Scale Integr. VLSI Syst. (2008)
25. Di Carlo, S., Prinetto, P., Savino, A.: Software-based self-test of set-associative cache memories. IEEE Trans. Comput. (2010)
26. Elver, M., Nagarajan, V.: McVerSi: a test generation framework for fast memory consistency verification in simulation. In: The 22nd Symposium on High Performance Computer Architecture (2016)
27. Riga, M., Sanchez, E., Reorda, M.S.: On the functional test of L2 caches. In: IEEE 18th International On-line Testing Symposium (2012)
28. Acle, J.P., Cantoro, R., Sanchez, E., Reorda, M.S.: On the functional test of the cache coherency logic in multi-core systems. In: 6th Latin American Symposium on Circuits and Systems (2015)
29. Qin, X., Mishra, P.: Automated generation of directed tests for transition coverage in cache coherence protocols. In: Design, Automation & Test in Europe Conference & Exhibition (DATE) (2012)

An (Accidental) Exploration of Alternatives to Evolutionary Algorithms for SBSE

Vivek Nair$^{(\boxtimes)}$, Tim Menzies, and Jianfeng Chen

North Carolina State University, Raleigh, USA
vivekaxl@gmail.com

Abstract. SBSE researchers often use an evolutionary algorithm to solve various software engineering problems. This paper explores an alternate approach of sampling. This approach is called SWAY (Sampling WAY) and finds the (near) optimal solutions to the problem by (i) creating a larger initial population and (ii) intelligently *sampling* the solution space to find the best subspace. Unlike evolutionary algorithms, SWAY does not use mutation or cross-over or multi-generational reasoning to find interesting subspaces but relies on the underlying dimensions of the solution space. Experiments with Software Engineering (SE) models shows that SWAY's performance improvement is competitive with standard MOEAs while, terminating over an order of magnitude faster.

Keywords: Search-based SE · Sampling · Evolutionary algorithms

1 Introduction

Finding solutions to problems in Software Engineering is challenging since it often means accommodating competing choices. When stakeholders propose multiple goals, SBSE methods can reflect on goal interactions to propose novel solutions to hard optimization problems such as configuring products in complex product lines [23], tuning parameters of a data miner [26], or finding best configurations for clone detection algorithms [28]. For these tasks, many SBSE researchers use evolutionary algorithms (EA):

1. *Generate* population $i = 0$ by selecting at random across known ranges.
2. *Evaluate:* all individuals in population i.
3. Repeat
   (a) *Cross-over:* make population $i + 1$ by combining elite items;
   (b) *Mutation:* make small changes to individuals in population i;
   (c) *Evaluate:* all individuals in population i;
   (d) *Selection:* choose some elite subset of population i;

EAs can be slow due to the "Repeat" loop of step3; or the need to evaluate every candidate in step2a; or the polynominal-time cost of processing each population in step2c (a rigorous selection step requires $O(N^2)$ comparisons of all pairs). So can we do better than EA for Search-based SE? That is, are there faster alternatives to EA?

This paper experimentally evaluates one such alternative which we call SWAY (short for the Sampling WAY):

© Springer International Publishing AG 2016
F. Sarro and K. Deb (Eds.): SSBSE 2016, LNCS 9962, pp. 96–111, 2016.
DOI: 10.1007/978-3-319-47106-8_7

1. As above, *generate* population $i = 0$;
2. Intelligently *select* the cluster within population 0 with best scores.

Until recently, we would have dismissed SWAY as an ineffective method for exploring multi-goal optimization since its search is very limited. The main criticism against sampling techniques were:

– SWAY quits after the initial generation;
– SWAY makes no use of mutation or cross-over so there is no way for lessons learned to accumulate as it executes;
– Depending on the algorithm, not all members of population will be evaluated–e.g. active learners [14] only evaluate a few representative examples.

Nevertheless, quite by accident, we have stumbled onto evidence that has dramatically changed our opinion about SWAY. Recently we were working with an algorithm called GALE [14]. GALE is an evolutionary algorithm includes SWAY as a sub-routine:

$$evolution = (mutation + crossover + sampling) * generations$$
$$SWAY \quad = GALE - evolution$$

While porting GALE from Python to Java, we accidentally disabled evolution. To our surprise, that "broken" version of GALE (that only used SWAY) worked as well, or better, than the original GALE. This is an interesting result since GALE has been compared against dozens of models in a recent TSE article [14] and dozens more in Krall's Ph.D. thesis [13]. In those studies, GALE was found to be competitive against widely used evolutionary algorithms. If Krall's work is combined with the results from our accident, then we conjecture that the success of EAs is due less to "evolution" than to "sampling" many options. This, in turn, could lead to a new generation of very fast optimizers since, as we show below, sampling can be much faster than evolving.

This paper documents that accidental discovery, as follows. After answering some frequently asked questions, we present some multi-goal SE problems followed by several algorithms which could explore them. All those models are then optimized using the EAs and our sampling techniques. Our observations after conducting the study are:

– Mutation strategy of a recently published EA algorithm (GALE) adds little value;
– GALE without evolution (SWAY) runs an order of magnitude faster than EAs;
– Optimizations found by SWAY are similar to those found by SBSE algorithms.

Our conclusion will be that sampling is an interesting research approach for multi-dimensional optimization that deserves further attention by the SBSE community.

1.1   Frequently Asked Questions

This section comments on several issues raised while discussing GALE and SWAY. Firstly, when we say "faster processing", we mean "reducing the number of candidate evaluations". Merely measuring runtime can conflate the intrinsic merit of an algorithm with (a) the implementation language for that algorithm and (b) whether or not some static code analysis has been applied to improve the performance of that code. Hence, we count "runtime" in EAs and SWAY in terms of number of evaluations.

Secondly, sampling with SWAY is not some universal panacea that will simplify all SBSE problems. Some tasks do not need a hundred-fold speed up. For example, the core of next release planning problems is very small and evaluates very fast [30]. Similarly, sampling may not improve standard "lab problems" (e.g. DTLZ, Fonseca, etc [8]) used to evaluate MOEA algorithms since these are also very small and very fast to evaluate. However, there exists SBSE tasks which could definitely benefit from fast sampling techniques. Some models takes hours to make a single evaluation (e.g. the aeronautics software requirements model explored by Krall et al. [14]). For such models, it is very useful if we perform fewer evaluations. Also, when there are very many options to explore (e.g. 9.3 million candidate configurations for software clone detectors [28]) then sampling would be useful to reduce the number of explored candidates. Finally, if it is proposed to put humans-in-the-loop to help guide the evaluations [22], then sampling becomes a very useful method for reducing the effort required of those humans.

Finally, we make a note that our main observation "SWAY works as well as EAs with far fewer evaluations" is consistent over other "lab problems" such as DTLZ, Fonseca, Golinski, Srinivas, etc [8]. Those results are not included here since, in our experience, results from those small maths models are less convincing to the SBSE community than results from software models.

scale factors (exponentially decrease effort)	prec: have we done this before?
	flex: development flexibility
	resl: any risk resolution activities?
	team: team cohesion
	pmat: process maturity
upper (linearly decrease effort)	acap: analyst capability
	pcap: programmer capability
	pcon: programmer continuity
	aexp: analyst experience
	pexp: programmer experience
	ltex: language and tool experience
	tool: tool use
	site: multiple site development
	sced: length of schedule
lower (linearly increase effort)	rely: required reliability
	data: 2nd memory requirements
	cplx: program complexity
	ruse: software reuse
	docu: documentation requirements
	time: runtime pressure
	stor: main memory requirements
	pvol: platform volatility

Fig. 1. XOMO inputs range $1 \leq x \leq 6$.

2   Materials

This section describes our models, optimizers, and statistical analysis. The implementation and all experimental data are available at http://tiny.cc/Sway

2.1   Models

XOMO: This section summarizes XOMO. For more details, see [14,16–18]. XOMO [16–18] combines four software process models from Boehm's group at the University of Southern California. XOMO's inputs are the project descriptors of Fig. 1 which can (sometimes) be changed by management decisions. For example, if a manager wants to (a) *relax schedule pressure*, they set *sced* to its minimal value; (b) to *reduce functionality* they halve the value of *kloc* and reduce minimize the size of the project database (by setting *data=2*); (c) to *reduce quality* (in order to race something to market) they might move to lowest reliability, minimize the documentation work and the complexity of the code being written, reduce the schedule pressure to some middle value. In the language of XOMO, this last change would be *rely=1, docu=1, time=3, cplx=1*.

XOMO derives four objective scores: (1) project *risk*; (2) development *effort*; (3) predicted *defects*; (4) total *months* of development (*Months* = *effort* / *#workers*). Effort and defects are predicted from mathematical models derived from data collected from hundreds of commercial and Defense Department projects [2]. As to the *risk* model, this model contains rules that triggers when management decisions decrease the odds of successfully completing a project: e.g. demanding *more* reliability (*rely*) while *decreasing* analyst capability (*acap*). Such a project is "risky" since it means the manager is demanding more reliability from less skilled analysts. XOMO measures *risk* as the percent of triggered rules.

The optimization goals for XOMO are to *reduce* all these values.

- Reduce risk;
- Reduce effort;
- Reduce defects;
- Reduce months.

Note that this is a non-trivial problem since the objectives listed above as non-separable and conflicting in nature. For example, *increasing* software reliability *reduces* the number of added defects while *increasing* the software development effort. Also, *more* documentation can improve team communication and *decrease* the number of introduced defects. However, such increased documentation *increases* the development effort.

POM3 – A Model of Agile Development: According to Turner and Boehm [3], agile managers struggle to balance *idle rates, completion rates* and *overall cost*.

- In the agile world, projects terminate after achieving a *completion rate* of $(X < 100)\%$ of its required tasks.
- Team members become *idle* if forced to wait for a yet-to-be-finished task from other teams.
- To lower *idle rate* and increase *completion rate*, management can hire staff–but this increases *overall cost*.

Short name	Decision	Description	Controllable
Cult	Culture	Number (%) of requirements that change.	yes
Crit	Criticality	Requirements cost effect for safety critical systems.	yes
Crit.Mod	Criticality Modifier	Number of (%) teams affected by criticality.	yes
Init. Kn	Initial Known	Number of (%) initially known requirements.	no
Inter-D	Inter-Dependency	Number of (%) requirements that have interdependencies. Note that dependencies are requirements within the *same* tree (of requirements), but interdependencies are requirements that live in *different* trees.	no
Dyna	Dynamism	Rate of how often new requirements are made.	yes
Size	Size	Number of base requirements in the project.	no
Plan	Plan	Prioritization Strategy (of requirements): one of 0= Cost Ascending; 1= Cost Descending; 2= Value Ascending; 3= Value Descending; 4 = $\frac{Cost}{Value}$ Ascending.	yes
T.Size	Team Size	Number of personnel in each team	yes

Fig. 2. List of inputs to POM3. These inputs come from Turner & Boehm's analysis of factors that control how well organizers can react to agile development practices [3]. The optimization task is to find settings for the controllables in the last column.

Hence, in this study, our optimizers tune the decisions of Fig. 2 in order to

- Increase completion rates;
- Reduce idle rates;
- Reduce overall cost.

Those inputs are used by the POM3 model to compute completion rates, idle times and overall cost. For full details POM3 see [1, 21]. For a synopsis, see below.

To understand POM3 [1, 21], consider a set intra-dependent requirements. A single requirement consists of a prioritization *value* and a *cost*, along with a list of child-requirements and dependencies. Before any requirement can be satisfied, its children and dependencies must first be satisfied. POM3 builds a requirements heap with prioritization values, containing 30 to 500 requirements, with costs from 1 to 100 (values chosen in consultation with Richard Turner [3]). Since POM3 models agile projects, the *cost,value* figures are constantly changing (up until the point when the requirement is completed, after which they become fixed).

Now imagine a mountain of requirements hiding below the surface of a lake; i.e. it is mostly invisible. As the project progresses, the lake dries up and the mountain slowly appears. Programmers standing on the shore study the mountain. Programmers are organized into teams. Every so often, the teams pause to plan their next sprint. At that time, the backlog of tasks comprises the visible requirements.

For their next sprint, teams prioritize work for their next sprint using one of five prioritization methods: (1) cost ascending; (2) cost descending; (3) value ascending; (4) value descending; (5) $\frac{cost}{value}$ ascending. Note that prioritization might be sub-optimal due to the changing nature of the requirements *cost,value* as the unknown nature of the remaining requirements. Another wild-card that POM3 has contains an *early cancellation probability* that can cancel a project after N sprints (the value directly proportional to number of sprints). Due to this wild-card, POM3's teams are always racing to deliver as much as possible before being re-tasked. The final total cost is a function of:

(a) Hours worked, taken from the *cost* of the requirements;
(b) The salary of the developers: less experienced developers get paid less;
(c) The critically of the software: mission critical software costs more since they are allocated more resources for software quality tasks.

Scenarios: Our studies execute XOMO and POM3 in the context of seven specific project-specific scenarios. For XOMO, we use four scenarios taken from NASA's Jet Propulsion Laboratory [18]. As shown in Fig. 3, FLIGHT and GROUND is a general description of all JPL flight and ground software while OSP and OPS2 are two versions of the flight guidance system of the Orbital Space Plane.

For POM3, we explore three scenarios proposed by Boehm (personnel communication). As shown in Fig. 4: POM3a covers a wide range of projects; POM3b represents small and highly critical projects and POM3c represent large projects that are highly dynamic (ones where cost and value can be altered over a large range).

project	feature	ranges low	high	values feature	setting
FLIGHT:	rely	3	5	tool	2
	data	2	3	sced	3
	cplx	3	6		
JPL's flight	time	3	4		
software	stor	3	4		
	acap	3	5		
	apex	2	5		
	pcap	3	5		
	plex	1	4		
	ltex	1	4		
	pmat	2	3		
	KSLOC	7	418		

project	feature	ranges low	high	values feature	setting
GROUND:	rely	1	4	tool	2
	data	2	3	sced	3
	cplx	1	4		
JPL's ground	time	3	4		
software	stor	3	4		
	acap	3	5		
	apex	2	5		
	pcap	3	5		
	plex	1	4		
	ltex	1	4		
	pmat	2	3		
	KSLOC	11	392		

project	feature	ranges low	high	values feature	setting
OSP:	prec	1	2	data	3
	flex	2	5	pvol	2
	resl	1	3	rely	5
Orbital space	team	2	3	pcap	3
plane nav&	pmat	1	4	plex	3
gudiance	stor	3	5	site	3
	ruse	2	4		
	docu	2	4		
	acap	2	3		
	pcon	2	3		
	apex	2	3		
	ltex	2	4		
	tool	2	3		
	sced	1	3		
	cplx	5	6		
	KSLOC	75	125		

project	feature	ranges low	high	values feature	setting
OSP2:	prec	3	5	flex	3
	pmat	4	5	resl	4
	docu	3	4	team	3
OSP	ltex	2	5	time	3
version 2	sced	2	4	stor	3
	KSLOC	75	125	data	4
				pvol	3
				ruse	4
				rely	5
				acap	4
				pcap	3
				pcon	3
				apex	4
				plex	4
				tool	5
				cplx	4
				site	6

Fig. 3. Four project-specific XOMO scenarios. If an attribute can be varied, then it is mutated over the range *low* to *high*. Otherwise it is fixed to one *setting*.

	POM3a A broad space of projects.	POM3b Highly critical small projects	POM3c Highly dynamic large projects
Culture	$0.10 \leq x \leq 0.90$	$0.10 \leq x \leq 0.90$	$0.50 \leq x \leq 0.90$
Criticality	$0.82 \leq x \leq 1.26$	$0.82 \leq x \leq 1.26$	$0.82 \leq x \leq 1.26$
Criticality Modifier	$0.02 \leq x \leq 0.10$	$0.80 \leq x \leq 0.95$	$0.02 \leq x \leq 0.08$
Initial Known	$0.40 \leq x \leq 0.70$	$0.40 \leq x \leq 0.70$	$0.20 \leq x \leq 0.50$
Inter-Dependency	$0.0 \leq x \leq 1.0$	$0.0 \leq x \leq 1.0$	$0.0 \leq x \leq 1.0$
Dynamism	$1.0 \leq x \leq 50.0$	$1.0 \leq x \leq 50.0$	$40.0 \leq x \leq 50.0$
Size	$x \in [3,10,30,100,300]$	$x \in [3, 10, 30]$	$x \in [30, 100, 300]$
Team Size	$1.0 \leq x \leq 44.0$	$1.0 \leq x \leq 44.0$	$20.0 \leq x \leq 44.0$
Plan	$0 \leq x \leq 4$	$0 \leq x \leq 4$	$0 \leq x \leq 4$

Fig. 4. Three specific POM3 scenarios.

2.2 Optimizers

The optimizers studied here assume the existence of some model (e.g. POM3, XOMO) that can convert *decisions* "*d*" into *objective* scores "*o*"; i.e.

$$o = model(d)$$

In this framework, each pair (d, o) is an *individual* within a *population*. Some individuals *dominate;* i.e. are better than others. Two forms of domination are *binary* and *continuous* domination. In *binary domination*, one individual x dominates y if all of x's objectives are never worse than the objectives in y but at least one objective in solution x is better than its counterpart in y; i.e.

$$\{\forall o_j \in objectives \mid \neg(o_{j,x} \prec o_{j,y})\} \wedge \{\exists o_j \in objectives \mid o_{j,x} \succ o_{j,y}\}$$

where $(\prec, \succ)$ tests if an objective score in one individual is (worse, better) than the other individual. An alternate culling method is the *continuous domination* predicate [31] that favors y over x if x "losses" least:

$$
\begin{aligned}
x \succ y &= loss(y, x) > loss(x, y) \\
loss(x, y) &= \sum_j^n -e^{\Delta(j,x,y,n)}/n \\
\Delta(j, x, y, n) &= w_j(o_{j,x} - o_{j,y})/n
\end{aligned}
\tag{1}
$$

where "n" is the number of objectives; $w_j \in \{-1, 1\}$ shows if we seek to maximize o_j.

Domination is used in *selection* step2d of the EA algorithm described in the introduction. For example, consider NSGA-II [7] and SPEA2 [32][1]:

– SPEA2's [32] *selection* sub-routine favors individuals that dominate the most number of other solutions that are not nearby (and to break ties, it favors items in low density regions).

---

[1] We use these NSGA-II and SPEA2 since, in his survey of the SSBE literature in the period 2004 to 2013, Sayyad [24] found 25 different algorithms. Of those, NSGA-II [7] or SPEA2 [32] were used four times as often as anything else. For comments on newer algorithms (NSGA-III and MOEA/D) see our *Future Work* section.

- NSGA-II [7] uses a non-dominating sorting procedure to divide the solutions into *bands* where $band_i$ dominates all of the solutions in $band_{j>i}$. NSGA-II's elite sampling favors the least-crowded solutions in the better bands.
- GALE [14] only applies domination to two distant individuals X, Y. If either dominates, GALE ignores the half of the population near to the dominated individual and recurses on the point near the non-dominated individual.

NSGA-II and SPEA2 use binary domination. Binary domination has issues for multi-goal optimization [25] since, as the objective dimensionality grows, large sets of individuals become non-dominated. Accordingly, other EAs such as GALE use continuous domination since it can distinguish better individuals

```
 1 | def SWAY( population, better= continuousDomination)  :
 2 |    # ------------------- top-down clustering
 3 |    def cluster(items, out):
 4 |        if    len(items) < enough:
 5 |               out += [items]
 6 |        else: west, east, westItems, eastItems = split(items, len(items/2))
 7 |               # if either dominates, ignore half. else, recurse on both
 8 |               if not better(west,east):  cluster( eastItems, out )
 9 |               if not better(east,west):  cluster( westItems, out )
10 |        return out
11 |    # ------------------- split items by proximity to 2 distant items
12 |    def split(items, middle):
13 |        rand = random.choose( items) # 'FASTMAP', step1
14 |        east = furthest(rand, items) # 'FASTMAP', step2
15 |        west = furthest(east, items) # east,west are now 2 distant items
16 |        c    = distance(west, east)
17 |        for x in items:
18 |            a    = distance(x,west)
19 |            b    = distance(x,east)
20 |            # find the distance of 'x' along the line running west to east
21 |            x.d = ( a*a + c*c - b*b )/( 2*c+ 0.0001 ) # cosine rule
22 |        items = sorted(items, key = d) # sorted by 'd'
23 |        return west, east, items[:middle], items[middle:]
24 |    # -------------------
25 |    def furthest( Apoint, items, most=-1, out=None):
26 |        #-- return the point which is furthest from Apoint within items
27 |        return furthestPoint
28 |    # ------------------- euclidean distance
29 |    def distance(xs, ys):
30 |        #-- normalize  x in xs, and y in ys to (value - min)/(max-min)
31 |        #-- let tmp be the sum of  (x-y)^2
32 |        #-- let n be the number of decisions
33 |        return sqrt(tmp) / sqrt(n) # so  0 <= distance <= 1
34 |    # ------------------- main
35 |    enough= max(sqrt(len(population)),20) # why 20? central limit theorem
36 |    return cluster(population, [])
```

Fig. 5. The SWAY is a recursive exploration of pairs of distant points east, west. Terminates when the size of the divided items is less than enough (used on line 4, set on line 34). Equation cdom defines continuousDomination which is used to define better (and is used on lines 8,9). For finding two distant points, lines 14,154,16 uses the FASTMAP heuristic [11] which locates two distant points in a population of size n after just $2n$ distance calculations. This linear-time search is much faster than a $O(n^2)$ time search needed to find the two *most* distant points (which in practice, is rarely much more distant than the two found by FASTMAP).

in multi-goal contexts (which according to Sayyad et al. [25] is for three goals or more).

Note that, GALE apart from Fig. 5, included a mutation strategy. GALE's recursive splitting of the n items in population i resulted in leaf populations of total size m. To build population $i + 1$, GALE then used a domination function to find which of two distant individuals X, Y in each leaf is "better". All the m individuals in those leaves were mutated towards the "better" end of their leaf. GALE then builds the population $i + 1$ back up to size n, by rerunning *generate* (step1 of EA) $n - m$ times. Also note unlike NSGA-II and SPEA-2, GALE only evaluates $2 \log n$ individuals (east, west pairs in its recursive binary chop) rather than n individuals. SWAY evaluates even fewer individuals than GALE since it terminates after the first generation.

2.3   Performance Measures

We use three metrics to evaluate the quality of optimization:

- **#Evaluations:** Number of times an optimizer calls a model or evaluate a model.
- **Spread:** Deb's *spread* calculator [7] includes the term $\sum_{i}^{N-1}(d_i - \overline{d})$ where d_i is the distance between adjacent solutions and $\overline{d}$ is the mean of all such values. A "good" spread makes all the distances equal ($d_i \approx \overline{d}$), in which case Deb's spread measure would reduce to some minimum value.
- **HyperVolume:** The hypervolume measure was first proposed in [33] to quantitatively compare the outcomes of two or more MOEAs. Hypervolume can be thought of as 'size of volume covered'.

Note that hypervolume and spread are computed from the population which is returned when these optimizers terminate. Also, *higher* values of hypervolume are *better* while *lower* values of spread and #evalautions are *better*.

These results were studied using non-parametric tests (the use non-parametrics for SBSE was recently endorsed by Arcuri and Briand at ICSE'11 [19]). For testing statistical significance, we used non-parametric bootstrap test 95 % confidence [10] followed by an A12 test to check that any observed differences were not trivially small effects; i.e. given two lists X and Y, count how often there are larger numbers in the former list (and there there are ties, add a half mark): $a = \forall x \in X, y \in Y \frac{\#(x>y)+0.5*\#(x=y)}{|X|*|Y|}$ (as per Vargha [27], we say that a "small" effect has $a < 0.6$). Lastly, to generate succinct reports, we use the Scott-Knott test to recursively divide our optimizers. This recursion used A12 and bootstrapping to group together subsets that are (a) not significantly different and are (b) not just a small effect different to each other. This use of Scott-Knott is endorsed by Mittas and Angelis [19] and by Hassan et al. [12].

3   Experiments with SWAY

In the following, we compare EA vs SWAY for 20 repeats of our two models through our various scenarios. All the optimizers use the population size recommended by their original authors; i.e. $n = 100$. But, in order to test the effects of increased sample, we run two versions of SWAY:

– SWAY2 : builds an initial population of size $10^2 = 100$.
– SWAY4: builds an initial population of size $10^4 = 10,000$.

One design choice in this experiment was the evaluation budget for each optimizer:

– If we allow infinite runs of EA that would bias the comparison towards EAs since better optimizations might be found just by blind luck (albeit at infinite cost).
– Conversely, if we restrict EAs to the number of evaluations made by (say) SWAY4 then that would unfairly bias the comparison towards SWAY since that would allow only a generation or two of EA.

To decide this issue, we returned to the motivation for SWAY discussed in Sect. 1.1 of this paper. SWAY is most useful when evaluating a solution using the model is expensive. Hence, our evaluation budget was selected to demand that SWAYing had to work using far fewer evaluations that EA. We found the median number of evaluations $e_1 = 50$ seen across all our slowest versions of SWAY (which is SWAY4), then allowed EA to evaluate 40 times the value of e_1 and we call this e_2 ($e_2 = \Delta e_1$, where $\Delta = 40$).

3.1   Results

Figure 6 shows the #evaluations for our optimizers. Note that:

– GALE requires more evaluations than SWAY since SWAY terminates after one generation while GALE runs for multiple evaluations.
– Even though SWAY4 explores 100 times the population of SWAY2, it only has to evaluate logarithmically more individuals- so the total number of extra evaluations for SWAY4 may only increase 2 to 4 times from SWAY2.
– The standard optimizers (NSGA-II and SPEA2) require orders of magnitude more evaluations. This is because these optimizers evaluate all n members of each population, GALE and SWAY, on the other hand, only evaluate $2 \log n$ members.

Figure 7 shows results obtained by all the optimizers, compared to the results obtained using SWAY techniques. The figure shows the median (**med.**) and inter quartile range (**IQR** 75th-25th value) for all the optimizers and SWAY techniques. Horizontal quartile plots show the median as a round dot within the inter-quartile range. In the figure, an optimizer's score is ranked 1 (**Rank**=1) if other optimizers have (a) worse medians; and (b) the other distributions are significantly different (computed via Scott-Knott and bootstrapping); and (c) differences are not a small effect (computed via A12).

The left-hand-side column of Fig. 7 shows the spread results and can be summarized as: the spreads found by standard EAs (NSGA-II and SPEA2) were

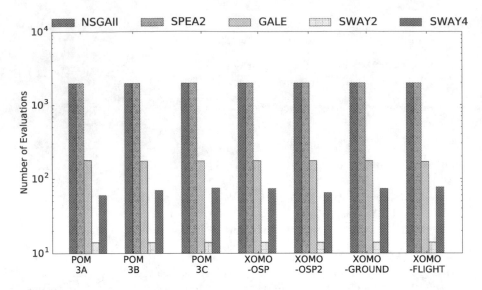

Fig. 6. Median evaluations, 20 repeats.

always ranked last in all scenarios. That is, for these scenarios and models, to achieve a good distribution of results, it is better to sample than evolve.

The right-hand-side of Fig. 7 shows the hypervolume results and can be summarized as: GALE and SWAY2 were always ranked last in all scenarios. That is, for these scenarios and models, to find best optimization solutions, it is insufficient to explore just a few evaluations of a small population (e.g. the 100 instances explored by SWAY2 and GALE).

Having made a case against SWAY2, GALE, and our EAs, this leaves SWAY4. We note that SWAY4's spread is never worse than standard EAs (and sometimes it is even best: see the Pom3s spread results). As to the SWAY4 hypervolume results, in one case (Pom3b), SWAY4 is clearly inferior to standard EAs (NSGA-II and SPEA2). But in all the other results, SWAY4 is an interesting option. Often it is ranked second after EAs but those statistical rankings do not always pass a "reasonableness" test. Consider the hypervolumes achieved in Pom3a: 106,106,104,102,100 where the best hypervolume (of 106) came from SPEA2 while SWAY4 generated very similar hypervolumes of 104. Our statistical tests divide optimizers with median values of 106,106,104,102,100 into four **Ranks**: which may not be "reasonable". As pragmatic engineers, we are hard-pressed to recommend evaluating a very slow model $2,000$ times to achieve a hypervolume of 106 (using SPEA2) when 50 evaluations of SWAY4 would achieve a hypervolume of 104. In Fig. 7, we mark all the results that we think are "reasonable close" to the top-ranked result with a red "•" dot. SWAY4 is always marked as "reasonable close" to the EAs.

We acknowledge that the use of the "reasonableness" measure in the last paragraph is somewhat subjective assessment. Also, for some ultra-mission

Rank	using	med.	IQR		Rank	using	med.	IQR	
Pom3a					**Pom3a**				
1	SWAY 2	91	22		1	SPEA 2	106	0	
1	GALE	99	18		1	NSGA-II	106	0	
1	SWAY 4	104	13		2	SWAY 4	104	0	
2	NSGA-II	151	13		3	SWAY 2	102	3	
2	SPEA 2	156	17		4	GALE	100	2	
Pom3b					**Pom3b**				
1	GALE	93	46		1	NSGA-II	202	27	
1	SWAY 4	102	15		1	SPEA 2	184	8	
2	SWAY 2	126	39		2	SWAY 4	137	10	
2	NSGA-II	135	16		3	GALE	95	23	
2	SPEA 2	143	10		3	SWAY 2	91	12	
Pom3c					**Pom3c**				
1	SWAY 4	75	7		1	NSGA-II	105	0	
1	SWAY 2	84	25		1	SPEA 2	105	0	
2	GALE	99	10		2	SWAY 4	103	1	
3	NSGA-II	112	24		3	SWAY 2	101	1	
3	SPEA 2	128	20		3	GALE	100	1	
Flight					**Flight**				
1	GALE	100	15		1	NSGA-II	147	1	
2	SWAY 2	130	31		1	SPEA 2	147	1	
2	SWAY 4	131	24		2	SWAY 4	140	5	
2	NSGA-II	143	12		3	GALE	100	3	
2	SPEA 2	144	12		3	SWAY 2	100	9	
Ground					**Ground**				
1	GALE	100	48		1	NSGA-II	205	1	
1	SWAY 2	126	37		1	SPEA 2	204	1	
2	SWAY 4	169	15		2	SWAY 4	196	11	
2	NSGA-II	169	23		3	SWAY 2	157	52	
2	SPEA 2	180	20		3	GALE	100	17	
OSP					**OSP**				
1	SWAY 2	88	20		1	NSGA-II	261	1	
1	GALE	100	31		1	SPEA 2	261	1	
2	SWAY 4	152	17		2	SWAY 4	245	8	
2	SPEA 2	152	9		3	SWAY 2	148	70	
2	NSGA-II	155	9		3	GALE	100	0	
OSP2					**OSP2**				
1	GALE	100	85		1	NSGA-II	171	1	
2	SWAY 2	210	115		1	SPEA 2	171	0	
2	SWAY 4	281	17		2	SWAY 4	163	10	
3	SPEA 2	311	34		3	SWAY 2	101	29	
4	NSGA-II	355	38		3	GALE	100	46	

a. Spread (*less* is *better*)   b. Hypervolume (*more* is *better*)

Fig. 7. Spread and hypervolumes seen in 20 repeats. **Med** is the 50th percentile and **IQR** is the *inter-quartile range*; i.e. 75th-25th percentile. Lines with a dot in the middle (e.g. ⟶•) show the median as a round dot within the IQR (and if the IQR is vanishingly small, only a round dot will be visible). All results sorted by the median value: spread results are sorted ascending (since *less* spread is *better*) while hypervolume results are sorted descending (since *more* hypervolume is *better*). The left-hand side columns **Rank** the optimizers. The *Smaller* the **Rank**, the *better* the optimizer; e.g. top-left, SWAY2, GALE, SWAY4 are top ranked for spread within Pom3a with a **Rank** of "1". One row has a larger "**Rank**" than the next if (a) its median values are worse and (b) a statistical hypothesis test concurs that the distributions in the two rows are different (with a non-small effect size). **Rank** is computed using Scott-Knott, bootstrap 95% confidence, and the A12 test (see text for details). Red dots "•" denote median results that are "reasonable close" to the top-ranked result (see text for details). (Color figure online)

critical domains, it might indeed be required to select optimizers that generate hypervolumes that are $\frac{106-104}{104} = 2\%$ better than anything else. However, we suspect that many engineers would gladly use a method that is 50 times faster and delivers (very nearly) the same results.

4   Conclusions and Future Work

Based on the above results, we recommend SWAY4 (and not SWAY2 or GALE) for ultra-rapid multi-objective optimization.

Since SWAY4 is just GALE without evolution (plus a larger initial sample) , we must conclude that there is little value in GALE's mutation operators. Hence, we attribute Krall's results (where GALE performed similar to NSGA-II and SPEA2 for multiple models [13,14]) to *sampling*, and not *evolution*. However, a limitation of this analysis is that only reports results from two models and compare against two EAs and the subsequent work should compare SWAY to a broader array of models and EAs.

But even before looking at more models and more EAs, it is still insightful to ask: why can SWAY work as well, or better than EAs? The latter evaluate more candidates– should not they do better than the partial sampling of SWAY? Our answer to these questions suggests some interesting directions for future work.

To define that future work, we first we report of a current trend in machine learning research. Dasgupta and Freund [5] comment that:

> A recent positive in that field has been the realization that a lot of data which superficially lie in a very high-dimensional space R^D, actually have low intrinsic dimension, in the sense of lying close to a manifold of dimension $d \ll D$.

One way to discover those lower dimensions is the random projection method [5]; i.e. k times construct a line between two random points on the surface of a sphere containing the decisions; then project the data down to each of those k lines; then return the line that maximizes the distance of the data along the k-th line. For low-dimensional data, k can be quite small; e.g. McFee and Lanckriet [15] merely used $k = 20$ for their data mining experiments.

It turns out that SWAY is a random projection algorithm. Whereas McFee and Lanckriet find the dimension that most separates the data using $k = 20$ random projections, SWAY approximates that process using a technique proposed by Faloutsos [11] (see lines 14,15,16 of Fig. 5). This observation has three implications:

1. SBSE might be another example of the kind of domains discussed by Dasgupta and Freund; i.e. underneath the large R^D space of decisions explored by EAs is a much smaller space defined by $d \ll D$ dimensions.
2. Simple algorithms like SWAY would be expected to be successful, since they are more direct way of exploring the underlying $d \ll D$ dimensions of model decisions.

3. There might be algorithms *better* than SWAY for exploring the low dimensional space. Exploring low-dimensional manifolds is an active are of interesta [4,6,9,15] generating efficient algorithms – some of which could well outperform SWAY.

Hence, our future direction is clear– explore more of the low dimensional manifold literature and experiment with applying those algorithms to SBSE. As a specific example, consider how we might apply low-dimensional manifolds to optimizing newer generations of MOEA algorithms such as NSGA-III [20] and MOEA/D [29]:

– The core of both those algorithms is an EA search. Perhaps, for each generation, we could over-generate new candidates then prune them back using something like SWAY4. The results of this paper suggest that such over-generate-and-prune could lead to better results with fewer evaluations.
– Another approach would be to use the clustering method of SWAY to simplify the Tchebycheff space explored by MOEA/D or the vectors connection reference points in NSGA-III.

Our ideas for optimizing NSGA-III and MOEA/D with SWAYing are still in the early stages so we have no results to present at this time. Nevertheless, our preliminary results are encouraging and we hope that, using SWAY, we can generate new algorithms that will significantly advance the state of the art, and scale to very complex problems.

Finally, we remark on the obvious question raised by this work: "if such simple sampling techniques (like SWAY) is similar to very expensive evolutionary algorithm, why was it not discovered earlier?". We have no definitive answer, except for the following comment. It seems to us that the culture of modern SE research rewards complex elaboration of existing techniques, rather than the careful reconsideration and simplification. Perhaps it is time to reconsider the old saying "if it ain't broke, don't fix it". Our revision to this saying might be "if it ain't broke, keep cutting the crap till it breaks". The results of this paper suggest that "cutting the crap" can lead to startling and useful results that challenge decades-old beliefs.

References

1. Boehm, B., Turner, R.: Using risk to balance agile and plan-driven methods. Computer **36**, 57–66 (2003)
2. Boehm, B.W., Horowitz, E., Madachy, R., Reifer, D., Clark, B.K., Steece, B., Winsor Brown, A., Chulani, S., Abts, C.: Software Cost Estimation with COCOMO II. Prentice Hall, Upper Saddle River (2000)
3. Boehm, B., Turner, R.: Balancing Agility and Discipline: A Guide for the Perplexed. Addison-Wesley Longman Publishing Co., Inc., Boston (2003)
4. Cannings, T.I., Samworth, R.J.: Random projection ensemble classification. arXiv preprint arXiv:1504.04595 (2015)
5. Dasgupta, S., Freund, Y.: Random projection trees and low dimensional manifolds. In: 40th ACM Symposium on Theory of Computing (2008)

6. Dasgupta, S., Sinha, K.: Randomized partition trees for nearest neighbor search. Algorithmica **72**(1), 237–263 (2015)
7. Deb, K., Pratap, A., Agarwal, S., Meyarivan, T.: A fast elitist multi-objective genetic algorithm: NSGA-II. IEEE Trans. Evol. Comput. **6**(2), 182–197 (2000)
8. Deb, K., Thiele, L., Laumanns, M., Zitzler, E.: Scalable Test Problems for Evolutionary Multi-Objective Optimization. TIK report 1990, Computer Engineering and Networks Laboratory (TIK), ETH Zurich, July 2001
9. Durrant, R.J., Kabán, A.: Random projections as regularizers: learning a linear discriminant from fewer observations than dimensions. In: Asian Conference on Machine Learning (2013)
10. Efron, B., Tibshirani, R.J.: An Introduction to the Bootstrap. CRC, Boca Raton (1993)
11. Faloutsos, C., Lin, K.-I. FastMap: a fast algorithm for indexing, data-mining and visualization of traditional and multimedia datasets. In: ACM SIGMOD International Conference on Management of Data (1995)
12. Ghotra, B., McIntosh, S., Hassan, A.E.: Revisiting the impact of classification techniques on the performance of defect prediction models. In: 37th IEEE International Conference on Software Engineering, May 2015
13. Joseph Krall. Faster Evolutionary Multi-Objective Optimization via GALE, the Geometric Active Learner. Ph.d thesis, West Virginia University (2014). http://goo.gl/u8ganF
14. Krall, J., Menzies, T., Davies, M.: Gale: geometric active learning for search-based software engineering. IEEE Trans. Softw. Eng. **41**(10), 1001–1018 (2015)
15. McFee, B., Lanckriet, G.: Large-scale music similarity search with spatial trees. In: 12th International Society for Music Information Retrieval Conference (2011)
16. Menzies, T., El-Rawas, O., Hihn, J., Feather, M., Madachy, R., Boehm, B.: The business case for automated software engineerng. In: 22nd IEEE/ACM International Conference on Automated Software Engineering (2007)
17. Menzies, T., Williams, S., El-Rawas, O., Baker, D., Boehm, B., Hihn, J., Lum, K., Madachy, R.: Accurate estimates without local data? Softw. Process Improv. Pract. **14**, 213–225 (2009)
18. Menzies, T., Williams, S., El-Rawas, O., Boehm, B., Hihn, J.: How to avoid drastic software process change (using stochastic stability). In: 31st International Conference on Software Engineering (2009)
19. Mittas, N., Angelis, L.: Ranking and clustering software cost estimation models through a multiple comparisons algorithm. IEEE Trans. Softw. Eng. **39**(4), 537–551 (2013)
20. Mkaouer, W., Kessentini, M., Bechikh, S., Deb, K., Cinnelde, M.O. High dimensional search-based software engineering: finding tradeoffs among 15 objectives for automating software refactoring using NSGA-III. In: ACM Genetic and Evolutionary Computation Conference (2014)
21. Port, D., Olkov, A., Menzies, T.: Using simulation to investigate requirements prioritization strategies. In: 23rd International Conference on Automated Software Engineering (2008)
22. Reed, P., Kollat, J.B., Devireddy, V.K.: Using interactive archives in evolutionary multiobjective optimization: a case study for long-term groundwater monitoring design. Environ. Model. Softw. **22**(5), 683–692 (2007)
23. Sayyad, A., Ingram, J., Menzies, T., Ammar, H. Scalable product line configuration: a straw to break the camel's back. In: 28th International Conference on Automated Software Engineering (2013)

24. Sayyad, A., Ammar, H.: Pareto-optimal search-based software engineering (POS-BSE): a literature survey. In: 2nd International Workshop on Realizing Artificial Intelligence Synergies in Software Engineering (2013)
25. Sayyad, A.S., Menzies, T., Ammar, H.: On the value of user preferences in search-based software engineering: a case study in software product lines. In: 35th International Conference for Software Engineering (2013)
26. Tantithamthavorn, C., McIntosh, S., Hassan, A.E., Matsumoto, K.: Automated parameter optimization of classification techniques for defect prediction models. In: 38th International Conference on Software Engineering (2016)
27. Vargha, A., Delaney, H.D.: A critique and improvement of the CL common language effect size statistics of McGraw and Wong. J. Educ. Behav. Stat. **25**(2), 101–132 (2000)
28. Wang, T., Harman, M., Jia, Y., Krinke, J.: Searching for better configurations: a rigorous approach to clone evaluation. In: 9th Joint Meeting on Foundations of Software Engineering, ACM (2013)
29. Zhang, Q., Li, H.: MOEA/D: a multiobjective evolutionary algorithm based on decomposition. IEEE Trans. Evol. Comput. **11**(6), 712–731 (2007)
30. Zhang, Y., Harman, M., Mansouri, S.A.: The multi-objective next release problem. In: ACM Genetic and Evolutionary Computation Conference (2007)
31. Zitzler, E., Künzli, S.: Indicator-based selection in multiobjective search. In: Yao, X., Burke, E.K., Lozano, J.A., Smith, J., Merelo-Guervós, J.J., Bullinaria, J.A., Rowe, J.E., Tiño, P., Kabán, A., Schwefel, H.-P. (eds.) PPSN 2004. LNCS, vol. 3242, pp. 832–842. Springer, Heidelberg (2004). doi:10.1007/978-3-540-30217-9_84
32. Zitzler, E., Laumanns, M., Thiele, L.: SPEA2: improving the strength pareto evolutionary algorithm for multiobjective optimization. In: Giannakoglou, K., Tsahalis, D., Periaux, J., Papailiou, K., Fogarty, T. (eds.) Evolutionary Methods for Design Optimisation, and Control. CIMNE, Barcelona (2002)
33. Zitzler, E., Thiele, L.: Multiobjective optimization using evolutionary algorithms — a comparative case study. In: Eiben, A.E., Bäck, T., Schoenauer, M., Schwefel, H.-P. (eds.) PPSN 1998. LNCS, vol. 1498, pp. 292–301. Springer, Heidelberg (1998). doi:10.1007/BFb0056872

Improved Crossover Operators for Genetic Programming for Program Repair

Vinicius Paulo L. Oliveira[1], Eduardo F.D. Souza[1], Claire Le Goues[2],
and Celso G. Camilo-Junior[1(✉)]

[1] Instituto de Informatica - Universidade Federal de Goias (UFG),
Goiania, GO, Brazil
{viniciusdeoliveira,eduardosouza,celso}@inf.ufg.br
[2] School of Computer Science, Carnegie Mellon University (CMU), Pittsburgh, USA
clegoues@cs.cmu.edu

Abstract. GenProg is a stochastic method based on genetic programming that presents promising results in automatic software repair via patch evolution. GenProg's crossover operates on a patch representation composed of high-granularity edits that indivisibly comprise an edit operation, a faulty location, and a fix statement used in replacement or insertions. Recombination of such high-level minimal units limits the technique's ability to effectively traverse and recombine the repair search spaces. In this work, we propose a reformulation of program repair operators such that they explicitly traverse three subspaces that underlie the search problem: Operator, Fault Space and Fix Space. We leverage this reformulation in the form of new crossover operators that faithfully respect this subspace division, improving search performance. Our experiments on 43 programs validate our insight, and show that the UNIF1SPACE without memorization performed best, improving the fix rate by 34 %.

Keywords: Automatic software repair · Automated program repair · Evolutionary computation · Crossover operator

1 Introduction

Software maintenance is expensive, usually substantially more so than initial development. Maintenance has been estimated to dominate the life cycle cost of software, consuming up to 70 % of those costs [22]. One class of techniques proposed to help mitigate these costs draws on search-based software engineering by applying meta-heuristic search techniques like Genetic Programming [11] to *evolve* program repairs, to improve or mitigate the cost of the bug fixing process [5,20]. The goal is to explore the solution space of potential program improvements, seeking modifications to the input program that, e.g., fix a bug without reducing other functionality, as revealed by test cases.

An important research innovation in this space represents candidate solutions as small *edit programs*, or *patches* to the original program. This is by contrast

© Springer International Publishing AG 2016
F. Sarro and K. Deb (Eds.): SSBSE 2016, LNCS 9962, pp. 112–127, 2016.
DOI: 10.1007/978-3-319-47106-8_8

to earlier work, which adapted more traditional tree-based program representations for repaired program variants [29]. The patch-based representation has significant benefits to both scalability and expressive power in the bug repair domain [17]. It is now commonly used across the domain of Genetic Improvement, a field which treats the program itself as genetic material and attempts to improve it with respect to a variety of functional and quality concerns [26].

Our core contention is that the current formulation of the patch representation overconstrains the search space by conflating its constituent subspaces, resulting in a more difficult to traverse landscape. Consider GenProg [16,29], a well-known program repair method that uses a customized Genetic Programming heuristic to explore the solution space of possible bug fixes represented as patches. The genome consists of a variable-length sequence of tree-based edits to be made to the original program code, with the edits themselves constituting the genes. Each edit takes the following form: `Operation`(*Fault,Fix*). `Operation` is the selected edit operator (one of *insert, delete,* or *replace*); *Fault* represents the modification point for the edit; and *Fix* captures the statement that will be inserted whenever necessary, such as when `Operation` is a replacement or insertion. That is, each edit contains information along the three subspaces underlying the program repair problem (operator, fault, and fix) [13].

This high gene granularity is considered important to scalability. However, this high granularity for the purposes of crossover limits the search ability to identify, recombine, and propagate the small, low-order building blocks that form the core of a healthy fitness landscape for the purposes of evolutionary computation [10]. Crossover cannot combine partial templates or schema of information along a single subspace, or even two of the three, because the edits themselves are indivisible. We speculate that this is one (though certainly not the only) reason that existing evolutionary program improvement techniques are historically poor at finding multi-edit patches [24].

We therefore propose a novel representation for patch-based evolutionary program improvement, particularly for crossover, to affect a smaller-granularity representation without substantial scalability loss. We instantiate this approach in the GenProg technique for automatic defect repair. Our overall hypothesis is that this new representation and associated crossover operators enable the productive traversal and recombination of information across the actual subspaces of the program improvement problem, and thus can improve performance.

Thus, the main contributions of this paper are:

- An explicit consideration of the implications of schema theory on genetic programming for program repair.
- A new representation to use specifically for crossover that provides a traversal and recombination between repair subspaces.
- Six new crossover operators that more effectively explore the search space.
- Experiments demonstrating improvement in fix effectiveness.

The remainder of this paper is organized as follows. Section 2 presents background on genetic programming, and GenProg in particular; Sect. 3 describes our new representation and operators; Sect. 4 presents experimental setup, results, and discussion. Section 5 discusses related work; we conclude in Sect. 6.

2   Background

Search-based program improvement leverages metaheuristic search strategies, like genetic programming, to automatically evolve new programs or patches to improve an input program.[1] These improvements can be either functional (e.g., bug fixing [13], feature grafting [12]) or quality-oriented (e.g., energy usage [25]). We focus on automatic program repair, GenProg in particular, but anticipate that our innovations for patch representation should naturally generalize. In this section, we provide background on Genetic Programming in general (Sect. 2.1) and its instantiation for repair in GenProg (Sect. 2.2).

2.1   Genetic Programming

Genetic Programming (GP) is a computational method inspired by biological evolution that evolves computer programs. GP maintains a population of program variants, each of which corresponds to a candidate solution to the problem at hand. Each individual in a GP population is evaluated for its *fitness* with respect to a given fitness function, and the individuals with the highest fitness are more likely to be selected to subsequent generations. Domain-specific *mutation* and *crossover* operators modify intermediate variants and recombine partial solutions to produce new candidate solutions, akin to biological DNA mutation and recombination.

In the context of the Evolutionary Algorithms (EA), a *schema* is a template that identifies a subset of strings (in a GA) or trees (in a GP) with similarities at certain positions (gene) [8]. The fitness of a schema is the average fitness of all individuals that match (or include) it. Holland's *schema theorem*, also called the fundamental theorem of genetic algorithms [10], says that short, low-order schemata with above-average fitness increase exponentially in successive generations. The schema theorem informs the *building block hypothesis*, namely that a genetic algorithm seeks optimal performance through the juxtaposition of such short, low-order, high-performance schemata, called *building blocks*. Ideally, crossover combines such schemata into increasingly fit candidate solutions; this is a feature of a healthy adaptive GP algorithm.

2.2   GenProg for Program Repair

GenProg overview. GenProg is a program repair technique predicated on Genetic Programming. GenProg takes as input a program and a set of test cases, at least one of which is initially failing. The search goal is a patch to that input program

---

[1] We restrict attention to background necessary to understand our contribution; We discuss related work more fully in Sect. 5.

that leads it to pass all input test cases. Using test cases to define desired behavior and assess fitness is fairly common in research practice [18,19,23]. Although test cases only provide partial specifications of desired behavior, they are commonly available and provide efficient mechanisms for constraining the space and assessing variants. Experimental results demonstrate that GenProg can be scalable and cost-effective for defects in large, real-world open-source software projects [13]. However, there remain a large proportion of defects that it cannot repair. We focus particularly on the way that GenProg's patch representation results in a suboptimal fitness landscape for the purposes of a healthy adaptive algorithm.

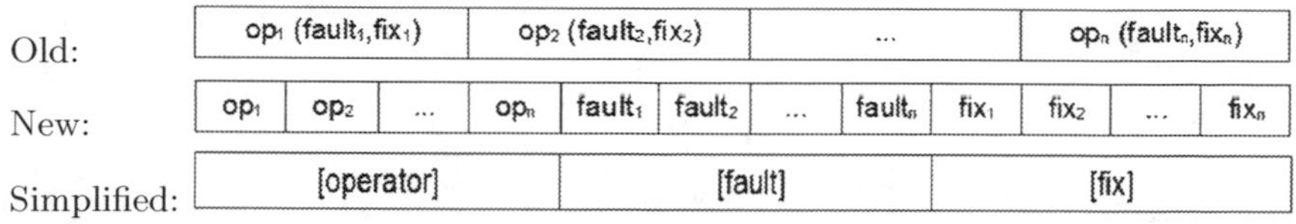

Old:	op_1 (fault$_1$,fix$_1$)		op_2 (fault$_2$,fix$_2$)			...			op_n (fault$_n$,fix$_n$)	
New:	op_1	op_2	...	op_n	fault$_1$	fault$_2$	...	fault$_n$	fix$_1$	fix$_2$ ... fix$_n$
Simplified:	[operator]				[fault]				[fix]	

Fig. 1. Old representation (top); New representation (middle); and simplified (bottom).

Search space. The program repair search problem can be formulated along three subspaces: the `Operation`, or the possible modifications that can be applied; the *fault location(s)*, or the set of possibly-faulty locations where the modifications shall be applied; and the *fix code*, or the space of code that can be inserted into the faulty location [14,28]. GenProg constrains this infinite space in several ways: (1) it uses the input test cases to *localize* the defect to a smaller, weighted program slice, (2) it uses coarse-grained perturbation operators at the C statement level (*insert*, *replace*, and *delete*), and (3) it restricts fix code to code within the same program or module, leveraging the *competent programmer hypothesis* while substantially reducing the space of possible fix code.

Representation and mutation. GenProg's patch representation (Fig. 1, top) is composed of a variable-length sequence of high-granularity edit operations. Each edit takes the form: `Operation`(*Fault,Fix*), where `Operation` is the edit operator; *Fault* is the modification location; and *Fix* captures the statement that will be inserted when `Operation` is a replacement or insertion. The mutation operation consists of appending a new such edit operation, constructed pseudo-randomly, to the existing (possibly empty) list of edits that describe a given variant.

Crossover. Crossover combines partial solutions and can improve the exploitation of existing solutions and implicit genetic memory. It takes two *parent* individuals from the population to produce two *offspring* individuals. GenProg uses a one-point crossover over the edits composing each of the parents. It selects a random cut point in each individual and then swaps the tails of each list to produce two new offspring that each contain edit operations from each parent. This does not create new edits; this power is currently reserved for mutation. Our illustrative example (Sect. 3.1) indicates the ways that this representation limits the recombination potential offered by crossover (Fig. 2).

3   Approach

Our high-level goal is to enable efficient recombination of genetic information while maintaining the scalability and efficiency of the modern patch representation. The building block hypothesis states, intuitively, that crossover should be able to recombine small schemata into large schemata of generally increasing fitness. Instead of building high-performance strings by trying every conceivable combination, better solutions are created from the best partial solutions of past generations. We posit that the current patch representation for program repair does not lend itself to the recombination of such small building blocks, because each edit combines information across all three subspaces, and edits are indivisible for the purposes of crossover. Partial information about potentially high-fitness features of an individual (e.g., accurate fault localization, a useful edit operator) cannot be propagated or composed between individuals.

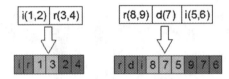

Fig. 2. Example of mapping an individual to the new representation. Each subspace is represented by a color: Yellow is the Operator subspace, blue is the Fault subspace and red is the Fix subspace. The character i = Insert, r = Replace, d = Delete. (Color figure online)

We propose to explicitly conceive of the schemata in this domain as a template of edit operations, where certain operations and their order is necessary to represent key individual information. We instantiate this conception in a new intermediate representation and then new crossover operators that leverage it. We begin with a running example that we will use to illustrate the approach (Sect. 3.1). We propose a new representation and a mapping to it from the existing patch representation (Sect. 3.2). We then present six new crossover operators (Sect. 3.3: OP1SPACE, UNIF1SPACE, and OPALLS, and then each of these new operators with memorization.

3.1   Illustrative Example

Consider a bug that requires two edits to be repaired:[2] Insert(*1,9*) Delete(*3,*). Consider also two candidate patches that contain all the genetic material necessary for this repair: (A) Insert(*1,2*)Replace(*3,4*) and (B) Replace(*8,9*) Delete(*3,*)Insert(*5,6*). The deletion in candidate (B) is correct as is and only

---

[2] We use integer indices to denote numbered statements taken from a pool of potential faulty locations and candidate fix code, as is standard.

needs to be combined with the appropriate insertion. The current crossover operator can propagate this deletion into subsequent generations.

However, constructing the Insert(*1,9*) cannot be accomplished through crossover alone, even though the insertion in candidate (A) is only one modification from the solution along the fix space, and (B) contains the correct code in its first replacement. Crossover cannot change the Fix element in (A) from 2 to 9, because the gene is treated as an indivisible unit. The only way to achieve the desired solution is via a combination of edits that compose semantically to the desired solution, or by relying on mutation to produce the insertion from whole-cloth.

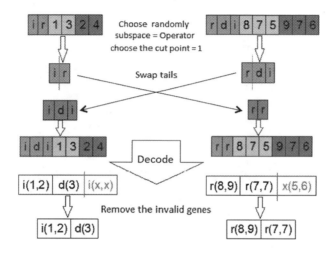

Fig. 3. Example of OP1SPACE applied to a pair of variants.

3.2   Decoupled Representation

We begin by decoupling the three subspaces in the representation to decrease edit granularity. We map variants to a new representation that imposes independence of subspaces, shown in the middle of Fig. 1. This decoupled representation has fixed positions to improve genetic memory. To simplify presentation, this representation can be further reduced to a one dimensional array by concatenating the three subspace arrays, shown in the bottom of Fig. 1. To simplify subsequent crossover operations while maintaining variant integrity, we add to the Delete operator a ghost *Fix* value, equal to its *Fault* value.

Note that we maintain the original patch representation for non-crossover steps because it is beneficial for mutation and because doing so allows us to focus our study on the effects of crossover specifically. A mapping transformation (*encode*) is thus applied to each individual immediately before crossover, which is applied to pairs of individuals selected in the standard way. We then apply a *decode* transformation to the offspring to return them to the canonical representation for selection and mutation. As will be shown, *Decode* can cause a loss of information. We therefore propose a memorization system to repair broken individuals, which we discuss subsequently.

3.3   New Crossover Operators

We propose six crossover operators to leverage and analyze the proposed representation in search-based program repair. OP1SPACE and UNIF1SPACE apply to a single subspace, while OPALLS applies to the whole chromosome. These three operators augmented with memorization mechanism result in six total proposed operators.

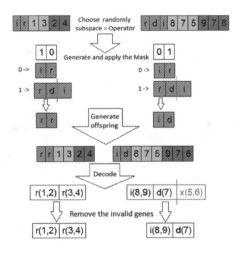

Fig. 4. Example of UNIF1SPACE applied in the Operator subspace.

One Point Crossover on a Single Subspace (OP1SPACE). OP1SPACE applies one-point crossover to a single subspace (see Fig. 3 for a visual presentation). It therefore explores new solutions in a single neighborhood, while maintaining potentially important blocks of information in the other subspaces. Given two parent variants *encoded* into the new representation, OP1SPACE chooses one of the three subspaces uniformly at random, and then randomly selects a cut point. Because the patch representation is of variable length, this number must be bounded by the minimum length of the chosen subspace so as to result in a valid point in both parents. We swap the tails beyond this cut point between parents, generating two offspring. The portion of the individuals relative to the unselected subspaces are unchanged.

Finally, *decode* is applied. *Decode* to unchanged parents is simply the inverse of *encode*. However, this crossover operator can *break* edit operations in offspring when the parents are of different lengths, resulting in either excess or missing data in the unchanged subspaces (e.g., an insert operation without a corresponding fix statement ID; Fig. 3 provides an example). For this operator, decode simply drops invalid genes.

Uniform Single Subspace (UNIF1SPACE). A *uniform* crossover operator combines a uniform blend of data from each parent [4], promoting greater exploration. However, in certain domains, a uniform operator be problematically destructive [17]. We thus propose a uniform operator along a single subspace, promoting a constrained exploration. As with OP1SPACE, UNIF1SPACE selects a subspace at random. It then generates a random binary mask of length equal to the smaller of the two subspaces chosen. Genes are swapped between parents to create offspring according to this mask. As with OP1SPACE, invalid genes are dropped in decode. Figure 4 shows the behavior of this operator on the running example. It can create highly diverse offspring, but may also dissolve many basic blocks.

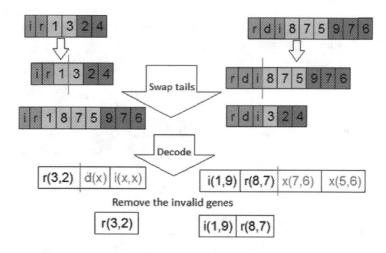

Fig. 5. Example of OPALLS.

One Point Across All Subspaces (OPALLS). OPALLS follows the same rules for cut point selection as OP1SPACE, but without the restriction to a single subspace. The crossover point is based on the length of the entire individual. It swaps large parts of the entire individual, simultaneously mixing subspaces. This operator can thus maintain larger basic blocks than UNIF1SPACE, with a greater capacity for information exchange than OP1SPACE. Large blocks containing valuable information within at least one subspace cannot be dissolved, so this operator prevents the destruction of some good information in such subspaces. However, it can completely change certain operations by affecting an entire subspace. For example, this crossover can keep all the original values for "Operator", but, unlike OP1SPACE, will still change all the Fix values and part of the Fault values. We illustrate with the running example in Fig. 5.

Memorization. As the previous discussion demonstrated, crossover on the decoupled representation presents a possibility of data loss. We therefore propose a *memorization* scheme to help reconstruct valid from invalid genes. Memorization maintains, for each individual, a cache of pieces of genes unused after crossover operations, distinguishing between the Operator, Fix and Fault spaces. It then tries to use values from this cache to fix broken genes on demand. This cache is maintained throughout the evolution process.

For example, in Fig. 3, the operation "i" in the first offspring and the fault and fix values 5 and 6 in the second would be stored in the cache for use in subsequent generations. Assuming the existence of data from previous variants in the cache, the memorization algorithm will try to find a Fault and Fix value to repair the first offspring, and an Operator to repair the second. If such values are available, they will be selected between at random, removed from the cache, and inserted into the associated individual.

Thus, we propose the three previously-described crossover operators, as well as the same three operators implemented with memorization, hypothesizing that memorization may decrease data loss and increase the number of solutions through the evolution process.

4   Experiments

In this section, we present experiments that compare the proposed crossover operators to the canonical one-point patch representation crossover operator. We hypothesize that the proposed crossover operators can increase the fix rate.

4.1   Setup

Table 1. Benchmarks, test cases, and buggy versions of each program.

Program	Tests	Versions
gcd	11	1
zune	24	1
checksum	6	7
digits	6	7
grade	7	7
median	7	7
smallest	7	7
syllables	6	6

Benchmarks. Table 1 shows the C programs we use in our evaluation. gcd and zune have classically appeared in previous assessments of program repair.[3] Both include infinite loop bugs. The other six program classes are drawn from IntroClass [15],[4] a set of student-written versions of small C programming assignments in an introductory C programming course. IntroClass contains many incorrect student programs corresponding to each problem. We chose 6–7 random programs for each assignment, for a total of 43 defective programs. We use the higher-quality black box tests provided with the benchmark to assess correctness.

Each program version itself is small, but this is important for our evaluation. First, it allows us to run many random trials for more iterations than is typical in program repair evaluations, without a prohibitive computational

---

[3] Both available from the GenProg project: http://genprog.cs.virginia.edu/.
[4] Available at http://repairbenchmarks.cs.umass.edu/.

time. Second, our small programs are fully covered/specified by their black box tests, which allows for a separation of concerns with respect to fitness function quality and completeness. That is: the tests provided with real-world programs can be *weak proxies* for correctness, increasing the risk of low-quality patches. We sidestep this issue by evaluating on small but very well-specified programs (as validated by their designers, manually, and experimentally [27]).

Parameters and metrics. We executed 30 random trials for each program version. The search concludes either when it reaches the generational limit or when it finds a patch that causes the program to pass all provided test cases. The parameters used for all runs are: Elitism = 3, Generations = 20, Population size = 15, Crossover rate = 0.5, Mutation rate = 1, Tournament k = 2. The evaluation metrics are the success rate and the number of test suite evaluations to repair, a machine and test-suite independent measure of time.

4.2 Results

Table 2 presents the success rate of experiments for all operators and problems (higher is better). Table 3 presents test suite evaluations, or average fitness evaluations, to repair (lower is better). In the latter table, we omit grade and syllables, as no repairs were found in any run.

Table 2. Success rate (percentage) over all runs. We aggregate across IntroClass problems for presentation.

Memorization?	Original	OP1SPACE		UNIF1SPACE		OPALLS	
	N/A	No	Yes	No	Yes	No	Yes
gcd	0.70	**0.80**	0.63	0.67	0.70	0.73	**0.80**
zune	0,66	0.70	0.97	**1.00**	0.97	0.93	0.93
checksum	0.00	0.00	0.01	**0.03**	0.00	0.00	0.00
digits	0.27	0.25	0.31	**0.29**	0.27	0.26	0.28
grade	0.00	0.00	0.00	0.00	0.00	0.00	0.00
median	0.28	**0.50**	0.48	0.48	0.49	**0.50**	0.49
smallest	0.51	0.51	0.58	**0.64**	0.57	**0.64**	0.60
syllables	0.02	0.16	0.16	0.16	0.16	0.16	0.16
Average	0.305	0.365	0.392	**0.408**	0.395	0.402	0.407

Success rate. UNIF1SPACE without memorization presents the best success rate, as can be seen in Table 2. Overall, the UNIF1SPACE was the best operator, producing a 34 % improvement the fix rate over the Original baseline. A Wilcoxon rank-sum test, at $\alpha = 0.05$, establishes that the observed difference in performance between all operators without memorization and the Original crossover are statistically significant. A Vargha-Delaney test supports the observation that all operators outperformed the Original operator, with effect sizes between 0.532 and 0.564, indicating a small but observable effect size. The effect size is greatest for UNIF1SPACE, as compared to the Original baseline.

Although UNIF1SPACE produced consistently strong results, it is not the best across all problems. At a per-problem level, for the checksum problem, UNIF1SPACE without memorization is best, but in general, checksum appears to be difficult for all operator. We speculate that this is because most of checksum defects require a specific modification that is difficult to produce with the current operators in short programs. On digits programs, OP1SPACE with memorization was the best, followed by UNIF1SPACE without memorization. In the gcd problem, all operators produced a high fix rate, but OP1SPACE without memorization and OPALLS with memorization were best. In the median problem, OP1SPACE and OPALLS without memorization were best, but all proposed operators are comparable. For zune, UNIF1SPACE without memorization achieved the maximum fix rate; the other proposed operators were all still better than the original baseline. Finally, for syllables, all proposed operators reached the same results and outperformed the original.

Table 3. Test suite evaluations to repair. We aggregate across IntroClass problems for presentation. We omit grade because no repairs were found. N/A is used when no repair was found.

Memorization?	Original	OP1SPACE		UNIF1SPACE		OPALLS	
	N/A	No	Yes	No	Yes	No	Yes
gcd	10.88	**5.04**	6.20	10.94	7.77	5.91	7.47
zune	3.90	**3.00**	3.30	3.83	3.87	3.22	3.01
checksum	**27.22**	69.50	35.67	47.00	N/A	56.25	N/A
digits	14.53	13.17	17.63	14.90	**9.94**	15.63	13.64
median	**16.07**	37.94	41.48	34.38	40.91	33.30	41.78
smallest	**16.40**	37.59	44.77	65.26	48.33	56.73	46.40
syllables	**20.53**	27.30	27.30	28.97	30.90	25.40	27.13
Average	**15.59**	27.64	25.19	29.32	23.62	28.06	19.91

Efficiency. Table 3 presents the average fitness evaluations to repair for each operator. Overall, the operator with the best success rate was not the most efficient. This is consistent with our expectations: the more difficult problems are harder to solve, and thus succeeding in them (having greater success) can pull up the average time to repair [17]. This behavior may also be explained by the fact the operators that focus on a single subspace, OP1SPACE and UNIF1SPACE, are less destructive in recombining variants, which may lead to a slower search process as compared to Original and OPALLS. However, overall, the differences are not large, and it may be reasonable to exchange a slight loss of efficiency in favor of a more effective search strategy. On the other hand, the operator OPALLS with memorization presented a success rate almost the same as UNIF1SPACE without memorization, but presented a considerable smaller time to repair, so it may present a desirable cost-benefit tradeoff.

At a per-problem level, the Original crossover operator outperforms the others for checksum, but as the success rate is low, high variability is unsurprising. The second best operator here is OP1SPACE without memorization. For digits, the UNIF1SPACE with memorization was best, followed by OP1SPACE without memorization. In gcd OP1SPACE without memorization significantly outperformed Original; OPALLS without memorization performed second best. The zune presents a low discrepancy within operators, but OP1SPACE without memorization was the most efficient. The smallest and median the Original was much better than others. For syllables, Original was best, followed by OPALLS without memorization.

Memorization results. Memorization does not appear to increase success rate, as we can see particularly in the best operators according to this metric (UNIF1SPACE followed by OPALLS, both without memorization). We speculate that the loss of incomplete genes in decode can reduce unnecessary modifications that hinder repair performance. One general lesson is that there may be a benefit to mitigating code bloat throughout the program improvement process. However, in aggregate, comparing each operator with memorization to the same operator without, the version with memorization is more efficient, supporting the general potential of the mechanism. This is particularly true of OPALLS, where memorization provided a significant efficiency benefit. This may suggest that memorization is more beneficial for the more destructive operators, allowing them to avoid large losses of genetic material. As a final note, our maximum generation count was relatively low, reducing the potential utility of a genetic memorization mechanism. We expect the memorization approach may perform better in longer runs.

New representation. In general, on average, crossover using our new representation outperformed the standard representation, even when genes are lost in decode. This indicates the new representation *in particular* has important potential to improving the performance of patch-based program improvement heuristic techniques. In terms of scalability, the new representation does not use considerably more memory over the standard representation, and the computational cost of transforming between them was low. Although we do not directly analyze the progression of schema through the search, our results are affirmed by underlying theory suggesting that the representation improves GenProg's ability to construct and propagate building blocks.

4.3   Threats to Validity

On threat to the validity of our results is that they may not generalize, because our dataset may not be indicative of real-world program improvement tasks. We selected our programs because they allowed us to minimize other types of noise, such as test suite quality, which allowed for a more focused study of operator effectiveness; we view this as a necessary tradeoff. Another important concern in program improvement work is output quality, as test-case-driven program improvement can overfit to the objective function or be misled by weak tests. We mitigate this risk by using high-coverage, high-quality test suites [27]. Note that output quality is not our core concern, and the new representation and operators are parametric with respect to fitness functions and mutation operators, and thus should generalize immediately to other patch-based program improvement techniques that produce program improvements. Further tests and analysis are required to fully explain the operators' behavior, enabling understanding of why any one operator performed better than another.

5   Related Work

Most innovations in the Genetic Programming (GP) space for program improvement involve new kinds of fitness functions or application domains; there has been less emphasis on novel representations and operators, such as those we explore. However, there are exceptions to this general trend. Orlov and Sipper outline a semantics-preserving crossover operator for Java bytecode [21]. Ackling et al. propose a patch-based representation to encode Python rewrite rules [1]; Debroy and Wong investigate alternative mutation operators [6]. Forrest et al. quantified operator effectiveness, and compared crossback to traditional crossover [7]. Le Goues et al. examined several representation, operator and other choices used for evolutionary program repair [17], quantified the superiority of the patch representation over the previously-common AST alternative, and demonstrated the importance of crossover to success rate in this domain. Although they do examine the role of crossover, they do not attempt to decompose the representation to improve evolvability, as we do, rather focusing on the effects of representation and parameter weighting in particular. These results corroborate Arcuri's [2] demonstrating that parameter and operator choices have tremendous impact on search-based algorithms generally. Our research contributes to this area, presenting a new way to represent and recombine parents and demonstrating the influence of crossover operators on algorithmic performance.

Our results demonstrate that in theory our new representation combined with the crossover operators can improve the creation and propagation of the build blocks, but does not directly investigate the role of schema evolution in this phenomenon; we leave this to future work. For example, Burlacu [3] presents a powerful tool for theoretical investigations on evolutionary algorithm behavior concerning building blocks and fitness.

Informed by the building blocks hypothesis, Harik proposed a compact genetic algorithm, representing the population as a probability distribution over a solution set, which is operationally equivalent to the order-one behavior of a simple GA with uniform crossover [9]. He concluded that building blocks can be tightly coded and propagated throughout the population through repeated selection and recombination. His theory suggests that knowledge about the problem domain can be inserted into the chromosomal features, and GA can use this partial knowledge to link and build information blocks. The difficulty in representing a program in repair problem can be one of the reasons for its complexity.

6 Conclusion

Supported by the Schema Theorem and Building Blocks Hypothesis, our primary contribution in this paper is a new low-granularity patch representation and associated crossover operators to enable better parental recombination in a search-based program improvement algorithm. We also presented a novel memorization process that shows a possibility to repair problematic genes, that even not showing results better than without memorization, it can be useful to develop new ways to solve the broken genes problem. Our objective was to improve the algorithm's ability to traverse the fitness landscape, improving success rate. Our results suggest that this targeted approach is promising: our best new crossover operator, Unif1Space without memorization, demonstrated an increase of 34 % in the success rate over the baseline. However, our results also showed that operator success varied across the different program classes studied. The results suggest that it may be possible to achieve both the scalability benefits of the patch representation for program improvement as well as more effective recombination over the evolutionary computation, motivating future work on such novel evolutionary operators and associated parameters.

References

1. Ackling, T., Alexander, B., Grunert, I.: Evolving patches for software repair. In: Genetic and Evolutionary Computation, pp. 1427–1434 (2011)
2. Arcuri, A.: Evolutionary repair of faulty software. Appl. Soft Comput. **11**(4), 3494–3514 (2011)
3. Burlacu, B., Affenzeller, M., Winkler, S., Kommenda, M., Kronberger, G.: Methods for genealogy and building block analysis in genetic programming. In: Borowik, G., Chaczko, Z., Jacak, W., Łuba, T. (eds.) Computational Intelligence and Efficiency in Engineering Systems, Part I. SCI, vol. 595, pp. 61–74. Springer, Heidelberg (2015). doi:10.1007/978-3-319-15720-7_5
4. Chawdhry, P.K., Roy, R., Pant, R.K.: Soft Computing in Engineering Design and Manufacturing. Springer, Heidelberg (2012)
5. de Oliveira, A.A.L., Camilo-Junior, C.G., Vincenzi, A.M.R.: A coevolutionary algorithm to automatic test case selection and mutant in mutation testing. In: Congress on Evolutionary Computation, pp. 829–836 (2013)
6. Debroy, V., Eric Wong, E.: Using mutation to automatically suggest fixes for faulty programs. In: International Conference on Software Testing, Verification, and Validation, pp. 65–74 (2010)
7. Forrest, S., Nguyen, T., Weimer, W., Goues, C.L.: A genetic programming approach to automated software repair. In: Genetic and Evolutionary Computation Conference (GECCO), pp. 947–954 (2009)
8. Goldberg, D.E.: Genetic Algorithms in Search, Optimization and Machine Learning, 1st edn. Addison-Wesley Longman Publishing Co., Inc., Reading (1989)

9. Harik, G.R., Lobo, F.G., Goldberg, D.E.: The compact genetic algorithm. IEEE Trans. Evol. Comput. **3**(4), 287–297 (1999)
10. John, H.: Adaptation in natural and artificial systems (1992)
11. Koza, J.R.: Genetic Programming: On the Programming of Computers by Means of Natural Selection. MIT Press, Cambridge (1992)
12. Langdon, W.B., Harman, M.: Grow and graft a better CUDA pknot-sRG for RNA pseudoknot free energy calculation. In: Genetic and Evolutionary Computation Conference, GECCO Companion 2015, pp. 805–810 (2015)
13. Le Goues, C., Dewey-Vogt, M., Forrest, S., Weimer, W.: A systematic study of automated program repair: fixing 55 out of 105 bugs for $8 each. In: International Conference on Software Engineering, pp. 3–13 (2012)
14. Le Goues, C., Forrest, S., Weimer, W.: Current challenges in automatic software repair. Softw. Qual. J. **21**(3), 421–443 (2013)
15. Le Goues, C., Holtschulte, N., Smith, E.K., Brun, Y., Devanbu, P., Forrest, S., Weimer, W.: The ManyBugs and IntroClass benchmarks for automated repair of C programs. IEEE Trans. Softw. Eng. **41**, 1236–1256 (2015)
16. Le Goues, C., Nguyen, T.V., Forrest, S., Weimer, W.: GenProg: a generic method for automatic software repair. IEEE Trans. Softw. Eng. (TSE) **38**, 54–72 (2012)
17. Le Goues, C., Weimer, W., Forrest, S.: Representations and operators for improving evolutionary software repair. In: Genetic and Evolutionary Computation Conference (GECCO), pp. 959–966 (2012)
18. Long, F., Rinard, M.: Automatic patch generation by learning correct code. In: Principles of Programming Languages, POPL 2016, pp. 298–312 (2016)
19. Mechtaev, S., Yi, J., Roychoudhury, A.: Angelix: scalable multiline program patch synthesis via symbolic analysis. In: International Conference on Software Engineering, ICSE 2016, pp. 691–701 (2016)
20. Nunes, B., Quijano, E.H.D., Camilo-Junior, C.G., Rodrigues, C.: SBSTFrame: a framework to search-based software testing. In: International Conference on Systems, Man, and Cybernetics (2016)
21. Orlov, M., Sipper, M.: Flight of the FINCH through the Java wilderness. IEEE Trans. Evol. Comput. **15**(2), 166–182 (2011)
22. Pressman, R.S.: Software Engineering: A Practitioners Approach. Palgrave Macmillan, London (2005)
23. Qi, Y., Mao, X., Lei, Y., Dai, Z., Wang, C.: The strength of random search on automated program repair. In: Proceedings of the 36th International Conference on Software Engineering, pp. 254–265. ACM (2014)
24. Qi, Z., Long, F., Achour, S., Rinard, M.: An analysis of patch plausibility and correctness for generate-and-validate patch generation systems. In: International Symposium on Software Testing and Analysis, pp. 24–36 (2015)
25. Schulte, E., Dorn, J., Harding, S., Forrest, S., Weimer, W.: Post-compiler software optimization for reducing energy. In: Architectural Support for Programming Languages and Operating Systems, pp. 639–652 (2014)
26. Silva, S., Esparcia-Alcázar, A.I. (eds.): Genetic and Evolutionary Computation Conference, GECCO 2015, Companion Material Proceedings, Workshop on Genetic Improvement. ACM (2015)
27. Smith, E.K., Barr, E., Goues, C.L., Brun, Y.: Is the cure worse than the disease? Overfitting in automated program repair. In: Joint Meeting of the European Software Engineering Conference and ACM SIGSOFT Symposium on the Foundations of Software Engineering (ESEC/FSE), pp. 532–543 (2015)

28. Weimer, W., Fry, Z.P., Forrest, S.: Leveraging program equivalence for adaptive program repair: models and first results. In: Automated Software Engineering (ASE), pp. 356–366 (2013)
29. Weimer, W., Nguyen, T., Le Goues, C., Forrest, S.: Automatically finding patches using genetic programming. In: International Conference on Software Engineering (ICSE), pp. 364–374 (2009)

Scaling up the Fitness Function for Reverse Engineering Feature Models

Thammasak Thianniwet and Myra B. Cohen[(⊠)]

Department of Computer Science and Engineering,
University of Nebraska-Lincoln, Lincoln, NE 68588-0115, USA
{tthianni,myra}@cse.unl.edu

Abstract. Recent research on software product line engineering has led to several search-based frameworks for reverse engineering feature models. The most common fitness function utilized maximizes the number of matched products with an oracle set of products. However, to calculate this fitness each product defined by the chromosome has to be enumerated using a SAT solver and this limits scalability to product lines with fewer than 30 features. In this paper we propose SAT_{ff}, a fitness function that simulates validity by computing the difference between constraints in the chromosome and oracle. In an empirical study on 101 feature models comparing SAT_{ff} with two existing fitness functions that use the enumeration technique we find that SAT_{ff} shows a significant improvement over one, and no significant difference with the other one. We also find that SAT_{ff} requires only 7% of the runtime on average scaling to feature models with as many as 97 features.

Keywords: Genetic algorithms · Software product lines · Reverse engineering · Feature models · Fitness function

1 Introduction

Software product line (SPL) engineering is a development paradigm that builds families of related of products using common platforms combined with variable features [14]. Developers and maintainers of the SPL utilize a *feature model* to describe the supported set of products. A feature model consists of a set of Boolean constraints combined with a hierarchical tree representation. However, in practice feature models are often missing or may not be updated as the SPL evolves [12]. To address this problem, researchers have developed techniques to reverse engineer feature models from either a set of products or from the set of constraints describing the SPL.

Several search-based frameworks have been proposed which use genetic algorithms for reverse engineering feature models [8,9,17]. While effective, the evaluations of these frameworks have been performed on feature models with less than 30 features. As we have tried to reproduce these studies, we have learned that the feature size limitation may not be random, but is in fact due to the high cost

© Springer International Publishing AG 2016
F. Sarro and K. Deb (Eds.): SSBSE 2016, LNCS 9962, pp. 128–142, 2016.
DOI: 10.1007/978-3-319-47106-8_9

of calculating the fitness functions. Typically, the fitness functions for reverse engineering aim to match the set of valid products within the product line. Variations exist that place different weights on the number of matched, missed and additional products, but they all require enumeration of the full set of products in each changed model. Since the number of products grows exponentially with the number of features, and this computation must be done repeatedly, it is a performance bottleneck.

Many real product lines have more than 30 features (we reverse engineer a real application with over 90 features in our study), meaning this fitness calculation will limit the effectiveness of the current reverse engineering techniques. Therefore we ask if it is possible to compute validity in an alternative way. Our intuition is that we may be able to obtain similar information from examining only the representation of the set of products – the set of constraints.

In this paper we propose a new fitness function, SAT_{ff}, that mimics validity by computing the tautological implication of the sets of constraints in each model against the original. This estimates the distance between two models. We then perform an empirical study to evaluate both its effectiveness and its efficiency on over 100 feature models ranging in the number of features from 9 to 97. We compare the quality of SAT_{ff} against two state of the art validity fitness functions proposed in two different reverse engineering frameworks. We find that SAT_{ff} shows a significant improvement over one of these across all models, and no significant difference with the other one, suggesting a similar effectiveness. However, SAT_{ff} requires only 7 % of the runtime on average, scaling to feature models with as many as 97 features.

The contributions of this work are:

1. A new fitness function, SAT_{ff} aimed to measure the valid products based on computing the tautological implication of the sets of constraints in each model
2. An empirical study showing that the new fitness function scales to models that have over 90 features

In the next section we present some background, related work and motivate the need for a new fitness function. We then present SAT_{ff} in Sect. 3, followed by the empirical study in Sects. 4 and 5. Finally we conclude and present future work in Sect. 6.

2   Motivation and Related Work

Figure 1(a) is an example of a Mobile Media software product line that manipulates different types of media on a mobile device [5]. On the left (a), we see a feature model that describes the product line. The root of the feature model is the feature *Mobile Media v7*. There are three mandatory features that are required, *Album Mgmt*, *Media Mgmt*, and *Media Selection*, denoted by a filled circle at the end of the line. The filled arc under the *Media Selection* represents an or-group relationship. This means that one or more media (*Photo, Music,*

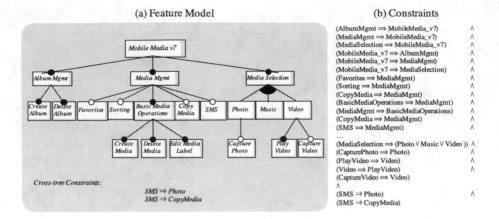

Fig. 1. Mobile media v7 SPL: a feature model and its constraints

Video) can be selected. There are four optional features for managing the media, *Favorites*, *Sorting*, *Copy Media*, and *SMS*, denoted by an open circle. The *Basic Media Operations* and its three sub-operations are required for all mobile devices. There are also two additional constraints not in the diagram. We call these the cross-tree constraints. *SMS* $\Longrightarrow$ *Photo* represents a constraint that *SMS* can be selected only when *Photo* is selected.

The usefulness of the feature model is that it is human readable, providing an abstraction for the whole product line. Underlying the feature model is a set of constraints (shown as Fig. 1(b)). (The mapping of the constraints will be discussed in the next section.) This set of constraints can be used for further analysis, such as to compute the number of products or to list the valid product configurations.

The existing work that reverse engineers feature models uses a genetic algorithm to search for a correct feature model that closely describes a set of known valid products [8,9,17]. The input to the framework is either a set of products, or the set of equations from which the products can be enumerated (without the tree hierarchy). This is the oracle for driving the search fitness. At each search iteration, for each member of the population, the set of products that the model represents is also enumerated, and compared to the oracle set. In a model with 27 features (the largest model evaluated in these papers) there are as many as 2^{27} or $134,217,728$ products (or product configurations) to be enumerated. Although there may be constraints in the models that reduce this space to some degree, the genetic algorithm has to be able to refactor models up to this value. Other work synthesizes a feature model directly from a set of constraints [1,16]. However, this provides the same solution each time and it may not be an optimal solution for the modeler. We believe that the evolutionary algorithm is more flexible, given that it will find different solutions in the search space and provides an opportunity to balance validity with additional objectives.

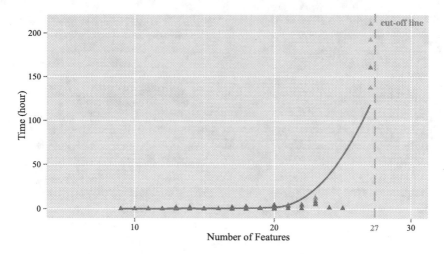

Fig. 2. Exponential execution time of the current fitness function

While there is existing research that uses multi-objective search on feature models with more than 500 features, the goal is to find optimal configurations for building a software product with specific quality objectives [6,15]. These do not attempt to optimize the feature model itself (our focus), and do not, therefore use fitness functions that require the enumeration of all products.

Some real-world software product lines, such as Linux, have been reported to have extremely high variability with more than 11,000 features, and the possibility of more than (2^{11000}) product configurations [12]. This makes it impossible to enumerate all of the products in order to evaluate fitness. While we do not necessarily achieve this level of scalability in this work, we believe that any improvement in our ability to work on larger product lines is valuable. In Fig. 2, we show efficiency using $Validity_{ff}$ within SPLRevO (the most accurate fitness function in [17]) on varying size feature models. We see that the execution time increases exponentially as the number of features increases (the number of iterations for the search is kept constant). The y-axis is the time in hours for the search with a limit of 100 generations, while the x-axis is the number of features. There are five runs for each feature model, denoted by triangles. As can be seen, once there are more than 20 features in the model, the runtime jumps. It takes more than 200 h to find a correct feature model with 27 features. In our experiments we were unable to find any solutions for feature models larger than 27 features (beyond the cut-off line). We also note that in our experiments we have been able to reverse engineer a feature model with 97 features in about the same time (200 h).

While the number of products grows exponentially in these systems, a recent study by Nadi, et al. [12] shows that the Linux system has only 12,758 constraints, 4,999 hierarchical constraints and 7,759 cross-tree constraints. If we examine the Mobile Media SPL shown in Fig. 1, we see that it has 184 different mobile media products, however there are only 32 constraints that describe it. The implication is that we may be able to reason about validity using the set of constraints directly, instead of requiring an enumeration of the products.

2.1 Existing Reverse Engineering Frameworks

Two existing frameworks for reverse engineering feature models are the Software Product Line Reverse Engineering Optimization framework (SPLRevO) [17] and the Evolutionary algoriTHm for Optimized feature Models (ETHOM) [8]. Both use genetic algorithms to perform a single-objective optimization. The frameworks use slightly different chromosomes and evolutionary operators, and contain different fitness functions, but the primary objective of both frameworks are the same. In SPLRevO, the basic chromosome consists of two parts, the feature diagram, and the cross-tree constraints. The feature diagram part of the chromosome describes the relationships between features. Each relationship contains one or more children, the parent, and a relationship type. The relationships for a single child can be either a Hierarchy or Mandatory. For a group of children, the supported relationships are Mutex, Or, or Xor. The cross-tree constraints are represented by their expression tree. The encoding of the Mobile Media feature model from Fig. 1 is shown in Fig. 3. Figure 3(a) is the feature diagram and Fig. 3(b) is the set of cross-tree constraints in tree form (they are flattened into an array form in our implementation).

2.2 Existing Fitness Functions

SPLRevO has one fitness function, called $Validity_{ff}$ in this paper. ETHOM has three fitness functions, the most accurate of which is $MinDiff_{ff}$ [9]. Both frameworks can incorporate different fitness functions, hence either one can be used

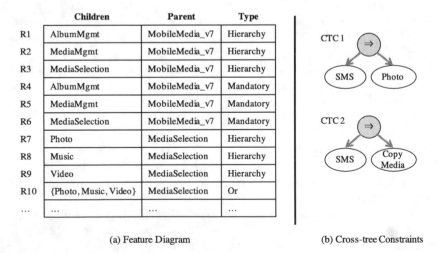

	Children	Parent	Type
R1	AlbumMgmt	MobileMedia_v7	Hierarchy
R2	MediaMgmt	MobileMedia_v7	Hierarchy
R3	MediaSelection	MobileMedia_v7	Hierarchy
R4	AlbumMgmt	MobileMedia_v7	Mandatory
R5	MediaMgmt	MobileMedia_v7	Mandatory
R6	MediaSelection	MobileMedia_v7	Mandatory
R7	Photo	MediaSelection	Hierarchy
R8	Music	MediaSelection	Hierarchy
R9	Video	MediaSelection	Hierarchy
R10	{Photo, Music, Video}	MediaSelection	Or
...	...	...	...

(a) Feature Diagram   (b) Cross-tree Constraints

Fig. 3. Encoding of feature model for mobile media v7 SPL: (a) diagram (b) CTCs

to run experiments for comparison. We show the *Validity$_{ff}$* fitness as (3) and the *MinDiff$_{ff}$* as (4) below. *Validity$_{ff}$* is used to measure how close an evolved feature model is to the given set of valid products, based on the number of matching products. It is the ratio of the number of matching products and the number of desired products, penalized by the number of additional products that over describe the evolved feature model. The final fitness has a range from 0 to 100 and is maximizing. 100 is the correct model. *MinDiff$_{ff}$* is a fitness function that minimizes the dissimilarity between the feature models in the evolution and the given set of valid products. It minimizes both the missing and additional products in the feature model, by summing the differences together.

$$\#addi(sfs, fm) = |fm| - \#matched(sfs, fm) \tag{1}$$

$$\#missing(sfs, fm) = |sfs| - \#matched(sfs, fm) \tag{2}$$

$$Validity_{ff}(sfs, fm) = \frac{\frac{\log_2(\#matched(sfs,fm)+1)}{-0.1\cdot\log_2(\#addi(sfs,fm)+1)}}{\log_2(|sfs|+1)} \cdot 100 \tag{3}$$

$$MinDiff(sfs, fm) = \#missing(sfs, fm) + \#addi(sfs, fm) \tag{4}$$

In order to calculate these fitness functions, several intermediate calculations are needed. In these equations *sfs* and *fm* are the set of desired products and an evolved feature model, respectively. $|fm|$ can be obtained by asking the *ProductsQuestion* in FaMa, *the Feature Model Analyzer* framework, which is an analysis framework for working with software product lines [3,4]. FaMa consists of several reasoners and supports questions such as enumerating and counting products of the feature model, or checking if a specific product is valid. *#matched(sfs, fm)* represents the number of matching products between *sfs* and *fm*. *#addi(sfs, fm)* represent the number of additional products found in *fm*, but not in *sfs*. *#missing(sfs, fm)* represent the number of missing products not found in *fm*. The matching products can be determined by asking the *ValidProductQuestion* for each product in *sfs* on *fm* in FaMa.

3   Satisfiable Validity Fitness Function (SAT_{ff})

Both *MinDiff$_{ff}$* and *Validity$_{ff}$* validate an evolved feature model based on the number of products. In this section, we present a more scalable fitness function SAT_{ff}, that utilizes the observation of others that the number of constraints is usually significantly smaller than the number of features [12]. We show an example of the computation of SAT_{ff} in Fig. 4.

In Fig. 4, the input of SAT_{ff} can be either an existing feature model or source code. When the input is a feature model, it will be transformed to a set of constraints, and evolved to find an alternative feature model having the same constraints. In this paper, we use the same approach as Benavides et al. [2]

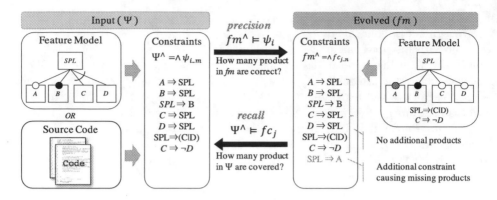

Fig. 4. The Computation of SAT_{ff}

to transform a feature model to a set of constraints. We also eliminate the redundant constraints, for instance, for the alternative group. The research of Nadi et al. [12] provides a way to extract constraints directly from C source code using their analysis tools TypeChef [7] and the FeAtuRe Constraint Extractor (FARCE) [13]. In this case, we can use these constraints directly to feed into our fitness function.

SAT_{ff} works directly on the set of constraints simulating the validity. It estimates the difference between the given input constraints and the evolved feature models in terms of tautological implication ($\models$). This idea was used by Nadi et al. to determine if their constraints that they extract are correct [12]. To compute the fitness function, the evolved feature model will be transformed to a set of constraints using the same approach as used to transform the original feature model. There are two steps to compute SAT_{ff}. First, we compute precision, and then we compute recall, both of which are described next.

Computing the precision tells us how many of the products in the new feature model are correct (top portion of Fig. 4). Let $\Psi^\wedge = \wedge_{i=1}^{m}\psi_i$ be a conjunction of all m individual constraints ψ_i from the given input Ψ. Let $fm^\wedge = \wedge_{j=1}^{n}fc_j$ be a conjunction of all n individual constraints fc_j from an evolved feature model fm. In Fig. 4, we see that all of the input constraints have been recovered by the evolved feature model. This implies that the evolved feature model has, at least, the same set of restrictions on which products configurations are valid. The number of input constraints recovered can, therefore, estimate how many correct products are in the evolved feature model. We present this estimation as $precision_{SAT}$; ranging from 0 to 100.0. $precision_{SAT}(\Psi, fm) = 100$ if and only if $fm^\wedge$ tautologically implies ψ_i ($fm^\wedge \models \psi_i$) for all $\psi_i \in \Psi$. This indicates that the evolved feature model has at least the same restrictions on the valid products as the given input (hence no additional product). However, this is not enough since we might also have additional products that the original model did not contain. If there exists any ψ_i such that $\neg(fm^\wedge \models \psi_i)$ is true, there exist some additional products in the evolved feature model.

In Fig. 4, we also see an additional constraint ($SPL \implies A$) in the evolved feature model. That means feature A is mandatory for the evolved feature model but it is optional in the input. This constraint limits products without feature A, causing some missing valid product configurations. The number of evolved constraints, therefore, can estimate how many valid products are recovered. We present this estimation as $recall_{SAT}$; ranging from 0 to 100.0. The $recall_{SAT}(\Psi, fm) = 100$ if and only if $\Psi^{\wedge}$ tautologically implies fc_j ($\Psi^{\wedge} \models fc_j$) for all $fc_j \in fm$. This indicates that the evolved feature model covers all the products of the given input (hence no missing product). If there exists any fc_j such that $\neg(\Psi^{\wedge} \models fc_j)$ is true, some products of the given input are uncovered. The precision and recall of retrieving the product configurations of the given input using constraint satisfiability are shown in (5) and (6), respectively.

$$precision_{SAT}(\Psi, fm) = \frac{|\{\psi_i | \psi_i \in \Psi, fm^{\wedge} \models \psi_i\}|}{m} \qquad (5)$$

$$recall_{SAT}(\Psi, fm) = \frac{|\{fc_j | fc_j \in fm, \Psi^{\wedge} \models fc_j\}|}{n} \qquad (6)$$

To find the correct feature model, both precision and recall must be maximized, hence minimizing the missing and additional products. SAT_{ff} balances both precision and recall. We use $F_{\beta=4}$ *measure* for computing this fitness value. We believe that recovering most of valid products of the given input is more important than minimizing additional products. Thus, we heuristically choose the value of $\beta = 4$ (greater than 1) to emphasize the $recall_{SAT}$. The computation of the SAT_{ff} is given in (7).

$$SAT_{ff}(\beta = 4) = \frac{(\beta^2 + 1) \cdot precision_{SAT} \cdot recall_{SAT}}{\beta^2 \cdot precision_{SAT} + recall_{SAT}} \qquad (7)$$

4   Empirical Study

In this section, we evaluate the performance of the new validity fitness function (SAT_{ff}) compared with the two traditional validity fitness functions, $MinDiff_{ff}$ and $Validity_{ff}$. We aim to answer the following research questions.[1]
RQ1: How well does the quality of feature models generated using SAT_{ff}, compare to those using the existing fitness functions, $MinDiff_{ff}$ and $Validity_{ff}$?
RQ2: How well does SAT_{ff} scale to larger feature models?

4.1   Subjects

We used 101 subjects for our experiments. 100 are originally from the SPLOT feature model repository [11]. These models are derived from real applications and are provided for the community as benchmarks. We categorize these subjects into small, medium, large, and extra large based on the number of features. We

---

[1] http://cse.unl.edu/~myra/artifacts/ssbse2016/.

Table 1. Subjects used in experiments

Group	Total models	Features	Products (avg.)
Small	22	9 - 10	21.7
Medium	54	11 - 19	104.6
Large	15	20 - 27	227.9
XLarge	9	30 - 97	N/A
Real C Code	1	52	N/A
Total	101	9 - 97	184.2

show details of these subjects in the Table 1. There are 22 small feature models with between 9 and 10 features, 54 medium models (11–19 features) and 15 large models (20–27 features). The small, medium, and large subjects have been used in existing work on reverse engineering [8,17]. We also include 9 extra large feature models (30–97 features) as well as a model extracted directly from the source code of a C application, nano-2.4.2[2] with 52 features. The last column of the table shows the average number of products in each SPL. Since we use FaMa to compute the number of products, we were unable to compute the number of products for the XLarge and Real C Code subjects. We note that the number of valid products in a real product line is often much smaller than the potential product space. For instance, we have on average of 228 products in the large models (with a max of 810 products). However, during the search, as constraints are relaxed, this number can increase (theoretically to the upper bound that is possible). To verify this, we did a quick search of the logs for a feature model with 27 features, and found an individual with with 1.2 million products.

4.2   Metrics Used

We evaluate the effectiveness of the fitness functions by comparing the desired set of products (products in the starting model) with the products in the evolved feature model. We count the matched, missing and additional products in each model, and calculate the *precision, recall,* and the F_β-*measure* as measures of effectiveness. F_β *measure* is the weighted harmonic mean of precision and recall. We use F_1, where $\beta = 1$, that weights precision and recall equally [10]. A high F_1-measure is our primary goal since this is the metric that indicates how close we are to our desired solution. The calculations for our metrics are shown in Eqs. (8)–(10). We also record the execution time that each experiment takes to measure efficiency.

$$precision(sfs, fm) = \frac{\#matched(sfs, fm)}{|fm|} \cdot 100 \qquad (8)$$

---

[2] http://www.nano-editor.org.

$$recall(sfs, fm) = \frac{\#matched(sfs, fm)}{|sfs|} \cdot 100 \qquad (9)$$

$$F_{\beta=1}(sfs, fm) = \frac{2 \cdot precision(sfs, fm) \cdot recall(sfs, fm)}{precision(sfs, fm) + recall(sfs, fm)} \qquad (10)$$

4.3 Methods

We implemented SAT_{ff} in the SPLRevO framework [17]. We added $MinDiff_{ff}$ which originated in the ETHOM framework [9] so that all experiments are run on the same platform (SPLRevO). We run all experiments 5 times for all subjects within SPLRevO using each of $MinDiff_{ff}$, $Validity_{ff}$ and SAT_{ff}. We use a rank selection and a one-point crossover (with a 100 % crossover rate), and a 1 % mutation applied to both the feature diagram and the cross-tree constraints. We set the population size of the feature models to 100. We run the experiments up to 100 generations. The algorithm stops early if there is no improvement of fitness value after 25 consecutive generations. These parameter settings are chosen to be consistent with prior work [8, 17].

To compute $MinDiff_{ff}$ and $Validity_{ff}$, we use FaMa [3] with the Choco solver to obtain the number of products, the list of all product configurations, and valid products. For SAT_{ff}, the input of the existing feature models are first converted to a set of conjunctive constraints. We use JavaBDD [18] to compute tautological implication for SAT_{ff}.

For nano-2.4.2, we use TypeChef [7] and FARCE [13] to extract constraints from the code. There are 72 possible features (obtained by grep) of which 52 are binary. We provide TypeChef only with the list of binary features for compatibility with the framework. We run all experiments on the same computing cluster with AMD Opteron(TM) CPUs running at 2300MHz. Each individual configuration was submitted to a separate node with a maximum Java memory pool of 32GB, and 10 days wall clock time.

5   Results

In this section, we answer each research question in turn. To answer RQ1, we turn to Tables 2 and 3, and the boxplots shown in Figs. 5 and 6. In Table 2, we show the average fitness value (FFvalue), average precision, recall, and F_1 for the feature models from $MinDiff_{ff}$, $Validity_{ff}$, and SAT_{ff} in each category. We see that $Validity_{ff}$ gives the highest F_1 of 76.2 on average, while SAT_{ff} is slightly lower. However, we see an improvement of F_1 of SAT_{ff} over $Validity_{ff}$ on large models up to 58.9 for SAT_{ff} versus 55.4 for $Validity_{ff}$. The worst F_1 measure is that of $MinDiff_{ff}$. Note that we do not show data for either $MinDiff_{ff}$ and $Validity_{ff}$ for extra large models, because the search times out or runs out of memory. Since the precision, recall, and F_1 are computed based on the number of matching products and we cannot enumerate all the products of XLarge model, these metrics are not available. We show the graphical distribution of these results as boxplots in Fig. 5.

Table 2. Result of feature models from three fitness functions

Fitness/Models	FFvalue	Precision (%)	Recall (%)	F_1	Time (minute)
$MinDiff_{ff}$	86.8	32.4	20.7	23.7	11.8
Small	10.4	68.2	42.8	49.2	1.9
Medium	79.7	26.6	17.3	19.8	10.4
Large	224.5	0.7	0.5	0.6	31.6
$Validity_{ff}$	92.8	69.1	98.2	76.2	147.9
Small	94.5	76.5	99.3	84.1	2.3
Medium	93.6	71.1	99.0	78.8	21.8
Large	87.1	51.3	93.9	55.4	815.2
SAT_{ff}	98.8	65.4	97.2	74.1	86.9
Small	99.2	73.4	100.0	82.1	0.1
Medium	99.1	66.3	98.2	74.9	0.2
Large	98.6	50.2	89.7	58.9	0.3
XLarge	89.4	-	-	-	973.0
Real C Code	95.4	-	-	-	1.8

Table 3. Significance test of F_1 and execution time on SAT_{ff} compared to $MinDiff_{ff}$ and $Validity_{ff}$

Fitness/Models	F_1		Time	
	ΔF_1	p-value	ΔTime (%)	p-value
$MinDiff_{ff}$	57.63	<0.05	−96.00	<0.05
Small	31.76	<0.05	−84.98	<0.05
Medium	56.20	<0.05	−91.40	<0.05
Large	57.63	<0.05	−96.00	<0.05
$Validity_{ff}$	−2.43	0.35	−93.41	<0.05
Small	−1.50	0.47	−86.15	<0.05
Medium	−3.79	0.23	−94.80	<0.05
Large	1.18	0.55	−99.02	<0.05

We next ran the Mann-Whitney-Wilcoxon Test (in R) to determine if these results are significant. We compare the F_1 between SAT_{ff} and both $MinDiff_{ff}$ and $Validity_{ff}$, using a 0.05 significance level. The null hypothesis is that there is no significance improvement in this measure of SAT_{ff} over the existing fitness functions, $MinDiff_{ff}$ and $Validity_{ff}$. The result for this analysis is shown in Table 3. We show the different of those measures associated with p-value. To see the effectiveness of SAT_{ff}, we turn to F_1 in this table. We see p-value > 0.05 in $Validity_{ff}$. Therefore, we accept the null hypothesis and conclude that SAT_{ff} effectively find a correct feature model as good as $Validity_{ff}$. However, we see a

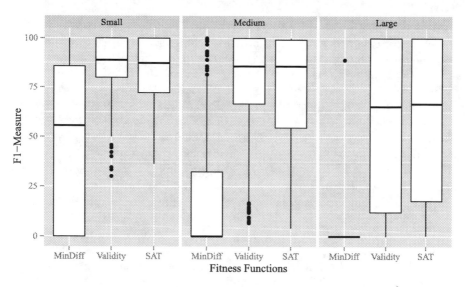

Fig. 5. F_1-measure of small, medium, and large feature models from three fitness functions

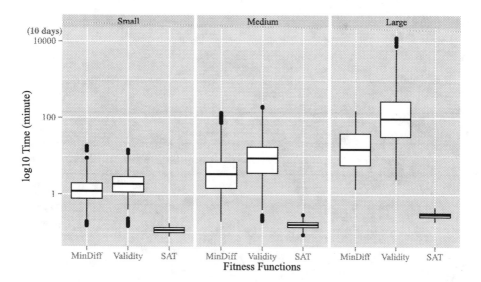

Fig. 6. Execution time of small, medium, and large feature models from three fitness functions

slightly better result for the large model, 1.2 % improvement. When turn to the F_1 of $MinDiff_{\!f\!f}$, we see p-value <0.05. Therefore, we reject the null hypothesis and conclude that $SAT_{\!f\!f}$ provides a significance improvement over $MinDiff_{\!f\!f}$, up to 57.63 % of F_1 on average.

Summary of RQ1. Based on this result we can conclude that SAT_{ff} produces accurate feature models with an F_1 measure as high as the existing fitness function $Validity_{ff}$. It shows that we can simulate the distance of the feature models not only from the products, but also from the constraints that define them.

To answer RQ2, we first look at the boxplots in Fig. 6. We can see that for each of the groups of subjects, the SAT_{ff} fitness is much lower than the other two fitness functions. The significance results are shown in Table 3. We next turn to the plot in Fig. 7. In this figure, we plot the best optimization time of each iteration from three fitness functions on every subject versus the number of features. The results from $MinDiff_{ff}$, $Validity_{ff}$, and SAT_{ff} are plotted as blue squares, red triangles, and gray circles, respectively. We also show the trend of each fitness function as the smooth lines using local polynomial regression fitting method (loess) in R. We use a logarithmic scale for the execution time. We see that both $MinDiff_{ff}$ and $Validity_{ff}$ exponentially increase execution time when the number of features increases. Although $MinDiff_{ff}$ requires slightly less time, it also has the worst F_1. On the other hand, we see a promising result from our new fitness function SAT_{ff}. We see the highest efficiency using SAT_{ff}. As the result in Table 3, it reduces a significant execution time exponentially compared to the others, 96 % on $MinDiff_{ff}$ and 93 % on $Validity_{ff}$ (99 % on large models).

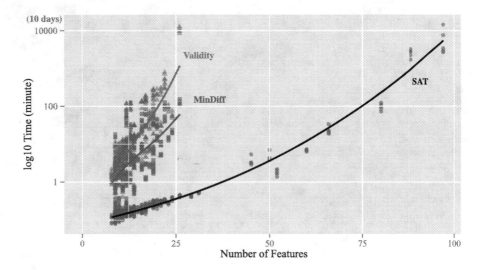

Fig. 7. Execution time versus the number of features

Summary of RQ2. Based on this data we can conclude that SAT_{ff} is a scalable alternative validity fitness function. It computes faster and provide correctness as good as the traditional $Validity_{ff}$.

5.1 Discussion and Limitations

In this paper, we have successfully shifted from enumerating an exponential number of products to symbolically satisfying the finite number of constraints of feature models. However, we still see some limitations. While we more than tripled the number of features that we could previously handle in the search frameworks, we were unable to scale beyond 100 features. We used JavaBDD to compute the tautology between the input constraints and the evolved feature models. This requires more memory when the number of features increases, and we found that this was a limiting factor. Second, while the size of the input constraints is a fixed number, the constraints the in evolution can be arbitrary large and complex. In addition, we need to compute the tautology simulating the distance for each of the chromosomes in the population for a number of generations. This also may hinder further scalability. We plan to revisit these issues in future work to see if we can simplify constraints first, before the evaluations, and/or to implement some sort of incremental solving.

6 Conclusions and Future Work

In this paper, we have presented a new validity fitness function SAT_{ff} for reverse engineering feature models when using a genetic algorithm. SAT_{ff} estimates the distance between the input constraints and the evolved feature models using tautological implications. We implemented SAT_{ff} in the SPLRevO framework and compared the effectiveness and efficiency to the two validity fitness functions $MinDiff_{ff}$ and $Validity_{ff}$ that compute validity using the number of products. Our results show that SAT_{ff} produces feature models (in terms of the F_1 measure) as good as the best existing fitness function $Validity_{ff}$, yet it significantly reduces the execution time. We are also able to scale our search to product lines with as many as 100 features. In future work, we will look at ways to scale the fitness function further through incremental solving and by pre-simplification of constraints. We also plan to incorporate additional fitness objectives and to implement a multi-objective approach.

Acknowledgments. This research was supported in part by the National Science Foundation under award number CCF-1161767.

References

1. Andersen, N., Czarnecki, K., She, S., Wąsowski, A.: Efficient synthesis of feature models. In: Proceedings of the 16th International Software Product Line Conference, vol. 1. pp. 106–115. SPLC (2012)
2. Benavides, D., Segura, S., Trinidad, P., Ruiz-Cortés, A.: A first step towards a framework for the automated analysis of feature models. In: Managing Variability for Software Product Lines: Working With Variability Mechanisms (2006)

3. Benavides, D., Segura, S., Trinidad, P., Ruiz-cortés, A.: FaMa: tooling a framework for the automated analysis of feature models. In: Proceeding of the First International Workshop on Variability Modelling of Software Intensive Systems VAMOS, pp. 129–134 (2007)
4. Benavides, D., Segura, S., Trinidad, P., Ruiz-cortés, A.: FAMA, a framework for automated analyses of feature models (2014). http://www.isa.us.es/fama/
5. Figueiredo, E., Cacho, N., Sant'Anna, C., Monteiro, M., Kulesza, U., Garcia, A., Soares, S., Ferrari, F., Khan, S., Castor Filho, F., Dantas, F.: Evolving software product lines with aspects: an empirical study on design stability. In: International Conference on Software Engineering, pp. 261–270. ICSE (2008)
6. Henard, C., Papadakis, M., Harman, M., Le Traon, Y.: Combining multi-objective search and constraint solving for configuring large software product lines. In: International Conference on Software Engineering, pp. 517–528. ICSE (2015)
7. Kenner, A., Kästner, C., Haase, S., Leich, T.: Typechef: toward type checking #ifdef variability in c. In: International Workshop on Feature-Oriented Software Development, pp. 25–32. FOSD (2010)
8. Lopez-Herrejon, R.E., Galindo, J.A., Benavides, D., Segura, S., Egyed, A.: Reverse engineering feature models with evolutionary algorithms: an exploratory study. In: Fraser, G., Teixeira de Souza, J. (eds.) SSBSE 2012. LNCS, vol. 7515, pp. 168–182. Springer, Heidelberg (2012)
9. Lopez-Herrejon, R.E., Linsbauer, L., Galindo, J.A., Parejo, J.A., Benavides, D., Segura, S., Egyed, A.: An assessment of search-based techniques for reverse engineering feature models. J. Syst. Softw. **103**, 353–369 (2014)
10. Manning, C.D., Raghavan, P., Schütze, H.: Introduction to Information Retrieval. Cambridge University Press, Cambridge (2008)
11. Mendonca, M., Branco, M., Cowan, D.: S.P.L.O.T.: Software product lines online tool (2014). http://www.splot-research.org/. Generative Software Development Lab. Computer Systems Group, University of Waterloo
12. Nadi, S., Berger, T., Kästner, C., Czarnecki, K.: Mining configuration constraints: static analyses and empirical results. In: International Conference on Software Engineering, pp. 140–151. ICSE (2014)
13. Nadi, S., Berger, T., Kästner, C., Czarnecki, K.: Where do configuration constraints stem from? An extraction approach and an empirical study. IEEE Trans. Softw. Eng. **41**(8), 820–841 (2015)
14. Pohl, K., Böckle, G., van der Linden, F.: Software Product Line Engineering. Springer, Berlin (2005)
15. Sayyad, A., Ingram, J., Menzies, T., Ammar, H.: Scalable product line configuration: a straw to break the camel's back. In: International Conference on Automated Software Engineering (ASE), pp. 465–474 (2013)
16. She, S., Lotufo, R., Berger, T., Wąsowski, A., Czarnecki, K.: Reverse engineering feature models. In: Proceedings of the 33rd International Conference on Software Engineering (ICSE), pp. 461–470 (2011)
17. Thianniwet., T., Cohen, M.B.: SPLRevO: optimizing complex feature models in search based reverse engineering of software product lines. In: First North American Search Based Software Engineering Symposium (NasBASE 2015), February 2015
18. Whaley, J.: JavaBDD - Java Binary Decision Diagram library. http://javabdd.sourceforge.net

A Multi-objective Approach to Prioritize and Recommend Bugs in Open Source Repositories

Duany Dreyton$^{(\boxtimes)}$, Allysson Allex Araújo, Altino Dantas, Raphael Saraiva, and Jerffeson Souza

Optimization in Software Engineering Group, State University of Ceará, Doutor Silas Munguba Avenue, 1700, Fortaleza 60714-903, Brazil
{duany.dreyton,allysson.araujo,altino.dantas,jerffeson.souza}@uece.br,
raphael.saraiva@aluno.uece.br
http://goes.uece.br

Abstract. Bugs prioritization in open source repositories poses as a challenging and complex task, given the significant number of reports and the impact of a wrong bug assignment to the software evolution. Deciding the most suitable bugs in order to be solved can be considered as an optimization problem. Thus, we propose a search-based approach supported by a multi-objective paradigm to tackle this problem, aiming to maximize the resolution of the most important bugs, while minimizing the risk of later resolution of the most severe ones. Furthermore, we propose a strategy to avoid the developer's effort when choosing a solution from the Pareto Front. Regarding the empirical study, we evaluate the performance of three metaheuristics and investigate the human competitiveness of the approach. Overall, the proposal can be said human competitive in a real-world scenario and the NSGA-II outperformed both MOCell and IBEA in the adopted quality measures.

Keywords: Bugs prioritization · Multi-objective optimization · SBSE

1 Introduction

After a system has been deployed, it inevitably has to change if it is to remain useful [1]. The developers add new features, correct previous mistakes and misunderstandings, and react to the requirements, technologies, and knowledge volatility as it plays out through the time [2]. Software evolution claims that the system must evolve to meet changing user needs and may be triggered by several issues, including the reports and correction of software bugs found in operation [3]. Intrinsically addressed to the software evolution, we shall use the term maintenance in this paper to refer to the general process of changing a system after it has been delivered. These changes range from simple modifications, for instance, correcting coding errors, to more difficult ones, as significant enhancements to correct specification errors [4]. According to the Lehman's laws of software evolution [5], the system tends to be more complex and challenging as it grows, unless explicit steps are taken to reorganize the overall design.

© Springer International Publishing AG 2016
F. Sarro and K. Deb (Eds.): SSBSE 2016, LNCS 9962, pp. 143–158, 2016.
DOI: 10.1007/978-3-319-47106-8_10

Aiming to cope with all these unavoidable changes, large open source software projects usually provide a bug repository to their communities, such as KDE and Eclipse. This feature has a vital role in the software quality, specially because it encourages the developer's engagement and helps to deal with the high number of vulnerabilities daily reported. Given this critical scenario, "In which order should the bugs be fixed?" is a frequent and complex problem to be discussed, because it involves different variables, such as the experience of each developer, which bugs have more urgency to be fixed and which ones are duplicated of those already in the repository [6]. The difficulty of assigning new bug's report to the appropriate developer is known as Bug Triage Problem [7].

Nevertheless, the single most important requirement of an open source software system is that its source code must be freely available to everyone who wishes to examine or change it [8]. This process is human-oriented and each developer decides on his/her own which bug will be fixed by him/her. Generally, these decisions are often based on some personal criteria and, sometimes, this means that much of the effort concentrates on what part-time programmers find interesting, rather than on what might be more essential [9]. This particularity raises relevant questions, such as: how to stimulate the development effort towards overall promising goals regarding the system? How to reduce the developers wasted time used examining a large list of reports?

In addition, we verify that the currently repositories do not provide a *satisfactory* support decision to their community. With *satisfactory*, we refer to friendly and easily recommend a prioritized list of bugs which can be suitable for each developer. Through this strategy, our assumptions are (i) encouraging the development of what is essential and (ii) decreasing the developer's effort at defining, among many bugs, a specific list suited for his/her experience.

We believe that this strategy can, at least in part, be automated. Thus, Search-based Software Engineering (SBSE) rise as an promising alternative because it proposes to reformulate complex Software Engineering problems as search problems. There are only two key ingredients to explore SBSE: the representation of the problem and the definition of the fitness function [10].

A proposal to automatically prioritize bugs in open source repositories has been introduced in [11]. In this work, a weighted single-objective formulation composed of the votes given by the community, besides the priority and severity levels of each bug was presented. However, the present paper significantly extends the previous work in three major aspects: (i) mathematically formulates the problem as multi-objective (ii) proposes a strategy based on the compatibility between developer's experience and the experience level required by a bug to avoid the effort when choosing a solution from the Pareto Front and (iii) extends the empirical evaluation with novel research questions, including a participant-based experiment. In summary, the primary contributions of this work are:

- The presentation of a novel multi-objective formulation for the problem;
- The proposal of a strategy to choose a solution from Pareto Front suitable to the developer's experience.
- Experimental analyses considering the multi-objective approach;

This paper is organized as follows. Section 2 discusses the related work. The problem of prioritizing bugs in open repositories and the overall multi-objective approach are described in Sect. 3. Section 4 reports the empirical study designed to evaluate the proposal. Finally, Sect. 5 concludes the paper and points out some future works.

2   Related Work

As previously mentioned, an automated approach to prioritize bugs was presented in [11]. It was proposed as a single-objective version composed of metrics identified from the Kate Editor repository. Experimental results have demonstrated as feasible to the user adjust which option better suits to his/her needs.

Anvik, Hiew and Murphy [6] investigate the usage of a machine learning algorithm to learn the kinds of reports that each developer resolves. When a new report arrives, a small number of developers is suggested. It was reached precision levels of 57 % and 64 % on the Eclipse and Firefox projects, respectively. Similarly, Anvik [12] proposes a recommender that produces a set of possible developers to whom a bug might reasonably be assigned. Such recommender is constructed by providing an algorithm with information about previously fixed bug reports to create a model of expertise of the developers. Kanwal and Maqbool [13] suggest classification-based approach to create a bug priority recommender, which assigns a priority level to new bug reports in a repository. The results indicate the feasibility of classification techniques for automatic priority assignment.

No prior work has considered the priorities of developers in bug repositories and its applications. Thus, Xuan *et al.* [14] model the developer prioritization using a socio-technical approach to improve typical tasks in bug repositories. They generate the developer prioritization by ranking all the participant developers. The experiments show that the developer prioritization is helpful to improve the predicting tasks in bug repositories. As far as we know, the present approach is the first work that explores multi-objective optimization to prioritize bugs.

3   Prioritizing Bugs in Open Source Repositories

Uncovered failures are daily reported in open bugs repositories. This task is encouraged by community because one potential advantage of an open bug repository allows more bugs to be identified and solved, improving the quality of the produced software [15]. However, handling these reports manually is time consuming, and often it results in delaying the resolution of important bugs [13].

Due to this limitation, deciding which bugs must be fixed and in which order poses as a relevant challenge to be addressed. Aiming to tackle this problem, our search-based approach, called as **PRBugs**, consists of two stages: **Prioritization Stage** and **Recommendation Stage**. In the first one, a subset of all available bugs is prioritized considering the opinion of the developer responsible for triaging the bugs, as well as the feedback from the community. In the second stage, a solution from the Pareto Front is recommended to a developer, which presents more compatibility with his/her experience. A Pareto Front is a set of solutions that are non-dominated with respect to each other [16].

Bug tracking or issue tracking systems, such as Bugzilla, JIRA and Github, are used to report bugs or other issues and keep the tracking of what have been fixed [1]. We analyzed these three systems and three roles were generalized to be used in our proposal:

- **Contributor:** it represents any user of the bug repository. This role can report new problems, monitor corrections evolution, discuss through the comments and vote about which bugs must be fixed;
- **Domain expert:** it does the same tasks such as a contributor, but also has knowledge about the repository's domain. The responsibility of this role is to manage the repository to assure that it contains only valid bugs;
- **Developer:** besides the tasks of a contributor, this role requires technical knowledge about the development task, the language programming employed or the documentation process, for instance.

Figure 1 shows an overview of our approach, which is composed of 5 steps in 2 stages (Prioritization and Recommendation). This approach intends to be generic enough to be employed by any bug tracking system. First of all, a contributor reports (1) a bug and its *Severity* to be triaged (2) by an expert domain. A triagers task manages the repository so that it contains only valid bugs and defines *Priority* and *Experience Level* values of each one. When a bug is accepted

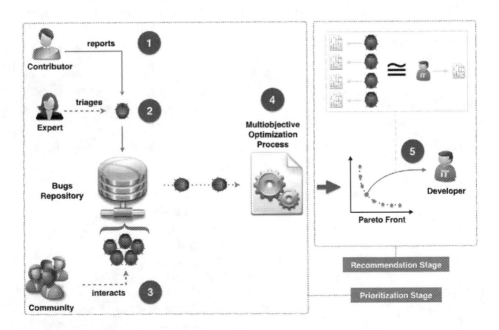

Fig. 1. PRBugs overview.

in the repository, the community can discuss and express its *Relevance* through the number of votes, for example, or another interaction mechanism. As can be seen, until this step, all the process is human-oriented. Considering the reported bugs and its information (*Relevance, Priority, Experience Level* and *Severity*) in the repository, the multi-objective optimization process (4) is applied and, consequently, the Prioritization Stage is fulfilled. At the end of the multi-objective optimization process, the developer would select the preferred solution from the Pareto Front. However, besides requiring more effort, this can be a difficult task for large Pareto Fronts [17]. For this reason, we propose a Recommendation Stage, which consists of choosing a solution from the Pareto Front (5) properly suited to the developer's experience rate. This experience rate is gathered through the historical analysis of the bugs previously resolved by the developer, in other words, it is verified the which areas he/she usually contributes. For example, we assume that a developer with 3 fixes in the system, 2 of which in a area of interest (experience rate 66 %), may be considered more likely to fix bugs in such area than a developer that has 1000 fixes in the system overall but only 500 in this supposed area (experience rate 50 %).

Such as defined in the approach overview, we may formalize the *information* from the bugs repositories that we use as input and which role has to provide it:

- *Severity:* it represents how serious the impact caused by a bug for the software operation is. In this case, technical knowledge is not necessary and its value may be informed by any role previous defined;
- *Relevance*: it expresses the overall community concerns about the report. Once again, no technical knowledge is required and any role may inform its value;
- *Priority*: it defines the precedence level that resolution of a bug presents in relation to others. This information must be given by the domain expert (triager) with technical background to determine if the correction of a bug is more urgent than the correction of others;
- *Experience Level*: it represents the technical opinion from the domain expert about how much it is estimated from experience rate in each area of the system to the bug be resolved;
- *Technical Precedence:* it informs when a bug fixing depends on correction of another one, that is, the relations between the bugs. Technical and domain knowledge from the domain expert is required because these relations may involve every part of the software.

These input values are not strictly dependent, given that increase one does not necessarily imply in increase another. For example, a bug may has a low *severity* and, in the expert domain opinion's, presents a high *priority*. However, it is very plausible consider scenarios where such values also collaborates to the expert domain made his/her decisions.

3.1 Mathematical Modelling

As previously established, the **PRBugs** is divided in two stages, called as **Prioritization Stage** and **Recommendation Stage**, respectively. Therefore, each stage is mathematically modelled as follows.

The proposed **Prioritization Stage** consists of finding the best order of bugs to be fixed, taking into account the (i) community feedback and (ii) expert domain opinion. The community feedback is captured through the *Severity* and *Relevance* values assigned for each bug, respectively specified at steps 1 and 3, as shown by Fig. 1. The expert domain opinion is gathered through the definition of a *Priority* value during the triage process at step 2.

Consider $B = \{b_1, b_2, b_3, \cdots, b_N\}$ a set of all N reported bugs which are available to be prioritized. Consider $P = \{p_1, p_2, p_3, \cdots, p_M\}$ as problem solution that is a vector which contains elements of B, where M is a parameter defined before starting optimization process which defines the number of bugs in a solution P. Thus, the model proposed in this work consists of:

$$\begin{aligned} \text{maximize} \quad & importance(P), \\ \text{minimize} \quad & risk(P), \\ \text{subject to:} \quad & pos(P, b_i) < pos(P, b_j), if\ b_i \prec b_j\ and\ b_j \in P, \end{aligned} \tag{1}$$

where $pos(P, b_i)$ returns the position of a bug b_i at P if $b_i \in P$, and ∞ otherwise. The constraint $b_i \prec b_j$ represents the *Technical Precedence*, fixing a bug b_j depends on previously fixing a bug b_i. Thus, P vector represents a candidate solution for the problem.

Generally, the bugs available in the repository may present different priority values assigned by the domain expert. Thus, the *importance(P)* function encourages an early resolution of the bugs with more *Priority* and *Relevance*. This function is calculated as follows:

$$importance(P) = \sum_{i=1}^{N} \left[\frac{priority_i + relevance_i}{2} \times (M - pos(P, b_i) + 1) \times isIn(P, b_i) \right] \tag{2}$$

where $priority_i$ indicates the *Priority* value given by the expert domain for a bug b_i and $relevance_i$ represents the community feedback about the bug b_i. Both values of $priority_i$ and $relevance_i$ are expressed by $x = \{x \in \mathbb{R} | 0 \le x \le 1\}$. Function $isIn(P, b_i)$ indicates when b_i is in P, it returns 1 if $b_i \in P$, otherwise 0. Thus, given the maximization context, as bugs with high *Priority* and *Relevance* values are in the first positions of P, the higher *importance(p)* value.

On the other hand, the *risk(P)* function encourages an early resolution of bugs specified as more severe by the community. The higher the *Severity* value from a bug, the earlier should be its correction. Basically, we aim at minimizing the risk of later resolution of the most severe bugs. This function is given by:

$$risk(P) = \sum_{i=1}^{N} severity_i \times pos(P, b_i) \times isIn(P, b_i) \tag{3}$$

where $severity_i$ is a value assigned during the report step and can be given by any member of the community. Similarly to the $priority_i$ and $relevance_i$ values, the $severity_i$ must be expressed by $x = \{x \in \mathbb{R} | 0 \le x \le 1\}$. Hence, the $risk(P)$

function is directly impacted by the bugs positioning in P and, consequently, its values decrease by allocations of bugs with high *Severity* at first positions of P.

As previously discussed, we propose a strategy to mitigate the developer's effort in selecting a solution from the Pareto Front. A simple strategy could be the selection of a solution that balances both objectives, looking for minimizing the losses of the two axis of search space. However, there is no confidence that the selected solution is properly suited to the developer's experience.

The **Recommendation Stage** consists of selecting a solution from the Pareto Front aiming at increasing the compatibility between the developer's experience rate and the *Experience Level* required to fix the bug. In other words, given a developer, it is recommended a solution composed of bugs more likely to be chosen/resolved by him/her. We consider *experience* as the ratio between the number of bugs resolved by a developer in a specific area of the system and the total number of bugs fixed by him/her. Thus, two important pieces of information are required to achieve the recommendation process: (i) the developer's historical contribution to verify the areas of the system in which he/she usually cooperates and (ii) the *Experience Level* required by a bug to be resolved.

Consider $C = \{c_1, c_2, c_3, \cdots, c_D\}$ the set of all areas of the system in which a bug b_i may belong to, where D is the total of areas. Consider $H_d = \{h_1, h_2, h_3, \cdots, h_D\}$ the set of developers' experience in each software area, where $h_i = \{x \in \mathbb{R} | 0 \leq x \leq 1\}$ represents how experient is a developer d in the area c_i. Also consider $E_b = \{e_1, e_2, e_3, \cdots, e_D\}$ as the set of *Experience Level* values needed to resolve a bug b in which is assigned by the domain expert, where $e_i = \{x \in \mathbb{R} | 0 \leq x \leq 1\}$ represents the *Experience Level* required by a bug b_i in software area c_i. Hence, the compatibility between the developer's experience and the *Experience Level* is given by:

$$compatibility(P, C, H_d, E_b) =$$

$$\left[\frac{(M+1)M}{2} \right] - \left\{ \sum_{i=1}^{M} \left[\sqrt{\sum_{j=1}^{D} (e_j - h_j)^2 \times req(b_i, e_j)} \right] \times (M - i + 1) \right\} \quad (4)$$

where M is the number of bugs in the solution P. The $req(b_i, e_j)$ function indicates whether a bug b_i requires or not some experience in the area c_j, returning 1 if $e_j > 0$, otherwise 0.

As can be seen, the $compatibility(P, C, H_d, E_b)$ function calculates the euclidean distance [18] between values of experience required by a bug b_i and values of developer's experience, both measures related to an area c_j. Then, the result is multiplied by the complement of bug position at P, so that distances in bugs allocated at first positions have a negative impact more significant for the solution. Thus, as higher value obtained by $compatibility(P, C, H_d, E_b)$ function, more compatible is the suggested set of bugs to the developer's experience.

4   Empirical Study

In this section, we discuss how the empirical study was conducted, the achieved results and, finally, the threats to validity.

4.1   Experimental Design

The instance set employed in this empirical study is composed of real-world and artificial data. The real-world instance was based on the Kate Editor bugs repository. We collect those bugs that could be fixed by the developers until February 19th, 2016, whose status are unconfirmed, confirmed and reopened. At the end, it was identified that a total of 280 bugs were able to be prioritized.

As the information formalization suggests, the bugs repository have to provide four major informations to be used as an input to our approach. Analyzing the Kate Editor repository, we may identify as:

- *Severity:* when a contributor reports a bug, he/she must indicate the *Severity* value in which it belows. There are five nominal types: Wish-list, Minor, Average, Crash, Major, Severe and Critical. To allow data manipulation, we considered the five different nominal types as numeric values as follows: 0.1. 0.25, 0.4, 0.55, 0.7, 0.85 and 1.0, respectively;
- *Relevance:* to represent this information we used the number of votes, which represent the overall interest of the community to resolve a bug without a direct compromise with a technical perspective;
- *Priority:* when a bug is triaged, the expert domain assigns a *Priority* value expressed according to five nominal types, similar to the *Severity*. These five values are Very Low, Low, Normal, High and Very High and were respectively quantified as 0.2, 0.4, 0.6, 0.7 and 1.0;
- *Experience Level:* this information currently does not exist in the Kate Editor bugs repository and we had to simulate it. Following the constraints stated in the mathematical modelling, we randomly defined in which area a bug belongs to, as well as the *Experience Level* expected by each one. There are 16 areas established in the repository;
- *Technical Precedence:* this information currently exists in the Kate Editor bugs repository and it informs when there is a bug that either blocks or depends on the fixing of another bug. It is represented by a bug ID or a collection of bugs ID's.

As previously discussed, two pieces of information are necessary to realize the Recommendation Stage: (i) the developer's experience and (ii) the *Experience Level* required from a bug to be resolved. To obtain the first one, it was analyzed the developer's historical contribution and counted how many bugs each developer fixed in each of the 16 areas. Consequently, this data reflects in which area of the system concentrates on the experience of each developer. As presented earlier, the *Experience Level* was artificially generated. At the end, it was identified as a total of 508 developers.

Regarding the data extraction process, the number of votes was obtained using data scraping techniques, that consists of running through the elements from Document Object Model on the web page and obtain the required information. *Priority* and *Severity* values, *Technical Precedence*, and information about the developer's historical contribution, were obtained using a JavaScript Object Notation (JSON) API and querying to the Remote Procedure Call (RPC) server provided by the repository in which offers JSON format responses.

The artificial instance was designed to represent the data collected from a hypothetical bug repository of Scholar Management system. It was generated 100 bugs and defined three areas in which a bug may belongs: User Interface, Core and Database. Referring to the *Severity, Relevance, Priority, Experience Level* and *Technical Precedence*, we randomly generated these values following the constraints defined in the mathematical model.

The empirical study conducted in this work consists of two experiments: Artificial Experiment and Participant-based Experiment. In the first one, the objective is to evaluate the approach's behavior using different search-based algorithms, over artificial and real-world instances. Complementing this one, the second experiment aims at investigating the feasibility's proposal with a group of 5 developers. The participants have between 2 and 12 years of experience in software engineering, totalizing 32 years of experience, and an average of 6.4 years of experience per person. In a scale of 0 (low) to 3 (high), one participant rated at 3, three as 2 and one as 1, his/her practical software development experience. Regarding the software maintenance experience in a scale of 0 to 3, one developer rated his/her experience at 3 and the others indicated their experience as 2.

First of all, each participant was briefed about (a) the task they were supposed to perform, which were the chosen bugs to be fixed and (b) the scenario, tool usage and instance in which they would be working with. Only the artificial instance was used in this experiment, given the lack of domain knowledge of the participants with the software in which the real-world instance was based on. The experiment procedure was divided in three moments: (i) we require to the participant an estimation value about his/her experience in each one of the three areas (User Interface, Core and Database); (ii) aiming at simulating an usual bug repository, we show to the developer a list with the descriptions of all available bugs and we ask: "Given this list of bugs, if you consider fixing any bugs, which ones would you choose and in which order?"; (iii) finally, the approach was executed and solutions showed to the participant, in other words, a suggested prioritized list of bugs suitable to his/her experience.

Concerning to the multi-objective techniques to be compared in the empirical study, we investigated the NSGA-II, MOCell and IBEA. In addition, we considered the Random Search to be used as sanity check, as recommended by Harman [19]. For the experiments, the parameters were empirically obtained. For the four search-based approaches, we defined 100,000 evaluations as stopping criteria. Regarding the multi-objective evolutionary algorithms, we configured 250 individuals per population; binary tournament as selection method; 90 %

for single-point crossover; 1 % for bitflip mutation. Concerning to the external archive, we used 100 for both MOCell and IBEA. Finally, the feedback value required by the MOCell was configured as 20.

Moreover, the real Pareto Front is unknown to the instances evaluated in this study. Thus, we used the procedure presented by Zhang [20] to generate a reference Pareto Front (PF_{ref}) to be used in further performance comparisons. Considering 3,000,000 as the maximum number of evaluations, each multi-objective technique obtains a known Pareto Front for each instance and the best non-dominated solutions found are the respective PF_{ref}.

4.2   Results and Analysis

This experiment was conducted in order to answer two research questions:

- **RQ₁**: Which search-based technique, among the evaluated ones, produces better results regarding Hypervolume (HV), Generational Distance (GD) and Spread (SP) metrics?
- **RQ₂**: Can the results generated by PRBugs be said to be human competitive?

Aiming to deal with the stochastic nature and produce a fair comparison, each search-based technique was performed 30 times for each evaluated instance [21]. In the end, both quality metrics adopted in this work (HV, GD e SP) and the respective averages were collected.

Initially, we conducted a linear correlation analysis of the two objective proposed in this work: importance and risk. Generally, the goal is to quantify the association, investigate the relationship between these objectives and obtain a correlation coefficient to represent these particularities [22]. A correlation coefficient of 0.964 and 0.726 was obtained to artificial and real-world instances used in this work, respectively. These values imply in a very strong positive correlation, concluding both objectives addressed in the fitness function are conflicting.

Table 1 presents the average and standard deviation from the metrics values (HV, GD e SP) collected for each search-based approach evaluated, considering both real-world and artificial instances.

Hypervolume reflects the convergence and dispersion of the solutions regarding the Pareto Front. Thus, the higher the value of this metric is, it is closer

Table 1. Average and standard deviation of the metrics collected for 30 runs and different instances. Best values achieved for each metric are highlighted in bold.

Metrics	Search techniques							
	NSGA-II		MOCell		IBEA		**Random Search**	
	Artificial	Real-world	Artificial	Real-world	Artificial	Real-world	Artificial	Real-world
HV	**0.80±0.03**	**0.89±0.05**	0.78±0.04	0.80±0.06	0.76±0.04	0.86±0.05	0.12±0.02	0.24±0.03
GD	**0.00±0.00**	**0.01±0.00**	0.01±0.00	0.07±0.03	0.00±0,00	0.01±0,00	0.02±0.00	2.65E+06 ±1.06E+05
SP	1.04±0.07	1.60±0.10	0.81±0.06	**0.70±0.13**	1.32±0.05	1.41±0.13	**0.61±0.01**	1.50±0.00

to the PF_{ref} is the known Pareto Front. As seen in the Table 1, the NSGA-II achieved the highest average in HV for both instances, while the Random Search presents the worst performance. Analyzing the artificial instance, the NSGA-II was 2.6 % and 5.2 % superior than MOCell and IBEA, respectively. To the real-world instance, the NSGA-II outperforms both multi-objective techniques in 11.2 % and 3.5 %. The highest HV reached was 0.89 using the NSGA-II to the real-world instance and the lowest value was obtained by the Random Search with the artificial instance. Naturally, this Random Search performance is normal, since it is expected that the quality of the solutions generated by heuristics strategies is greater than those generated randomly [23].

Generational Distance contributes to calculate the distance between the known Pareto Front obtained by the optimization technique and the PF_{ref}. In this case, the lower is the obtained value, it is closer to the PF_{ref} the known Pareto Front is. Analyzing the GD values in the Table 1 we may identify the NSGA-II and IBEA results are the best ones and quite similar for both instances, being superior to the MOCell and the Random Search.

Spread denotes the diversity accounted in a known Pareto Front. How close to 0 this value is, more indicates a distributed and sparse set of non-dominated solutions. As the Table 1 reports, the MOCell reaches the best results for the real-world instance, being 43.7 % and 49.6 % to the NSGA-II and IBEA, respectively. Despite of the Random Search achieves the lowest value in Spread, the known Pareto Front generated is considerably outlying from the PF_{ref} as discussed in the previous analyses. Excluding the random results, the MOCell still outperforms the NSGA-II and IBEA for both instances.

Aiming to provide an intuitive visualization of the results, the Fig. 2 shows the known Pareto Fronts obtained by each search-based algorithm evaluated for each instance, as well as the values achieved by the metrics analyzed. In synthesis, there is possible to corroborate the conclusions previous discussed, such as the closeness of the NSGA-II to the PF_{ref} in terms of HV and GD, or the advantage of the MOCell in SP. In addition, we can verify the superiority of all heuristic approaches regarding the Random Search which suggests the proposed approach passes the sanity check as recommended by Harman [19].

Concerning to the statistical analysis, we followed the guidelines suggested by Arcuri and Briand [21]. We used the Wilcoxon rank sum test with the Bonferroni adjustment method to calculate the statistical difference considering a 95 % confidence level, while the Vargha-Delaney's $\hat{A}_{12}$ test was used to measure the effect sizes. The measures the probability that a run with a particular Algorithm 1 yields better values than a Algorithm 2.

Analyzing the HV metric in the Table 2, we may conclude that NSGA-II outperforms all other techniques with statistical difference. In all cases this superiority is higher than 60 % and, when specifically compared to MOCell, reaches higher values in 90 % of the time. Regarding the SP results, we may identify that for real-world instance, in 100 % of the time, MOCell achieves lower values than NSGA-II and IBEA, being this last one with statistical difference. On the other hand, the Random Search overcomes with statistical difference all results

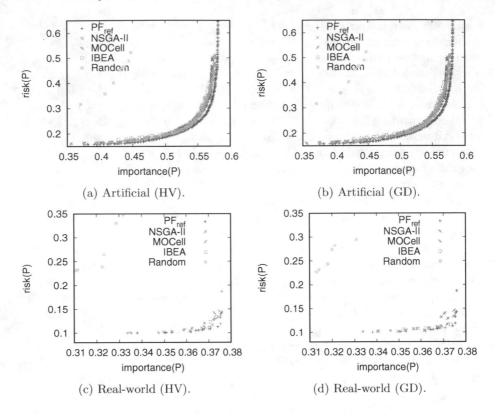

(a) Artificial (HV).

(b) Artificial (GD).

(c) Real-world (HV).

(d) Real-world (GD).

Fig. 2. Known Pareto Fronts for each instance and metric.

Table 2. Effect Size values obtained by the Vargha-Delaney's $\hat{A}_{12}$ test. Values in bold represent statistical difference considering a 95 % confidence level.

Algorithms	Metrics	Real-world instance			Artificial instance		
		IBEA	MOCell	NSGA-II	IBEA	MOCell	NSGA-II
MOCell	HV	0.22	–	–	**0.66**	–	–
	SP	**0**	–	–	**0**	–	–
	GD	1	–	–	0.77	–	–
NSGA-II	HV	**0.71**	**0.90**	–	**0.80**	**0.62**	–
	SP	0.89	1	–	**0**	0.99	–
	GD	–	**0**	–	**0.41**	**0.15**	–
Random	HV	0	0	0	0	0	0
	SP	–	1	**0.10**	**0**	**0**	**0**
	GD	1	1	1	1	1	1

reached by the remaining algorithms. Finally, investigating the GD, the NSGA-II outperforms with statistical difference the MOCell in 100 % and 85 % of the time considering the real-world and artificial instances, respectively. Comparing the NSGA-II with IBEA, there is no statistical difference between them evaluating the real-world instance and, taking into account the artificial one, the NSGA-II reaches lower values in 59 % of the time.

Complementing the previous results and analyses, we will analyze the human competitiveness of the approach using the results obtained from Participant-based Experiment. Table 3 shows the *importance* and *risk* values of the solutions respectively produced by the approach and the ones manually selected by the human subjects. We notice that PRBugs results outperforms in *importance* the ones manually selected by 4 of 5 participants. Regarding to *risk* values obtained from human-based solutions, only 1 of 5 participants achieved better results then those generated by our proposal.

To aggregate such discussion, Fig. 3 shows the average values achieved by manual and automatic solutions for each objective. As can be seen, taking into account the average results for all participants, the *importance* average values of the solutions manually obtained were less than ones achieved by the proposed approach. This result favors the approach, since greater *importance* values suggest that the more essential bugs are prioritized. In addition, we verified that *risk* average value from human-based solutions was higher than ones reached by the algorithm which is interesting, given that qualified solutions have to present lower *risk* values.

Table 3. Values of *importance* (*I*) and *risk* (*R*) achieved by the PRBugs and manually.

Participant	#1		#2		#3		#4		#5		mean	
	I	*R*	*I*	*R*	*I*	*R*	*I*	*R*	*I*	*R*	*I*	*R*
PRBugs	0.39	0.19	0.08	0.08	0.46	0.39	0.46	0.39	0.12	0.07	0.30	0.22
Manually	0.26	0.54	0.05	0.11	0.05	0.11	0.35	0.62	0.24	0.55	0.19	0.39

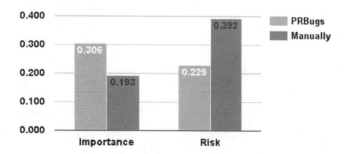

Fig. 3. Average *importance* and *risk* values of PRBugs and manually solutions.

Summarizing, the *importance* and *risk* values generated by the Participant-based Experiment strongly suggest that the results generated by the proposal can be said to be human competitive, in other words, the approach is able to generate potential solutions more accurate than ones manually selected.

Lastly, analyzing the Feedback Questionnaire fulfilled by the participants after the experiments, we may also point out some interesting insights. For example, a significant diversity among their adopted criteria. While a participant choose the bugs which they think to be more easy to fix, another one opted for the bugs which the description suggests to be more critical in technical terms. Regarding their inclination to use the approach in a real context of open source development, on a scale of 0 to 5, three participants rated at 4 and two at 3. When the participants were asked whether open source repositories would have to implement the proposed recommendation system, on a scale of 0 to 5, one participant rated at 5, three at 4 and one at 3. These feedbacks encourages the evolution of the PRBugs.

4.3   Threats to Validity

We discuss below the threats to the validity of our empirical evaluation, classifying them into Internal, External, Construction and Conclusion validity [24].

Regarding the Internal threats, we had to randomly define the values of *Experience Level* to the real-world instance generated, because this information does not currently exists in the Kate Editor bugs repository. Consequently, this decision may impact the bugs suggested in the Recommendation Stage. Despite of the parameters used in the tests being empirically obtained, a tuning parametrization would lead to better results [25]. In order to encourage the user engagement in the Participant-based Experiment, we present to each developer the major aspects of proposed scenario, including the prioritization task, tool usage and instance evaluated. Regarding External threats, we considered five participants, four search-based techniques, one artificial instance and one real-world instance, with 100 and 280 bugs, respectively. Replications on a wider range of repositories with a high number of participants are desirable to achieve more generalizable results. Concerning the Construct, we used metrics which has been successfully applied in several research work [26]. Referring to the Conclusion, to counter the stochastic nature of search techniques and ensure a fair comparison, each algorithm and instance was performed 30 times in the Artificial Experiment. In addition, statistical analyses were conducted in order to measure the statistical difference and effect size between the samples.

5   Conclusions

In this paper, an automated approach called PRBugs is proposed to prioritize and recommend bugs in open source repositories. This proposal does not intend to select the most skilled developer to fix a bug, but to suggest the most suitable solution to each developer considering his/her usual areas of contributions. Two experiments were performed and the results were able to show that (i) the NSGA-II outperforms the other search-based algorithms regarding the Hypervolume, while in terms of Spread, the MOCell solutions was superior. In addition, it was verified that the NSGA-II and IBEA were equally good in Generational Distance; (ii) The proposed approach can, indeed, be said to be human competitive.

Regarding the future works, we intend to include the concepts of Robust Optimization to deal with the uncertainties of the values used as input and to develop a strategy to automatically predicts which area a bug belongs considering its textual similarity to other bugs previously reported.

References

1. Sommerville, I.: Software Engineering, 9th edn. Addison-Wesley (2010)
2. Rajlich, V.: Software evolution and maintenance. In: Proceedings of the on Future of Software Engineering, pp. 133–144. ACM (2014)
3. Lehman, M.M., Ramil, J.F.: Software evolution background, theory, practice. Inf. Process. Lett. **88**(1), 33–44 (2003)
4. Bennett, K.H., Rajlich, V.T.: Software maintenance, evolution: a roadmap. In: Proceedings of the Conference on the Future of Software Engineering, pp. 73–87. ACM (2000)
5. Lehman, M.M., Ramil, J.F., Wernick, P.D., Perry, D.E., Turski, W.M.: Metrics and laws of software evolution-the nineties view. In: 4th International Software Metrics Symposium, Proceedings, pp. 20–32. IEEE (1997)
6. Anvik, J., Hiew, L., Murphy, G.C.: Who should fix this bug? In: Proceedings of the 28th International Conference on Software Engineering, pp. 361–370. ACM (2006)
7. Reis, C.R., de Mattos Fortes, R.P.: An overview of the software engineering process and tools in the mozilla project (2002)
8. Feller, J., Fitzgerald, B., et al.: Understanding Open Source Software Development. Addison-Wesley, London (2002)
9. Godfrey, M.W., Qiang, T.: Evolution in open source software: a case study. In: International Conference on Software Maintenance, Proceedings, pp. 131–142. IEEE (2000)
10. Harman, M., McMinn, P., de Souza, J.T., Yoo, S.: Search based software engineering: techniques, taxonomy, tutorial. In: Meyer, B., Nordio, M. (eds.) Empirical Software Engineering and Verification. LNCS, vol. 7007, pp. 1–59. Springer, Heidelberg (2012)
11. Dreyton, D., Araújo, A.A., Dantas, A., Freitas, Á., Souza, J.: Search-based bug report prioritization for kate editor bugs repository. In: Barros, M., Labiche, Y. (eds.) SSBSE 2015. LNCS, vol. 9275, pp. 295–300. Springer, Heidelberg (2015)
12. Anvik, J.: Automating bug report assignment. In: Proceedings of the 28th International Conference on Software Engineering, pp. 937–940. ACM (2006)
13. Kanwal, J., Maqbool, O.: Bug prioritization to facilitate bug report triage. J. Comput. Sci. Technol. **27**(2), 397–412 (2012)
14. Xuan, J., Jiang, H., Ren, Z., Zou, W.: Developer prioritization in bug repositories. In: 34th International Conference on Software Engineering (ICSE), pp. 25–35. IEEE (2012)
15. Raymond, E.: The cathedral and the bazaar. Knowl. Technol. Policy **12**(3), 23–49 (1999)

16. Konak, A., Coit, D.W., Smith, A.E.: Multi-objective optimization using genetic algorithms: a tutorial. Reliab. Eng. Syst. Saf. **91**(9), 992–1007 (2006)
17. Zio, E., Bazzo, R.: A comparison of methods for selecting preferred solutions in multiobjective decision making. In: Kahraman, C. (ed.) Computational Intelligence Systems in Industrial Engineering, vol. 6, pp. 23–43. Springer (2012)
18. Danielsson, P.-E.: Euclidean distance mapping. Comput. Graph. Image Process. **14**(3), 227–248 (1980)
19. Harman, M.: The current state and future of search based software engineering. Future Softw. Eng. 342–357 (2007)
20. Zhang, Y.: Multi-Objective Search-based Requirements Selection and Optimisation. University of London (2010)
21. Arcuri, A., Briand, L.: A hitchhiker's guide to statistical tests for assessing randomized algorithms in software engineering. Softw. Test. Verification Reliab. **24**(3), 219–250 (2014)
22. Deb, K., Saxena, D.K.: On finding pareto-optimal solutions through dimensionality reduction for certain large-dimensional multi-objective optimization problems. Kangal report 2005011 (2005)
23. Harman, M., Jones, B.F.: Search-based software engineering. Inf. Softw. Technol. **43**(14), 833–839 (2001)
24. de Oliveira Barros, M., Dias-Neto, A.C.: 0006/-threats to validity in sbse empirical studies. RelaTe-DIA, 5(1) (2011)
25. Arcuri, A., Fraser, G.: On parameter tuning in search based software engineering. In: Cohen, M.B., Ó Cinnéide, M. (eds.) SSBSE 2011. LNCS, vol. 6956, pp. 33–47. Springer, Heidelberg (2011)
26. Deb, K.: Multi-objective Optimization Using Evolutionary Algorithms, vol. 16. Wiley, Chichester (2001)

Search Based Clustering for Protecting Software with Diversified Updates

Mariano Ceccato[1], Paolo Falcarin[2(✉)], Alessandro Cabutto[2],
Yosief Weldezghi Frezghi[1], and Cristian-Alexandru Staicu[3]

[1] Fondazione Bruno Kessler, Trento, Italy
{ceccato,frezghi}@fbk.eu
[2] University of East London, London, UK
{falcarin,a.cabutto}@uel.ac.uk
[3] Department of Computer Science, TU Darmstadt, Darmstadt, Germany
cristian-alexandru.staicu@crisp-da.de

Abstract. Reverse engineering is usually the stepping stone of a variety of attacks aiming at identifying sensitive information (keys, credentials, data, algorithms) or vulnerabilities and flaws for broader exploitation. Software applications are usually deployed as identical binary code installed on millions of computers, enabling an adversary to develop a generic reverse-engineering strategy that, if working on one code instance, could be applied to crack all the other instances. A solution to mitigate this problem is represented by Software Diversity, which aims at creating several structurally different (but functionally equivalent) binary code versions out of the same source code, so that even if a successful attack can be elaborated for one version, it should not work on a diversified version. In this paper, we address the problem of maximizing software diversity from a search-based optimization point of view. The program to protect is subject to a catalogue of transformations to generate many candidate versions. The problem of selecting the subset of most diversified versions to be deployed is formulated as an optimisation problem, that we tackle with different search heuristics. We show the applicability of this approach on some popular Android apps.

Keywords: Software diversity · Clustering · Obfuscation · Security

1 Introduction

The latest BSA Global Software Piracy Study[1] states that 39 % of software installed on computers around the world in 2015 is not properly licensed, amounting to \$52 billion in losses due to unlicensed software; the same study shows that malware often spreads through unlicensed software distributed on the internet, causing a wider number of security attacks and consequent revenue losses. In particular, the 98 % of mobile apps lack binary code protection and they can be

---

[1] BSA Global Software Piracy Survey: http://globalstudy.bsa.org/2016/.

© Springer International Publishing AG 2016
F. Sarro and K. Deb (Eds.): SSBSE 2016, LNCS 9962, pp. 159–175, 2016.
DOI: 10.1007/978-3-319-47106-8_11

easily reverse engineered and modified[2]. Software vendors need effective solutions to contrast Man-At-The-End attacks [11], where the end user is the attacker, owning the device running the software, and able to reverse engineer and modify the code, in order to use and spread unlicensed copies.

Obfuscation is a common protection against reverse engineering, and it consists of semantic-preserving code transformations that make a program more difficult to understand by changing its structure, while keeping the original functionalities. A multitude of techniques to perform code obfuscation have been proposed [8]. From a security viewpoint, obfuscation can help software diversity so that an attacker can find more difficult to map critical code in one release to another one.

Diversified updates is a software protection technique that aims at mitigating the risk of such attacks. When a program is frequently updated with a different version, then an available crack can be used for a limited amount of time, until a diversified update is pushed. The deployed versions should be pairwise different from the ones previously deployed, such that an attack available for one version cannot be easily replayed on another version.

The open problem we want to tackle is how to determine whether the subsequent diversified version maximizes its own diversity with respect to the previous versions, mitigating the security risks by maximizing diversity.

In this paper, we propose a novel approach to generate diversified versions of the program to protect. These can be used in an update strategy aimed at limiting the time available to an attacker to be successful. Given the availability of a catalogue of transformations, first of all we propose a novel strategy to filter those that are not effective in achieving diversification. These transformations that remain after filtering are combined in all the possible permutations, to form the complete set of the candidate versions. Then, our second novel contribution is to formulate the identification of diversified versions as a clustering problem, to be addressed with search based optimization heuristics.

The paper is structured as follows. Section 2 presents our approach to generate diversified versions for updates. Then, in Sect. 3 we introduce our setting for the empirical validation, while Sect. 4 presents and comments the experimental results. Section 5 compares our approach to the related literature while Sect. 6 concludes the paper.

2   Automatic Generation of Maximally Diversified Versions

Software diversity aims at distribution of unique binaries, so that it become much less likely that a single attack will affect large numbers of targets, and as a consequence the impact of reverse engineering attacks will be reduced. The distribution of unique binaries also has the effect that attackers cannot simply

---

[2] State of Application Security: https://www.arxan.com/resources/state-of-application-security/.

analyse their own software copies to locate critical code in certain binary code sections, because such code might have been relocated in different sections due to binary code diversity.

2.1 Approach Overview

Our code protection technique based on diversified updates, consists in generating several structurally different (but functionally equivalent) binary code versions out of the same source code such that they maximise their pairwise diversity. This protection strategy aims at reducing the exploitation of reverse engineering attacks: a successful attack on one code instance cannot be easily replayed on a diversified update.

Our approach is composed of the subsequent steps:

- A catalogue of code transformations are applied separately to the program to protect, so as to generate several distinct versions of the initial program;
- These versions are analysed, to filter out transformations that do not work well on the current program;
- The remaining transformations are combined together (in all the possible combinations) to generate many versions candidate for updates;
- We measure the similarity among all the pairs of versions;
- Candidate versions are subject to clustering, to group in the same cluster all the versions that are very similar to one another;
- We select one version from each distinct cluster. Since the version selected in this way are different from one another, they can be used to support diversified updates.

2.2 Program Transformations

Code obfuscation aims at transforming a program such that it becomes much harder to understand and reverse engineer, while its observable behaviour remains the same.

Code obfuscation represents an available approach to generate versions with a high level of diversity, with the added value of thwarting code comprehension.

We adopted Zelix KlassMaster[3] a commercial obfuscation tool for Java and Android. Zelix KlassMaster provides several activation points for obfuscating Java classes. It also provides a way to prevent methods, classes and packages from being obfuscated, or to identify the portion of code to protect with obfuscation. The tool can be streamlined by the use of scripts, which make it very easy to automate.

Zelix KlassMaster supports 15 distinct configuration parameters to control which transformations are activated and how they are configured. Among them, 8 parameters supports binary values, other 3 parameters have three possible values each, and the other two parameters allow four values each. This means

---

[3] http://www.zelix.com/klassmaster/.

that, potentially, a total of $2^8 * 3^3 * 4^2 = 110{,}592$ distinct obfuscated versions can be generated using this tool, just by resorting to its different configurations. Moreover, the number of versions can be further increased by selecting the subset of methods and/or classes on which to apply the obfuscation (instead of the whole application), but this dimension is not investigated in this study.

2.3 Similarity Metric

To quantify the similarity between two versions, we rely on the Normalized Compression Distance (NCD [14])[4]. The formula used to compute similarity is shown in Eq. 1, where NCD is the Normalized Compression Distance and C_{rzip}[5] is the size of the compressed text.

$$S(v1, v2) = 1 - NCD(v1, v2) = 1 - \frac{C_{rzip}(v_1 v_2) - min(C_{rzip}(v_1), C_{rzip}(v_2))}{max(C_{rzip}(v_1), C_{rzip}(v_2))} \quad (1)$$

This metric is based on *rzip*, a lossless compression algorithm, to estimate the amount of common information shared among two documents. In fact, size reduction is achieved by removing repeated sub-sequences of bits.

If two versions v_1 and v_2 are very similar, the compression of the concatenation $v_1 v_2$ will not bring additional information and it will result in a size closer to the smaller of the two versions. Thus, the NCD distance will tend to zero and similarity (that is $1 - NCD$) will be close to 1.

Conversely, when v_1 and v_2 are different the size of the compression of the concatenation would tend to reach the sum of the sizes of v_1 and v_2, the distance will tend to one and similarity will tend to 0.

We base similarity computation on the textual representation of the Java code, obtained by executing the *javap* disassembler. We drop irrelevant information for disassembled code, such as constant headers, compilation info, comments, white lines and we replace the identifiers with labels. Eventually, we compute the similarity as specified in Eq. 1 using *rzip* as compression algorithm. We used NCD metric implementation with *rzip* algorithm because its history buffer is wider than gzip, which is limited to 32 Kbytes [5].

2.4 Filtering Twin Obfuscations

Many versions can be generated by blindly combining all the available code obfuscation transformations. However, some of these distinct transformations in the catalogue could generate programs that are not so different, so they should be detected and excluded.

Since transformations can be combined, let's call the transformations in the catalogue the *atomic* obfuscations. If we consider m atomic obfuscations, we can elaborate $n = 2^m$ distinct combinations of atomic obfuscations to deliver n

---

[4] Our approach is general, and it is compatible with any other pairwise similarity metric.

[5] https://rzip.samba.org/.

candidate *versions* for updates. Since the number of versions n is exponential in the number of atomic obfuscations m, we need to carefully select the m atomic obfuscation to keep, i.e. only the relevant ones.

When two atomic obfuscations are just small variations of the same transformation algorithm, or when they are two different algorithms that emit very similar obfuscated code (for example an atomic obfuscation only targeting and rewriting exception handling code may have little effect on an original application with few exception code blocks), it does not make sense to consider both of them for diversity. Including one of the two similar variants is enough, and the other can be considered redundant: we propose to apply a preliminary filtering to drop some of the m atomic obfuscations from the search space, when they are not promising as a diversifier component for the application. When two atomic obfuscations a and b are very similar to each other, we call a and b *twin* obfuscations.

Our approach to detect twin obfuscations and filter them out is as follows:

- We consider only the atomic obfuscations, i.e. each version is obtained by applying only an atomic obfuscation from the catalogue: in this way, we only obtain m versions;
- We compute the pairwise similarity of these m versions. Similarity values are stored in a similarity matrix of size $m \times m$. A value in the similarity matrix in the i-th row and j-th column represents the similarity between version i and version j;

  For each atomic obfuscation a, the a-th row in the similarity matrix represents the *signature vector* X_a. The signature vector contains the similarity values between a and all the other $m - 1$ obfuscated versions. The b-th element of this vector, namely $X_a(b)$, represents the similarity between code obfuscated with a and code obfuscated with b.
- Two atomic obfuscations are *twins* when their signature vectors are very similar, i.e. the two transformations generate code with the same values of similarity when compared with the same alternative versions. We compute the *twin value* $t_{a,b}$ between atomic obfuscation a and b as the square of the distance between their signature vectors X_a and X_b with the sum of squared residuals:

$$t_{a,b} = \sum_{i=1..n, i \neq a, i \neq b} (X_a(i) - X_b(i))^2$$

- When all the pairwise twin values $t_{x,y}$ are available (one for each obfuscation pair (x, y)), we sort them in ascending order to detect the most likely twins;
- We exclude the twins by excluding the atomic obfuscations with lowest *twin values*. Let us say that $t_{a,b}$ is the smallest value among all the twin values (first value in the sorted set). At this stage, we can exclude either a or b. To decide which one to exclude, we consider the next twin value $t_{x,y}$ (in the sorted twin values in ascending order). There could be three cases:
  - $(x = a) \lor (y = a)$: we make the decision to exclude a;
  - $(x = b) \lor (y = b)$: we make the decision to exclude b;

- $(x \neq a) \wedge (y \neq a) \wedge (x \neq b) \wedge (y \neq b)$: we make no decision at this point and we iterate. We consider the next twin value $t_{w,z}$ in the sorted list, and we compare a and b with w and z.

There are multiple strategies to decide when to stop excluding twin obfuscations. A possible strategy is to set a threshold and exclude atomic obfuscations whose twin values are below the threshold. Alternatively, we can set a target size m_{max} for the number of atomic obfuscations and stop filtering when this target is met, i.e. when $m \leq m_{max}$.

In this work, we opted for the second strategy. We set the upper limit to the number of versions n_{max} to 500. Therefore, the number of atomic obfuscations m is approximately[6] $9(2^9 = 512)$. Eventually, the number of pairwise similarity values k to measure is 130,816, in fact the distinct pairs of n versions are $k = n(n-1)/2$.

Anyway, this filtering strategy is required to keep the number of versions to generate and the number similarity values to measure limited to a tractable size. Anyway, the exact solution to the clustering problem is still intractable (see Sect. 2.5).

2.5   Clustering Based on Similarity

We formulate the problem of computing the set of maximally dissimilar versions as a clustering problem, as shown in the example in Fig. 1. Clustering is used to partition the available versions into groups that contain very *similar* versions, three groups in the example. Versions from the same cluster (e.g., in C_1) are very similar to each other, so they cannot be used in the same update plan. The final set of versions to be used as updates is selected by taking just one element from each high-similarity group, they are the black elements in Fig. 1. In this way, very similar versions are never used in the update plan. Clustering is driven by the similarity metric defined in Eq. 1.

Given a partition of all the available versions into similarity clusters, we define the *intra-similarity* A_i of the cluster i as the average similarity of all the pairs of elements in the cluster:

$$A_i = \frac{\sum_{v_1,v_2} S(v_1, v_2)}{|C_i|(|C_i| - 1)/2}, \quad \forall v_1, v_2 \in C_i \tag{2}$$

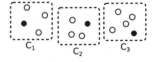

Fig. 1. Diversified updates based on clustering for similarity.

---

[6] The number of atomic obfuscations m can be actually larger, because some combinations cause an error in the obfuscation tool, or simply do not work. Thus, more atomic obfuscations are required to meet the target number of versions n.

We define the *inter-similarity* between two clusters C_i and C_j as the average similarity of the versions from the two clusters:

$$E_{i,j} = \frac{\sum_{v_1,v_2} S(v_1,v_2)}{|C_i|\,|C_j|} \quad v_1 \in C_i, v_2 \in C_j \tag{3}$$

Considering that our objective is to search for a clustering configuration whose clusters contains elements as similar as possible (high intra-similarity) and low similarity between elements from different clusters (low inter-similarity), we define the overall *similarity quality* among the clusters as the average intra-similarity minus the average of all the inter-similarity:

$$SQ = \frac{1}{n_c} \sum_{i=1}^{n_c} A_i - \frac{1}{\frac{n_c(n_c-1)}{2}} \sum_{i,j=1}^{k} E_{i,j} \tag{4}$$

where n_c is the number of clusters in the partition to evaluate.

At this stage, the software diversity problem can be expressed as a search problem, aiming at finding the clustering partition that maximize the similarity quality SQ.

2.6   Search Strategies

The analytic solution of clustering is intractable [24], because the number of potential solutions to the clustering problem is exponential in the number of elements to cluster. Considering that the number of candidate versions for update are hundreds of thousands, we adopt search heuristics. They are *Greedy agglomerative clustering*, *Hill climbing* and *Single objective genetic algorithm*.

Greedy agglomerative clustering: Agglomerative clustering is a greedy algorithm to find a candidate good partition in the search space. This algorithm starts from an initial configuration, where each element is assigned to a different cluster. At each step, inter-/intra-similarity are computed and the two most similar clusters (those with the highest inter-similarity) are merged to form a single cluster. This process is iterated and, at each step, the total number of cluster decreases by 1. The iteration terminates when all the clusters are merged in a single final big cluster.

During this process, we record the similarity quality SQ of all the visited configurations, and the one with the highest value represents the final optimal solution.

This algorithm produces candidate clustering configurations with decreasing number of clusters, in the interval $[0, n]$. However, solutions with too few clusters are not relevant to solve our problem, even if their similarity quality SQ would be very high, because not enough versions would be available for updates. Thus, we consider interesting only those clustering configurations with a number of clusters above a threshold, that we set to 10.

Hill climbing: Hill-climbing starts from an initial random configuration of clustering. At each step, neighbour solutions are considered and one of them is randomly chosen among those that improve the fitness function SQ of the current clustering configuration. This process is iterated until no better solution can be found in the neighbourhood. However, given the huge space of the neighbour configurations, only a subset of it is probed, and this subset is selected choosing 100 configuration with uniform probability among all the neighbour cases.

Neighbour solutions consist of all the clustering configurations that can be obtained from the current clustering configuration with an atomic change. An atomic change consists of applying one of these mutation operators:

 (i) Moving one element from a cluster to another cluster; and
(ii) Removing one element from a cluster and create a brand new cluster with just this element;

The search stops when no neighbour can be found that improve the fitness function or the search budget is consumed.

Single objective genetic algorithm: Genetic algorithms are a family of optimization heuristics inspired by biological evolution. A population of solutions is evolved by giving higher probability of recombining to solutions with higher values of a *fitness function*. The aim is to push the population to evolve and explore the part of the solution space with better and better values of fitness function. In particular, we adopt a steady state genetic algorithm. In this variant, offspring replace the parents at each iteration regardless of their fitness function [2].

In our case, the population of solutions is represented by clustering configurations. For a clustering configuration, the fitness function is represented by the similarity quality SQ.

The initial population is represented by 100 versions, including random clustering configuration. At each evolution iteration, we *select* 70 % of the population, using linear ranking selection with a selection pressure sp of 1.5. The selected versions are paired randomly. Each of these pairs of solutions undergoes *crossover* with rate of 0.5.

Crossover, consists in elaborating two brand new solutions (offspring), based on the two selected solutions (parents). Let's assume that the two parents, namely clustering C_1 and clustering C_2, contain respectively n_1 and n_2 clusters. Two cross points r_1 and r_2 are randomly selected, such that $r_1 < n_1$ and $r_2 < n_2$. Then, r_1 clusters are randomly selected from C_1 and r_2 clusters from C_2 to form the new C_3 offspring configuration. The remaining $n_1 - r_1$ clusters from C_1 and $n_2 - r_2$ clusters form C_2 are used to create the new C_4 offspring configuration.

At this stage C_3 and C_4 could be invalid clustering configurations, because they could contain repeated elements or they could miss elements, so they should be fixed. In case an element is repeated, one instance of the repeated element is randomly selected and removed. Conversely, if an element is missing, it is added to a random cluster.

In steady state GA, when crossover takes place, only offspring survives for the next generation while parents do not [23]. Otherwise, if there is no crossover, the parents survive for the next generation. The offspring is subject to mutation with a rate of 0.03. Mutation operators are the same operators used to visit the neighbourhood in hill climbing search strategy.

The search stops when the search budget is consumed or when a plateau is reached, i.e. no improvement in the population after 100 iterations.

3   Experimental Settings

3.1   Research Questions and Variables Selection

Our experimental investigation aims at answering the following research questions:

- **RQ_0:** What is the interval of validity of the normalized compression distance?
- **RQ_1:** What is the distribution of *Similarity* among all the version pairs?
- **RQ_2:** Is filtering effective in discarding useless obfuscations?
- **RQ_3:** How many diversified versions can be identified by the search heuristics?

RQ_0 is a sanity check, to verify that we are using the metric in the correct interval of validity. RQ_1 aims at studying how values of Similarity are spread. Then, RQ_2 is intended to validate the filtering procedure that we proposed. We adopted a filtering procedure to control the (exponential) number of versions to consider, by excluding those obfuscations that are not effective in generating diversified versions. Eventually, the last research question RQ_3 directly compares the search strategies, to identify the most effective to solve the software diversity problem.

To answer these research questions, we measure and collect the following variables:

- *Similarity:* the similarity among version pairs based on the compression size (as defined in Sect. 2.3);
- *Similarity Quality:* the fitness function (as defined in Sect. 2.5) to compare clustering configurations; and
- *Number of Clusters:* how many clusters are in a clustering configuration. This number corresponds to the number of diversified versions that can be used as diversified updates.

3.2   Experimental Procedure

The empirical investigation is conducted according to the following experimental procedure:

- The original version of an app (as it is distributed by the apps market) is subject to all the atomic obfuscation transformations available in Zelix Klass-Master (no combinations of obfuscations);

- Twin obfuscations are then detected and excluded for this particular app;
- The remaining atomic obfuscation transformations are applied to the app, in all the possible combinations, resulting in the versions candidate for diversified updates;
- Pairwise similarity is computed among all the pairs of these versions;
- The search heuristics (agglomerative clustering, hill climbing and genetic algorithm) are applied to compute optimal clustering based on similarity.

Agglomerative clustering is a deterministic algorithm and it requires a fixed number of fitness function evaluations, that is equal to the number of versions to group into the clusters. Conversely, hill climbing and genetic algorithm are non-deterministic, so we set a search budget: in particular, they are stopped after 100.000 fitness function evaluations or when a plateau (a local optimum) is detected.

3.3   Subject Apps

We apply the experimental procedure on several real world Android apps. We select 10 from the most popular apps as ranked in the official Android store, namely Google Play (data collected in 2013). They spread on different categories (utility, social network, games, voip, internet browser) and their popularity goes from half a million to 500 millions of downloads. Their size is between 100 kB to almost 10 MB. The smallest apps contain about 200 classes, while the largest apps contain about 10,000 classes.

Despite we selected popular apps from different categories, they could be prone to the app sampling problem [22]. This represents a threat to the external validity of our results. Only replications of this study with more apps would confirm or disprove our findings.

4   Results

4.1   RQ0: Validity of the Normalized Compression Distance

As shown by Cebrián et al. [5], metrics based on the Normalized Compression Distance provide reliable results in an limited interval. In particular, NCD metrics give unreliable results when size of the file to compress is lager than the sliding window used by the compression algorithm. For example, Cebrián et al. reports that *gzip* can be used for files up to 32 Kb.

Here we adopt a validation procedure similar to the one used by Cebrián et al., i.e. we study the *idempotency* property of NCD based on *rzip* that requires $NCD(x,x) = 0$. We take a large text file and we truncate it to have a shorter file x. Then we plot $NCD(x,x)$ for increasing size of x, from 0 to 1 GB with steps of 16 MB.

Results are shown in Fig. 2, left-hand side plot. The most interesting region is highlighted in yellow and detailed in the right-hand side plot. The idempotency

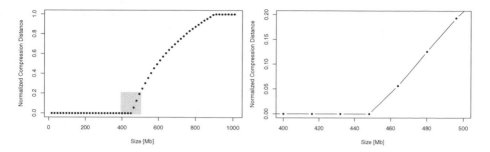

Fig. 2. Interval of validity of the Normalized Compression Distance. (Color figure online)

property (zero distance between x and x) is satisfied when the size of files is lower than 448 MB. NCD values are not reliable for larger files.

For the subsequent experiments, the size of decompiled code will be lower than 20 MB, so the NCD metric is used in its interval of validity.

4.2 RQ1: Distribution of Similarity

First of all, we examine the distribution of the values of similarity. Figure 3 show the histogram of *Similarity* for *Skype*. The histogram contains all the versions, after filtering twin obfuscations, for approximately 130,000 pairs.

As we can see, values of similarity are clustered in two groups. A first group that contains quite dissimilar pairs is centred in 0.4, ranging mostly in the interval $[0.1, 0.5]$. The second group contains quite similar pairs and it is centred in 0.8. Probably, diversified updates will be selected among versions whose similarity falls in the first group.

4.3 RQ2: Effectiveness of Filtering

Table 1 shows which atomic obfuscations remain after applying filtering, more precisely, which atomic obfuscations are combined to diversify the code. A check mark shows when an atomic obfuscation (column) passes filtering and so it is used to generated candidate diversified versions for a case study (row). The last row summarizes on how many apps each obfuscation has been applied. As we can see, the set of obfuscations that passes filtering is quite different among different apps. Some obfuscations are applied to most of the case studies (two obfuscations are applied to all 10 apps, an obfuscation to 9 apps and four obfuscations are applied to 8 apps), while others are used less frequently (one obfuscation is applied on 2 apps and two obfuscations are applied to 3 apps).

This suggests that the filtering step is quite app dependent, because the effectiveness of atomic obfuscation transformations in diversifying the code indeed depends on the code to transform. Thus, there is no universal rule on what atomic obfuscations to adopt in general when diversifying the code. The filtering step shall be repeated for each app that we want to diversify.

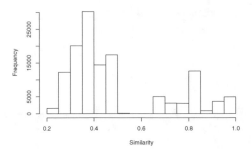

Fig. 3. Histogram of similarity in Skype.

Table 1. Obfuscation transformations that pass filtering.

App	Atomic obfuscations															
	1	2	3	4	5	6	7	8	9	10	11	12	13	14	15	16
airdroid	√		√		√	√	√		√	√	√	√		√	√	√
chrome	√	√	√		√		√				√	√	√		√	√
contacts	√	√	√	√			√	√			√	√	√		√	√
esx-filexplorer	√		√	√	√					√	√	√	√		√	√
facebook	√		√		√		√		√		√	√	√		√	√
gotetris	√	√	√	√	√		√	√		√			√	√		√
opera	√	√	√	√	√					√		√	√	√		√
skype	√	√	√	√	√					√	√	√	√		√	√
twitter	√	√	√	√		√	√	√	√	√	√	√	√	√	√	√
wordfriends	√		√				√				√	√			√	√
Total	10	6	9	7	7	2	7	3	3	7	8	8	8	4	8	10

It should be noted that this filtering step is fully automatic, based on the algorithm presented in Sect. 2.4.

Due to the fact that the obfuscation tool Zelix KlassMaster (that we do not control) fails to generate certain configurations, the number N of the atomic obfuscations required to reach n_{max} combinations is different for different case study apps.

4.4   RQ3: Diversified Versions

After filtering twin obfuscations, we applied the three search heuristics to the subject apps, to see how many diversified versions they are able to identify.

Table 2 compares the results of the three search heuristics on the 10 apps, relevant values are highlighted in boldface. We observe negative values of similarity quality SQ when, according to Eq. 4, the inter-similarity term $E_{i,j}$ prevails on the intra-similarity term A_i.

Table 2. Results of clustering.

App	Agglomerative clust.		Hill climbing		Genetic algorithm	
	SQ	N	SQ	N	SQ	N
airdroid	**0.3533**	13	0.3377	24	0.2093	**35**
chrome	**0.4547**	10	0.4148	28	0.2332	**35**
contacts	**0.5431**	15	0.4786	23	0.2447	**34**
esx-filexplorer	0.1637	11	**0.3193**	27	0.2068	**107**
facebook	−0.5674	14	**0.0017**	17	−0.1105	**27**
gotetris	**0.3927**	12	0.3711	32	−0.0346	**34**
opera	0.2934	16	**0.3854**	26	0.2360	**41**
skype	**0.4351**	10	0.4287	32	0.2502	**96**
twitter	**0.4337**	13	0.4255	24	0.2562	**41**
wordfriends	−0.5792	12	**0.0011**	10	−0.1991	**15**
Average	0.1923	13	0.3164	24	0.1292	46

Agglomerative Clustering was able to elaborate the most diversified versions for the majority of the cases (for 6 out of 10 apps), because the corresponding clustering configurations score the highest values of Similarity Quality. Hill climbing elaborated configurations that were always more diversified in the other four cases.

Considering the number of clusters, the Genetic Algorithm was able to identify the largest set of diversified versions in almost all the apps (9 out 10 apps). In two of them, the number of diversified versions was quite impressive (107 versions for *esx-filexplorer* and 96 versions for *skype*) however the corresponding Similarity Quality was low, but still comparable with the values obtained with the other two approaches. Hill Climbing elaborated optimal configurations with many clusters for the remaining app (i.e., *opera*). Eventually, the greedy algorithm elaborated large sets of diversified versions for no app.

5   Related Work

The concept of software diversity has interested researchers for many years [12], but only recently software diversity has become practical due to cloud computing enabling the computational power to perform massive diversification [19]. In the existing literature [1, 10, 13, 17], software diversity relied on random generation of different diversified copies, starting from the same source code. A recent survey from Larsen et al. [20] compares the different approaches for software diversity in terms of performance and security.

Most of the past software diversity approaches have been based on some form of obfuscation [7], load-time binary transformation [18], virtualization obfuscation based on customized virtual machines [16], or operating system randomization [31]. Current software diversity approaches exploit the intrinsic randomness of compiler optimizations, extending the initial idea of Forrest et al. [12] of compiler-guided code variance. Other approaches rely on binary transformation based on a random seed [27], or multi-compilers and cloud computing [13] to create a unique diverse binary version of every program, and they apply such diversification for mobile apps [17]. The XIFER framework [10] randomly diversifies Android apps at load-time by means of a binary rewriter. However, such diversifier can be disabled or tampered with because it is running on the Android device and because the original app is available to the attacker before it is loaded and diversified by the XIFER framework.

A previous work by Anckaert et al. [1] applied regular compiler transformations (e.g., optimizations) in a stochastic manner to generate diversified binary code versions, with random seeds to vary compiler parameters. However, there is no guarantee that two versions generated with different random seeds will not converge to "similar" code. Anckaert et al. do not tackle the problem of measuring the diversity among the different versions, which is necessary for performing a diversity evaluation. Coppens et al. [9] apply binary diversification changing a random seed and they iteratively compare it with the previous one till they get a new version different enough from the previous version; however they search just one version, and not the best subset of versions like in our approach. Diversity has also been applied to improve security in different research lines: code randomization has been used to defend against code-reuse attacks [26], return-oriented programming attacks [15], code injection attacks [29].

The novelty of our approach is that we are the first to tackle the problem of searching the most diversified versions with meta-heuristics, to guarantee that the deployed versions will be effectively different from one another, basing on the similarity metric chosen. Similarity can be measured with source code metrics to detect plagiarism in text and programs [14], or binary metrics in antivirus systems [30]. Other approaches using search-based heuristics, like genetic programming, to achieve code transformation [21,28], but with a different goal, i.e. to automatically find patches to fix bugs. Portions of the programs are replaced by their mutated versions that convey different semantics: mutation continues until the bugs are fixed and all test cases pass. In software diversity instead, we do not change the semantics of the program, but only its structure. Interesting developments can investigate the use of similarity metrics based on clone detection [3], which detects code shared by two software versions, or software birthmark [25], which compares intrinsic software properties rather than binary code structure. Other works [4,6] evaluated the code complexity introduced by different obfuscation algorithms by using structural metrics, that should be instead kept low in refactoring.

6   Conclusion

In this work, we tackle the problem of maximizing software diversity by searching the best subset of diversified code versions to be deployed in parallel or within an update plan. Many candidate diversified versions are generated using combinations of off-the-shelf obfuscation transformations, which can generate a huge number of possible versions; we proposed an algorithm to reduce the number of versions to generate, by discarding redundant obfuscations for the particular application code, and then we use clustering to identify the most different versions to deploy. The empirical assessment shows that our approach works in diversifying 10 popular Android apps.

As future work, we intend to investigate alternative metrics to compute similarity in a way that approximate more appropriately program difference from an attacker point of view. Moreover, we intend to conduct a user study where we measure the actual learning effect when attacking two consecutive versions. The aim of this study would be to quantify for real the effort required to adapt an attack when receiving an update.

Acknowledgement. The authors want to thank Prof. Mark Harman who was involved in the initial stages of this work, and contributed by suggesting the use of clustering for this search problem. This research has been funded by the European Union 7th Framework Programme (FP7/2007-2013), under grant agreement number 609734 - ASPIRE project (Advanced Software Protection: Integration Research and Exploitation), http://www.aspire-fp7.eu/.

References

1. Anckaert, B., De Sutter, B., De Bosschere, K.: Software piracy prevention through diversity. In: Proceedings of the 4th ACM workshop on Digital Rights Management, pp. 63–71. ACM (2004)
2. Arcuri, A., Fraser, G.: On parameter tuning in search based software engineering. In: Cohen, M.B., Ó Cinnéide, M. (eds.) SSBSE 2011. LNCS, vol. 6956, pp. 33–47. Springer, Heidelberg (2011)
3. Bellon, S., Koschke, R., Antoniol, G., Krinke, J., Merlo, E.: Comparison and evaluation of clone detection tools. IEEE Trans. Softw. Eng. **33**(9), 577–591 (2007)
4. Capiluppi, A., Falcarin, P., Boldyreff, C.: Code defactoring: evaluating the effectiveness of java obfuscations. In: Proceedings of the 19th Working Conference on Reverse Engineering, WCRE 2012, pp. 71–80. IEEE (2012)
5. Cebrián, M., Alfonseca, M., Ortega, A., et al.: Common pitfalls using the normalized compression distance: what to watch out for in a compressor. Commun. Inf. Syst. **5**(4), 367–384 (2005)
6. Ceccato, M., Capiluppi, A., Falcarin, P., Boldyreff, C.: A large study on the effect of code obfuscation on the quality of java code. Empirical Softw. Eng. **20**(6), 1486–1524 (2015)
7. Cohen, F.B.: Operating system protection through program evolution. Comput. Secur. **12**(6), 565–584 (1993)
8. Collberg, C., Nagra, J.: Surreptitious Software: Obfuscation, Watermarking, and Tamperproofing for Software Protection. Addison-Wesley Professional, Boston (2009)
9. Coppens, B., De Sutter, B., Maebe, J.: Feedback-driven binary code diversification. ACM Trans. Archit. Code Optim. **9**(4), 24:1–24:26 (2013)
10. Davi, L., Dmitrienko, A., Nürnberger, S., Sadeghi, A.R.: XIFER: a software diversity tool against code-reuse attacks. In: 4th ACM International Workshop on Wireless of the Students, by the Students, for the Students (S3 2012), August 2012

11. Falcarin, P., Collberg, C., Atallah, M., Jakubowski, M.: Guest editors' introduction: software protection. IEEE Softw. **28**(2), 24–27 (2011)
12. Forrest, S., Somayaji, A., Ackley, D.H.: Building diverse computer systems. In: The Sixth Workshop on Hot Topics in Operating Systems, pp. 67–72, May 1997
13. Franz, M.: E unibus pluram: massive-scale software diversity as a defense mechanism. In: Proceedings of the 2010 Workshop on New Security Paradigms, pp. 7–16. ACM (2010)
14. Freire, M., Cebrian, M., del Rosal, E.: Uncovering plagiarism networks. arXiv preprint cs/0703136 (2007)
15. Gupta, A., Kerr, S., Kirkpatrick, M.S., Bertino, E.: Marlin: a fine grained randomization approach to defend against ROP attacks. In: Lopez, J., Huang, X., Sandhu, R. (eds.) NSS 2013. LNCS, vol. 7873, pp. 293–306. Springer, Heidelberg (2013)
16. Holland, D.A., Lim, A.T., Seltzer, M.I.: An architecture a day keeps the hacker away. ACM SIGARCH Comput. Archit. News **33**(1), 34–41 (2005)
17. Jackson, T., et al.: Compiler-generated software diversity. In: Jajodia, S., Ghosh, A.K., Swarup, V., Wang, C., Wang, X.S. (eds.) Moving Target Defense: Creating Asymmetric Uncertainty for Cyber Threats, Advances in Information Security. Advances in Information Security, vol. 54, pp. 77–98. Springer, New York (2011). doi:10.1007/978-1-4614-0977-9_4
18. Just, J.E., Cornwell, M.: Review and analysis of synthetic diversity for breaking monocultures. In: Proceedings of the 2004 ACM Workshop on Rapid Malcode, pp. 23–32. ACM (2004)
19. Larsen, P., Brunthaler, S., Franz, M.: Security through diversity: are we there yet? IEEE Secur. Priv. **12**(2), 28–35 (2014)
20. Larsen, P., Homescu, A., Brunthaler, S., Franz, M.: SoK: automated software diversity. In: 2014 IEEE Symposium on Security and Privacy (SP), pp. 276–291, May 2014
21. Le Goues, C., Nguyen, T., Forrest, S., Weimer, W.: GenProg: a generic method for automatic software repair. IEEE Trans. Softw. Eng. **38**(1), 54–72 (2012)
22. Martin, W., Harman, M., Jia, Y., Sarro, F., Zhang, Y.: The app. sampling problem for app. store mining. In: 2015 IEEE/ACM 12th Working Conference on Mining Software Repositories, pp. 123–133. IEEE (2015)
23. McMinn, P.: Search-based software test data generation: a survey. Softw. Test. Verification Reliab. **14**(2), 105–156 (2004)
24. Michael, R.G., David, S.J.: Computers and Intractability: A Guide to the Theory of NP-Completeness. W.H. Freeman & Co., San Francisco (1979)
25. Myles, G., Collberg, C.S.: Detecting software theft via whole program path birthmarks. In: Zhang, K., Zheng, Y. (eds.) ISC 2004. LNCS, vol. 3225, pp. 404–415. Springer, Heidelberg (2004)
26. Shioji, E., Kawakoya, Y., Iwamura, M., Hariu, T.: Code shredding: byte-granular randomization of program layout for detecting code-reuse attacks. In: Proceedings of the 28th Annual Computer Security Applications Conference, ACSAC 2012, pp. 309–318. ACM (2012)
27. Van Put, L., Chanet, D., De Bus, B., De Sutter, B., De Bosschere, K.: Diablo: a reliable, retargetable and extensible link-time rewriting framework. In: 2005 Proceedings of the Fifth IEEE International Symposium on Signal Processing and Information Technology, pp. 7–12. IEEE (2005)
28. Weimer, W., Nguyen, T., Le Goues, C., Forrest, S.: Automatically finding patches using genetic programming. In: Proceedings of 31st International Conference on Software Engineering, pp. 364–374 (2009)

29. Williams, D., Hu, W., Davidson, J.W., Hiser, J.D., Knight, J.C., Nguyen-Tuong, A.: Security through diversity: leveraging virtual machine technology. IEEE Secur. Priv. **7**(1), 26–33 (2009)
30. Wong, W., Stamp, M.: Hunting for metamorphic engines. J. Comput. Virol. **2**(3), 211–229 (2006)
31. Xu, J., Kalbarczyk, Z., Iyer, R.K.: Transparent runtime randomization for security. In: 2003 Proceedings of the 22nd International Symposium on Reliable Distributed Systems, pp. 260–269. IEEE (2003)

Test Data Generation Efficiency Prediction Model for EFSM Based on MGGP

Weiwei Wang, Ruilian Zhao[✉], Ying Shang, and Yong Liu

College of Information Science and Technology,
Beijing University of Chemical Technology,
Beijing 100029, People's Republic of China
rlzhao@mail.buct.edu.cn

Abstract. Most software testing researches on Extended Finite State Machine (EFSM) have focused on automatic test sequence and data generation. The analysis of test generation efficiency is still inadequate. In order to investigate the relationship between EFSM test data generation efficiency and its influence factors, according to the feasible transition paths of EFSMs, we build a multi-gene genetic programming (MGGP) predictive model to forecast EFSM test data generation efficiency. Besides, considering standard genetic programming (GP) and neural network are commonly employed in predictive models, we conduct experiments to compare MGGP model with GP model and back propagation (BP) neural network model on their predictive ability. The results show that, MGGP model is able to effectively predict EFSM test data generation efficiency, and compared with GP model and BP model, MGGP model's predictive ability is stronger. Moreover, the correlation among the influence factors will not affect its predictive performance.

Keywords: Multi-gene genetic programming · Extended finite state machine · Test data generation efficiency predictive model

1 Introduction

Software testing is an indispensable stage in software development process. It can effectively ensure the quality of software system and improve software reliability [24]. One of the most challenging task in software testing is test case generation [22]. During test case automatic generation procedure, its efficiency is a main emphasis that needs to be focused on, as it directly relates to whether this generation technique can be applied to the real industry programs.

Experimental work in software testing has generally focused on comparing and evaluating the effectiveness and efficiency of different coverage criteria on various source code levels [15,16,21]. Gallagher et al. [4] reported the factors, the number of test data variables being generated and the length of test path, which affect the performance of the test data generator for Ada software system. However, the paucity of the efficiency analysis on test data generation at the model level of abstraction means that the software tester has little knowledge

© Springer International Publishing AG 2016
F. Sarro and K. Deb (Eds.): SSBSE 2016, LNCS 9962, pp. 176–191, 2016.
DOI: 10.1007/978-3-319-47106-8_12

on potential factors that affecting the efficiency of test data generation in EFSM models. EFSMs are widely used in software modeling and a great volume of research exists in the area of state-based testing from EFSMs [3]. At present most researches on EFSM have focused on automatic test sequence and data generation [2,18,19]. The analysis of test data generation efficiency has profound guiding significance for test generation, but it is still insufficient and need a further research.

R. Zhao et al. [23] conducted an empirical study on 8 EFSM models to investigate effectiveness of the test generation approach and identified the key factors affecting the efficiency of test generation in EFSM models. Also they have preliminarily analysed the correlation between the influence factors and the efficiency. Furthermore, Jiang et al. [11] used a multiple linear regression predictive model and a BP neural network predictive model respectively to conduct the analysis of efficiency-factors for path-oriented test generation on EFSM. The experimental results demonstrated that, compared with the multiple linear regression model, the BP neural network is more suitable to build the predictive model. But the experiment also showed that the correlation between input variables sometimes may prevent the results to achieve convergence. In order to solve this problem, they adopted Principal Component Analysis (PCA) [1] to extract principal factors from all the influence factors according to accumulating contribution rate. Though PCA can eliminate the factors which have dependency with other factors, it leads to inaccuracy of the predictive model [6].

Due to inaccuracy of the predictive model, we explore a nonlinear regression prediction model which can be unconstrained to strong correlation among influence factors to analyse the correlation between the efficiency and influence factors. As stated above, some influence factors have strong correlation among each other, even multicollinearity exists. MGGP is a new nonlinear system modeling approach that integrates the capabilities of standard GP and classical regression [7]. A. Garg and K. Tai compared the performance of regression analysis, artificial neural network and MGGP in handling the multicollinearity problem. They found that MGGP regression can be more accurate and efficient than others for modeling nonlinear problems [6].

So, in this paper, we are the first to propose a new approach based on MGGP to predict the test generation efficiency. Namely the MGGP predictive model is established for test case generation on EFSM to inspect the nonlinear correlation between the test generation efficiency and influence factors. And then PCA are further used to validate whether the principal influence factors only can lead to inaccuracy of predictive model. In addition, considering GP and neural network are commonly employed in predictive models, we establish the GP model to be compared with MGGP model and BP model. The empirical study shows that the GP model has a better predictive ability than BP model and the MGGP model performs better than the others.

The primary contributions of this paper are as follows:

1. MGGP is firstly used to set up a predictive model for path-oriented test generation on EFSM.

2. PCA is employed to extract the irrelevant influence factors from original factors. And then these irrelevant factors are taken to build a PCA-MGGP predictive model. Experimental results show that MGGP predictive model is more precise than PCA-MGGP model.

3. Empirical study is conducted to compare MGGP model with standard GP model and BP model. The results show that MGGP predictive model performs better.

The remainder of this paper is organized as follows. Section 2 describes EFSM and MGGP algorithm. Section 3 introduces how to apply MGGP to establish a predictive model for path-oriented test generation on EFSM. Section 4 reports the experimental results and discussion. Section 5 gives the conclusion of this paper.

2   Background

2.1   EFSM and Influence Factors

An extended finite state machine (EFSM) model is formally represented as a 6-tuple (S, S_0, I, V, O, T), where S is a finite set of states, $S_0 \in S$ is an initial state named START, I is a set of input declarations, V is a finite set of internal/context variables, O is a set of output declarations, T is a finite set of transitions. Each member of I is expressed as event(input parameters) meaning event occurs with a list of input parameters. Each member of O is described as action. Each transition $t \in T$ is represented by a 5-tuple ⟨source(t), target(t), event(t),condition(t), action(t)⟩, where $source(t) \in S$ is the start state of transition t, $target(t) \in S$ is the target state, $event(t) \in I$ is an incentive event or empty, condition(t) is the preconditions performing transition t, and action(t) represents a sequence of actions [12,13].

A state transition t occurs when one of the machine's transitions is taken. If a transition t has a condition c on the internal variables and input parameters, then c must be satisfied in order for t to be taken [23]. Considering a test data required to traverse a feasible transition path, all the conditions, input parameters and actions in the path will influence test data generation. If the conditions are rare or easily satisfied and the input parameters and actions are simple in that path, test data can be generated effortlessly. Otherwise, test data will be hard to generate or the generation time would greatly increase.

As discussed in [23], for different feasible transition paths on EFSM, there is a very strong exponential relationship in EFSM test case generation, for example test generation cost and Length of Path with Events Variables (LPEV), test generation cost and Number of Numerical Event Variables on a path (NNEV). In those relations, LPEV and NNEV are called influence factors. The influence factors and corresponding marks in this paper are showed in Table 1. The first column in the table represents influence factors for path-oriented test generation on EFSM. The second column is the corresponding marks of influence factors. For example, in one feasible path of EFSM, the influence factors and their values

Table 1. Factors affecting test data generation of EFSM

Influencing factor	Representation
Length of path (LP)	X1
Number of variables (NV)	X2
Number of variables defined in event (NVDE)	X3
Number of variables defined in actions (NVDA)	X4
Number of variables used in conditions (NVUC)	X5
Number of variables used in actions (NVUA)	X6
Number of variables defined in event and used in conditions (NVDEUC)	X7
Number of variables defined in actions and used in conditions (NVDAUC)	X8
Number of conditions (NC): The number of nonempty conditions in a path	X9
Number of sub-conditions (NSC)	X10
Number of equal operators in conditions (NEOC)	X11
Number of numerical equal operator in conditions (NNEOC)	X12
Length of path with event variables (LPEV)	X13
Number of numerical variables (NNV)	X14
Number of numerical event variables (NNEV)	X15

are $\{X1 : 4, X2 : 5, \ldots, X15 : 2\}$. It means that length of the path is 4, the number of variables is 5 and so on.

2.2 MGGP Algorithm

MGGP was developed by Hinchliffe et al., and Hiden [6]. GP is a biologically inspired machine learning method that evolves computer programs to perform a task [20]. Unlike common optimization methods such as GA, in which potential solutions are represented as numbers, GP represents the potential solutions by structural based on so-called tree representation [14]. This property makes evolutionary process more flexible. The main advantage of GP over other regression analysis and statistical modeling techniques is having the ability of generating the mathematical expressions without assuming any prior form of the existing relationships [10]. The GP method automatically evolves the model structure and its coefficients [8].

MGGP is a robust variant of GP, which effectively combines the model structure selection ability of the standard GP with the parameter estimation power of classical regression. Instead of the complex rules and mathematical routines, the MGGP is able to learn the key information patterns within the multidimensional information domain in high efficiency. Recently, MGGP have been used successfully for engineering modeling problems, such as permeability estimation in heterogeneous oil reservoirs [14], materials and structural engineering [5], microbial fuel cell evaluation [9] and so on.

Specifically, the key difference between GP and MGGP is that, in GP model there is only one tree to represent the evolution formula, but the MGGP model participating in the evolution is the combination of several sets of genes/trees. Each of these trees can be considered to be a gene, which means each of them is a traditional GP tree. MGGP assigns weights to each gene to generate the final model as a linear combination of the sub-programs [17]. MGGP can be expressed as follows:

$$y = \alpha_0 + \alpha_1 gene_1 + \alpha_2 gene_2 + \cdots + \alpha_n gene_n . \tag{1}$$

Where α_0 represents the bias of offset term, $\alpha_1 \cdots \alpha_n$ are the gene weights and n is the number of genes (i.e. trees) that constitute the available individuals. These weights are automatically determined by the least squares procedure for each multi-gene individual.

MGGP algorithm process is presented in Fig. 1, where MaxGene and Max-Tree refer to the maximum number of genes and the maximum depth of trees in each of gene. They are set in advance, thus the complexity of predictive model can be constrained. When applying MGGP to a problem, there are five major preparatory steps. These five steps involve determining (1) the set of terminals, (2) the set of primitive functions, (3) the fitness measure, (4) the parameters for controlling the run, and (5) the method for designating a result and the criterion for terminating a run. The terminals can be viewed as the inputs to the as-yet-undiscovered predictive model. The set of terminals (along with the set of functions) are the ingredients from which genetic programming attempts to construct a computer program to solve, or approximately solve the problem. The set of functions are used to generate the mathematical expression that attempts to fit the given finite sample of data. Fitness is naturally measured by the error produced by the computer program. The closer this error to 0, the better the computer program. In the evolutionary process, reproduction, crossover and mutation genetic operations are similar to GA operations.

3   Approach

In this section, we will present detailed implementation of the predictive model for EFSM test case generation efficiency based on MGGP. So as to investigate the relationship between test data generation efficiency and its influence factors, we regard the influence factors as independent variables, the test generation cost as a dependent variable, then build a MGGP predictive model to forecast EFSM test data generation efficiency.

The corresponding values of factors that affect test generation efficiency on EFSM can be expressed as matrix $X = (x_{ij})_{m \times n}$ (i=1,...,m; j=1,...,n), where m is the number of paths, n is the number of influence factors, x_{ij} is the value of the jth influence factor on the ith path. Taking account of test generation

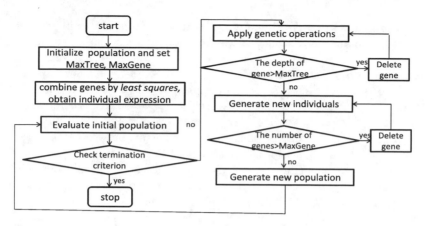

Fig. 1. The process of MGGP algorithm

efficiency on EFSM Y_i, we extend X to $X' = (x_{ij})_{m \times (n+1)}$, where $X_{i \times (n+1)} = Y_i = (y_i)_{m \times 1}$ is the iteration number of test generation of ith path on EFSM.

Influence factors and efficiency which are from early experiments are used to establish the predictive model. This model can forecast test generation cost according to influence factors. For one feasible path of EFSM, the correlation between test generation cost and influence factors can be expressed as:

$$y = f(x_1, x_2, \cdots, x_n, C)(i = 1, \ldots, n) . \tag{2}$$

where y is test generation cost, x_i is the ith influence factor, C is a random constant, and f is the mapping relation between x and y. The various forms of f are different individuals of MGGP. Each individual consists of some certain genes whose weights are automatically determined by the least squares procedure.

When MGGP is adopted to establish a predictive model, there are five key parameters as in Sect. 2.2 to be confirmed firstly. Therefore, firstly this section explains how to design the key parameters, and then describes the process of applying MGGP to predict test generation efficiency on EFSM.

3.1   Setup Parameters in MGGP

The Set of Terminals. The terminals set of MGGP generally includes input variables and random constants. The predictive model is based on the correlation between efficiency and factors of the known paths on EFSM. The main purpose of this model is to forecast test generation cost of unknown paths with given influence factors. Its input variables are specific values of influence factors that are included in Table 1. Moreover, during the modeling process by MGGP, test generation cost of the known paths on EFSM is used to guide the individual evolutionary direction. So in this study, the set of terminals can be designed as test generation cost and influence factors matrix $X' = (x_{ij})_{m \times (n+1)}$ and random constants.

The Set of Functions. As MGGP has the ability of automatically evolving the model structure and its coefficients, the functions set can consist of many functions in theory, such as basic mathematical operators $(+,-,\times,\div$ etc.), boolean algebra operators (AND and OR) as well as other defined operators. During the evolutionary process, the redundant function will be weeded out automatically. However, this will expand the search space of MGGP, thereby decrease the efficiency of MGGP algorithm.

As we know, there exists a nonlinear relationship between test generation efficiency and influence factors on EFSM. So the set of functions can join the commonly used nonlinear functions such as exp, $square$, log and $tanh$ and also basic mathematical operators $(+,-,\times,\div)$ had been used. Among these operators, $\div$ is protective division which means when the divisor is 0 the result is 0. exp is the exponent function whose base is e. log is natural logarithm function. $tanh$ is hyperbolic tangent function.

Fitness Function. The MGGP predictive model makes use of test generation influence factors on EFSM to forecast test generation cost. So, the expected value more approximate to the actual value means the performance of predictive model is better. Mean Square Error (MSE) can be treated as fitness function to represent proximity between the expected value and actual value of test generation cost on EFSM. The mathematical formula of MSE as follows:

$$MSE = \frac{1}{n} \sum_{k=1}^{n} (y_k - f(x_k))^2 \ . \tag{3}$$

In MSE formula, n is population size; y_k is the actual value of the kth individual; $f(x_k)$ is the expected value of the kth individual. The smaller fitness indicates that the expected value is more approximate to the actual value and the individual is better.

The Parameters for Controlling the Run. Some parameters make a big difference to the efficiency of MGGP algorithm, such as population size, number of generations, the maximum tree depth, the maximum number of genes, crossover rate, mutation rate and direct reproduction. In this paper, when using the MGGP algorithm, various parameters must be adjusted to increase the rate of convergence. These parameters are selected based on trial and error approach or some previously suggested values.

The Criterion for Terminating a Run. The termination criterion is the maximum number of generations or the threshold error of the model in the evolutionary process. When an individual fitness reaches the setting threshold value, it represents the best individual has been gained and the evolution process succeeds. When individual generation iteration reaches to the maximum number, it represents the evolution process fails.

Both situations above can be viewed as our termination criterion. If the individual meets the former, the MGGP predictive model for test generation efficiency on EFSM is successful. On the contrary, the predictive model fails.

3.2   The MGGP Predictive Model Construction

In this section, we propose the predictive model based on MGGP to forecast test case generation efficiency. The steps followed by the computing techniques to find optimal predictive models are generally similar. The specific steps to derive the model for path-oriented test generation efficiency on EFSM are displayed at Fig. 2.

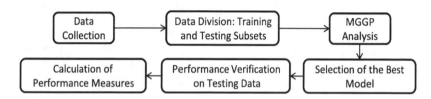

Fig. 2. Steps for developing a MGGP predictive model for EFSM test generation efficiency

Firstly, data of influence factors and efficiency from test generation on EFSM were collected. Secondly, the gathered database was divided into training and testing data. Thirdly, MGGP was run on the training data to find a computer program which can connect the input variables to the output (test case generation efficiency). Next, the MGGP model was chosen considering both simplicity and the best performance on the training data. Finally, the MGGP model was run for the testing data to prove its generalization capability when dealing with unseen data in its future applications.

The MGGP algorithm for modeling test generation efficiency in terms of influence factors on EFSM is described in Algorithm 1. The input of this algorithm is composed of influence factors and efficiency matrix . The output is the predictive value of test generation cost. Step 1 is to set the parameters for controlling the run of this algorithm; Step 2 is to define the set of functions; Step 4–6 describe the population initialization. That is to produce genes by terminals and functions randomly. The depth of each gene is set less than $MaxTree$ and the number of combination genes by the least squares procedure is set less than $MaxGene$. The combination genes are individual expression. Step 7 calculates the fitness of individuals in population; Step 8–15 express genetic operations and reproduction during iterating process; Step 16 signifies that when the population satisfies the termination criterion then return the final result. If the individual in the population reaches the fitness threshold, then it is set as the best predictive model. If no individuals reach the threshold during the maximum iteration process, then it represents the predictive model evolves abortion.

Algorithm 1. The MGGP algorithm for test generation efficiency predictive model

---

Input: Test generation influence factors and efficiency matrix $X' = (x_{ij})_{m \times (n+1)}$
Output: The predictive value of test generation cost $Y'_i = (y_i)_{m \times 1}$
 1: *set : runcontrol.pop_size, runcontrol.num_gen, MaxTree, MaxGene,*
       fitness.terminate_value
 2: *define functions*$\{+, -, \times, \div, exp, square, log, tanh\}$
 3: $t \leftarrow 0$
 4: *initialize Population(t) :*
 5: *generate genes randomly*
 6: *generate individuals :   combine genes by least squares*
 7: *fitness* $\leftarrow$ *evaluate Population(t)*
 8: **while** *fitness*$! = fitness.terminate\_value$ **and** $t <= runcontrol.num\_gen$ **do**
 9:       $t \leftarrow t + 1$
10:       *select Population(t) from Population(t − 1) :*
11:       *generate new genes*
12:       *generate new individuals*
13:       *alter Population(t)*
14:       *fitness* $\leftarrow$ *evaluate Population(t)*
15: **end while**
16: *Return results*

---

4   Empirical Study and Discussion

This section describes the details of experiments and results. The following research questions motivate our experiments:

1. RQ1: Does the proposed predictive model based on MGGP algorithm perform effectively to forecast path-oriented test generation efficiency on EFSM?
2. RQ2: Do the influence factors excluded by PCA have an effect on the effectiveness of the MGGP predictive model?
3. RQ3: Does the MGGP model outperform GP and BP model in their predictive ability?

4.1   Experiment Setup

Data Collection and Analysis. For EFSM, the previous work had conducted a substantial number of experiments for the 8 EFSM subjects. For each subject, test cases were generated by GA for potential (K) complete feasible transition paths (FTPs) [23] with different lengths. A large amount of FTPs property information and test generation cost were recorded. According to these data, we make use of MGGP to analyze the mapping relation between test generation influence factors and efficiency, and establish the predictive model.

The specific EFSMs we use in this paper are presented in Table 2. A sample data is composed by the corresponding values of test generation influence factors and cost for one certain path on EFSM. We select a number of sample data from

Table 2. EFSMs used in the experiment

Model name	The number of states	The number of transfers	The range of path length	The number of paths
ATM	9	23	[4,50]	2040
ATM-noexit	9	24	[5,50]	1901
Cashier	5	17	[4,34]	1450
Cashier-noexit	12	22	[5,30]	575
CruiserControl	12	21	[4,20]	814
CruiserControl-noexit	5	18	[4,30]	796
FuelPump	13	25	[11,50]	1999

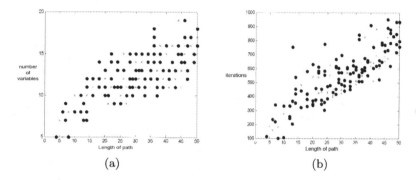

(a)   (b)

Fig. 3. Examples of data distribution based on Kennard-Stone algorithm

FTPs and split them into training data set and test data set. The training set consists of a set of data used only for learning. The test set is a set of data used to assess the generalization performance of a trained model.

The accuracy and generalization performance of a model is close to whether the training process is sufficient in the modeling procedure. So it is crucial to select training data set which can represent original data set. Kennard-Stone algorithm widely used can pick out the proper subset in the whole dataset. The subset data can be evenly distributed in whole dataset space. So Kennard-Stone algorithm is used to pick out 70 % sample data as training data. The rest of 30 % sample data is viewed as test data to examine the extrapolation and generalization ability of the models while only the training is used for formulating the models. Taking data distribution of ATM model as an example, the results are as Fig. 3(a) and (b). In these figures, "•" represents data points of training set, "×" represents data points of test set. As the figures show, training data set selected by Kennard-Stone algorithm is evenly distributed in given data domain. Its distribution can represent the whole dataset distribution.

The Evaluation Criterion of MGGP Model. To evaluate the MGGP predictive model generalization on the test generation efficiency, the performance of the model is expressed in terms of square linear correlation coefficient (R^2) between test generation cost on EFSM and the model output. The R^2 is evaluation criterion, and its formula is as follows:

$$R^2 = \frac{\sum_{i=1}^{n}(y_i' - \bar{y})^2}{\sum_{i=1}^{n}(y_i - \bar{y})^2} = 1 - \frac{\sum_{i=1}^{n}(y_i - y_i')^2}{\sum_{i=1}^{n}(y_i - \bar{y})^2} . \tag{4}$$

Where y_i' is the model output; y_i is the actual test generation cost on EFSM; $\bar{y}$ is the average value of all the actual test generation cost; n is the number of sample data. R^2 closer to 1 indicates that the expected value of test generation cost on EFSM is closer to the actual value. That is to say, the MGGP predictive model is better. On the contrary, R^2 closer to 0 indicates the MGGP predictive model becomes worse.

4.2   Experimental Design

To answer RQ1, we establish 8 MGGP predictive models on 8 EFSMs and compare the actual test generation efficiency with the model output on test data set. Furthermore, for RQ2, we establish two predictive models respectively for each EFSM to see through the effect of influence factors excluded by PCA clearly. One adopts original influence factors and efficiency to build predictive model, the other uses PCA to deal with original influence factors. In addition, for RQ3, we establish the GP model and compare MGGP predictive model with standard GP model and BP neural network model on their predictive ability.

4.3   Experimental Results

The Performance of MGGP Model. The MGGP predictive model is to analyze the correlation of efficiency-factors for path-oriented test generation on EFSM and forecast the test generation cost with given factors. The MGGP model established by original influence factors and efficiency on EFSM makes use of the test data set to evaluate its performance. Figure 4 shows the predictive effectiveness of 8 MGGP models for different EFSMs. The abscissa axis in Fig. 4 denotes the number of test data samples and the vertical axis represents test generation cost. We have normalized sample data. R^2 of each model can be calculated. R^2 of ATM, ATM_noexit, Cashier, Cashier_noexit, CruiserControl, CruiserControl_noexit, FuelPump, FuelPump_noexit are 0.92169, 0.9315, 0.88692, 0.92038, 0.87931, 0.93557, 0.97338, 0.89594. It can be seen that R^2 of overall test data in 8 EFSMs is close to 1. This indicates that the MGGP model is able to effectively predict test generation efficiency on EFSM. So the RQ1 has been answered.

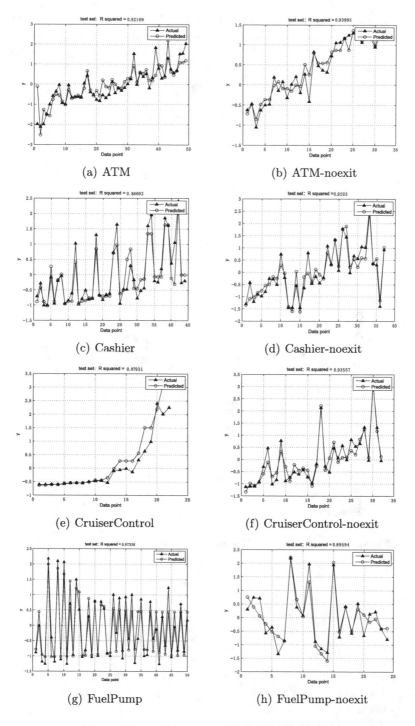

(a) ATM   (b) ATM-noexit

(c) Cashier   (d) Cashier-noexit

(e) CruiserControl   (f) CruiserControl-noexit

(g) FuelPump   (h) FuelPump-noexit

Fig. 4. The performance of MGGP on EFSMs

The PCA-MGGP Model & MGGP Model. To solve RQ2, a new MGGP model is further established with test generation influence factors extracted by PCA for EFSM. We call it PCA-MGGP predictive model. The extracted key influence factors of ATM are X1, X9, X10, X11; ATM-noexit are X1, X3, X6, X13; Cashier are X1, X2, X3, X15; Cashier-noexit are X5, X6, X7, X15; CruiserControl are X1, X2, X3, X5, X6, X7, X10; CruiserControl-noexit are X1, X2, X3, X13, X15; FuelPump are X1; FuelPump-noexit are X1, X10.

In order to ulteriorly compare the PCA-MGGP predictive model and the original MGGP predictive model, both models are used to conduct experiments on 8 EFSMs. The results are as Fig. 5. The abscissa axis in Fig. 5 denotes the different EFSMs and the vertical axis represents R^2. As the Fig. 5 shows, the original MGGP model achieves a larger value of R^2 than PCA-MGGP predictive model in every EFSM. It denotes that MGGP algorithm can be unconstrained to the dependency among influence factors and build a more precise model. Thus the influence factors excluded by PCA have an effect on the predictive model and can lead to inaccuracy of the prediction model.

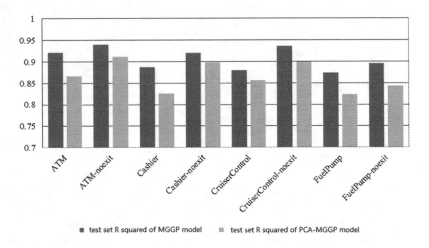

Fig. 5. Comparison predictive models of MGGP with PCA-MGGP

Effectiveness Comparison of Various Prediction Models. So as to further investigate the capability of the MGGP model in test generation efficiency prediction, the MGGP model is compared with BP model, GP model, PCA-GP model and PCA-MGGP model. The results are summarized in Table 3.

The first column in Table 3 is different EFSMs and the second column is different R^2 of test data sets on different predictive models. According to the experimental results, R^2 of test data sets on MGGP predictive model is generally closer to 1 than on other predictive models. Comparing BP model with PCA-GP model and PCA-MGGP model, we can see that genetic programming is better than neural networks on their predictive ability when using the same influence

Table 3. Comparison of PCA-BP, PCA-GP, PCA-MGGP, GP and MGGP

Model name	R^2				
	BP	PCA-GP	PCA-MGGP	GP	MGGP
ATM	0.8022	0.8576	0.8666	0.89232	0.92169
ATM-noexit	0.81295	0.87886	0.91118	0.90117	0.93995
Cashier	0.80241	0.81537	0.82535	0.85565	0.88692
Cashier-noexit	0.83271	0.86876	0.89762	0.89279	0.92038
CruiserControl	0.84139	0.84409	0.85703	0.86047	0.87931
CruiserControl-noexit	0.81237	0.89706	0.89998	0.90211	0.93557
FuelPump	0.79892	0.82385	0.82385	0.84399	0.87338
FuelPump-noexit	0.79893	0.85067	0.84335	0.88464	0.89594

factors to predict test generation efficiency. Compared with the GP model, the MGGP model performs better. The comparison results have answered the RQ3. It shows that the MGGP model notably outperforms those models and the MGGP model is more effective and accurate.

4.4 Discussion

During data preprocessing procedure, we define outlier as the data which has a long distance from corresponding average value of random variables. This distance is three times of the standard deviation. This is called 3 sigma principles. This method is widely used, but the existence of outliers can disturb computing the standard deviation. So this method may leave outliers and exclude helpful data. As the effectiveness of modeling method based on evolution algorithm depends on selected data set and data preprocessing, thus there is a need to further research on outliers.

In this paper, MGGP is used to establish predictive models for eight different EFSMs. Nevertheless, the scale of EFSMs is small. A problem that whether the EFSMs complexity influence prediction accuracy appears. Existing research shows that the prediction accuracy is related to the scale of training data set, the outliers, the missing values, features and algorithm itself. So we don't think the EFSMs complexity affect prediction accuracy. We will further conduct experiments to validate this question in the future.

5   Conclusions

In this study, we focus on test data generation efficiency on FTPs for EFSM. According to the FTPs of EFSMs, MGGP is adopted to establish test generation efficiency predictive model. The empirical study demonstrates that it is effective to forecast test data generation efficiency. In contrast with PCA-MGGP model, the results show that, MGGP algorithm can be unconstrained to the dependency among influence factors and able to effectively build a more accurate predictive model with the test generation original influence factors on EFSM. Besides, compared with standard GP model and BP neural network model on their predictive ability, the performance of MGGP model is the best.

References

1. Abdi, H., Williams, L.J.: Principal component analysis. Wiley Interdisc. Rev.: Comput. Stat. **2**(4), 433–459 (2010)
2. Anand, S., Burke, E.K., Chen, T.Y., Clark, J., Cohen, M.B., Grieskamp, W., Harman, M., Harrold, M.J., McMinn, P., et al.: An orchestrated survey of methodologies for automated software test case generation. J. Syst. Softw. **86**(8), 1978–2001 (2013)
3. Asoudeh, N., Labiche, Y.: Multi-objective construction of an entire adequate test suite for an EFSM. In: 2014 IEEE 25th International Symposium on Software Reliability Engineering (ISSRE), pp. 288–299. IEEE (2014)
4. Gallagher, M.J., Narasimhan, V.L.: ADTEST: a test data generation suite for Ada software systems. IEEE Trans. Softw. Eng. **23**(8), 473–484 (1997)
5. Gandomi, A.H., Alavi, A.H.: A new multi-gene genetic programming approach to nonlinear system modeling. Part I: materials and structural engineering problems. Neural Comput. Appl. **21**(1), 171–187 (2012)
6. Garg, A., Tai, K.: Comparison of regression analysis, artificial neural network and genetic programming in handling the multicollinearity problem. In: 2012 Proceedings of International Conference on Modelling, Identification & Control (ICMIC), pp. 353–358. IEEE (2012)
7. Garg, A., Tai, K.: Stepwise approach for the evolution of generalized genetic programming model in prediction of surface finish of the turning process. Adv. Eng. Softw. **78**, 16–27 (2014)
8. Garg, A., Tai, K., Gupta, A.: A modified multi-gene genetic programming approach for modelling true stress of dynamic strain aging regime of austenitic stainless steel 304. Meccanica **49**(5), 1193–1209 (2014)
9. Garg, A., Vijayaraghavan, V., Mahapatra, S., Tai, K., Wong, C.: Performance evaluation of microbial fuel cell by artificial intelligence methods. Expert Syst. Appl. **41**(4), 1389–1399 (2014)
10. Han, C., Wang, J., Zheng, M., Wang, E., Xia, J., Li, G., Choe, S.: New variogram modeling method using MGGP and SVR. Earth Sci. Inf., 1–17
11. Jiang, L., Zhao, R., Li, Z.: Analysis of efficiency-factors model of test data generation based on extended finite state machine specifications. J. Comput. Appl. **33**(A02), 229–234 (2013)
12. Kalaji, A.S., Hierons, R.M., Swift, S.: Generating feasible transition paths for testing from an extended finite state machine (EFSM) with the counter problem. In: 2010 Third International Conference on Software Testing, Verification, and Validation Workshops (ICSTW), pp. 232–235. IEEE (2010)
13. Kalaji, A.S., Hierons, R.M., Swift, S.: An integrated search-based approach for automatic testing from extended finite state machine (EFSM) models. Inf. Softw. Technol. **53**(12), 1297–1318 (2011)
14. Kaydani, H., Mohebbi, A., Eftekhari, M.: Permeability estimation in heterogeneous oil reservoirs by multi-gene genetic programming algorithm. J. Petrol. Sci. Eng. **123**, 201–206 (2014)

15. Lin, X., Pomeranz, I., Reddy, S.M.: Techniques for improving the efficiency of sequential circuit test generation. In: Proceedings of the 1999 IEEE/ACM International Conference on Computer-Aided Design, pp. 147–151. IEEE Press (1999)
16. Mahajan, M., Kumar, S., Porwal, R.: Applying genetic algorithm to increase the efficiency of a data flow-based test data generation approach. ACM Sigsoft Softw. Eng. Not. **37**(5), 1–5 (2012)
17. Mohammadzadeh, D., Bazaz, J.B., Yazd, S.V.J., Alavi, A.H.: Deriving an intelligent model for soil compression index utilizing multi-gene genetic programming. Environ. Earth Sci. **75**(3), 1–11 (2016)
18. Panthi, V., Mohapatra, D.P.: Automatic test case generation using sequence diagram. In: Aswatha Kumar, M., Selvarani, R., Kumar, T.V.S. (eds.) Proceedings of ICAdC. AISC, vol. 174, pp. 277–284. Springer, Heidelberg (2013)
19. Schrammel, P., Melham, T., Kroening, D.: Generating test case chains for reactive systems. Int. J. Softw. Tools Technol. Transf., 1–16 (2014)
20. Searson, D.P., Leahy, D.E., Willis, M.J.: Gptips: an open source genetic programming toolbox for multigene symbolic regression. In: Proceedings of the International Multiconference of Engineers and Computer Scientists, vol. 1, pp. 77–80. Citeseer (2010)
21. White, T.: Increasing the efficiency of search-based unit test generation using parameter control, pp. 1042–1044 (2015)
22. Zhang, J., Yang, R., Chen, Z., Zhao, Z., Xu, B.: Automated EFSM-based test case generation with scatter search. In: Proceedings of the 7th International Workshop on Automation of Software Test, pp. 76–82. IEEE Press (2012)
23. Zhao, R., Harman, M., Li, Z.: Empirical study on the efficiency of search based test generation for EFSM models. In: Third International Conference on Software Testing, Verification, and Validation Workshops, pp. 222–231. IEEE (2010)
24. Zhou, X., Zhao, R., You, F.: EFSM-based test data generation with multi-population genetic algorithm. In: 2014 5th IEEE International Conference on Software Engineering and Service Science (ICSESS), pp. 925–928 IEEE (2014)

Search-Based Generalization and Refinement of Code Templates

Tim Molderez[✉] and Coen De Roover[✉]

Software Languages Lab, Vrije Universiteit Brussel, Brussels, Belgium
{tmoldere,cderoove}@vub.ac.be

Abstract. Several tools support code templates as a means to specify searches within a program's source code. Despite their ubiquity, code templates can often prove difficult to specify, and may produce too many or too few match results. In this paper, we present a search-based approach to support developers in specifying templates. This approach uses a suite of mutation operators to recommend changes to a given template, such that it matches with a desired set of code snippets. We evaluate our approach on the problem of inferring a code template that matches all instances of a design pattern, given one instance as a starting template.

Keywords: Templates · Evolutionary algorithms · Recommender systems

1 Introduction

In program search and transformation tools, source code templates are a means to concisely describe source code snippets of interest. For example, templates can describe all instances of a particular bug, snippets that need to be refactored or transformed, instances of design patterns, ... However, code templates can still prove difficult to specify: when a user has little experience working with templates, or needs to write a larger or more complex template, the templates may not always produce the desired results. A template could be too general and produce too many matching snippets. It could also be too specific and produce too few matches. In this paper, we introduce a search-based [10] approach and a suite of mutation operators to assist users of EKEKO/X [5], a template-based search and transformation tool for Java.[1]

Automated generalization and refinement - When a template produces too few or too many matches, the EKEKO/X user can mark which ones are either undesired or missed, and invoke our search-based approach. It automatically looks for a sequence of mutations to the template, so it does produce *only* the desired matches. This approach uses a single-objective evolutionary algorithm

---

[1] The EKEKO/X program transformation tool and the extensions presented in this paper are available at: https://github.com/cderoove/damp.ekeko.snippets.

© Springer International Publishing AG 2016
F. Sarro and K. Deb (Eds.): SSBSE 2016, LNCS 9962, pp. 192–208, 2016.
DOI: 10.1007/978-3-319-47106-8_13

(EA). To evaluate this EA, we perform an experiment in the context of generalizing design pattern instances: the EA is given one instance of a design pattern, and is then tasked to find a template to match all instances of that pattern.

Mutation operators - A key component of the EA is its suite of mutation operators, which determine the different types of modifications that the EA can perform on a template. Important to note is that these mutation operators can also be used directly by the EKEKO/X user to edit templates. This provides two benefits: first, mutation operators can only be applied if they lead to a syntactically valid template, which prevents syntax errors. Second, some of the operators automate common scenarios such as abstracting away the name of a particular variable declaration and its uses.

In summary, after giving a brief overview of the EKEKO/X tool in Sect. 2, this paper presents the following contributions: Sect. 3 provides a suite of all template mutation operators. Section 4 presents our search-based approach to automatically generalize and refine code templates. Finally, Sect. 5 discusses the experiment to evaluate whether the approach is able to automatically find a suitable solution.

2 The EKEKO/X Program Transformation Tool

2.1 Overview

EKEKO/X is a program search and transformation tool for Java, where searches and transformations are specified in terms of code templates. A code template is a snippet of Java code, in which parts (corresponding to AST nodes) can be replaced by wildcards and metavariables, and different annotations called *directives* can be added. These constructs are used to either add or remove constraints to/from parts of a template. The process of *matching* a template involves looking for all concrete snippets of Java code that satisfy all constraints specified in that template. A simple example of a template is the following:

```
public class ...  {[public void toString(){...}]@[match|set]}
```

It describes any public class that defines a `toString` method. To abstract away the class name and the `toString` method body, wildcards (shown as "...") are used. A `match|set` directive is also attached to the `toString` method; it indicates there may be other class members beside the `toString` method. If the directive were absent, the template would describe classes that *only* define `toString`. In general, attaching one or more directives to a piece of code uses the following notation: `[code]@[directives]`.

EKEKO/X also provides support for template *groups*, in which multiple templates can be related to each other. An example of such a template group is given in Fig. 1. This example can be used to check the code convention that fields should not be accessed directly if a getter method is available. Any matches produced by this template group indicate a violation against the code convention. An example match is shown in Fig. 2. The group consists of two templates: the

```
1   public class ... {[
2     [private ... ?field;        // Field
3      public ... ... () {         // Getter method
4           return [...]@[(refers-to ?field)];}
5   ]@[match|set]}
6
7   public ... ... (...) {
8     [...]@[(refers-to ?field) child*]}
```

Fig. 1. Any direct field reference for which a getter is available

```
public class Square extends Shape {
    private int length = 5;
    public Square(int length) {this.length = length;}
    public int getLength() {return length;}}

public int area(Square s) {return s.length*s.length;}
```

Fig. 2. One of the matches of the template group

first (lines 1–5) describes a class with a field and its getter method; the second (lines 7–8) describes a method containing a reference to that field.

Aside from wildcards and directives, this example also makes use of *metavariables* (shown as an identifier starting with a "?"). These are logic variables whose values are concrete snippets of code. Directives can also refer to metavariables. In line 4, the `refers-to` directive has `?field` as its operand. Because the directive has an operand, it is contained in parentheses. The directive specifies that the variable in the return statement must directly refer to the value of `?field`. This ensures that the method in line 3–4 is the getter method of field `?field`.

The second template describes a method declaration, also using the `refers-to` directive to specify that there should be a reference to `?field` in the method's body. It also has a second directive, `child*`. This indicates that the reference to `?field` may occur anywhere in the method body (at any nesting depth). Without this directive, the method body's would consist *only* of the field reference.

2.2   Definitions

To define our suite of different mutation operators, we should first make some of the core concepts related to templates more precise:

Template - A template is a snippet of code, where parts can be replaced by wildcards or metavariables, and parts can be annotated with directives. To make this more precise, it is more convenient to define a template as a tree structure rather than a piece of text. In particular, a template is a decorated abstract syntax tree (AST), where every node is decorated with a set of directives.

We will refer to these decorated AST nodes as *template nodes*, or simply nodes. When referring to AST nodes that are part of the program being searched, we will call these *source nodes*.

Template group - A template group is a set of templates. Relations between templates in a group can be established as well: if a metavariable occurs in multiple templates, these occurrences all refer to the same metavariable. In the example of Fig. 1, the `?field` metavariable is used to link both templates.

Metavariable - A metavariable is a variable (in a logic programming context) of which the value is a source node.

Directive - A directive attaches additional constraints to a node. These constraints will be taken into account whenever the template is matched. A directive is always attached to one node in a template, which is referred to as the *subject*. A directive can also have operands, where most directives use metavariables as operand values.

Matching - A template group produces a match if a mapping is found between template nodes and source nodes, such that all of the template group's constraints are satisfied.

Note that, while this is not visible in the textual representation of a template, all nodes except the root implicitly have a directive (typically the `child` directive), which adds the constraint that this node should be a child of its parent. This is necessary to reflect the template's tree structure in the list of constraints.

Matching node - During matching, when a mapping is found between a template node and a source node, that source node is called the *matching node*. For example, there is a mapping between the wildcard template node in line 1 of Fig. 1 and `Square`, the corresponding matching node in Fig. 2.

3   Mutation Operator Suite

An operator, or "mutation operator" in full, performs a modification in a template group. An operator is always applied to one node, also referred to as the operator's subject. There are two types of operators: *atomic* and *composite* operators. Atomic operators only modify a single node in a template; composite operators may modify multiple nodes in multiple templates of a group.

3.1   Atomic Operators

An overview of all available atomic operators is given in Table 1, listing each operator's name and its operands, which subjects it can be applied to, and a brief description. We will then highlight a selection of operators in more detail:

Replace by variable (var) - The subject and its children are replaced by a metavariable node. Any directives present in the subject are preserved, except `match`. Additionally, a directive is added that will bind the matching node to the given metavariable (var). In the following example, the operator is applied to the "Hello world" string, such that the resulting template matches any `println` call, and metavariable `?arg` is bound to the call's actual argument:

```
System.out.println("Hello world");
```

$\Rightarrow$ *Subject "Helloworld", Operands* $\langle ?arg \rangle$

```
System.out.println(?arg);
```

Table 1. Overview of atomic operators related to program search

Operator	Subject	Description
Replace by variable (?var)	Any non-root, non-protected	Replaces the subject with a metavariable.
Replace by wildcard	Any non-root, non-protected	Replaces the subject with a wildcard.
Add directive (dir, operands)	Depends on selected directive	Adds a directive to the subject, with the given operand values.
Remove directive (dir)	Any	Removes a given directive from the subject.
Remove node	Non-mandatory child of parent, non-protected	Removes the subject node.
Insert node at (type, index)	List	Inserts a new node of the given type into the subject list, at the given index.
Replace node (type)	Non-primitive, non-root and non-protected	Replaces the subject by a new node of the given type.
Replace value (value)	Primitive, non-protected	Replaces the subject by the given value.
Replace parent statement	Statement in body of another Statement	Statement in which the subject occurs is replaced by the subject.
Erase list	List	Removes all list elements of the subject.

Add directive (dir, operands) - This operator attaches the given directive, with the given operand values, to the subject node. As there are several directives available, shown in Tables 1, 2 we only highlight a selection:

- `child/child+/ child*`- This directive relates the subject to its parent node x. In case of `child`, x's matching node is the parent of the subject's matching node. For `child*`, x's matching node is a direct or indirect ancestor of the subject's matching node. For `child+`, it is an indirect ancestor. Exactly one of these three directives must be present in every template node (except the root).
- `(invoked-by ?call)` - This directive adds a constraint that relates a method call to a method declaration. Consider that the subject is a method declaration in class x. This method declaration should be invoked by `?call`, a method call where the receiver's static type is x.
- `protect` - "Protects" the subject and all of its parents. If a node is protected, it cannot be accidentally removed or abstracted away, because any operators that could do so are now disallowed. This means the `protect` directive only affects the subject applicability of other operators, and does not add any constraints.

Table 2. Overview of the available matching directives

Directive signature	Subject	Description
`child,child+, child*`	Any	Relates the subject node to its parent template node x. The matching node of x is the parent (`child`) / indirect ancestor (`child+`) / ancestor (`child*`) of the subject's matching node.
`(equals ?var)`	Any	The subject now unifies with the given metavariable.
`match`	Any	Checks that the subject node type and its properties correspond to the matching node's.
`match|set`	List	The list elements of the subject must also appear (in any order) in the matching node's list elements.
`(type ?type)`, `(type|sname <str>)`, `(type|qname<str>)`	Type, variable declaration/reference or expression	The matching node should resolve to or declare the given type. (specified as a metavariable, its simple name or its qualified name)
`(subtype + /* ?type)`, `(subtype|sname+/* <str>)`, `(subtype|qname + /* <str>)`,	Type, variable declaration/reference or expression	The matching node should resolve to or declare a (reflexive) transitive subtype of the given type.
`(refers-to ?var)`	Identifier in method body	Matching node lexically refers to a local variable, parameter or field denoted by the argument.
`(referred-by ?expr)`	Field/var. decl. or formal method parameter	Matching node declares a local variable, parameter or field lexically referred to by `?expr`.
`(invokes ?method)`, `(invokes|qname <string>)`	Method call	Matching node is an invocation to the given method, considering the receiver's static type.
`(invoked-by ?call)`	Method declaration	Inverse of the above: matching node is a method declaration that was invoked by `?inv`.
`(constructed-by ?ctor)`	Constructor	Matching node is a constructor that was invoked by `?ctor`instantiation.
`(constructs ?ctor)`	Instantiation expression	Matching node is an instantiation that invokes the constructor `?ctor`.
`(overrides ?methdecl)`	Method declaration	Matching node is a method declaration that overrides the `?methdecl` declaration.
`protect`	Any	Prevents operators from removing or abstracting away this node

3.2   Composite Operators

The list of available composite operators is given in Table 3. A selection of these operators is highlighted in more detail:

Table 3. Overview of all composite operators

Operator	Subject applicability	Description
Isolate statement in block	Statement, cannot have protected ancestor	Parent is replaced by any block in which the subject statement occurs as a descendant.
Isolate stmt/expr in method	Statement/ Expression, cannot have protected ancestor	Method body in which the subject occurs is replaced by any method body in which the subject occurs as a descendant.
Generalize references	Local var., field decl. or formal parameter	Abstract away the name of a variable, both in the declaration and all lexical references to it.
Generalize types (qname)	Type, non-protected	Abstracts away all occurrences of a particular type (while preserving its qualified name).
Extract template	Any non-root, non-primitive	Extracts the subject into a new, additional template in the template group.
Generalize invocations	Method/ctor. decl	Abstracts away all invocations to the subject

Isolate statement in method - The method body in which the subject occurs is replaced with "any method body that contains the subject". This is useful in cases where we are only interested in one particular statement of a method. This composite operator repeatedly applies the "Replace parent statement"-operator, until the statement appears directly in the method body. All other statements are removed from the body, and a `match|set` is added. Finally, a `child*` is added to the subject. This example isolates the `insertPointAt` call such that any `splitSegment` method containing this call will match:

```
public int splitSegment(int x, int y) {
    int i = findSegment(x, y);
    if (i != -1){insertPointAt(new Point(x, y), i+1);}
    return i+1;}
```

$$\Rightarrow Subject insertPointAt(new Point(x,y), i+1);$$

```
public int splitSegment(int x, int y) {
    [[insertPointAt(new Point(x, y), i+1);]@[child*]]@[match|set]}
```

Generalize types - This operator abstracts away the name of a particular type, while preserving the information that all occurrences of that type still have the same type. This is done by replacing each occurrence of the type by a wildcard, and attaching a `type` directive to it with the given metavariable. In this example all instances of type `Expression` have been abstracted away:

```
public class ... extends Statement {
    private ASTId<Expression> ...;
    public ASTId<Expression> getExpression() {...}
    public void setExpression(ASTId<Expression> e) {...}}
```

$$\Rightarrow SubjectExpression, Operands \langle ?etype \rangle$$

```
public class ... extends Statement {
    private ASTId<[...]@[(type ?etype)]> ...;
    public ASTId<[...]@[(type ?etype)]> getExpression() {...}
    public void setExpression(ASTId<[...]@[(type ?etype)]> e) {...}}
```

4 Recommending Template Mutations

After providing an overview of our suite of mutation operators, this section introduces our search-based approach, which uses an EA to automatically generalize or refine a template until it matches only with a desired set of snippets.

4.1 Evolutionary Algorithm

The idea is that the user first creates a rough draft of the desired template group, which may produce too few or too many matches. The user then marks which results were missed and/or which matches are undesired. Next, the EA is invoked, which continually modifies the template group with the aim of improving its match results. This continues until either a solution is found that matches exactly the desired set of source nodes, or the user interrupts the search process and uses the best template groups produced up to now.

Our motivation for choosing a search-based approach is three-fold: first, it is a relatively simple solution to a complex problem. Second, even if the approach does not find a solution that produces the desired matches exactly, it can still recommend a template group that is an improvement over the initial group. Third and finally, using this approach the suite of operators and directives of Sect. 3 can be extended without altering the EA.

The EA we are using in particular is single-objective. The individuals in the EA are represented directly as template groups. Pseudocode of the EA is presented as the *evolve* function in Fig. 3. This function takes a set of template groups (*init_templates*) and a set of desired source nodes (*d_matches*) as input. The *cur_gen* variable contains the current generation of template groups. Initially, it contains the input template group(s). Every iteration of the EA's while loop produces a new generation of template groups based on the previous one, until one of the groups has a *fitness* of 1, which indicates we found a solution that produces only the set of desired matches. The fitness function, which computes fitness values, is described in more detail in the next section.

```
evolve(init_templates, d_matches) {
    cur_gen := init_templates
    history := init_templates
    while(∄t∈ cur_gen : fitness(t, d_matches)= 1) {
        selections := ∪ˢᵢ₌₁ tourn_select(cur_gen, d_matches, R)
        mutants := ∪ᴹᵢ₌₁ ∃t : t = mutate(tourn_select(cur_gen, d_matches, R))
            and fitness(t,d_matches) ≠ 0 and t ∉ history
        cur_gen := selections ∪ mutants
        history := history ∪ mutants}}
```

Fig. 3. Pseudocode describing the evolutionary algorithm

Creating a new generation is done only by a process of selections and mutations. The *selections* set is created by performing tournament selection S times in the current generation, where S is user-chosen. Tournament selection chooses one template group by randomly picking R (user-chosen) groups from the current generation, and returning the one with the best fitness out of those R.

A *mutants* set is also created: M (user-chosen) template groups are chosen via tournament selection, followed by applying a mutation operator to each group. This is done by first randomly choosing a subject node in one of templates of a template group. Next, a mutation operator is chosen at random from the operators presented in Sect. 3, followed by randomly choosing operand values. Most operators use metavariables as operands. To find operand values, a metavariable is chosen that already occurs in the template group, or a new one is generated.

Once a mutation is applied, it becomes part of the next generation on two conditions: first, it cannot have a fitness value of zero. This typically indicates that the mutant does not produce any matches whatsoever, and is highly unlikely to lead the search process in the right direction. Second, the new generation cannot contain mutants that were already seen in earlier generations, which is checked using the *history* set. The new generation is then created by concatenating the *selections* and *mutants* sets, and the EA can either move on to the next generation, or stop if a solution is found.

4.2 Fitness Function

We make use of a single-objective EA; there is a single fitness value that it aims to optimize. In our case, the fitness value is a real number in the [0,1] range, where higher is better. The fitness function, which computes the fitness of a template group, is defined in Fig. 4. It is given a template group t and a set of desired matches m as input. It is defined in terms of the F_1 score and the *partial score*, where each component is given a user-specified weight (W_1 and W_2).

The main component of the fitness value is the F_1 score, a number in the [0,1] range defined in terms of how many desired (true positives, tp) and undesired (false positives, fp) matches were found by a template group, as well as how many desired matches were not found (false negatives, fn). The closer it is to 1, the closer the template group is to producing *only* the desired matches. If false

$$fitness(t, m) = W_1.F_1(t, m) + W_2.partial(t, m)$$
$$, \text{ where } W_1 + W_2 = 1 \text{ and } W_1 \geq 0 \qquad partial(t, m) = (\sum_{i=1}^{n} \frac{matchCount(t, m_i)}{nodeCount(t)})/n$$

$$F_1(t, m) = \frac{prec(t, m).rec(t, m)}{prec(t, m) + rec(t, m)} \qquad prec(t, m) = \frac{tp(t, m)}{tp(t, m) + fp(t, m)} \qquad rec(t, m) = \frac{tp(t, m)}{tp(t, m) + fn(t, m)}$$

Fig. 4. Computing the fitness of a template group t

positives are found, the score lowers, which prevents the EA from producing solution template groups that simply match with anything.

While the F_1 score in itself is sufficient to recognize a solution template group, it also is a rather coarse-grained measure. It often takes a sequence of several mutations before a template group's F_1 score increases. For example, several wildcards may need to be introduced to produce an additional match. To make the fitness function more fine-grained, a second component is necessary, the partial score. The idea is that a template group that *almost* produces an additional desired match is better than one that does not. We want to measure how "close" a template group is to matching with each of the desired matches: for each of the desired matches, the template group is applied only against this desired match. Every node that is successfully mapped is one step closer to the template group actually producing that desired match. The ratio of mapped nodes ($matchCount$) to the total number of nodes in the template group ($nodeCount$) indicates how close the template group is to finding this desired match. The average of these ratios (one per desired match) is the partial score.

4.3 Reducing the Search Space

An important factor to consider in search problems is the size of the search space. To reduce it, we have taken several design decisions:

The first is related to the fact that many directives use metavariables in their operands. For the directive to have any effect, that metavariable must be bound to a value elsewhere: if a mutation adds an `invoked-by`, the operand needs to be bound to a method declaration. If it is not bound yet, the mutation operator also adds an `equals` directive to a method declaration in the template group. We use this shorthand, where an `equals` directive is automatically added, for the following directives: `invokes`, `invoked-by`, `refers-to`, `referred-by`, `overrides`, `constructs`, `constructed-by` and all variants of the `type` directive.

A second decision is the lack of crossover operations, where two new template groups are created by swapping a randomly chosen subtree in one template group, with a random subtree in another template. We found that crossovers mostly produce invalid templates, or templates that do not produce any matches.

The third decision is the ability to choose which operators need to be enabled or disabled. This is useful to reduce the search space as there are several "redundant" directives that are the inverse of each other, e.g.`invokes` and `invoked-by`.

The final decision concerns the use of the `protect` directive. While it prevents users from accidentally removing or abstracting away an important node, the same holds true for the EA. Adding a `protect` is useful to avoid getting the EA stuck in a local optimum, because it abstracted away too much information.

5   Generalizing Design Pattern Templates

To evaluate the EA's ability to automatically generalize or refine a template group, we will use it in the context of design patterns [7]. Given one instance of a particular design pattern as an input template group, and all instances of the pattern as the set of desired matches, the EA is tasked to find a template group that produces all desired matches. We have chosen this context, as most design patterns involve multiple roles, played by different classes, which are related to each other in various ways. To represent a design pattern as a template group then involves multiple templates making use of several different directives. As such, we consider design patterns well-suited to put the EA to the test. The main research question to be answered in this experiment is how effective the algorithm is at finding a solution template group.[2] Can a solution be found? How many generations are required to find a solution, and how much time?

5.1   Experiment Setup

For this experiment, we chose two Java applications of a reasonable size, and where design pattern instances have been documented in the P-MARt dataset [8]: the JHotDraw v5.1 drawing application (16019 LOC; 173 classes; 1134 methods), and the Nutch v0.4 web crawler (37108 LOC; 321 classes; 1864 methods). For JHotDraw, we generalized the observer, prototype, template method, strategy and factory method patterns. For Nutch, we generalized the template method, strategy and bridge patterns. Other patterns in these projects were excluded either because the pattern documentation in P-MARt was incomplete, or because the pattern only has one instance (so there is nothing to generalize).

For each of the selected design patterns, the experiment is set up as follows. We first need to ensure an exact solution (with a fitness equal to 1) exists in the EA's search space: if it is unknown whether a solution exists, the experiment would simultaneously evaluate how expressive our template language is, which complicates evaluating the EA's effectiveness. We ensure there is an exact solution by designing it manually using only our suite of mutation operators.

Next, one instance of the design pattern is used as the EA's input template group. We do perform some preprocessing on this template by removing irrelevant methods and adding `protect` directives to those parts of the template that may not be removed. Our assumption is that the user has a notion of which parts are considered important. While this preprocessing is optional, the odds of only finding a local optimum are greater because the EA could abstract away too much (otherwise protected) information by e.g. replacing a node with a wildcard. An example of an input template group for the factory method pattern

---

[2] Experiment data and instructions to reproduce the experiment are available at the EKEKO/X website: https://github.com/cderoove/damp.ekeko.snippets.

Table 4. Experiment results

Pattern	TG	Match	Succ	Time (m)	BestFit	StdDev	GenTS	Rand	Hill
Observer	3	21	7	13.22	0.922	0.098	26.428	0.422	0.526
Prototype	3	27	4	6.75	0.814	0.231	46.75	0.172	0.307
Template method	2	47	5	76.43	0.817	0.170	56.8	0.271	0.369
Strategy	3	13	2	58.52	0.660	0.186	110.5	0.176	0.200
Factory method	3	22	2	99.68	0.682	0.187	118.5	0.201	0.239
Template method	2	7	9	18.27	0.977	0.052	83.888	0.368	0.459
Strategy	3	74	1	91.49	0.545	0.279	51	0.100	0.124
Bridge	3	69	0	64.24	0.803	0.120	-	0.168	0.260

```
1    public interface Figure extends Storable, Cloneable, Serializable {
2         [[public Connector connectorAt( int x, int y);]@[protect]]@[match|set]}
3
4    public class RoundRectangleFigure extends AttributeFigure {
5         [public Connector connectorAt( int x,  int y) {
6              return [new ShortestDistanceConnector(this)]@[protect];}]@[match|set]}
7
8    public interface Connector extends Serializable, Storable {
9         [public abstract Figure owner();
10        public abstract Rectangle displayBox();
11        public abstract boolean containsPoint(int x, int y);]@[match|set]}
```

Fig. 5. Input template group

is shown in Fig. 5: most of the methods irrelevant to the pattern are removed.[3] The factory method itself is important for the pattern, and so is the fact that it instantiates something, so both have a `protect` directive (lines 2 and 6).

Finally, the EA is started using the input template group, and all instances of the design pattern as desired matches. The configuration we have used is the following: $S = 8$; $M = 22$; $R = 5$; $W_1 = 0.6$; $W_2 = 0.4$; the maximum number of generations is 150. Each generation contains 30 individuals, of which 8 are selections, and 22 are mutants. Tournament selection is performed using 5 rounds. The F_1 score is given a weight of 0.6; the partial score has a weight of 0.4, which we will discuss in Sect. 5.2. S, M and R are chosen based on the Essentials of Metaheuristics book [14]. The number of individuals was kept fairly low as template matching is memory-intensive, especially because the fitness of individuals is computed in parallel.[4] Finally, the following 16 operators are enabled for all experiments: Replace by wildcard/variable, Add directive (`equals`, `invokes`, `constructs`, `overrides`, `refers-to`, `type`, `subtype*`, `child*`, `match|set`), isolate expression in method, generalize references/types/invocations/construc-

---

[3] If a method is removed, `match|set` is always added so the template still matches.
[4] The system used in the experiment has 16GB RAM and an Intel Core i7 (Haswell).

tor invocations. The disabled operators are either inverse relations of other directives, or would insert/remove AST nodes, which is unlikely to produce templates with any matches.

5.2   Experiment Results

The results of our experiment are presented in Table 4. The top 5 rows are JHotDraw patterns, and the bottom 3 are Nutch patterns. For each pattern, 10 runs were executed. The following data is provided in the table: the no. of templates in each template group (TG); the no. of desired matches (Match); no. of runs (out of 10) that found an exact solution (Succ); total time taken on average, in minutes (Time); average best fitness (BestFit); standard deviation of best fitness (StdDev); for runs that found an exact solution, the average no. of generations needed to find the solution (GenTS); average best fitness found by a random search algorithm (Rand); average best fitness found by a hill climbing algorithm (Hill). Figure 6 gives an idea of how the best fitness evolved per generation for one run of each pattern. Figure 7 shows the evolution of F_1 and partial score fitness components seperately (for one run of the factory method pattern); it clearly shows the fine-grained nature of the partial score, compared to the coarse F_1 score. Because we gave the partial score a weight of 0.4, it can cause the F_1 score to temporarily lower, as can be seen around generation 75. This can occur when the EA is close to finding many more true positives, and may need to temporarily tolerate an increase in false positives.

An example solution that was generated for the factory method pattern in JHotDraw is shown in Fig. 8. It was generated from the input template of Fig. 5. The three templates respectively represent the creator (line 1–2), concrete creator (line 4–6), and product (line 8) roles of the design pattern. As the EA chooses random metavariable names, we renamed them here to improve readability. The EA has abstracted away several parts with wildcards, but retained just enough information: the `connectorAt` factory method in line 2 (which appears in all instances), the instantiation expression in line 6 and which types need to be either classes or interfaces. More importantly, the EA added directives to relate the three templates to each other: the concrete creator must be a subtype of the creator interface due to the `type` and `subtype` directives in lines 1 and 4. The factory method must return an instance of the product due to the `type` directives in lines 5 and 8. Additionally, due to the `child*` directive in line 5, the factory method may also a return a generic type where the product is a parameter. This is needed, as some instances of the pattern return a `Vector` of the product type.

Based on the data of Table 4, we observe that the search algorithm is able to find solutions producing only the desired matches in several runs. However, we do not consistently find exact solutions in all runs, and in case of Nutch's bridge pattern no solutions were found. This indicates that the search process can get stuck in a local optimum. This happens for several reasons; for example: 1. a wildcard is added too eagerly and abstracts away information that is needed later on; 2. a relation may need to be established between two nodes using a common metavariable, but both have already been bound to two different metavariables,

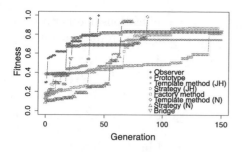

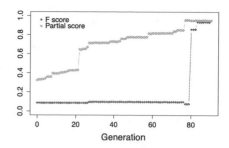

Fig. 6. Overall fitness   **Fig. 7.** Fitness components

```
1  public interface [...]@[(type ?creator)] extends ... {
2      [[public ... connectorAt(... x,   ... y)...]]@[protect]]@[match|set]}
3
4  public class ?creator-impl extends [...]@[(subtype* ?creator)] {
5      [public [[...]@[(type ?product)]]@[child*] ...(...)... {
6          [[....new ...(...)]@[child* protect]]@[match|set]}]@[match|set]}
7
8  public interface [...]@[(type ?product)] extends ... {...}
```

Fig. 8. Generated solution for the factory method pattern

or 3. the fitness score was increased by relating a subclass to a superclass, but it would be better to relate it to its interface. The current suite of operators is primarily designed for ease-of-use when editing templates manually, which may not entirely correspond to operators designed for an EA. Improving the current suite to this end is considered future work.

As a basic comparison, we also performed the same experiments using a random search algorithm, as well as a hillclimbing algorithm (also 10 runs per pattern). The random algorithm continually produces random template groups, and only keeps the one with the best fitness. To generate a random group, a random number (between 0 and 50) of mutations is applied to the initial input group. Our reasoning here is that, considering the number of operations we needed to manually construct a solution, solutions must be within 50 mutations of the input template group, which is a much smaller search space than generating entirely random template groups from scratch. The hillclimbing algorithm continually applies a random mutation to the best template group. If the mutant has a better fitness, it becomes the best template group. Both the random and hillclimbing algorithm's maximum number of iterations is 500. We only show the average best fitness of both the hillclimbing and random search algorithm in Table 4, as neither of the algorithms could find an exact solution in any of its runs. This mainly indicates that the search space is too large to accidentally find a solution, and that it is possible to get stuck in local optima. As per the guidelines of Arcuri and Briand [2], we also performed a Mann-Whitney U-test to compare the BestFit with the Rand column, as well as the BestFit with the Hill column. In both cases we obtain a p-value smaller than 0.0001, confirming that the EA outperforms both the random search and hillclimbing algorithms.

5.3   Threats to Validity

The experiment was performed within only two software systems. While our focus is on snippets of code, the entire code base affects the fitness value.

Our experiment is focused on generalizing design pattern instances, so our results may not carry over to other uses of templates. While the EA itself should not change, the suite of mutation operators may need to be extended.

Finally, some combinations of directives on the same node, or a node and its children, are incompatible combinations, or require special-case behavior. We have discovered and fixed several bugs in our code because the search algorithm is exercising so many combinations of directives, but it is difficult to be exhaustive.

6   Related Work

Several program search and transformation tools exist that are, to some extent, based on code templates. This includes languages and tools such as Stratego [17], TXL [4] and JTransformer [12]. However, the constraints that are available for these languages is limited to expressing syntactic and structural characteristics, but not semantic ones (such as the directives `refers-to`, `invokes`, `overrides`, ...). The Coccinelle [3] tool does allow for semantic relations based on temporal logic within a function, but not between different functions.

A closely related tool is ChangeFactory, in which transformations can be generalized by attaching constraints/conditions to recorded changes. The conditions that can be specified are only of a syntactic nature, which limits expressivity. When considering languages that focus solely on program searches, such as BAZ [6], JQuery [11], CodeQuest [9] or PQL [15], these languages do support various semantic constraints, but they are not template-based.

With regards to our EA, several works in the field of program repair make use of genetic search or genetic programming techniques to either generate or evolve patches that fix an instance of a bug [1,13,18]. However, these approaches focus on repairing one instance, without looking for similar instances of the same bug. While our approach does not perform any program repairs, we can use it to describe multiple instances of a bug in one template. In this regard, the work of Meng et al. [16] is more closely related. Based on two sequences of source code modifications, each fixing an instance of the same bug, their approach can create a transformation that should find and fix all instances of a bug. The approach in this work however does not consider interprocedural modifications.

7   Conclusion and Future Work

In this work, we have presented a suite of mutation operators to modify template groups and a search-based approach that automatically generalizes and refines templates, which we have tested in the context of producing template groups that match with design pattern instances. While we found that the approach is able to either substantially improve a template or find solutions that match exactly with a desired set of snippets, a substantial amount of time is often required. However, time is less of an issue in our direction of future work. The current work has focused only on template groups performing program searches. This is a stepping stone towards also supporting program transformations, in which e.g. a patch/transformation that fixes one instance of a bug can be generalized to a transformation that fixes all instances of that bug.

References

1. Ackling, T., Alexander, B., Grunert, I.: Evolving patches for software repair. In: Proceedings of the 13th Annual Conference on Genetic and Evolutionary Computation, GECCO 2011, pp. 1427–1434. ACM (2011)
2. Arcuri, A., Briand, L.: A practical guide for using statistical tests to assess randomized algorithms in software engineering. In: 33rd International Conference on Software Engineering (ICSE), pp. 1–10 (2011)
3. Brunel, J., Doligez, D., Hansen, R.R., Lawall, J.L., Muller, G.: A foundation for flow-based program matching: Using temporal logic and model checking. In Proceedings of the 36th Annual ACM SIGPLAN-SIGACT Symposium on Principles of Programming Languages, POPL 2009, pp. 114–126 (2009)
4. Cordy, J.R.: The TXL source transformation language. Sci. Comput. Program. **61**(3), 190–210 (2006)
5. De Roover, C., Inoue, K.: The Ekeko/X program transformation tool. In: 2014 IEEE 14th International Working Conference on Source Code Analysis and Manipulation (SCAM), pp. 53–58, September 2014
6. De Roover, C., Noguera, C., Kellens, A., Jonckers, V.: The soul tool suite for querying programs in symbiosis with eclipse. In: Proceedings of the 9th International Conference on Principles and Practice of Programming in Java, pp. 71–80. ACM (2011)
7. Gamma, E., Helm, R., Johnson, R., Vlissides, J.: Design Patterns: Elements of Reusable Object-oriented Software, vol. 49(120), p. 11. Addison-Wesley, Reading (1995)
8. Guéhéneuc, Y.-G.: P-mart: pattern-like micro architecture repository. In: Proceedings of the 1st EuroPLoP Focus Group on Pattern Repositories (2007)
9. Hajiyev, E., Verbaere, M., de Moor, O.: *codeQuest*: scalable source code queries with datalog. In: Thomas, D. (ed.) ECOOP 2006. LNCS, vol. 4067, pp. 2–27. Springer, Heidelberg (2006)
10. Harman, M., Mansouri, S.A., Zhang, Y.: Search-based software engineering: trends, techniques and applications. ACM Comput. Surv. **45**(1), 11:1–11:61 (2012)
11. Janzen, D., De Volder, K.: Navigating and querying code without getting lost. In: Proceedings of the 2nd International Conference on Aspect-Oriented Software Development, pp. 178–187. ACM (2003)
12. Kniesel, G., Hannemann, J., Rho, T.: A comparison of logic-based infrastructures for concern detection and extraction. In: Proceedings of the 3rd Workshop on Linking Aspect Technology And Evolution (LATE 2007). ACM (2007)
13. Le Goues, C., Nguyen, T., Forrest, S., Weimer, W.: Genprog: a generic method for automatic software repair. IEEE Trans. Softw. Eng. **38**(1), 54–72 (2012)
14. Luke, S.: Essentials of Metaheuristics. Lulu, 2nd edn. (2013). http://cs.gmu.edu/~sean/book/metaheuristics/

15. Martin, M., Livshits, B., Lam, M.S.: Finding application errors, security flaws using PQL: a program query language. In: Proceedings of the 20th Annual ACM SIGPLAN Conference on Object-Oriented Programming, Systems, Languages, and Applications, OOPSLA 2005, pp. 365–383 (2005)
16. Meng, N., Kim, M., McKinley, K.S.: LASE: locating and applying systematic edits by learning from examples. In: Proceedings of the International Conference on Software Engineering, pp. 502–511. IEEE Press (2013)
17. Visser, E.: Program transformation with Stratego/XT. In: Lengauer, C., Batory, D., Blum, A., Odersky, M. (eds.) Domain-Specific Program Generation. LNCS, vol. 3016, pp. 216–238. Springer, Heidelberg (2004)
18. Weimer, W., Nguyen, T., Le Goues, C., Forrest, S.: Automatically finding patches using genetic programming. In: Proceedings of the 31st International Conference on Software Engineering, pp. 364–374. IEEE CS (2009)

SBSE Challenge Papers

Amortised Deep Parameter Optimisation of GPGPU Work Group Size for OpenCV

Jeongju Sohn[✉], Seongmin Lee, and Shin Yoo

Korea Advanced Institute of Science and Technology, 291 Daehak Ro,
Yuseong Gu, Daejeon, Republic of Korea
kasio555@kaist.ac.kr

Abstract. GPGPU (General Purpose computing on Graphics Processing Units) enables massive parallelism by taking advantage of the Single Instruction Multiple Data (SIMD) architecture of the large number of cores found on modern graphics cards. A parameter called local
work group size controls how many work items are concurrently executed
on a single compute unit. Though critical to the performance, there is
no deterministic way to tune it, leaving developers to manual trial and
error. This paper applies amortised optimisation to determine the best
local work group size for GPGPU implementations of OpenCV template
matching feature. The empirical evaluation shows that optimised local
work group size can outperform the default value with large effect sizes.

1 Introduction

While Central Processing Units (CPUs) are keeping up with Moore's Law [7]
by increasing the number of cores on a single die, graphics processing units continue to increase their peak performance, outpacing Moore's Law [3]. While the
original purpose of this computation power is for 3D graphics, advances in pro-
grammable shaders led to General Purpose computing on Graphics Processing
Units (GPGPU), in which shaders concurrently execute the same general purpose program against a large volume of data [6]. OpenCV [5], a widely used
computer vision library, provides a transparent GPGPU layer, allowing users
to write a unified code that can be compiled to run on both CPUs and GPUs,
resulting in up to 30 speed-up [2].

One of the major factors that affect the performance is the number of work
items executed in a single GPU compute unit, called *local work group size*[1]. These
work items share the same local memory, which effectively acts as a cache for
the much slower global memory on the graphics card (which serves all compute
units). Assigning too few work items to a compute unit will underutilise the
GPU, whereas assigning too many work items to a compute unit will result in
missed cache and slow I/O to and from the global memory.

---

[1] On the other hand, the global work group size corresponds to the number of all
parallel work items.

F. Sarro and K. Deb (Eds.): SSBSE 2016, LNCS 9962, pp. 211–217, 2016.
DOI: 10.1007/978-3-319-47106-8_14

While the parameter has a critical impact on performance, there is no definite way to set a single value that works for all cases: the ideal value depends on combination of the application and its I/O requirements, as well as the specific hardware the kernel is currently running on. Consequently, the default values suggested by frameworks or vendors are usually based on a simple heuristic. Tuning work group size for maximum performance for a specific application remains an experimental trial-and-error process, resulting in a practical challenge [1,4].

This paper applies amortised optimisation [10] to the local work group size parameter in the GPGPU module of OpenCV in order to make it faster: it is a case of Deep Parameter Optimisation [9] as the work group size parameter has to be exposed to be explicitly controlled. With repetitive use of a specific OpenCV function, the amortised optimisation will guide the user to the local work group size best suited for the combination of user's graphics processing unit and the given GPGPU task. The results show that it is possible to improve OpenCV performance by reducing the execution time with statistical significance and large effect sizes.

2   Amortised Optimisation and OpenCV

Amortised optimisation aims to apply metaheuristic optimisations to certain control variables, step by step across multiple user executions, after deployment [10]. For example, with amortised hill climbing, a single step can be either submitting the next neighbouring solution to the program, or submitting a random solution to the program to initiate a random restart.

2.1   Amortised Hill Climbing for Local Work Group Size

We have manually exposed the local work group size used by our target OpenCV function. The Maximum Work Group size (M_{WG}), i.e. the maximum number of work items on a single compute unit, is restricted by the graphics processing unit device; this defines our search space. OpenCL [8], the underlying GPGPU platform, allows work group sizes for 2D image operations to be defined in a tuple, (wgs_1, wgs_2). This facilitates easier interpretation of parallelisation of operations on a specific subregion in the given image. The size of the actual workgroup is $wgs_1 \cdot wgs_2$.

It is important to specify and observe the allowed ranges for possible value. In particular, it is not possible to set values of (wgs_1, wgs_2) such that $wgs_1 \cdot wgs_2$ is larger than the device specific limit. Furthermore, since we are implementing the hill climbing algorithm, it is important that neighbours of the current solutions to become feasible values. Given (wgs_1, wgs_2), we define its neighbours as $\{(wgs_1 + step_1, wgs_2 + step_2), (wgs_1 - step_1, wgs_2 - step_2)\}$.

In order to adhere to these restrictions, we primarily control wgs_1 and set wgs_2 accordingly. The value of wgs_1 is initially chosen randomly, and its neighbours are obtained by adding or subtracting the step size, $step_1$ (which is set proportionally to the input image size). Subsequently, we use SETWGS2(), which

Algorithm 1. SetWGS2

Input: Max work group size, M_{WG}, the first workgroup size, wgs_1, the step size for wgs_1, $step_1$, the step size for wgs_2, $step_2$, and the current limit for wgs_2, $limit_2$

Output: A tuple $(wgs_{2_{new}}^-, wgs_{2_{new}}, wgs_{2_{new}}^+)$, in which $wgs_{2_{new}}^-$ is the new candidate value for the second work group size, and the other two are its neighbours for next iteration of hill climbing

(1) **if** $M_{WG}/(wgs_1 + step_1) + 1 \leq limit_2$

(2) $limit_2 \leftarrow M_{WG}/(wgs_1 + step_1) + 1$

(3)   **if** $1 \leq limit_2 \leq 2$

(4)   **return** $(1, 1, 1)$

(5)   **else if** $limit_2 = 3$

(6)   **return** $(1, 1, 2)$

(7)   **else**

(8)   **repeat**

(9) $step_2 \leftarrow step_2/(limit_2/3 + 1)$

(10)   **until** $step_2 \neq 0$

(11) $limit_2 \leftarrow limit_2 - 1$

(12) **repeat**

(13) $wgs_2 \leftarrow$ RAND$()\%(limit_2 + 1)$

(14) **until** $!(wgs_2 \leq step_2 | (wgs_2 + step_2) \cdot (wgs_1 + step_1) > M_{WG})$

(15) **return** $(wgs_2 - step_2, wgs_2, wgs_2 + step_2)$

takes wgs_1, global work group size and the step size for the 2nd dimension, $limit_2$ and $step_2$ respectively, as input.

Function SETWGS2() first readjusts $limit_2$ if necessary. If wgs_1 has increased, the maximum possible value for wgs_2 may need to decrease: wgs_2 should be between the quotient of M_{WG} divided by wgs_1 plus $step_1$ (Line 1). If, after adjustment, $limit_2$ becomes too small to be explored, SETWGS2() returns a tuple predetermined small values, corresponding to the new wgs_2 and its neighbours. Otherwise, we now adjust $step_2$ according to $limit_2$, sample a new wgs_2 from the new range determined by $limit_2$, and return $(wgs_2 - step_2, wgs_2, wgs_2 + step_2)$.

Given the relatively small search space and the noisy fitness function (i.e. execution time), we have borrowed features from tabu search to encourage exploration and avoid local optima. The algorithm maintains a record of attempted work group sizes; when current selected work group sizes have been visisted more than a predetermined number of times(limit of visiting count), the alogrithm restarts with new work group sizes which have not been visited more than the limit.

3   Experimental Setup

3.1   Subjects

Subject of our optimisation is the template matching function in OpenCV. Template matching is a technique which finds the areas of an image that match to a template image. Implementation are composed of 20 different pairs of images (collected from the internet) and templates (cropped from the images). The sizes of each image and template pairs are listed in Table 1. Five different template matching algorithms (TM_SQDIFF_NORMED, TM_CCORR, TM_CCORR_NORMED, TM_CCOEFF, TM_CCOEFF_NORMED) have been assigned to pairs randomly.

Table 1. Subject images/templates and corresponding OpenCV template matching function(⊙: TM_SQDIFF_NORMED, △: TM_CCORR, ▲: TM_CCORR_NORMED, ◇: TM_CCOEFF, ◆: TM_CCOEFF_NORMED)

Match	$width_i$	$height_i$	$width_t$	$height_t$	Function	Match	$width_i$	$height_i$	$width_t$	$height_t$	Function
1	454	338	50	97	◆	11	342	228	42	36	△
2	454	338	53	119	△	12	342	228	41	40	⊙
3	454	338	51	105	◆	13	890	639	80	72	▲
4	455	453	22	52	△	14	890	639	63	70	◆
5	463	280	31	28	△	15	890	639	96	92	△
6	463	280	33	41	⊙	16	890	639	79	80	◇
7	891	451	64	71	⊙	17	939	629	46	42	▲
8	891	451	60	70	△	18	499	256	87	75	⊙
9	891	451	100	88	⊙	19	938	633	118	105	△
10	342	228	40	39	△	20	671	448	115	64	◇

3.2 Evaluation

A single run of a pair contains 30 repeated matchings to smooth outliers. A single optimisation contains 20 runs with default setting, follows 80 runs with amortised optimisation, followed by 20 runs with optimised setting. To cope with the stochastic nature of the algorithm and the noisy fitness function, optimisation for each pair was repeated 20 times. All experiments have been performed on a machine with Intel Core i7 6700 K with 64.0 GB RAM, equipped with NVidia Titan X GPU, running OpenCV Ver. 3.10 and Ubuntu 14.04 LTS. The M_{WG} supported by Titan X is 1,024.

Our objective is to reduce the execution time. We use getTickCount and getTickFrequency from OpenCV to obtain execution time in seconds.

We use Mann-Whitney U test to compare the execution time with default setting to that with the optimised setting. Since the underlying probability distribution is not known, we use Mann-Whitney U test to check the statistical significance ($\alpha = 0.05$) of our alternative hypothesis H_1: the optimised setting produces shorter execution time than the default setting. Since we repeat the hypothesis test 20 times, we also report p–values with Bonferroni correction. Finally, effect sizes have been analysed using Vargha and Delaney's A_{12} statistics.

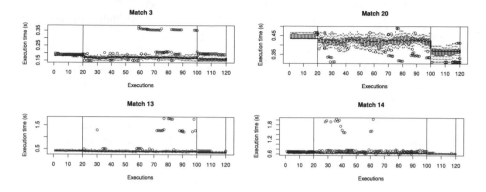

Fig. 1. Boxplots of 20 optimisations per pair.

4   Results

Figure 1 shows four representative boxplots of 20 optimisations[2], each of which contains 20 default runs, 80 amortised optimisation runs, followed by 20 optimised runs with the best parameter values found. The x-axis shows run sequence, while the y-axis shows the execution time for each execution. The boxplots show that the parameter values found during optimisation can outperform the default parameter values. For Match 3 and 20, the improvement is visible. However, detailed statistics in Table 2 confirms that other pairs also show statistically significant improvement with large effect size measured by A_{12}.

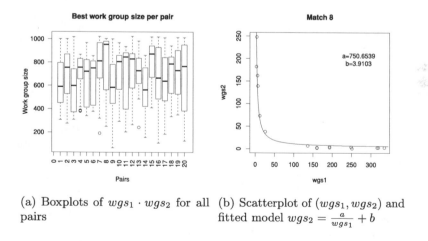

(a) Boxplots of $wgs_1 \cdot wgs_2$ for all pairs

(b) Scatterplot of (wgs_1, wgs_2) and fitted model $wgs_2 = \frac{a}{wgs_1} + b$

Fig. 2. Distribution and convergence of work group size

---

[2] Boxplots for all experiments can be found at http://coinse.kaist.ac.kr/projects/adpoopencv.

Table 2. Mean and standard deviation of default (μ_d, σ_d) and optimised (μ_o, σ_o) execution times, results of hypothesis testing (p, p_{bonf}), and effect sizes (A_{12})

Match	μ_d	σ_d	μ_o	σ_o	p	p_{bonf}	A_{12}	Match	μ_d	σ_d	μ_o	σ_o	p	p_{bonf}	A_{12}
1	0.190	0.007	0.179	0.012	< 1e-3	< 1e-3	0.225	11	0.089	0.003	0.060	0.004	< 1e-3	< 1e-3	0.000
2	0.093	0.002	0.081	0.002	< 1e-3	< 1e-3	0.000	12	0.106	0.001	0.068	0.002	< 1e-3	< 1e-3	0.000
3	0.182	0.003	0.163	0.014	< 1e-3	< 1e-3	0.140	13	0.405	0.028	0.362	0.024	< 1e-3	< 1e-3	0.120
4	0.172	0.007	0.133	0.006	< 1e-3	< 1e-3	0.000	14	0.653	0.014	0.625	0.014	< 1e-3	< 1e-3	0.084
5	0.164	0.006	0.129	0.005	< 1e-3	< 1e-3	0.000	15	0.429	0.012	0.355	0.024	< 1e-3	< 1e-3	0.000
6	0.176	0.005	0.132	0.005	< 1e-3	< 1e-3	0.000	16	0.645	0.012	0.587	0.025	< 1e-3	< 1e-3	0.002
7	0.383	0.023	0.350	0.028	< 1e-3	< 1e-3	0.197	17	0.418	0.014	0.390	0.015	< 1e-3	< 1e-3	0.108
8	0.329	0.004	0.299	0.022	< 1e-3	< 1e-3	0.050	18	0.129	0.002	0.109	0.004	< 1e-3	< 1e-3	0.000
9	0.257	0.001	0.244	0.007	< 1e-3	< 1e-3	0.001	19	0.569	0.020	0.485	0.037	< 1e-3	< 1e-3	0.006
10	0.086	0.003	0.060	0.003	< 1e-3	< 1e-3	0.000	20	0.444	0.013	0.363	0.024	< 1e-3	< 1e-3	0.000

Figure 2(a) shows the distribution of $wgs_1 \cdot wgs_2$, i.e. the actual work group size, for each pair. The median values vary across pairs, and are significantly different from M_{WG} supported by the device. Furthermore, Fig. 2(b) shows a case for which different optimisations for the same pair actually converge to the same work group size (i.e. $wgs_1 \cdot wgs_2$).

5   Conclusion

Local work group size is a GPGPU parameter whose optimal value is dependent on both the given task and the hardware environment. Default parameter heuristics are often not ideal for all tasks. This paper applies amortised optimisation to GPGPU layer of OpenCV. Results of empirical study suggest that amortised optimisation can take the burden of manual trial and error tuning off the user.

References

1. What is the algorithm to determine optimal work group size and number of workgroup? http://stackoverflow.com/questions/10096443/what-is-the-algorithm-to-determine-optimal-work-group-size-and-number-of-workgro
2. OpenCL Performance in OpenCV 3.0, May 2016. http://opencv.org/platforms/opencl.html
3. Chen, J.Y.: Gpu technology trends and future requirements. In: 2009 IEEE International Electron Devices Meeting (IEDM), pp. 1–6, December 2009
4. Intel Corporation: Work-group size considerations (2012). https://software.intel.com/sites/landingpage/opencl/optimization-guide/Work-Group_Size_Considerations.htm
5. Itseez: Open source computer vision library. https://github.com/itseez/opencv
6. Luebke, D., Harris, M., Krüger, J., Purcell, T., Govindaraju, N., Buck, I., Woolley, C., Lefohn, A.: GPGPU: General purpose computation on graphics hardware. In: ACM SIGGRAPH 2004 Course Notes, SIGGRAPH 2004. ACM (2004)
7. Moore, G.E.: Cramming more components onto integrated circuits. Electron. Mag. **38**, 114–117 (1965)

8. Stone, J.E., Gohara, D., Shi, G.: Opencl: A parallel programming standard for heterogeneous computing systems. IEEE Des. Test **12**(3), 66–73 (2010)
9. Wu, F., Weimer, W., Harman, M., Jia, Y., Krinke, J.: Deep parameter optimisation. In: Proceedings of the 2015 Annual Conference on Genetic and Evolutionary Computation, GECCO 2015, pp. 1375–1382. ACM, New York (2015)
10. Yoo, S.: Amortised optimisation of non-functional properties in production environments. In: Barros, M., Labiche, Y. (eds.) SSBSE 2015. LNCS, vol. 9275, pp. 31–46. Springer, Heidelberg (2015)

Automated Testing of Web Applications with TESTAR

Lessons Learned Testing the Odoo Tool

Francisco Almenar, Anna I. Esparcia-Alcázar[✉], Mirella Martínez,
and Urko Rueda

Research Center on Software Production Methods (PROS),
Universitat Politècnica de València, Camino de vera s/n, 46022 Valencia, Spain
{falmenar,aesparcia,mmartinez,urueda}@pros.upv.es
http://www.testar.org

Abstract. The TESTAR tool was originally conceived to perform automated testing of desktop applications via their Graphical User Interface (GUI). Starting from the premise that source code is not available, TESTAR automatically selects actions based only on information derived from the GUI and in this way generates test sequences on the fly. In this work we extend its use to web applications and carry out experiments using the Odoo open source management software as the testing object. We also introduce novel metrics to evaluate the performance of the testing with TESTAR, which are valid even when access to the source code is not available and testing is only possible via the GUI. We compare results obtained for two types of action selection mechanisms, based on random choice and Q-learning with different parameter settings. Statistical analysis shows the superiority of the latter provided an adequate choice of parameters; furthermore, the results point to interesting areas for improvement.

Keywords: Automated GUI testing · Testing metrics · Testing web applications · Q-learning

1 Introduction

TESTAR is an automated tool that performs testing via the GUI, using the operating system's Accessibility API to recognise GUI controls and their properties, and enabling programmatic interaction with them. It derives sets of possible actions for each state that the GUI is in and selects and executes appropriate ones, thus creating a test sequence on the fly. In previous work we have shown how TESTAR has been successfully applied to various commercial desktop applications [1,2,4,6], allowing automated testing of not just the GUI but of all the functionality that is accessible via the GUI, including e.g. databases.

In this work we report the first application of TESTAR to test a web application, namely the Odoo open source enterprise resource planning (ERP) system.

© Springer International Publishing AG 2016
F. Sarro and K. Deb (Eds.): SSBSE 2016, LNCS 9962, pp. 218–223, 2016.
DOI: 10.1007/978-3-319-47106-8_15

Testing web applications poses challenges that differ from those of desktop applications. For instance, web latency must be taken into account. Hence, the test automation tool must wait for the GUI to react before executing the next action. Also, we must avoid testing the *browser* rather than the application; for instance, we must filter out the search bar or the bookmarks.

We run experiments in three phases or iterations, refining the process after each phase. We used Q-learning with different parameter combinations as the action selection mechanism, and compare them using random action selection as a baseline. For the comparison we have introduced four new metrics that evaluate the quality of the testing; these metrics take into account that the source code of the software under test (SUT) is not available.

The rest of this paper is structured as follows. Section 2 explains the two main decisions taken by the human tester when testing with TESTAR, namely the action selection mechanism and the testing protocol. Section 3 introduces the metrics used for quality assessment of the testing procedure. Section 4 summarises the experimental set up, the results obtained and the statistical analysis carried out; it also highlights the problems encountered. Finally, in Sect. 5 we present some conclusions and outline areas for future work.

2   TESTAR Settings

The two main inputs for the human tester in TESTAR are the choice of an action selection mechanism and the protocol. We briefly describe these below.

Action selection. We have employed the *Q-learning* algorithm to guide the action selection process. Q-learning is a model-free reinforcement learning technique in which an agent, at a state S, must choose one among a set of actions A available at that state. By performing an action $a \in A$, the agent can move from state to state. Executing an action in a specific state provides the agent with a reward (a numerical score which measures the utility of executing a given action in a given state). The goal of the agent is to maximize its total reward, since it allows the algorithm to look ahead when choosing actions to execute. It does this by learning which action is optimal for each state. The action that is optimal for each state is the action that has the highest long-term reward.

Our version of the Q-learning algorithm is governed by two parameters: *maxReward* and *discount*. Depending on how these are chosen the algorithm will promote exploration or exploitation of the search space. The *maxReward* parameter determines the initial reward unexplored actions have; so, a high value biases the search towards executing unexplored actions. On the other hand, *discount* establishes how the reward of an action decreases after being executed. Small *discount* values decrease the reward faster and vice versa.

TESTAR protocol. A TESTAR custom protocol is a Java class that allows extending the basic functionality in order to implement complex action sets, specific filters and sophisticated oracles. Successive iterations allow the human tester to observe the problems encountered in the testing process and improve the protocol. In this work, three such iterations were carried out.

3   Metrics

Finding appropriate metrics for assessing the quality of the testing has been a long standing issue. For instance, [3] defines a number of metrics for GUI testing, but these imply having access to the code of the software under test (SUT); one of the strengths of TESTAR is precisely not relying on the assumption that this is the case. However, this also implies that specific metrics must be defined. In this work they were chosen as follows:

– **Abstract states.** This metric refers to the number of different states, or windows in the GUI, that are visited in the course of an execution.
– **Longest path.** Any automated testing tool must ensure the deepest parts of the GUI are tested. To measure whether the tool has just stayed on the surface or it has reached deeper, we define the longest path as the longest sequence of non-repeated (i.e. excluding loops) consecutive states visited.
– **Minimum and maximum coverage per state.** We define the *state coverage* as the rate of executed over total available actions in a given state/window; the metrics are the highest and lowest such values across all windows. This allows us to know to what extent actions pertaining to states were explored.

A consequence of not having access to the source code is that the metrics given above can be used to compare the efficiency of different testing methods, but not to assess the overall goodness of a method in isolation, because we do not know the global optima for each metric; for instance, we cannot know exactly how many different states there are.

4   Experiments and Results

4.1   Odoo - The Software Under Test (SUT)

Odoo[1] is an open source Enterprise Resource Planning software consisting of several enterprise management applications that can be installed or not depending on the user needs. It can be used to create websites, manage human resource (HR), finance, sales, projects and others. Odoo has a client-server architecture and uses a PostgreSQL database as a management system. Once deployed, we installed the mail, calendar, contacts, sales, inventory and project applications in order to test a wide number of options.

---

[1] See https://github.com/odoo/odoo for Odoo's *git* repository and issue tracker, including a manual with instructions on how to deploy the server and its requirements.

4.2 Procedure

In order to test Odoo with TESTAR a server version of Odoo must first be deployed[2]. Then TESTAR must be configured by supplying the URL that accesses the Odoo client and the browser that will be used to launch it. Next, we run TESTAR in *spy mode*; this uncovers possible problems with items that may not be detected well, such as emergent windows. In addition, it helps detecting undesired actions that might be performed by TESTAR that may bring problems such as involuntary file deletion. A number of parameters must also be set up, which are given in Table 1. With these settings and a first version of the TESTAR *protocol*[3] we carried out three iterations of the testing process, improving the protocol each time so as to remove the problems encountered.

Table 1. Experimental set up. We carried out three iterations involving the five sets. After each iteration the results obtained were used to refine the TESTAR protocol so as to better adapt it to the application.

Set	Max. actions per run	Runs	Action selection algorithm	Parameters $maxReward$	$discount$
Q1	1000	30	Q-learning	1	0.20
Q20	1000	30	Q-learning	20	0.20
Q99	1000	30	Q-learning	99	0.50
Q10M	1000	30	Q-learning	9999999	0.95
RND	1000	30	random	N/A	N/A

4.3 Statistical Analysis

We run the Kruskal-Wallis non parametric test on the results for the five sets. In iteration 3 the test shows that all the metrics have significant differences among the sets. Running pair-wise comparisons confirms this finding; results for all sets are given in Fig. 1, which shows how random selection can outperform some of the other sets. This highlights the importance of an adequate choice of parameters when using Q-learning for action selection.

4.4 Issues Encountered

Several issues arose when testing Odoo with TESTAR. The first one relates to the delays induced by network latency, which is to be expected in any web application. This can be circumvented via the TESTAR GUI, which allows the human tester to select the time to wait between actions. In addition, we have

---

[2] See the source install tutorial available from https://www.odoo.com/documenta tion/8.0/setup/install.html.

[3] For more details the reader is referred to the tutorial available from www.testar.org.

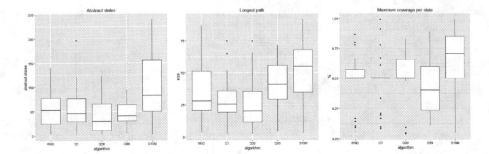

Fig. 1. Boxplots of the results obtained for 3 metrics in Iteration 3; Q10M beats the other options for these metrics, coming third in the remaining one (not shown here)

Table 2. Number of failures encountered per algorithm in the 3rd iteration. These failures coincide with known issues reported in https://github.com/odoo/odoo/issues

Set	Total failures	Unique failures
Q10M	3	1
Q99	0	0
Q20	6	2
Q1	2	1
RND	1	1

found that Odoo can display confirmation questions in the form of emerging windows that are not detected as a part of SUT by the accessibility API provided by Microsoft. This causes TESTAR to fail as it tries to find the SUT but is unable to, because the emerging window is in the foreground. Also, interactions coded via the CSS are usually not detected by the API, causing that actions available in emerging panels get mixed with those in the windows under them, which may cause the execution of unintended actions.

5   Conclusions

We have shown here the successful application of TESTAR to the automated testing of the Odoo management software - the first systematic experimentation of the testing tool to a web application. Two strategies for action selection were implemented within TESTAR: random and Q-learning. Four metrics were defined in order to evaluate the performance. Statistical analysis reveals the superiority of the Q-learning-based method, provided the parameters of the algorithm have been properly selected.

One metric we have not considered in the statistical analysis due to its low occurrence is the number of failures encountered, shown in Table 2.

Here we can see that although Q20 did not perform so well in the other metrics, it does on the other hand find the higher number of failures (which involve stopping the execution and hence having a lesser chance of increasing the value of other metrics); this must also be taken into account when evaluating the different algorithms.

Further work will involve exploring three areas. One is related to the improvement of the metrics; for instance [5] refers to the lack of correlation between coverage and faults found, so we need to investigate metrics that are closer to the latter.

We will also study the possible interest of replacing the current accessibility API with a more suitable one that better supports dynamic webs. In particular, we will look at the open source tool Selenium; we think its API Selenium-WebDriver, www.seleniumhq.org, can help us fix the current problems we have found when applying TESTAR to web testing. Finally, we will introduce new, more complex, metaheuristics for action selection, as a substitute for the relatively simple Q-learning algorithm.

Acknowledgments. This work was partially funded by projects **SHIP** (*SMEs and HEIs in Innovation Partnerships*, ref: EACEA/A2/UHB/CL 554187) and **PERTEST** (TIN2013-46928-C3-1-R).

References

1. Bauersfeld, S., de Rojas, A., Vos, T.: Evaluating rogue user testing in industry: an experience report. In: 2014 IEEE Eighth International Conference on Research Challenges in Information Science (RCIS), pp. 1–10, May 2014
2. Bauersfeld, S., Vos, T.E.J., Condori-Fernández, N., Bagnato, A., Brosse, E.: Evaluating the TESTAR tool in an industrial case study. In: 2014 ACM-IEEE International Symposium on Empirical Software Engineering and Measurement, ESEM 2014, Torino, Italy, p. 4, 18–19 September 2014
3. Memon, A.M., Soffa, M.L., Pollack, M.E.: Coverage criteria for GUI testing. In: Proceedings of ESEC/FSE 2001, pp. 256–267 (2001)
4. Rueda, U., Vos, T.E.J., Almenar, F., Martínez, M.O., Esparcia-Alcázar, A.I.: TESTAR: from academic prototype towards an industry-ready tool for automated testing at the user interface level. In: Canos, J.H., Gonzalez Harbour, M. (eds.) Actas de las XX Jornadas de Ingeniería del Software y Bases de Datos (JISBD 2015), pp. 236–245 (2015)
5. Schwartz, A., Hetzel, M.: The impact of fault type on the relationship between code coverage and fault detection. In: Proceedings of the 11th International Workshop on Automation of Software Test, AST 2016, pp. 29–35. ACM, New York (2016). http://doi.acm.org/10.1145/2896921.2896926
6. Vos, T.E.J., Kruse, P.M., Condori-Fernández, N., Bauersfeld, S., Wegener, J.: TESTAR: tool support for test automation at the user interface level. IJISMD **6**(3), 46–83 (2015). http://dx.doi.org/10.4018/IJISMD.2015070103

API-Constrained Genetic Improvement

William B. Langdon[✉], David R. White, Mark Harman, Yue Jia,
and Justyna Petke

CREST, University College London, London, UK
w.langdon@cs.ucl.ac.uk

Abstract. ACGI respects the Application Programming Interface whilst using genetic programming to optimise the implementation of the API. It reduces the scope for improvement but it may smooth the path to GI acceptance because the programmer's code remains unaffected; only library code is modified. We applied ACGI to C++ software for the state-of-the-art OpenCV SEEDS superPixels image segmentation algorithm, obtaining a speed-up of up to 13.2 % (±1.3 %) to the $50 K Challenge winner announced at CVPR 2015.

1   Introduction and Background

Genetic improvement uses computational search to find improved versions of existing software systems [6,8,11,19]. It usually does this by searching for a set of edits that are performed on the software system to be improved, such that the desired functional behaviour of the original is retained, while some functional [5,10] and/or non-functional [11,15] aspects are improved. There has been a recent upsurge of activity in this area, with results demonstrating that genetic improvement is able to improve many different properties of systems, including dynamic memory use [20], speed of execution [9,17] and energy consumption [1,14], as well as augmenting and fixing broken functionality [5,10].

One of the advantages of genetic improvement is that it uses unconstrained modifications to software systems, more akin to genetic programming [13], than traditional program transformation. As a result, the programmers' original version of the system, although improved, is also syntactically (and possibly semantically [9,15]) altered, making it less familiar to the programmer than the original. This lack of familiarity may pose a barrier to acceptance of genetically improved programs, and adoption of genetic improvement as a technique; developers may be concerned about ongoing maintenance and comprehension of the genetically improved program.

Ultimately, these concerns may be overcome by the advantages offered by genetic improvement: that which we currently regard as source code may, in future, become 'the new object code', to be manipulated freely by genetic improvement [6]. However, even if this vision were to be realised, there will remain a necessary transition period, during which we will need to support a 'mixed economy of software systems'. Systems, part produced by machine and

© Springer International Publishing AG 2016
F. Sarro and K. Deb (Eds.): SSBSE 2016, LNCS 9962, pp. 224–230, 2016.
DOI: 10.1007/978-3-319-47106-8_16

part produced by humans, will have to co-exist, symbiotically and seamlessly. This raises the fundamental question for genetic improvement of determining the best separation of concerns between human and machine: how they might collaboratively arrive at improved software systems that are acceptable to human developers?

We propose API-Constrained Genetic Improvement (ACGI), as a first attempt to identify such a suitable separation of concerns. The key insight underlying ACGI is that human programmers are *already* generally prepared to accept third-party software in the form of library code, accessed through API calls. Typical criteria for library code acceptance revolve around the performance of the library functions, and demonstration of acceptable behaviour with respect to a suite of test cases; exactly the criteria that are automatically and inherently assessed during the genetic improvement process. Using ACGI, we constrain genetic improvement to manipulate only the library's source code, leaving the API and application code unmodified.

Although library functions are inherently designed to be general solutions, the underlying implementation does not have to be the same for all client applications. Instead we suggest libraries offer opportunities for specialisation. With potentially multiple implementations, each tailored to the expected usage of the library by one or more applications. AGCI, we hope, can tailor library functions to each particular client application, providing evidence for improved performance and adequate testing.

In the next two sections we apply GI to just the C++ source code which implements the SEEDS picture segmentation [18]. This implementation won the State of the Art Vision Challenge (http://code.opencv.org/projects/opencv/wiki/VisionChallenge#Winners-by-Categories-all-are-winners-this-isnt-in-order-of-priority) last year at the 28th IEEE Conference on Computer Vision and Pattern Recognition (CVPR 2015) and was subsequently incorporated into the Open Source Computer Vision (OpenCV) library. Just acting on this source, using real run time on a real computer for fitness, GI was able to find an almost identical class which was on average more than 13 % faster on the images used in the State of the Art Challenge. (These images are 700 by 1000 full colour. None of them were used in training by our GI.)

2 Applying ACGI to OpenCV Image Segmentation

We used the new ACGI framework on the OpenCV C++ source code of SEEDS Superpixels. To identify the library methods used, we first profiled a simple client application of the SuperPixels library using valgrind. This highlighted the updatePixels() method of the `SuperpixelSEEDSImpl` class. Then we used ACGI (see Table 1) to apply mutations to just updatePixels() and fellow methods called by it. (I.e. update(), addPixel(), deletePixel(), probability(), threebyfour() fourbythree() and updateLabels(). In total 319 lines of code.)

Table 1. Evolve faster than state-of-the-art superPixel OpenCV segmentation

Representation:	list replacements, deletions, insertions and swaps (via BNF grammar)
Fitness:	Compile (gcc 4.8.5) modified code. Compare its segmentation of 2448 by 3264 colour training image with segmentation given by original code. If identical, fitness is nanoseconds to run SuperpixelSEEDS::iterate(pic,4) else mutant is killed. To reduce noise, run on local disk on otherwise idle networked Linux PC. For robustness to noise, fitness is 25th percentile (i.e. 3rd) of 11 sequential measurements.
Population:	Panmictic, non-elitist, generational. 100 members.
Parameters:	Initial population of random single mutants. 50 % truncation selection. 50 % two point crossover and 50 % mutation. (Mutations chosen equally between insert, delete, replace and swap.) No size limit. Stop after 200 generations

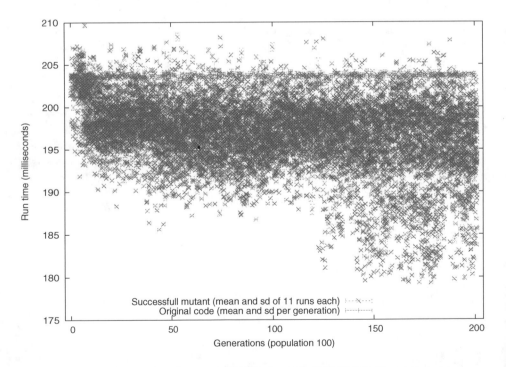

Fig. 1. Evolution of speed, on a 3.60 GHz Intel i7-4790 32 GB Centos7 desktop.

3   Results

3.1   Best of First Generation

In the first generation (left Fig. 1) all but five mutants compiled. (These five failed to compile due to a bug in the new swap mutation's use of scoping rules). Eight failed run time array bound checks. Four were aborted by the CPU limit of 5 s (all due to deleting the iteration increment part of `for` loops). 65 ran and terminated ok but at least one pixel (of 7 990 272) was different from the value calculated by the original code. Leaving 18 cases where the code was modified but gave exactly the same answer. It appears that the fastest of these improves the code by taking advantage of the fact that it is being run with its default settings. `<IF_updatePixels.cpp_267><IF_updatePixels.cpp_38>` replaces the condition of an `if` statement (`if( prior2 != 0 )` on line 267) with the `if` condition on line 38. As the compiler is now able to infer the condition will always be true, it can eliminate the `if` entirely. Whereas in the original code, although `prior2` is never zero, it is impossible for the compiler to know this.

3.2   Cleaning up the Best of Run Mutation

The best individual in generation 200 (right Fig. 1) gives exactly the same answer on all $2448 \times 3264 = 7\,990\,272$ pixels as the prize winning code and yet runs on average 9.7 % faster.

   The evolved program contains 22 changes. To determine which are essential, each was removed one at a time to create an intermediate of 21 changes whose performance on the same training image was measured as before. In six cases this made the mutant significantly more than 0.1 % worse. A new mutant was constructed from these six (in the same order as the best evolved program). (Notice we measured real runtime and so despite precautions some changes may still be included due to noise.) On the original training image it was 10.0 % faster than the original code and produced exactly the same answer. It was run on 447 new images. In 424 cases the new code produced identical answers. In all but five of the remaining 23 images less than nine (median 3) pixels were changed. The biggest difference was 71 out of 7 990 272 pixels. Overall $< 0.000\,000\,1$ of validation pixels are different. On average across the 447 new images the new code is 10.3 % ($\pm 1.4\,\%$) faster. On the six "bikes" images from the 2014 OpenCV challenge competition (which were not used for training), it always produces identical answers and is 13.2 % ($\pm 1.3\,\%$) faster. Taking the mutant and recompiling (gcc 4.8.4) for a virtualized Ubuntu 14.04.1 cloud server we get the same speed up, i.e. 13.1 % ($\pm 4.1\,\%$), however these savings did not carry over to a 1.6 GHz Apple MacBook Air laptop with a LLVM compiler. (Some semantics-preserving changes are available via https://github.com/Itseez/opencv_contrib/pull/687/.)

3.3   The Six Improvements in the Best of Last Generation

The six line changes are described and partially explained next. They are grouped by which method of the `SuperpixelSEEDSImpl` class they were made to.

`updatePixels()` Lines 113 and 114 are swapped (by swap mutation). No semantic changes are expected. However, it will change the order in which data are read. (Notice the image exceeds our desktop PC's cache of 8 Mbytes.)

A copy of line 59 is added to end of the first nested `for` loop which scans the whole image. Line 59 is in the nested `for` loop. It is a call to `update()`. It is difficult to see why this change is beneficial and perhaps it may change the program's output.

`probability()` Lines 279 and 281 are deleted. These are `case:` statements corresponding to values of `seeds_prior` which are never used *in these examples*. Reducing the number of cases in `switch( seeds_prior )` may make it faster for the cases that are used and in this code removing the unused options has no impact on the remaining cases.

`fourbythree()` Lines 338 and 345 are swapped. This has no impact on the output, but does change the order in which array elements are read.

A copy of line 199 (from `updatePixels()`) is inserted into `fourbythree()`. The line inverts global Boolean variable `forwardbackward`. However, `fourby three()` is always called twice, so the second call immediately inverts `forward backward` a second time, restoring the original behaviour. However, it is difficult to see why this mutation would make the program go faster.

4   Related and Future Work

Concerns about the maintainability of genetically improved code have partly been addressed by work on automatically generating documentation for the improvements [3]. Human-written documentation may suffer from all sorts of inconsistencies and omissions, whereas machine-generated documentation could, in principle, be more systematic and thorough.

Nevertheless, our experience of genetic improvement [1,9,20], is that we are at once *delighted* by the surprise of seeing the unexpected improvements that can be found, yet at the same time *challenged* to understand, interpret and explain them. It is one of the advantages of computational search that it can confound and surpass human expectations. Indeed, this 'surprisal' is the underpinning of most human competitive results, some of which have already been reported for SBSE in general [16], and for genetic improvement in particular [12].

The ability to find unexpected solutions is both a strength and a weakness of genetic improvement: It is a strength because it finds improved software that no human would be likely to find, but it can become a weakness if it finds solutions that few humans can understand. Our approach to genetic improvement, ACGI, isolates and contains the modified code, in much the way that a surgeon might seek to isolate a wound [2]. While the modified parts of the code are the source of improvement, to the programmer they might more closely resemble a 'wound'.

In focusing on library functions, our work is similar to the work on deep parameter optimisation [20], which exposes additional parameters to facilitate better tuning at the application layer. However, inserting additional parameters inherently disrupts the API layer. By contrast, the goal of ACGI is to minimally disrupt the API layer, so that details of the modifications that lead to improvements become relatively unimportant to the software engineer. In this way, our approach partly resembles the goal of 'obliviousness' in aspect oriented programming [7]; client code performance is improved, yet it remains oblivious to the changes made in the library functions, since the same API is maintained.

In future work, we will seek to investigate human programmer tolerance to genetically improved code, addressing the fundamental question "how much disruption is a software engineer prepared to tolerate for a given level of performance improvement for a given software engineering domain/application?".

5   Conclusions

We have introduced API-Constrained Genetic Improvement (ACGI) with the aim of bridging the gap between machine and human, to allay concerns about genetic improvement maintainability. Our initial experiments indicate that, despite ACGI's tight constraints, improvements can still be found automatically, in real-world software systems. E.g. compared to the winner of last year's image segmentation task in the OpenCV State of the Art Vision Challenge we find a speed up of 13 % (with little change in functionality).

Acknowledgement. We would like to thank Bobby R. Bruce. This work is part supported by the GGGP and DAASE [4] projects.

References

1. Bruce, B.R., Petke, J., Harman, M.: Reducing energy consumption using genetic improvement. In: GECCO, pp. 1327–1334 (2015). http://dx.doi.org/doi:10.1145/2739480.2754752

2. Cruse, P., Foord, R.: A five-year prospective study of 23,649 surgical wounds. Arch. Surg. **107**(2), 206–210 (1973)

3. Fry, Z.P., Landau, B., Weimer, W.: A human study of patch maintainability. In: ISSTA, pp. 177–187 (2012). http://dx.doi.org/doi:10.1145/2338965.2336775

4. Harman, M., Burke, E., Clark, J.A., Yao, X.: Dynamic adaptive search based software engineering (keynote paper). In: ESEM, pp. 1–8 (2012)

5. Harman, M., Jia, Y., Langdon, W.B.: Babel pidgin: SBSE can grow and graft entirely new functionality into a real world system. In: Le Goues, C., Yoo, S. (eds.) SSBSE 2014. LNCS, vol. 8636, pp. 247–252. Springer, Heidelberg (2014). http://dx.doi.org/10.1007/978-3-319-09940-8

6. Harman, M., Langdon, W.B., Jia, Y., White, D.R., Arcuri, A., Clark, J.A.: The GISMOE challenge: constructing the Pareto program surface using genetic programming to find better programs (keynote paper). In: ASE, pp. 1–14 (2012). http://dx.doi.org/doi:10.1145/2351676.2351678

7. Kiczales, G.: Aspect oriented programming. ACM SIGPLAN Not. **32**(10), 162 (1997). Table of contents includes this invited talk
8. Langdon, W.B.: Genetically improved software. In: Gandomi, A.H., et al. (eds.) Handbook of Genetic Programming Applications, pp. 181–220. Springer, Switzerland (2015). http://dx.doi.org/10.1007/978-3-319-20883-1_8
9. Langdon, W.B., Harman, M.: Optimising existing software with genetic programming. IEEE TEVC **19**(1), 118–135 (2015). http://dx.doi.org/doi:10.1109/TEVC.2013.2281544
10. Le Goues, C., Forrest, S., Weimer, W.: Current challenges in automatic software repair. Softw. Qual. J. **21**(3), 421–443 (2013). http://dx.doi.org/doi:10.1007/s11219-013-9208-0
11. Orlov, M., Sipper, M.: Flight of the FINCH through the Java wilderness. IEEE TEVC **15**(2), 166–182 (2011). http://dx.doi.org/doi:10.1109/TEVC.2010.2052622
12. Petke, J., Harman, M., Langdon, W.B., Weimer, W.: Using genetic improvement & code transplants to specialise a C++ program to a problem class. In: Nicolau, M., Krawiec, K., Heywood, M.I., Castelli, M., García-Sánchez, P., Merelo, J.J., Rivas Santos, V.M., Sim, K. (eds.) Genetic Programming. LNCS, vol. 8599, pp. 137–149. Springer, Heidelberg (2014). http://dx.doi.org/doi:10.1007/978-3-662-44303-3_12
13. Poli, R., Langdon, W.B., McPhee, N.F.: A field guide to genetic programming (2008). http://www.gp-field-guide.org.uk
14. Schulte, E., Dorn, J., Harding, S., Forrest, S., Weimer, W.: Post-compiler software optimization for reducing energy. In: ASPLOS, pp. 639–652 (2014). http://doi.acm.org/10.1145/2654822.2541980
15. Sitthi-amorn, P., Modly, N., Weimer, W., Lawrence, J.: Genetic programming for shader simplification. ACM TOG **30**(6), 152:1–152:11 (2011). http://dx.doi.org/doi:10.1145/2070781.2024186
16. Souza, J., Maia, C.L., de Freitas, F.G., Coutinho, D.P.: The human competitiveness of search based software engineering. IEEE SSBSE, 143–152 (2010). http://dx.doi.org/10.1109/SSBSE.2010.25
17. Swan, J., et al.: Gen-O-Fix: An embeddable framework for dynamic adaptive genetic improvement programming. Technical report CSM-195, University of Stirling (2014)
18. Van den Bergh, M., Boix, X., Roig, G., de Capitani, B., Van Gool, L.: SEEDS: superpixels extracted via energy-driven sampling. In: Fitzgibbon, A., Lazebnik, S., Perona, P., Sato, Y., Schmid, C. (eds.) ECCV 2012, Part VII. LNCS, vol. 7578, pp. 13–26. Springer, Heidelberg (2012). http://dx.doi.org/10.1007/978-3-642-33786-4_2
19. White, D.R., Arcuri, A., Clark, J.A.: Evolutionary improvement of programs. IEEE TEVC **15**(4), 515–538 (2011). http://dx.doi.org/doi:10.1109/TEVC.2010.2083669
20. Wu, F., Harman, M., Jia, Y., Krinke, J., Weimer, W.: Deep parameter optimisation. In: GECCO, pp. 1375–1382 (2015). http://dx.doi.org/doi:10.1145/2739480.2754648

Challenges in Using Search-Based Test Generation to Identify Real Faults in Mockito

Gregory Gay[✉]

University of South Carolina, Columbia, SC, USA
greg@greggay.com

Abstract. The cost of test creation can potentially be reduced through automated generation. However, to impact testing practice, automated tools must be at least as effective as manual generation. The Mockito project—a framework for mocking portions of a system—offers an opportunity to assess the capabilities of test generation tools on a complex real-world system. We have identified 17 faults in the Mockito project, added those to the Defects4J database, and assessed the ability of the EvoSuite tool to detect these faults. In our study, EvoSuite was only able to detect one of the 17 faults. Analysis of the 16 undetected faults yields lessons in how to improve generation tools. We offer these faults to the community to assist in benchmarking future test generation advances.

Keywords: Search-based testing · Automated unit test generation · Real faults

1 Introduction

Software testing is a notoriously expensive and difficult activity. With the exponential growth in the complexity of software, the cost of testing has only continued to rise. Much of the cost of testing can be traced directly to the human effort required to conduct most testing activities—such as producing test input and expected outputs. However, such effort is often in service of goals that can be framed as *search* problems, and automated through the use of optimization algorithms [1].

Test case generation can naturally be seen as a search problem. There are hundreds of thousands of test cases that could be generated for any particular SUT. From that pool, we want to select—systematically and at a reasonable cost—those that meet our goals and are expected to be fault-revealing [1]. Automated unit test generation tools have become very effective—even covering more code than tests manually constructed by developers [4]. However, to make an impact on testing practice, automated test generation techniques must be *as effective*, if not more so, at detecting faults as human-created test cases [7].

The Mockito project[1] offers an opportunity to assess the capabilities of test generation tools. Mockito is a *mocking framework* for Java unit testing, allowing

---

[1] http://mockito.org/.

© Springer International Publishing AG 2016
F. Sarro and K. Deb (Eds.): SSBSE 2016, LNCS 9962, pp. 231–237, 2016.
DOI: 10.1007/978-3-319-47106-8_17

users to create customized stand-ins (*mock objects*) for classes in a system, permitting testers to isolate units of a system from their dependencies. Rather than performing the functions of the mocked object, the mock instead issues preprogrammed output. Mockito is an essential tool of modern development, and is one of the most used Java libraries [8].

Mockito serves as an interesting benchmark for two reasons. First, it is a complex project. Much of its functionality is, naturally, related to the creation and manipulation of mock objects. The inputs required by many Mockito functions are complex objects—which are difficult for many test case generators to produce [2]. Second, Mockito is a mature project, having undergone eight years of active development. Recent Mockito faults are unlikely to be the simple syntactic mistakes modeled by mutation coverage. Faults that emerge in a mature project are more likely to require specific, difficult to trigger, combinations of input and method calls. If a test generation tool can detect such faults, then it is likely ready for real-world use. If not, then by studying these faults—and others like them—we may be able to learn lessons that will improve these tools.

We have identified 17 real faults in the Mockito project, and have added them to the Defects4J fault library [6]. We generated test suites using the search-based EvoSuite generation framework [3], and measured the suites' ability to cover the affected classes and detect each fault. EvoSuite was only able to detect one of the 17 faults discovered in the project. Some of the issues preventing fault detection include poor guidance for the fitness function, the need for complex input to methods and object constructors, specific environmental configurations and factors, uncertainty in which classes to generate tests for, and simplistic handling of interface changes between software versions. We have made this set of Mockito faults available to provide data and examples for benchmarking future test generation advances.

2   Study

Recent studies have assessed the capabilities of test generation tools on faults in open-source projects [7], but more data is needed to understand where such tools excel and where they need to be improved. In this study, we have generated tests using the search-based EvoSuite framework [3] on classes of the Mockito project. In doing so, we wish to answer the following research questions:

1. Can EvoSuite detect faults found in Mockito?
2. What factors prevented EvoSuite from detecting faults?

In order to answer these questions, we have performed the following experiment:

1. **Derived Faults:** We have identified 17 real faults in the Mockito project, and added them to the Defects4J fault database (See Sect. 2.1).
2. **Generated Test Cases:** For each fault, we generated tests on the fixed version of fault-affected classes. (See Sect. 2.2).

3. **Removed Non-Compiling Tests:** Any tests that do not compile or that fail on the fixed system are automatically removed (See Sect. 2.2).
4. **Assessed Fault-finding and Coverage:** For each suite and fault, we measure the number of tests that pass on the fixed version and fail on the faulty version. We also record the achieved code coverage.
5. **Analyzed Faults That Were Not Detected:** For each undetected fault, we examined the report and source code to identify possible detection-preventing factors.

2.1   Fault Extraction

Using Mockito's version control and issue tracking systems, we have identified 17 faults. Each fault is required to meet three properties. First, the fault must be related to the source code. For each reported issue, we attempted to identify a pair of code versions that differ only by the minimum changes required to address the fault. The "fixed" version must be explicitly labeled as a fix to an issue, and changes imposed by the fix must be to source code, not to other project artifacts such as the build system. Second, the fault must be reproducible—at least one test must pass on the fixed version and fail on the faulty version. Third, the fix to the fault must be isolated from unrelated code changes such as refactorings.

In order to focus on the faults typical of a mature project, we limited our extraction to the GitHub-based issue tracking system that Mockito began using in July 2014 (previously, Google Code was used). To help identify candidate faults, we used automation provided by Defects4J [6]—a library of faults from five open-source Java programs and tools for assessing tests intended to find such faults.

We have added Mockito as a sixth Defects4J project. This consisted of developing build files that work across project versions, extracting candidate faults, ensuring that each candidate could be reliable reproduced, and minimizing the "patch" used to distinguish fixed and faulty classes. Following this process, we extracted 17 faults from a pool of 89 candidate faults. Six of the 17 faults were "false-positives", fixes to issues reported in the old issue tracker that shared an issue ID with issues in the newer tracking system. As these six faults met reasonable system maturity and complexity thresholds, we also added them to Defects4J.

The faults used in this study can be accessed by cloning the `bug-mining` branch of https://github.com/Greg4cr/defects4j. Additional data about each fault can be found at http://greggay.com/data/mockito/mockitofaults.csv, including commit IDs, fault descriptions, and a list of triggering tests. We plan to add additional faults and improvements in the future.

2.2   Test Generation and Removal

EvoSuite applies a genetic algorithm in order to evolve test suites over several generations, forming a new population by retaining, mutating, and combining the strongest solutions. It is actively maintained and has been successfully applied to a variety of projects [7]. In this study, we used EvoSuite version 1.0.3 with the default fitness function—a combination of branch, context branch, line, exception, weak mutation, method-output, top-level method, and no-exception top-level method coverage. Given the potential difficulty in achieving coverage over Mockito classes, the search budget was set to 10 min. To control experiment cost, we deactivated assertion filtering—all possible regression assertions are included. All other settings were kept at their default values. As results may vary, we performed 30 trials for each fault by generating tests for the classes patched to fix the fault.

Tests are generated from the fixed version of the system and applied to the faulty version in order to eliminate the oracle problem. In practice, this translates to a regression testing scenario. Due to changes introduced to fix faults, such as altered method signatures or new classes, some tests may not compile on the faulty version of the system. We have automatically removed such tests. We have also removed tests that fail on the fixed version of the system, as these do not assist in identifying faults. On average, 4.48 % of the tests are removed from each suite. More statistics are included in Table 1.

3   Results and Discussion

The results of our experiment can be seen in Table 1. In our study, only one of the 17 faults was detected—Fault 2. This particular fault—revolving around incorrect handling of negative time values—is an excellent example of the kind of fault that automated test generation is able to handle. The code fix adds conditional behavior to handle time input. By covering the new branches, the tests are guided to detect the fault in all 30 trials. However, EvoSuite failed to detect the other 16 faults. Therefore, our next step was to examine these faults to identify factors preventing detection. These factors include:

Poor Guidance for the Fitness Function: While EvoSuite is often able to achieve reasonable levels of coverage across Mockito classes, coverage is sometimes quite low. While coverage does not guarantee fault detection, unexecuted code cannot reveal faults [5]. One reason coverage may not be achieved is that the code offers no guidance to the search tool in selecting *better* test suites.

Many fitness functions are designed to measure the distance from optimality of generated test cases. However, it is not always obvious how to calculate this distance. The code that must be covered to detect Fault 12[2] provides a good example. Both branches use the `instanceof` operator. Without a method of determining the "distance" between class types, the search devolves into a random search.

Complex Input is Required to Trigger a Fault: A challenge for test generation techniques is generating inputs of complex data types [2]. As Mockito generates objects that mimic other objects, many of its methods require complex

---

[2] https://github.com/mockito/mockito/commit/7a647a702c8af81ccf5d37b09c11529 c6c0cb1b7.

Table 1. Average test generation results for each fault—whether the fault was detected, number of generated tests, number of non-compiling tests, line coverage (LC), branch coverage (BC), exception coverage (EC), weak mutation coverage (WMC), method-output coverage (OC), method coverage (MC), no-exception top-level method coverage (MNEC), context branch coverage (CBC), and the resulting average across all coverage metrics.

ID	Fault Detected	# Tests Generated	# Tests Removed	% LC	% BC	% EC	% WMC	% OC	% MC	% MNEC	% CBC	Resulting % Coverage
1	X	4.23	0.00	10.00	7.00	100.00	2.00	2.00	25.00	8.00	3.00	20.00
2	✓	92.00	1.00	86.97	87.95	100.00	62.85	50.00	100.00	50.50	87.95	72.47
3	X	4.31	0.00	10.00	8.00	100.00	2.00	2.00	25.00	8.00	3.00	20.00
4	X	84.70	0.00	73.67	85.33	100.00	24.50	0.00	100.00	1.00	85.33	46.67
5	X	15.03	0.00	61.80	77.63	98.90	77.00	100.00	100.00	100.00	77.63	87.00
6	X	60.13	0.00	100.00	100.00	100.00	100.00	44.50	100.00	100.00	100.00	93.00
7	X	14.82	0.00	12.86	20.86	92.86	12.82	0.00	10.00	0.00	20.86	26.00
8	X	14.97	0.00	12.97	20.93	100.00	12.93	0.00	10.00	0.00	20.93	26.00
9	X	1.00	0.00	33.00	33.00	100.00	0.00	0.00	100.00	50.00	33.00	38.00
10	X	2.00	0.00	8.00	10.00	100.00	0.00	0.00	100.00	33.00	10.00	24.00
11	X	1.00	0.00	6.00	12.00	100.00	20.00	0.00	10.00	0.00	12.00	20.67
12	X	1.00	0.00	12.00	11.00	100.00	0.00	0.00	100.00	50.00	11.00	29.00
13	X	10.07	0.00	45.90	59.78	100.00	25.00	67.00	100.00	75.00	59.77	62.93
14	X	41.89	4.63	81.59	83.52	93.48	67.81	62.63	99.84	83.96	83.26	80.02
15	X	16.70	7.37	65.36	64.09	92.48	55.42	50.56	85.56	80.97	64.09	64.00
16	X	73.90	7.57	86.43	84.91	80.68	83.33	38.68	100.00	77.43	84.41	71.36
17	X	35.50	3.43	99.04	97.43	95.21	94.91	57.50	100.00	100.00	97.43	91.03

objects as input. Even in cases where coverage is high, test generators may have difficulty producing the intricate, highly-specific, input required to detect that fault.

Consider Fault 13[3], which occurs when Mockito's verification capabilities are invoked on a method call that, itself, has an embedded method call within it. Triggering this fault requires generating two different mock objects, then embedding a call to one object within a call to the second. Coverage alone is unlikely to suggest such input. Rather, fitness functions that incorporate domain expertise may be needed to help generate more complex input scenarios. Promising work has been conducted using grammars to produce complex input [2].

Complex Input is Required to *Generate Any Tests*: Unit tests instantiate an object and call the methods offered by that object. At times, objects must be provided with input when they are instantiated (there is no "default" constructor). Many of the code changes made to fix Fault 3[4] are contained within one method. EvoSuite not only fails to fully cover this method, it fails to invoke this method at all. In this case, EvoSuite attempts to instantiate the InvocationMaster class, but many of these attempts fail due to invalid input. EvoSuite cannot cover the methods of an object that it cannot instantiate.

---

[3] https://code.google.com/archive/p/mockito/issues/138.

[4] https://github.com/mockito/mockito/commit/3eec7451d6c83c280743c39b39c77a179abb30f9.

Faults Require Specific Environmental Factors: Fault 5^5 revolves around an undesired dependency on the JUnit framework. Fixing this fault requires code changes—yet, coverage of this code will not reveal this fault. Rather, the fault is detected when JUnit is removed from the local classpath. This is an example of a fault that depends on environmental factors—in this case, the classpath used to compile code. EvoSuite does manipulate certain environmental factors, such as file system access, but more examination of such factors is needed in future test generation research.

Fault Detection Requires Generating Tests for Related Classes: The classes affected by Fault 6^6 offer another interesting example. Mock objects can be configured to return different values based on the type of function input. Due to this fault, a mock can produce a value intended for certain data types when a `null` object is passed instead of the intended type. The fault-fixing changes are primarily in methods that do not require input—methods that are called by Mockito's argument matchers. Because these methods do not require input, this fault cannot be detected without generating tests for the argument matcher classes that, in turn, call these methods. Under normal circumstances, EvoSuite could produce the required `null` input, but tests would need to be generated for classes that do not contain faulty code, and instead depend on faulty code. Some consideration should be given to which classes are used when generating tests, and the dependencies between those classes.

Changes to Code Invalidate Test Cases: When tests are generated on one version of a system and applied to another, code changes such as the addition of new classes or altered method signatures can result in tests that do not compile on one version. In this study, we removed those tests. This may prevent fault detection. Fault 17^7 affects the ability to set mock objects as serializable. EvoSuite is correctly guided to create serializable mock objects. However, any time this occurs, interactions take place with a new class. These tests are removed, as they do not compile on the faulty version of the system. In normal practice, this is not an issue, as tests are generated on the version they are applied to, but during regression testing, similar issues may occur. Intelligent strategies are needed to generate tests that compile across multiple versions of systems.

4   Conclusion

The capabilities of test generation techniques have increased. Yet, from the examples extracted from the Mockito project, we can see that there are still fault-detection hurdles to overcome. EvoSuite was only able to detect one of the 17 faults. Some of the issues preventing fault detection include poor guidance for

---

[5] https://github.com/mockito/mockito/issues/152.

[6] https://github.com/mockito/mockito/commit/dc205824dbc289acbcde919e430176 ad72da847f.

[7] https://github.com/mockito/mockito/commit/77cb2037314dd024eb53ffe2e9e06304088a2d53.

the fitness function, the need for complex input to methods and object constructors, environmental factors, uncertainty in which classes to generate tests for, and simplistic handling of interface changes between multiple software versions. We hope that the set of faults extracted from Mockito will provide data and examples for benchmarking new test generation advances.

References

1. Ali, S., Briand, L.C., Hemmati, H., Panesar-Walawege, R.K.: A systematic review of the application and empirical investigation of search-based test case generation. IEEE Trans. Softw. Eng. **36**(6), 742–762 (2010)
2. Feldt, R., Poulding, S.: Finding test data with specific properties via metaheuristic search. In: 2013 IEEE 24th International Symposium on Software Reliability Engineering (ISSRE), pp. 350–359, November 2013
3. Fraser, G., Arcuri, A.: Whole test suite generation. IEEE Trans. Softw. Eng. **39**(2), 276–291 (2013)
4. Fraser, G., Staats, M., McMinn, P., Arcuri, A., Padberg, F.: Does automated whitebox test generation really help software testers? In: Proceedings of the 2013 International Symposium on Software Testing and Analysis, ISSTA 2013, pp. 291–301. ACM, New York (2013). http://doi.acm.org/10.1145/2483760.2483774
5. Gay, G., Staats, M., Whalen, M., Heimdahl, M.: The risks of coverage-directed test case generation. IEEE Trans. Softw. Eng. **PP**(99) (2015)
6. Just, R., Jalali, D., Ernst, M.D.: Defects4J: a database of existing faults to enable controlled testing studies for Java programs. In: Proceedings of the 2014 International Symposium on Software Testing and Analysis, ISSTA 2014, pp. 437–440. ACM, New York (2014). http://doi.acm.org/10.1145/2610384.2628055
7. Shamshiri, S., Just, R., Rojas, J.M., Fraser, G., McMinn, P., Arcuri, A.: Do automatically generated unit tests find real faults? an empirical study of effectiveness and challenges. In: Proceedings of the 30th IEEE/ACM International Conference on Automated Software Engineering (ASE), ASE 2015. ACM, New York (2015)
8. Weiss, T.: We analyzed 30,000 GitHub projects - here are the top 100 libraries in Java, JS and Ruby (2013). http://blog.takipi.com/we-analyzed-30000-github-projects-here-are-the-top-100-libraries-in-java-js-and-ruby/

Deep Parameter Optimisation for Face Detection Using the Viola-Jones Algorithm in OpenCV

Bobby R. Bruce[1](✉), Jonathan M. Aitken[2](✉), and Justyna Petke[1](✉)

[1] SSE Group, Department of Computer Science, CREST Centre, UCL, London, UK
r.bruce@cs.ucl.ac.uk , j.petke@ucl.ac.uk
[2] Department of Automatic Control and Systems Engineering,
University of Sheffield, Sheffield, UK
jonathan.aitken@sheffield.ac.uk

Abstract. OpenCV is a commonly·used computer vision library containing a wide variety of algorithms for the AI community. This paper uses *deep parameter optimisation* to investigate improvements to face detection using the Viola-Jones algorithm in OpenCV, allowing a trade-off between execution time and classification accuracy. Our results show that execution time can be decreased by 48 % if a 1.80 % classification inaccuracy is permitted (compared to 1.04 % classification inaccuracy of the original, unmodified algorithm). Further execution time savings are possible depending on the degree of inaccuracy deemed acceptable by the user.

Keywords: Deep parameter optimisation · Automated parameter tuning · Multi-objective optimisation · Genetic improvement · GI · SBSE · OpenCV · Viola-Jones Algorithm

1 Introduction

Traditional small mobile robotics applications have limited power and computing capacity. This is further complicated for Unmanned Aerial Vehicles (UAVs), which have limited battery-life and thus any excess weight is detrimental to the time that can be spent in the air. The efficiency and accuracy of the processing is thus essential in an Unmanned Aerial Vehicle (UAV) performing tasks. Typically these tasks can use visual servoing in order to direct flights to locate objects of interest [5], or to provide a larger field of view for ground-based vehicles [7]. This is especially important in areas in which the Global Positioning System (GPS) is unavailable, where an aerial vehicle can be used to localise a ground vehicle and provide extra information about routing [2].

For example, if the UAV is performing a visual survey of a region, any repetition of a route is wasteful. The optimisation of any visual processing is essential so that areas do not need to be re-covered and thus battery capacity is not wasted. Speeding up visual processing leads to images being processed at faster rates which allows the capture of more data [11].

© Springer International Publishing AG 2016
F. Sarro and K. Deb (Eds.): SSBSE 2016, LNCS 9962, pp. 238–243, 2016.
DOI: 10.1007/978-3-319-47106-8_18

Therefore, we propose to optimise OpenCV, a very popular computer vision library within the robotics community, using the recently introduced technique of *deep parameter optimisation* [14]. Our results show that we can achieve significant efficiency gains when we trade-off runtime and image classification accuracy. The following sections present the details of our approach.

2 OpenCV

OpenCV[1] is a library for computer vision [3]. It was developed by Intel, then Willow Garage, leading to its integration in the popular robotic development architecture – (ROS) [8] and wide uptake within the robotics as well as the computer vision community. It is now maintained by Itseez, a software company that specialises in optimisation of real-world applications in computer vision, pattern recognition and machine learning[2].

Face detection in OpenCV is commonly implemented using the Viola-Jones algorithm [12,13]. The Viola-Jones algorithm searches an image, at multiple scales, shifting through the image one pixel at a time, for a collection of haar features, which are shapes of binary values defining areas of light and darkness, components of the object separate from the background. The selected set of haar features defines the detected objects. There is a common set of haar features implemented in OpenCV that detects human faces, and a cascade classifier can be trained with an appropriate set.

3 Deep Parameter Optimisation

Deep parameter optimisation [14] is a technique that delves deeper into parameters that can affect non-functional program properties than traditional approaches (e.g., used in the machine learning community [6]). This forms a larger search-space opening new routes over which optimisation can be performed. There is a three-step process for performing deep parameter optimisation: (1) Discovery of the locations for deep parameters; (2) Exposing deep parameters to be available for tuning; (3) Search-based tuning of the exposed parameters.

4 Related Work

Previously studies have investigated the potential of optimising the Viola-Jones algorithm or adjusting it to perform more favourably under differing conditions [1,9,10].

Aby et al. [1] explored optimisation of the Viola-Jones algorithm on an embedded, single-board, computing platform – the Beagle Board. Rather than

---

[1] OpenCV's source code is available at: https://github.com/Itseez/opencv/.
[2] Itseez software company website: http://itseez.com/.

directly optimising the algorithm, they scheduled the heavy computational tasks on the Digital Signal Processor, freeing up the main ARM processor to complete ancillary computational tasks. Whilst this technique provides an improvement of processing time of the Viola-Jones algorithm it does not attempt to optimise the algorithm itself.

Rahmen et al. [9] developed an algorithm that uses skin colour and shape processing to detect faces. Initially this segments the images using typical skin colours before looking for smaller shapes that characterise faces. They achieved good performance, and indicate a favourable improvements in processing speed.

Ren et al. [10] applied a series of optimisation techniques in order to improve performance. They focused on removing the need to use dedicated extra processing power, rather than looking for software-based solutions. They tested three different optimisation approaches:

- Data Reduction – reducing the resolution of images used for face identification, increasing the shift between images from the standard one pixel, increasing the sizes used at each scale step and defining a larger minimum face size terminating the algorithm more quickly.
- Search Reduction – using key frames to limit the number of frames that need processing for a given video sequence.
- Numerical Reduction – using fixed-point formatted numbers rather than floating point to save on computation.

This paper provides an extension of this optimisation work as it applies deep parameter optimisation to the Viola-Jones algorithm itself. Rather than shifting processing, or attempting pre-filtering, we adjust the parameters themselves. Unlike the work of [10] the adjustments made throughout the optimisation are not limited to different areas, but operate across the complete algorithm. By using deep parameter optimisation, we can expose hidden options for optimisation.

5   Experimental Setup

Given OpenCV is a library, we developed a small command-line level program to utilise the OpenCV's functionality we wished to be optimised. This program, classify_images, took a directory of images as a lone argument. When executed classify_images produces output identifying which images contained faces and which did not. classify_images utilises the CascadeClassifier:: detectMultiScale method with CascadeClassifier initialised using haarcascade_frontalface_alt.xml (included by default in OpenCV).

We created a dataset of 10,000 images which contain faces[3] and 10,000 images which do not[4]. This was then split into a training set containing 1,500 images with faces and 1,500 without, and a test set containing 8,500 images with faces

---

[3] Obtained from the University of Massachusetts 'Labelled Faces In The wild' dataset - http://vis-www.cs.umass.edu/lfw/lfw.tgz.

[4] Obtained from the Caltech-256 dataset – http://www.vision.caltech.edu/ Image_Datasets/Caltech256/256_ObjectCategories.tar.

and 8,500 without. Prior to any form of optimisation `classify_images` incorrectly classified 0.90 % of the training set and 1.04 % of the test set.

We then profiled the software to find which files were the most heavily utilised in OpenCV when classifying images. We found that the top two files were `cascadedetect.cpp` and `cascadedetect.hpp`. We then proceeded to extract all integer constants from these files. This process involved using a regular expression to highlight all instances of integer constants. Before doing so we carried out a replacement of all occurrences of `[variable]++` to `[variable]+=1`, increasing the number of constants available for extraction.

We then replaced all instances of integer constants found with unique C Define Compilation Macros. These were extracted to a file called `defines.hpp` which was then included in both `cascadedetect.cpp` and `cascadedetect.hpp`. In total, `defines.hpp` contained 537 integer constants. `defines.hpp` can be seen as a source-code level configuration file which we altered.

While it would have been possible to proceed at this point with the parameter tuning process, considerable savings can be made by carrying out sensitivity analysis – the process of selecting a subset of parameters to optimise the desired non-functional properties.

For each of the 537 integer constants we first added one, compiled the OpenCV library, then run `classify_images` on a single face image randomly selected from the training set. If `classify_images` compiled, run, and produced a result without crashing, it passed what we refer to as 'stage 1'. If an integer passed 'stage 1' we then added 50 to the integer value. `classify_images` was then compiled with the modified OpenCV and run on the training set. To pass this stage ('stage 2') the modified version had to complete compilation and complete execution in a time different to the original (outside of the 95 % confidence interval for the original, unmodified, `classify_images` run 100 times on the training set). 'stage 1' can be viewed as a step to filter out parameters that are too sensitive, while 'stage 2' can be viewed as a step to filter out those that are not sensitive enough. After these two stages of sensitivity analysis we were left with 51 deep parameters for optimisation.

We tuned these parameters using the NSGA-II algorithm [4] implemented in the MOEA framework[5]. For the execution time objective we used UNIX's `time` utility on `classify_images` when classifying the training set. The second objective, classification inaccuracy, was calculated as a percentage of incorrect classifications by `classify_images` on the training set. NSGA-II attempts to minimize both of these objectives. We further reduced the search-space by only allowing parameters to be increased to a maximum of 64 and to be decreased to a minimum of 0.

We ran NSGA-II on 100 individuals over 10 generations in an Ubuntu 14.04.4 m4.large Amazon EC2 Instance (2 × 2.4 GHz Intel Xeon E5-2676 v3 processor, 8 GiB of memory, SSD Storage). The initial generation was seeded with an individual containing the original parameter settings. The remainder of the initial population was generated by iterating through the parameters and generating a variant equal to the original but with the parameter being increased by 1 or 2.

---

[5] MOEA framework available at: http://moeaframework.org/.

Once complete, the MOEA framework returned the Pareto front of solutions. To ensure these results were not over-fitted to the training set, we ran each Pareto optimal solution on the test set, removing any which crash or were dominated by other solutions to produce the final Pareto optimal set.

6   Results

The NSGA-II algorithm produced a Pareto front that contained 14 solutions when run on the training set. When ran each of these Pareto optimal solutions on the test set, one failed to complete execution and another was dominated by other solutions in the set thus leaving 12 Pareto optimal solutions and the original, unaltered program which was also found to be Pareto optimal when run on the test set[6]. These are shown in Fig. 1 (the original program included as the left-most solution).

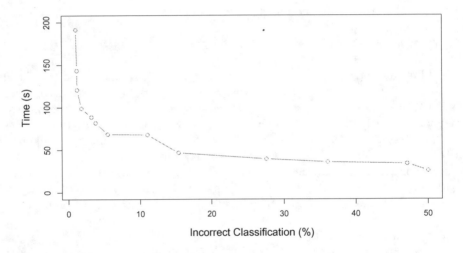

Fig. 1. The Pareto front of solutions when run on the test set of 17,000 images.

7   Conclusions

We used deep parameter optimisation to investigate improvements to face detection using the Viola-Jones algorithm in OpenCV, allowing for a trade-off between execution time and classification accuracy. In this study, a basic form of deep parameter optimisation decreased the execution time of the Viola-Jones algorithm by 48 % with a 1.80 % classification inaccuracy when evaluated on a test

---

[6] The source for the deep parameter optimisation algorithm we used and data discussed here is available from: https://github.com/BobbyBruce1990/DPT-OpenCV.git.

set of 17,000 images (compared to a 1.04 % inaccuracy when using the original algorithm). This technique shows the capacity for improvement within a widely used implementation of the Viola-Jones algorithm and provides a sound basis for further exploitation of more complex Search Based Software Engineering-(SBSE)methods. The source to achieve this has been made openly available on GitHub (See footnote 6).

References

1. Aby, P., Jose, A., Dinu, L., John, J., Sabarinath, G.: Implementation and optimization of embedded face detection system. In: International Conference on Signal Processing, Communication, Computing and Networking Technologies (ICSCCN), pp. 250–253 (2011)
2. Aitken, J.M., McAree, O., Veres, S.: Symbiotic relationship between robots - a ROS ARDrone/YouBot library. In: Proceedings of UKACC International Conference on Control (CONTROL) (2016)
3. Bradski, G., Kaehler, A.: Learning OpenCV: Computer Vision with the OpenCV Library. O'Reilly Media, Inc., Upper Saddle River (2008)
4. Deb, K., Pratap, A., Agarwal, S., Meyarivan, T.: A fast and elitist multiobjective genetic algorithm: NSGA-II. IEEE Trans. Evol. Comput. **6**(2), 182–197 (2002)
5. Goodrich, M.A., Morse, B.S., Gerhardt, D., Cooper, J.L., Quigley, M., Adams, J.A., Humphrey, C.: Supporting wilderness search and rescue using a camera-equipped mini UAV. J. Field Robot. **25**(1–2), 89–110 (2008)
6. Hoos, H.H.: Automated algorithm configuration and parameter tuning. In: Hamadi, Y., Monfroy, E., Saubion, F. (eds.) Autonomous Search, pp. 37–71. Springer, Heidelberg (2012). doi:10.1007/978-3-642-21434-9_3
7. Hsieh, M.A., Cowley, A., Keller, J.F., Chaimowicz, L., Grocholsky, B., Kumar, V., Taylor, C.J., Endo, Y., Arkin, R.C., Jung, B., Wolf, D.F., Sukhatme, G.S., MacKenzie, D.C.: Adaptive teams of autonomous aerial and ground robots for situational awareness. J. Field Robot. **24**(11–12), 991–1014 (2007)
8. Quigley, M., Conley, K., Gerkey, B., Faust, J., Foote, T., Leibs, J., Wheeler, R., Ng, A.Y.: ROS: an open-source robot operating system. In: ICRA Workshop on Open Source Software, vol. 3, p. 5 (2009)
9. Rahman, M., Ren, J., Kehtarnavaz, N.: Real-time implementation of robust face detection on mobile platforms. In: IEEE International Conference on Acoustics, Speech and Signal Processing, pp. 1353–1356 (2009)
10. Ren, J., Kehtarnavaz, N., Estevez, L.: Real-time optimization of Viola-Jones face detection for mobile platforms. In: IEEE Circuits and Systems Workshop: System-on-Chip-Design, Applications, Integration, and Software, pp. 1–4 (2008)
11. Shubina, K., Tsotsos, J.K.: Visual search for an object in a 3D environment using a mobile robot. Comput. Vis. Image Underst. **114**(5), 535–547 (2010)
12. Viola, P., Jones, M.: Rapid object detection using a boosted cascade of simple features. In: Proceedings of the IEEE Computer Society Conference on Computer Vision and Pattern Recognition, IEEE (2001)
13. Viola, P., Jones, M.: Robust real-time face detection. Int. J. Comput. Vis. **57**(2), 137–154 (2004)
14. Wu, F., Weimer, W., Harman, M., Jia, Y., Krinke, J.: Deep parameter optimisation. In: Proceedings of the 2015 on Genetic and Evolutionary Computation Conference, pp. 1375–1382 (2015)

Multi-objective Regression Test Suite Minimisation for Mockito

Andrew J. Turner[1]([✉]), David R. White[2], and John H. Drake[3]

[1] Department of Electronics, University of York, York YO10 5DD, UK
andrew.turner@york.ac.uk
[2] CREST, Department of Computer Science, University College London,
Gower Street, London WC1E 6BT, UK
david.r.white@ucl.ac.uk
[3] The OR Group, School of Electronic Engineering and Computer Science,
Queen Mary University of London, Mile End Road, London E1 4NS, UK
j.drake@qmul.ac.uk

Abstract. Regression testing is applied after modifications are performed to large software systems in order to verify that the changes made do not unintentionally disrupt other existing components. When employing regression testing it is often desirable to reduce the number of test cases executed in order to achieve a certain objective; a process known as test suite minimisation. We use multi-objective optimisation to analyse the trade-off between code coverage and execution time for the test suite of Mockito, a popular framework used to create mock objects for unit tests in Java. We show that a large reduction can be made in terms of execution time at the expense of only a small reduction in code coverage and discuss how the described methods can be easily applied to many projects that utilise regression testing.

1 Introduction

Search-based software engineering (SBSE) refers to methodologies that apply computational search techniques to software engineering problems [6]. Software testing is an extremely popular area for SBSE research, with a recent study suggesting that over half of the SBSE literature is concerned with software testing [7]. A key area of software testing that may be improved by search-based methods is regression testing.

Regression testing is performed when a system is updated from one version to the next, to check whether any of the new added features interfere with previous, existing features. Regression testing is also continuously performed during test driven development, where the aim is to produce a system that meets a specification embodied by a suite of tests. A *retest-all* approach executes an entire test suite on the system, however this can be extremely costly with respect to computational or time limitations. The fields of regression test suite minimisation, selection and prioritisation seek to optimise the amount of effort needed to perform regression testing on a particular system. For a detailed survey

© Springer International Publishing AG 2016
F. Sarro and K. Deb (Eds.): SSBSE 2016, LNCS 9962, pp. 244–249, 2016.
DOI: 10.1007/978-3-319-47106-8_19

of regression testing minimisation, selection and prioritisation, we direct the interested reader to Yoo and Harman [9].

Evolutionary Algorithms (EAs) are population-based metaheuristics inspired by the process of Darwinian evolution [1]. Given an initial population of candidate solutions, at each generation, strong solutions are chosen as parents to generate new solutions by recombination (crossover) and mutation. The newly generated solutions then compete with the original population for a place in the next generation. In the case of multi-objective optimisation, where multiple objectives are optimised simultaneously, a multi-objective EA (MOEA) attempts to find a set of *Pareto*-optimal solutions for which no improvement can be made in a single objective without having a detrimental effect on at least one of the other objectives [2]. This set of solutions, known as the Pareto front, gives a representation of the trade-off that exists between two conflicting objectives.

The nature of regression testing lends itself to formulation as a multi-objective problem, where the goal is to maximise the extent to which the test suite covers the target software whilst minimising the cost of executing that test suite. Indeed, many studies exist in the literature considering multi-objective regression testing [4,5,8], however these methods are still vastly outnumbered by studies considering single-objective variants.

Mockito (mockito.org) is a widely used Java-based framework for creating mock objects in automated unit testing. A mock object is used to mimic the behaviour of a real object when it is not possible to use the real object in a unit test, such as mocking the interface to a database. Thus, we are applying test suite optimisation to a set of tests written by programmers who are expert in testing; this offers a unique opportunity to examine the redundancy (with respect to code coverage) of a high-quality test suite. In this paper we apply the well-known multi-objective Non-dominated Sorting Genetic Algorithm II (NSGA-II) [3], to the test suite of the core components of a recent *beta* version of Mockito 2.0 (2.0.44). The objective of the optimisation algorithm is to minimise the running time of a selected subset of the test suite and maximise the proportion of the code-base covered by the selected tests in terms of branch coverage.

2   Methodology

The Mockito project uses the Gradle build system (gradle.org) to manage project structure, compilation and testing. The Gradle build system provides plugin support such that additional functionality can be executed as one or more 'tasks'. The standard plugin for Java (the language predominately used by Mockito) provides a *test* task. This task can be used to automatically run all unit tests associated with a project and produces information including pass/fail rates and time taken to execute each individual test. The specific tests to be executed may be manipulated by changing the Gradle build file (gradle.build). A further Gradle plugin provides support for using JaCoCo (eclemma.org/jacoco) that produces test coverage information of the executed unit tests. The JaCoCo plugin provides a range of common code coverage metrics including branch coverage and line coverage: we choose branch coverage in this work, but JaCoCo and similar plugins provide an easy route to apply other metrics. Both the Java and JaCoCo plugins provide high-level summaries as web-based report or comma separated value files, which can be easily parsed by external programs.

By specifying which specific tests are to be run via the *gradle.build* file, the Java and JaCoCo plugins can be used to measure the wall-clock time required to execute a subset of all available Mockitos unit tests and report code-coverage.

In this work a bit-string of length n, where n is the total number of available tests, is used to encode subsets of tests; where a '1' at position x in the bit-string represents than the xth test, out of all available tests, should be used and a '0' represents that it should be left out.

Using this encoding, we employ a multi-objective optimisation algorithm to search over the space of possible subsets. We use the NSGA-II [3] implementation from the MOEA framework (http://moeaframework.org/). The objectives optimised by NSGA-II are the elapsed wall-clock time from running a subset of tests (provided by the Java plugin) and the branch coverage of those tests (provided by the JaCoCo plugin).

2.1   Experimental Set-up

All of the results presented in this paper are based on version 2.0.44-beta of the Mockito framework. The parameters of NSGA-II were left at the defaults specified in the MOEA framework version 2.9; which include a population size of 100. NSGA-II was left to run for 5 h, which is an appropriate length of time to be incorporated into nightly builds i.e. ready to be used by the team of developers the following day. The experiments presented minimise the number of tests used by the core packages of the Mockito framework. The Mockito packages considered are: org.mockitousage.basicapi.*, org.mockitousage.bugs.*, org.mockitousage.misuse* and org.mockitousage.verification.*, which contain 420 individual tests in total.

3   Results and Discussion

The Pareto front of possible subsets of tests generated by applying NSGA-II to test suite minimisation of Mockito is given in Fig. 1. Running all available tests, for the packages described previously, requires 5.93 wall-clock seconds[1] and results in 47.82% branch coverage; the run time and branch coverage in Fig. 1 are in relation to these values. Although the time savings may appear small, even short pauses can have a significant impact in breaking a developer's "flow" during the repeated write-compile-test cycle.

As can be seen in Fig. 1, NSGA-II was able to significantly reduce the wall-clock time whilst maintaining a high proportion of the original branch coverage. Additionally, the generated Pareto front provides a graceful degradation in

---

[1] Running on an Intel © Core™ i7-4600U CPU @ 2.10 GHz x 2.

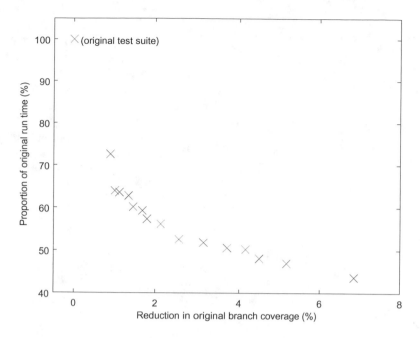

Fig. 1. Pareto front of regression test suite solutions found using NSGA-II

branch coverage as the wall-clock time is reduced. This demonstrates how the presented method could easily be incorporated into a decision support process; where a human in-the-loop decides what level of branch coverage degradation is acceptable given the computational speed-up in test cycle time. This would be particularly useful when applying minimisation to larger test suites.

In order to demonstrate how this significant reduction in wall-clock time is afforded, with minimal reduction in branch coverage, a detailed view of the effect of removing redundant tests is presented. Figure 2 shows the number of times each line of two Mockito source files are executed at least once by each test in the original test suite. These results are contrasted with employing a subset of tests found using NSGA-II. Lines not covered by any of the tests can also be identified in the given plots e.g. line 28 in Fig. 2a. The space between the bars represent non-executable lines i.e. comments and bracket placement.

As can be seen in Fig. 2, when using all available tests each line of a given source file is often evaluated by a large number of individual tests. This indicates that there is a high level of redundancy in the test suite. However, when applying a subsets of tests found using NSGA-II, the number of tests which execute the same lines is reduced. This is why very comparable levels of test coverage are maintained whilst utilising a reduced test suite; redundant tests have been removed. The compromise of this method is that a small number of lines which were previously covered may no longer be tested; such as line 56 in Fig. 2b.

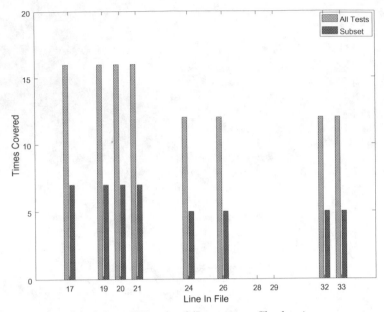

(a) *AtLeastXNumberOfInvocationsChecker.java*

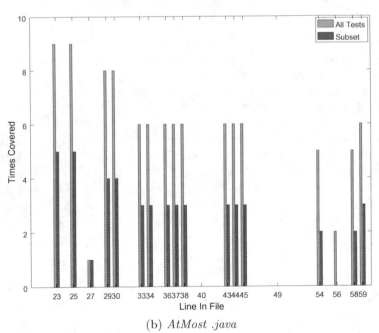

(b) *AtMost .java*

Fig. 2. Number of times each executable line of two Mockito source files are evaluated at least once by each individual employed test. Coverage from using all available tests and coverage from using a subsets of tests found using NSGA-II is shown.

4   Conclusions and Future Work

This paper applied test suite minimisation to a Java project through integration with the Gradle build system; no specific information regarding the Mockito was required. Therefore it is possible to apply the same approach to any project that uses Gradle, or even develop a plugin that automates the process. This is one instance of a wider trend in software development: the move towards automated build and deployment systems employing standardised interfaces represents an opportunity for the application and dissemination of SBSE.

Possible future work is to implement such a general plugin. The impact of test minimisation on the fault-finding ability of the test suite is of general interest and, by integrating with standard build tools as presented here, a larger-scale study could investigate this relationship.

In the described system all tests associated with each new candidate test suite were re-run in order to record overall converge and testing time; resulting in 5 h of training time. However, this can be dramatically reduced in future work by caching the coverage and elapsed time of each individual test. This means that no code has to be re-evaluated when assessing new candidate test suites, only a series of computationally cheap look-ups.

Multi-objective optimisation was successful in minimising the Mockito framework's regression suite. The wall-clock time required by the test suite was reduced by $\sim50\%$ whilst maintaining $\sim96\%$ of the original code coverage. Therefore using such methods can save significant developer time during the write-compile-test cycle with limited effect on the amount of code covered by the test suite.

References

1. Back, T., Fogel, D.B., Michalewicz, Z.: Handbook of Evolutionary Computation. IOP Publishing Ltd., Bristol (1997)
2. Deb, K.: Multi-Objective Optimization Using Evolutionary Algorithms, vol. 16. John Wiley & Sons, Hoboken (2001)
3. Deb, K., Pratap, A., Agarwal, S., Meyarivan, T.: A fast and elitist multiobjective genetic algorithm: NSGA-II. IEEE Trans. Evol. Comput. 6(2), 182–197 (2002)
4. Epitropakis, M.G., Yoo, S., Harman, M., Burke, E.K.: Empirical evaluation of Pareto efficient multi-objective regression test case prioritisation. In: Proceedings of the International Symposium on Software Testing and Analysis (2015)
5. Gu, Q., Tang, B., Chen, D.: Optimal regression testing based on selective coverage of test requirements. In: Proceedings of the Parallel and Distributed Processing with Applications (2010)
6. Harman, M., Burke, E., Clark, J.A., Yao, X.: Dynamic adaptive search based software engineering. In: Proceedings of the Empirical Software Engineering and Measurement (2012)
7. Harman, M., Mansouri, S.A., Zhang, Y.: Search-based software engineering: trends, techniques and applications. ACM Comput. Surv. 45(1), 11 (2012)
8. Yoo, S., Harman, M.: Pareto efficient multi-objective test case selection. In: Proceedings of the International Symposium on Software Testing and Analysis (2007)
9. Yoo, S., Harman, M.: Regression testing minimization, selection and prioritization: a survey. Softw. Test. Verification Reliab. 22(2), 67–120 (2012)

Searching for Configurations in Clone Evaluation – A Replication Study

Chaiyong Ragkhitwetsagul[1][(✉)], Matheus Paixao[1], Manal Adham[1],
Saheed Busari[1], Jens Krinke[1], and John H. Drake[2]

[1] University College London, London, UK
chaiyong.ragkhitwetsagul.14@ucl.ac.uk
[2] Queen Mary University of London, London, UK

Abstract. Clone detection is the process of finding duplicated code within a software code base in an automated manner. It is useful in several areas of software development such as code quality analysis, bug detection, and program understanding. We replicate a study of a genetic-algorithm based framework that optimises parameters for clone agreement (EvaClone). We apply the framework to 14 releases of Mockito, a Java mocking framework. We observe that the optimised parameters outperform the tools' default parameters in term of clone agreement by 19.91 % to 66.43 %. However, the framework gives undesirable results in term of clone quality. EvaClone either maximises or minimises a number of clones in order to achieve the highest agreement resulting in more false positives or false negatives introduced consequently.

1 Introduction

Code cloning is a common activity in software development. Clones can be created by reuse of well-written code or adaptation of functionality from existing code, and may lead to software maintenance issues. Numerous tools exist to detect clones in a given software system [4,8,10]. Not only do these tools differ in their detection approach, but they also come with a number of parameters to choose from which greatly affect their sensitivity [7]. The oracle problem in clone detection is the absence of the possibility to establish a ground truth, i.e. knowing if code is actually cloned. Therefore, multiple clone detectors are often used on the assumption that it is more likely that code is actually cloned when multiple clone detectors agree.

We perform a replication study of EvaClone [11] which uses a Genetic Algorithm to optimise clone detection tools parameters to maximise clone agreement, but in a different settings. We select four tools for this study: CCFinder [6], Deckard [5], NiCad [9], and Simian [2] and apply the framework to only a single subject, Mockito [1] (a mocking framework for unit testing within Java), over its 14 major releases. This experimental settings have not been explored yet in the previous study.

© Springer International Publishing AG 2016
F. Sarro and K. Deb (Eds.): SSBSE 2016, LNCS 9962, pp. 250–256, 2016.
DOI: 10.1007/978-3-319-47106-8_20

2   Optimising Parameters of Clone Detectors

Previous work by Wang et al. [11] has shown that a Genetic Algorithm (GA) is able to find a set of parameter values that maximise agreement between an ensemble of clone detection tools. They show that the derived optimised parameters provide better agreement among tools compared to using the tools' default settings, which are often used in empirical investigations in the literature. In this study, we adopt their EvaClone framework to search for configurations which maximise the level of agreement between the four clone detection tools.

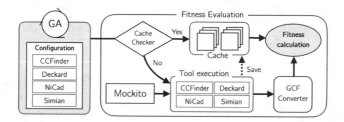

Fig. 1. A framework for optimising parameters of clone detectors using a GA

Figure 1 presents a high-level overview of the system. Given predefined configuration settings X, each tool generates a clone report containing either clone pairs or clone clusters in its own specific format. These output files are then converted into a General Clone Format (GCF) [11] so that they can be analysed in the same way. This is followed by fitness calculation of a given configuration X based on number of agreed clone lines. The fitness function computes the level of agreement between n different tools applied to detect clones in a subject system. $AgreedLines[i]$ is the number of lines where exactly i tools agree that they are part of a clone:

$$F(X) = \frac{\sum_i^n (i \times AgreedLines[i])}{n \times \sum_i^n AgreedLines[i]}$$

To search the space of configurations, we program the GA to initially generate a population of 100 feasible solutions (99 random individuals and one individual as the default configuration). Each individual solution encodes values for the 25 parameters of the four tools. These solutions are evolved using selection, crossover and mutation to create better quality solutions guided by the fitness value in each iteration. The crossover and mutation rate are the same as in [11], set at 0.8 and 0.1 respectively. We choose an elitism rate at 0.25.

The clone detectors selected for this study are representatives of (1) commonly used clone detection tools in research, and (2) different clone detection techniques, including string-based (Simian), parser-based (NiCad), token-based (CCFinder) and tree-based (Deckard). We reuse the default configurations given in [11] for CCFinder, NiCad, and Simian. Deckard has no default configuration so we choose the default parameters used in a recent study [10].

3   Experimental Study

We collected 14 major releases of Mockito from Google Code and GitHub repositories as subjects for this study. A manual investigation of the source code and release notes shows that 2 Java class files from Apache Commons have been included in the system since release 1.0 (*EqualsBuilder* and *ReflectionEquals*). The files are constantly modified over releases so we treat them as a part of Mockito. However, there are 2 complete libraries (*cglib* and *asm*) embedded in Mockito from release 1.5 to 1.9 which are used without modification. They make Mockito releases 1.5 to 1.9 grow three times bigger than release 1.4 and would introduce a strong bias to our results. Hence, we removed these two libraries out of the five releases. The size of the 14 releases (SLOC) after removal of the two libraries, and churn rates (inserted and deleted lines) are presented in Table 1.

Table 1. Mockito releases, their size (SLOC), size increment (%Inc) and churn rates

Release	0.9	1.0	1.1	1.2	1.3	1.4	1.5	1.6	1.7	1.8	1.9	1.10	2.0.0	2.0.44
SLOC	5500	6669	6784	6824	7239	7566	8364	8944	10143	12426	17876	22796	23555	25321
%Inc	N/A	21%	2%	1%	6%	5%	11%	7%	13%	23%	44%	28%	3%	8%
Insertions	N/A	1786	318	199	632	661	1494	1536	1445	5446	7151	7667	1452	13969
Deletions	N/A	618	204	157	218	335	656	989	245	3170	1765	2789	1577	11370

We are interested in three research questions, which will be individually presented and discussed.

RQ1 (optimised agreement): *how do the default parameters perform in terms of clone agreement on each Mockito release compared to the optimised ones?* This is to measure how good the default configuration is for each release compared to its optimised counterpart. If we can find a better configuration than the default, it should be used for finding clones in each particular release.

The experimental findings show that one can use EvaClone to find parameters that outperform the default parameters for all 14 releases. As depicted in Fig. 2,

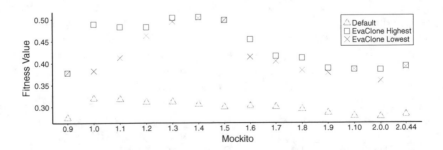

Fig. 2. Comparison of optimised tools agreement (the highest and the lowest in 20 runs) to the default agreement over 14 Mockito releases

the optimised parameters always provide a higher level of tools agreement than the default ones. The lowest clone agreement obtained from EvaClone among 20 runs (represented using × symbol) is still higher than using the default configuration. We calculated percentage of agreement improvement and found that the optimised one always outperform the default configuration ranging from 19.91 % up to 64.43 %. These findings support the results of Wang et al. [11] that the default parameters offer a poor level of clone agreement and one should optimise the tools' configurations for every subject system or for every release of a system to maximise agreement.

RQ2 (stability of optimised parameters): *are there noticeable differences in the values of optimised parameters over releases?* Since each release of Mockito contains several changes made to its code base, we are interested to see what the impact of these modifications is to the optimised parameters. If the optimised parameters are stable over releases, it means that we can use the same optimised parameters to detect clones in any Mockito release. If not, it means that one may need to optimise the parameters for each individual release.

With 20 GA runs for each release, we found several sets of distinct parameter settings that can achieve the same highest clone agreement level. Among sets of these equally-performing optimised parameters, we select one that has minimum amount of change from the optimised parameters chosen in the previous release[1] (using Euclidean distance). This method maximises the stability of optimised parameters over all releases. The optimised parameters over 14 Mockito releases are reported in Table 2 and can be used as a guideline for setting the parameters of these tools in further studies of clones or clone evolution in Mockito. We can see that none of the optimised parameters is stable over all releases. However, if we inspect each tool's settings individually, we notice some stability of specific parameters spanning over a number of releases. The parameters shown in bold (e.g. **50**, **inf**, **0.9**) represent parameters that are "dominant" in each specific release. Dominant parameters are those that have only a single value across all 20 runs. We can see that there are some parameters that are both dominant and stable over a number of releases. In addition, we observe that changing some parameters of Simian does not affect the tool's behaviour at all since they are subsumed by another parameter. For example, the `ignoreNumbers`, `ignoreCharacters`, and `ignoreStrings` flags are subsumed by a more general `ignoreLiterals` flag. These parameters can be changed without any effect if the `ignoreLiterals` flag is enabled. Their values are represented using * meaning they can be freely set to any value. We also found that changing the value of `ignoreIdentifierCase` does not have any effect at all. In summary, for Mockito, the optimised parameters are observed to be varied over 14 releases with some stability in a specific region of releases. There is no single set of optimised parameters that work well across all releases.

RQ3 (clones over releases): *how many clones in Mockito are reported with the highest agreement over releases?* We would like to observe the number of

---

[1] The full set of optimised parameters are at cragkhit.github.io/ssbsechallenge2016.

Table 2. Clone detection tools with their default configurations (DF) and optimised configurations per release. Bold parameters are dominant in each release (i.e. no variation found among 20 runs)

Tool/Parameter	DF	Optimised													
		0.9	1.0	1.1	1.2	1.3	1.4	1.5	1.6	1.7	1.8	1.9	1.10	2.0.0	2.0.44
CCFinder															
MinToken	50	10	70	70	70	80	80	80	80	10	10	10	10	10	10
TKS	12	10	16	18	19	18	18	19	20	14	17	10	10	10	10
Deckard															
MinToken	30	30	50	50	50	50	50	50	50	50	50	50	50	50	50
Stride	5	inf	8	8	8	5	8	8	8	16	5	inf	inf	inf	inf
Similarity	0.9	0.9	1.0	1.0	1.0	1.0	1.0	1.0	1.0	0.95	1.0	0.9	0.9	0.9	0.9
NiCad															
MinLine	6	5	7	7	7	6	6	6	7	6	5	5	5	5	5
MaxLine	1000	200	100	100	400	400	200	200	200	200	100	100	100	200	200
UPI	0.3	0.3	0.0	0.1	0.0	0.0	0.1	0.1	0.0	0.3	0.1	0.3	0.3	0.3	0.3
Blind	0	1	0	0	0	0	0	0	1	1	1	1	1	1	1
Abstract	0	4	6	6	6	6	5	5	6	6	2	4	4	4	4
Simian															
ignoreCurlyBraces	0	0	0	0	0	0	0	0	0	0	1	0	0	0	0
ignoreIdentifiers	0	1	0	0	0	0	0	0	0	1	1	1	1	1	1
ignoreIdentifierCase	0	*	*	*	*	*	*	*	*	*	*	*	*	*	*
ignoreStrings	0	1	0	0	0	0	0	0	0	1	0	*	*	*	*
ignoreStringCase	1	*	1	1	0	0	0	0	0	*	0	*	*	*	*
ignoreNumbers	0	1	0	1	0	1	1	0	1	1	0	*	*	*	*
ignoreCharacters	0	0	0	1	0	0	0	1	0	0	1	*	*	*	*
ignoreCharacterCase	1	0	0	*	1	1	0	*	1	1	*	*	*	*	*
ignoreLiterals	0	0	0	0	0	0	0	0	0	0	0	1	1	1	1
ignoreSubtypeNames	0	1	0	0	0	0	0	0	0	0	0	0	0	1	1
ignoreModifiers	1	1	1	0	1	0	0	0	0	0	0	1	1	1	1
ignoreVariableNames	0	1	0	0	0	0	0	0	0	1	1	0	0	0	1
balanceParentheses	0	0	1	1	1	1	1	1	1	0	0	0	0	0	0
balanceSquareBrackets	0	1	0	0	0	1	1	0	1	1	1	1	1	1	0
MinLine	6	5	6	6	6	6	6	6	6	7	7	5	5	5	5

clone lines (LOC) reported by the tools using optimised parameters in each release. This insight can support Mockito developers' decision to perform code refactoring in future releases and future research studying clone detection.

The number of agreed clone lines detected by EvaClone using optimised parameters agreed by exactly 1, 2, 3, and 4 tools over 14 releases are presented in Fig. 3. We can clearly see that there are spikes in the number of agreed clone lines in release 0.9 and from release 1.9 onwards compared to releases 1.0–1.8. In releases 1.0–1.8, the highest agreement has been achieved by drastically *decreasing* the overall number of cloned lines, while for the other releases it has been achieved by *increasing* the overall number of cloned lines. Moreover, Fig. 3 shows that a large percentage (40 %–50 %) of the code is identified as cloned by only one tool. A manual investigation of the clone reports from the four tools revealed that the cloned lines reported by only one tool in every release are 80.8 % generated by Deckard, 9.8 % by Simian, 4.8 % by CCFinder

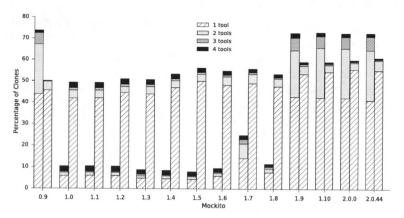

Fig. 3. Comparison of number of agreed clone lines (SLOC) for 1, 2, 3, and 4 tools reported by optimised parameters (left) and default parameters (right) in each release

and 4.6 % by NiCad for the optimised configurations and 87.9 %, 10.9 %, 0.7 %, and 0.5 % respectively for the default configurations. These fluctuations in the number of agreed clone lines reveal a weakness in the fitness function used by Wang et al. [11]: It increases agreement by significantly increasing or decreasing the number of cloned lines. The evaluation of the original study showed that EvaClone favours recall over precision [11], however, the drastic decrease in reported lines for releases 1.0–1.8 will reduce recall. Moreover, the large percentage of cloned lines in the default configuration suggests a low precision of at least one tool and the optimised configurations of release 0.9 and 1.9 onward decreases the precision even further. This phenomenon is not a desirable result in terms of clone quality since there will be either too many false positives or false negatives. Since the fitness evaluation function is also a component of the framework, one should find a better fitness function in order to overcome this problem. For example, the fitness function must not only rely on the number of cloned lines, but also include other aspects like how often a line is found to be cloned to other places.

Our replication study produced more evidence that designing a general fitness function that works well in all situations is a difficult task. Approaches to solve this problem of designing proper fitness functions are emerging [3]. Because of the large fluctuations in the number of clones reported by the framework, we decided not to draw any conclusion about clones in Mockito from these results.

4 Conclusion

We performed a replication study by applying EvaClone, a framework for optimising clone detection tool's configurations using a Genetic Algorithm, with four tools to 14 Mockito releases in order to study the optimised parameters and how variations in the analysed data impact the results of the Genetic Algorithm.

The results show that the optimised parameters given by the framework achieve a higher clone agreement among the tools over all releases of Mockito. Some of the optimised parameters are observed to be dominant in a single release or over some releases but there is no parameter set that consistently superior over all releases. We also discover a weakness in the fitness evaluation function, as it increases agreement by significantly increasing or decreasing the number of cloned lines, producing more false positives or false negatives respectively.

References

1. Mockito. http://mockito.org. Accessed 4 July 2016
2. Simian. http://www.harukizaemon.com/simian. Accessed 4 July 2016
3. Amal, B., Kessentini, M., Bechikh, S., Dea, J., Said, L.B.: On the use of machine learning and search-based software engineering for ill-defined fitness function: a case study on software refactoring. In: SBSE (2014)
4. Bellon, S., Koschke, R., Antoniol, G., Krinke, J., Merlo, E.: Comparison and evaluation of clone detection tools. TSE **33**(9), 577–591 (2007)
5. Jiang, L., Misherghi, G., Su, Z., Glondu, S.: DECKARD: scalable and accurate tree-based detection of code clones. In: ICSE (2007)
6. Kamiya, T., Kusumoto, S., Inoue, K.: CCFinder: a multilinguistic token-based code clone detection system for large scale source code. TSE **28**, 654–670 (2002)
7. Mondal, M., Roy, C.K., Rahman, M.S., Saha, R.K., Krinke, J., Schneider, K.A.: Comparative stability of cloned and non-cloned code. In: SAC (2012)
8. Roy, C.K., Cordy, J.R., Koschke, R.: Comparison and evaluation of code clone detection techniques and tools. Sci. Comput. Programm. **74**(7), 470–495 (2009)
9. Roy, C.K., Cordy, J.: NICAD: Accurate detection of near-miss intentional clones using flexible pretty-printing and code normalization. In: ICPC (2008)
10. Svajlenko, J., Roy, C.K.: Evaluating modern clone detection tools. In: ICSME (2014)
11. Wang, T., Harman, M., Jia, Y., Krinke, J.: Searching for better configurations: a rigorous approach to clone evaluation. In: FSE (2013)

Short Papers

AVMf: An Open-Source Framework and Implementation of the Alternating Variable Method

Phil McMinn[1]($^{(\boxtimes)}$) and Gregory M. Kapfhammer[2]

[1] University of Sheffield, Sheffield, UK
p.mcminn@sheffield.ac.uk
[2] Allegheny College, Meadville, USA
gkapfham@allegheny.edu

Abstract. The Alternating Variable Method (AVM) has been shown to be a fast and effective local search technique for search-based software engineering. Recent improvements to the AVM have generalized the representations it can optimize and have provably reduced its running time. However, until now, there has been no general, publicly-available implementation of the AVM incorporating all of these developments. We introduce AVMf, an object-oriented Java framework that provides such an implementation. AVMf is available from http://avmframework.org for configuration and use in a wide variety of projects.

1 Introduction

The Alternating Variable Method (AVM) is a local search method that was first applied to a search-based software engineering (SBSE) problem — the automatic generation of numerical test data — by Bogdan Korel in 1990 [12]. Despite the application of, supposedly more robust, global search techniques to this problem (e.g., Genetic Algorithms (GAs)), the AVM has stood the test of time. In 2007, Harman and McMinn [7] reported its effectiveness and efficiency for a series of C programs, and combined it with a GA to provide a "best of" Memetic Algorithm approach [8]. It has since been implemented into tools to generate test data for C programs (e.g., IGUANA [17] and AUSTIN [14,15]); generate Java test suites with EvoSuite [3,4]; create relational database data with the *SchemaAnalyst* tool [9,18]; and combined with dynamic symbolic execution in Microsoft's Pex tool [16]. The AVM has also found application to additional problems, including decision ordering for software product lines [22], balancing workload in requirements assignment [21], solving reliability-redundancy-allocation problems [20], as well as test case selection [19] and test suite prioritization [2].

Since Korel's original work, the AVM has been extended and improved for problems in SBSE: now it can handle more variable types, including fixed-point numbers [7] and strings [9,18], and can leverage new strategies proven to speed up the search for certain common types of objective function landscape [10,11].

© Springer International Publishing AG 2016
F. Sarro and K. Deb (Eds.): SSBSE 2016, LNCS 9962, pp. 259–266, 2016.
DOI: 10.1007/978-3-319-47106-8_21

The AVM is therefore capable of handling a variety of search representations and locating solutions to SBSE problems in a very efficient manner. Yet, to incorporate it into a project, a developer has previously had to understand the different variants of the algorithm and produce a faithful implementation, or, attempt to adapt the open-source of a less general version specifically written for test data generation (e.g., [15]). Either of these options represents a potentially time-consuming and error prone task. To address this, we have developed AVMf, a general, open-source object-oriented framework that implements different variants of the AVM and its representations in Java. AVMf is available for download from http://avmframework.org for deployment in SBSE projects. It is fully documented and comes with a series of examples demonstrating its usage.

2   The AVM and Recent Improvements to the Algorithm

The Original AVM. The AVM optimizes a vector $\vec{x} = (x_1, \ldots, x_{len})$ according to some objective function by taking, in turn, each variable $x_i, 1 \leq i \leq len$ of the vector and subjecting it to an individual search process. The original AVM used a variable search process subsequently named "Iterated Pattern Search" (IPS) [10,11], shown by lines 1–7 of Fig. 1. Here, we assume that $x_i \in \mathbb{Z}$, although later we explain how more complex types may also be handled by the approach. The initial part of the IPS algorithm involves making an increase and decrease of 1 to the value of the variable (lines 2–3), referred to as *exploratory moves*. If an exploratory move leads to an improvement in the objective value, a positive or negative "direction" is established for making further *pattern moves* (lines 4–6). Pattern moves of increasing size continue to be made while the objective value improves. When a pattern move fails to improve upon the objective value, the search has likely overshot an optimum, due to a pattern move that was larger than the difference between the current value of x_i and the optimal value. When this occurs, IPS loops back to the exploratory move process to re-establish a new direction. If exploratory moves do not lead to an improvement in objective value, IPS terminates and hands back control to the main loop, thus leading to the consideration of the next variable in the vector.

When all variables in the vector have been considered, the AVM wraps back to the first. When a cycle of all variables has completed without any improvement in the objective function, the AVM is lodged in a local optimum. At this point the search process can be restarted with a new (typically random) series of vector values. The AVM continues in this fashion until resources are exhausted (e.g., a maximum number of objective function evaluations or restarts have been expended, or a time limit has expired), or, the best outcome is attained — the optimal target vector is discovered. (For simplicity, these different termination criteria are not included as part of the algorithm definition in Fig. 1.)

New Variable Search Algorithms. Kempka et al. [10,11] proposed two new variable searches for the AVM, as shown in Fig. 1. Kempka et al. proved that these search techniques are more efficient than IPS for unimodal objective function landscapes. "Geometric Search" (GS) begins by performing exploratory

```
1:  while true do                                                        ▷ {IPS}
2:      if obj(x − 1) ≥ obj(x) and obj(x + 1) ≥ obj(x) return x          ▷ {IPS, GS, LS}
3:      if obj(x − 1) < obj(x + 1) then let k := −1 else let k := 1       ▷ {IPS, GS, LS}
4:      while obj(x + k) < obj(x) do                                     ▷ {IPS, GS, LS}
5:          let x := x + k, k := 2k                                      ▷ {IPS, GS, LS}
6:      end while                                                        ▷ {IPS, GS, LS}
7:  end while                                                            ▷ {IPS}
8:  let ℓ := min(x − k/2, x + k), r := max(x − k/2, x + k)               ▷ {GS, LS}
9:  while ℓ < r do                                                       ▷ {GS}
10:     if obj(⌊(ℓ + r)/2⌋) < obj(⌊(ℓ + r)/2⌋ + 1) then                  ▷ {GS}
11:         r := ⌊(ℓ + r)/2⌋                                             ▷ {GS}
12:     else                                                             ▷ {GS}
13:         ℓ := ⌊(ℓ + r)/2⌋ + 1                                         ▷ {GS}
14:     end if                                                           ▷ {GS}
15: end while                                                            ▷ {GS}
16: let n := min{n | F_n ≥ r − l + 2}                                    ▷ {LS}
17: while n > 3 do                                                       ▷ {LS}
18:     if ℓ + F_{n−1} − 1 ≤ r and obj(ℓ + F_{n−2} − 1) ≥ obj(ℓ + F_{n−1} − 1) then   ▷ {LS}
19:         let ℓ := ℓ + F_{n−2}                                         ▷ {LS}
20:     end if                                                           ▷ {LS}
21:     let n := n − 1                                                   ▷ {LS}
22: end while                                                            ▷ {LS}
23: x := ℓ                                                               ▷ {GS, LS}
```

Fig. 1. IPS, LS, GS algorithms for a variable $x \in \mathbb{Z}$. The function obj is equivalent to evaluating the objective function with a vector $\vec{x}$ with all components except x_i set to constants and x_i substituted by the free parameter x. F is the Fibonacci sequence starting from $F_0 = 0$. Each line is annotated to show the algorithm(s) it is a part of.

moves followed by pattern moves like IPS. Unlike IPS, however, it does not iterate after overshooting the optimum. Instead it uses past moves to "bracket" the upper and lower limits of the variable in which the optimum must lie, performing a binary search to finally locate it (lines 8–15 of Fig. 1). "Lattice Search" (LS) is a slightly faster alternative to GS where the unimodal assumption holds. LS converges on the optimum through moves that increase x_i from the lower value of the bracket through the addition of Fibonacci numbers (lines 16–22).

New Representations. Korel only demonstrated the original AVM with integer variables [12]. Harman and McMinn [7] extended this initial definition by allowing each variable to be specified with a set number of decimal places p, allowing fixed-point numbers to be handled. Exploratory moves correspond to the smallest possible increments and decrements of the variable (i.e., $\pm 10^{-p}$). Strings may also now be handled by the approach [9,18]. A string variable is essentially a sub-vector of the overall vector to be optimized. Their elements are characters that are individually manipulated by the local search routine. The length of this sub-vector is allowed to vary through a special sequence of moves that increase and decrease its size, supporting the optimization of variable-length strings.

3   The AVM Framework (AVMf)

The AVM Framework (AVMf) implements both the AVM algorithm and the subsequent enhancements to the original version proposed by Korel. The framework has been implemented with the aim of making the core algorithms as clear as possible, thereby closely matching the algorithmic definitions of Fig. 1, while still adhering to well-accepted principles of good object-oriented design. AVMf is publicly available from http://avmframework.org as a Git repository for inclusion in SBSE projects where the AVM may be the core search algorithm, or, a component of a more complex technique (e.g., a Memetic Algorithm) involving calls to algorithms in the framework. Or, the code can simply be lifted from the repository and adapted to a project as developers see fit.

To enable its algorithms to be easily used in SBSE projects, AVMf provides a framework of Java classes, which we now describe in detail. Each aspect of the framework is practically demonstrated by the source code of a series of examples in the repository, the simplest of which are introduced at the end of this section.

Configuring an AVM Search. The primary class is the `AVM` class in the root (i.e., `org.avmframework`) package. In order to construct an `AVM` instance, the developer must supply an instance of one of the variable search methods — `IteratedPatternSearch`, `GeometricSearch` or `LatticeSearch` — which reside in the `localsearch` package. The developer must also construct the `AVM` instance using a `TerminationPolicy` parameter, an object that decides when the AVM should terminate if a solution cannot be found. Options include a maximum number of objective function evaluations, a maximum number of restarts, or a time limit. Finally, constructing the `AVM` instance further requires two objects of type `Initializer` that are used to initialize variable vector values at the start of the search and re-initialize them on a restart. Default values may be used that can be specified for each variable, or random values can be chosen (through instances of either `DefaultInitializer` or `RandomInitializer`, two classes that both reside in the `initializer` package). To support the generation of random numbers, AVMf requires a `RandomGenerator` from the `org.apache.commons` library that provides an implementation of the Mersenne Twister algorithm.

In order to initiate a search process, the `search` method of the `AVM` instance must be invoked with an instance of a `Vector` class and an `ObjectiveFunction`, respectively. The `Vector` class describes the representation of the problem (i.e., the types of variables in the vector to be optimized), while the `ObjectiveFunction` class describes how instances of those vectors should be rewarded with objective values during the search.

Representation. In order to configure the search representation, an instance of the `Vector` class (in the root package) must be created, and variables added to it through the `addVariable` method, which accepts an instance of a `Variable`. Since the `Variable` class is abstract, an instance of one of its concrete subclasses must be provided (i.e., one of `IntegerVariable`, `FixedPointVariable`, `CharacterVariable` or `StringVariable`). Each variable must be constructed with information such as its minimum or maximum value (maximum length for strings), number of decimal places for fixed-point variables, and a "default" initial value in the search space (e.g., an empty string or a zero value). These values are used to initialize vector variables when the `DefaultInitializer` provides a starting point for the search, as previously described in this section.

Objective Function. In contrast to the rest of the framework, which requires configuring instances of existing classes, an objective function must be supplied to the search process by overriding the abstract `ObjectiveFunction` of the `objective` package. This involves providing an implementation of the `computeObjectiveValue` method that takes a `Vector` as a parameter and returns an instance of the abstract `ObjectiveValue` class. Since the AVM only needs to know whether one entity has a "better" objective value than another, exact numerical values are not needed, and so this class requires the "`betterThan`", "`worseThan`" and "`sameAs`" methods to be overridden. The `objective` package also supplies the concrete `NumericalObjectiveValue` class for returning higher-is-better or lower-is-better numerical objective values as needed.

Reporting. The `search` method of the `AVM` class returns an instance of the `Monitor` class, which can be used to find out interesting statistics regarding the search. These include the best vector found by the search, its objective value, the number of objective function evaluations that took place, the number of restarts that happened and the amount of time that the search took (in milliseconds). The `Monitor` class can also report the number of *unique* objective function evaluations. Employing the technique known as memoization, the objective function can make optional usage of a cache that maps previously observed vectors to objective values, avoiding the need to perform potentially costly re-evaluations.

Examples. AVM*f* comes with a series of examples demonstrating its use. Instructions on how to compile and run these examples are available in the project's `README.md` file located in the main directory of the code repository. The "`Quadratic`" example demonstrates the use of the AVM to solve a quadratic equation by finding one of its roots. "`AllZeros`" shows the optimization of an array of integers to zero values from arbitrary random values, while "`String`" optimizes a string value from an initially random string to a specified target.

Each example makes use of its own problem-specific fitness function, which forms part of its code definition. The following is taken from the `Quadratic` class, where the constants A, B and C correspond to the co-efficients of the equation (here, A = 4, B = 10 and C = 6). The function obtains the value of x from the (single variable) vector, and computes the value of y. The objective value is then assigned as the distance between y and zero, since intuitively, the closer the value of y to zero, the closer the search is to finding one of the roots of the equation:

```
ObjectiveFunction objFun = new ObjectiveFunction() {
    protected ObjectiveValue computeObjectiveValue(Vector vector) {
        double x = ((FloatingPointVariable) vector.getVariable(0)).asDouble();
        double y = (A * x * x) + (B * x) + C;
        double distance = Math.abs(y);
        return NumericObjectiveValue.LowerIsBetterObjectiveValue(distance, 0);
    }};
```

The following shows the output of the search process and the discovery of one of the equation's roots, -1.5. Re-running the search from different starting positions leads to the other root, -1, also being found.

```
Best solution: -1.5
Best objective value: 0.0
Number of objective function evaluations: 80 (unique: 80)
Running time: 3ms
```

As part of future work, we plan to extend the example set with case studies showing how the AVM is being or can be applied to real SBSE problems, such as test data generation. These will be made available via the code repository.

4   Conclusions and Future Work

This paper introduced AVMf, an open-source implementation of the AVM and a framework supporting its use in SBSE projects. AVMf is capable of advancing the AVM in both industrial practice and in the SBSE research community. Using AVMf, possible future applications of the AVM include the following:

Automatically Generating Readable Test Data. Generating readable tests that humans can easily understand has been a recent interest of search-based testing researchers (e.g., rewarding inputs that obtain a high score from a language model [1]). In a recent study evaluating test generation tools, participants also requested more readable values [5,6]. Given that the AVM employs a local search, it could start with examples of human-generated inputs and adapt them to new coverage targets — all without losing the qualities of the original data.

Automatically Determining Optimal Software Configuration Values. Highly configurable software tools, such as the GCC compiler, may be tunable through the use of search-based techniques such as genetic algorithms or the AVM [13]. In large search spaces of parameters, the AVM's exploratory move phase equips it to quickly discover which particular variables are relevant to the problem, while its phase of pattern moves allows it to determine the optimal values of parameters. Again, as a local search technique, the AVM is also well suited to taking an existing known-good human solution and improving upon it.

Automated Bug-Fixing. Recent experiments reveal that real-world bugs can occur as a result of mistakes made when defining constant variables and setting values in configuration files [23]. As such, the AVM could search for appropriate values that could potentially form the basis of a "fix". During its exploratory move phase the AVM could, by performing a quick sweep of small changes through the values involved and seeing how the resulting fitness values are affected, quickly determine which constants are relevant to the fix.

References

1. Afshan, S., McMinn, P., Stevenson, M.: Evolving readable string test inputs using a natural language model to reduce human oracle cost. In: Proceedings of ICST (2013)

2. Arrieta, A., Wang, S., Sagardui, G., Etxeberria, L.: Test case prioritization of configurable cyber-physical systems with weight-based search algorithms. In: Proceedings of GECCO (2016)
3. Fraser, G., Arcuri, A., McMinn, P.: Test suite generation with memetic algorithms. In: Proceedings of GECCO (2013)
4. Fraser, G., Arcuri, A., McMinn, P.: A memetic algorithm for whole test suite generation. JSS **103**, 311–327 (2015)
5. Fraser, G., Staats, M., McMinn, P., Arcuri, A., Padberg, F.: Does automated white-box test generation really help software testers? In: Proceedings of ISSTA (2013)
6. Fraser, G., Staats, M., McMinn, P., Arcuri, A., Padberg, F.: Does automated unit test generation really help software testers? a controlled empirical study. ACM TOSEM **24**, 23 (2015)
7. Harman, M., McMinn, P.: A theoretical and empirical analysis of evolutionary testing and hill climbing for structural test data generation. In: Proceedings of ISSTA (2007)
8. Harman, M., McMinn, P.: A theoretical and empirical study of search based testing: local, global and hybrid search. IEEE TSE **36**, 226–247 (2010)
9. Kapfhammer, G.M., McMinn, P., Wright, C.J.: Search-based testing of relational schema integrity constraints across multiple database management systems. In: Proceedings of ICST (2013)
10. Kempka, J., McMinn, P., Sudholt, D.: A theoretical runtime and empirical analysis of different alternating variable searches for search-based testing. In: Proceedings of GECCO (2013)
11. Kempka, J., McMinn, P., Sudholt, D.: Design and analysis of different alternating variable searches for search-based software testing. TCS **605**, 1–20 (2015)
12. Korel, B.: Automated software test data generation. IEEE TSE (1990)
13. Kukunas, J., Cupper, R.D., Kapfhammer, G.M.: A genetic algorithm to improve Linux kernel performance on resource-constrained devices. In: Proc. GECCO (2010)
14. Lakhotia, K., Harman, M., Gross, H.: AUSTIN: A tool for search based software testing for the C language and its evaluation on deployed automotive systems. In: SSBSE (2010)
15. Lakhotia, K., Harman, M., Gross, H.: AUSTIN: An open source tool for search based software testing of C programs. IST **55**, 112–125 (2013)
16. Lakhotia, K., Tillmann, N., Harman, M., de Halleux, J.: FloPSy - search-based floating point constraint solving for symbolic execution. In: Petrenko, A., Simão, A., Maldonado, J.C. (eds.) ICTSS 2010. LNCS, vol. 6435, pp. 142–157. Springer, Heidelberg (2010)
17. McMinn, P.: IGUANA: Input generation using automated novel algorithms. A plug and play research tool. Technical Report CS-07-14, Dept. Computer Science, University of Sheffield, UK (2007)
18. McMinn, P., Wright, C.J., Kapfhammer, G.M.: The effectiveness of test coverage criteria for relational database schema integrity constraints. ACM TOSEM **25**, 8:1–8:49 (2015)
19. Pradhan, D., Wang, S., Ali, S., Yue, T.: Search-based cost-effective test case selection for manual execution within time budget: an empirical study. In: Proceedings of GECCO (2016)
20. Qiu, X., Ali, S., Yue, T., Zhang, L.: Reliability-redundancy-location allocation with maximum reliability and minimum cost using search techniques. IST (2016, to appear)

21. Yue, T., Ali, S.: Applying search algorithms for optimizing stakeholders familiarity and balancing workload in requirements assignment. In: Proceedings of GECCO (2014)
22. Yue, T., Ali, S., Lu, H., Nie, K.: Search-based decision ordering to facilitate product line engineering of cyber-physical system. In: Proceedings of MODELSWARD (2016)
23. Zhong, H., Su, Z.: An empirical study on real bug fixes. In: Proceedings of ICSE (2015)

A Method Dependence Relations Guided Genetic Algorithm

Ali Aburas$^{(\boxtimes)}$ and Alex Groce

Oregon State University, Corvallis, OR 97330, USA
aburasali@gmail.com

Abstract. Search based test generation approaches have already been shown to be effective for generating test data that achieves high code coverage for object-oriented programs. In this paper, we present a new search-based approach, called GAMDR, that uses a genetic algorithm (GA) to generate test data. GAMDR exploits method dependence relations (MDR) to narrow down the search space and direct mutation operators to the most beneficial regions for achieving high branch coverage. We compared GAMDR's effectiveness with random testing, EvoSuite, and a simple GA. The tests generated by GAMDR achieved higher branch coverage.

Keywords: SBST · Genetic algorithm · Search space reduction · Java testing

1 Introduction

Different search-based testing techniques have been proposed to automatically generate unit tests for object-oriented programs, e.g., *TestFul* [4] and *EvoSuite* [7]. A major problem with most of the existing search based software testing (SBST) approaches is that they consider the whole search space of possible input values and method calls to the class under test (CUT). Thus, finding critical calls can be a challenge due to the large size of the search space.

In genetic algorithms (GA), the mutation operator plays an essential role: it modifies individuals (here, test cases) with a relatively small probability. Mutation operations (e.g., modifying input values or inserting method calls) are randomly performed to preserve diversity of populations, and prevent the search from being trapped in a local optima [11]. Nevertheless, whenever mutation occurs, the chance of choosing the method calls or primitive values that are most beneficial is very low. Such random mutation has two problems. First, it lacks guidance as to inputs, causing unnecessary computational expense [11]. This is due to an inability to explore promising areas in the search space. Second, randomly flipping methods or manipulating an input primitive value may fail to generate high quality new individuals. This can lead to an increase in the chances of premature convergence due to lack of diversity in the population [11].

© Springer International Publishing AG 2016
F. Sarro and K. Deb (Eds.): SSBSE 2016, LNCS 9962, pp. 267–273, 2016.
DOI: 10.1007/978-3-319-47106-8_22

In this short paper, we introduce a fully automated search-based testing approach for Java, called GAMDR. GAMDR implements a Genetic Algorithm (GA) that aims to cover *all* target branches. This implementation accelerates the search towards the global optimum because it does not waste time on infeasible branches [4,7]. GAMDR also exploits Method Dependence Relations (MDR) [14] to narrow down the search space and direct mutation operators to the most beneficial regions in the search space, leading to high CUT branch coverage.

2   Related Work

Harman et al. [9] were the first to theoretically and empirically explore search space reduction for SBST. Their empirical study targeted procedural programs and showed that irrelevant input removal improved the performance of local, global, and hybrid search algorithms. Barsei et al. [4] proposed a semi-automated approach to augment the efficiency and speed-up test generation with the Test-Ful tool. This was achieved by requiring the user to provide data regarding the effects of each method of the CUT. Ribeiro et al. [12] leveraged purity analysis [13] to reduce the input space of object-oriented programs. Harman et al. [10] also proposed a domain reduction technique to exclude irrelevant parameters in the search space for aspect-oriented programs. They performed backward slicing to identify such irrelevant parameters, after which evolutionary testing was conducted only on the remaining relevant parameters. Aburas and Groce [1] proposed a memetic algorithm exploiting MDR to improve the effectiveness of a hill climbing (HC) technique.

In contrast to the aforementioned approaches, our approach uses GA to generate test data and applies a static analysis to precisely identify only those member fields or parameters of the method under test that would be relevant for covering uncovered branches. Then, it leverages MDR to automatically direct the mutation operations to generate a sequence of method calls that produce the desired values for member fields or parameters, based on impact on target branches. Combining GA with MDR has a number of advantages. (**1**) it focuses on the root cause of the failure to cover target branches. (**2**) it focuses only on the relevant parts of the individuals (i.e., test cases) that affect the execution of the target branches. (**3**) it implements a domain reduction mechanism to speed search space exploration. Unlike previous search-based approaches, these strengths together enable the proposed approach to explore high complexity code in order to achieve high branch coverage.

3   GAMDR

GAMDR consists of three different components: the Instrumenter, Static Analyzer, and Genetic Tester components.

- **Instrumenter Component:** In this component, the original source code of the class under test (CUT) is instrumented at byte-code level to measure coverage values and calculate the fitness function. We use Soot[1] for analyzing and instrumenting Java byte-code.

- **Static Analyzer Component:** The key idea behind our approach is to use lightweight static analysis to identify relevant methods for each target branch, and then use them during mutation operations. To this end, we perform backward analysis for each target branch, and precisely identify if a parameter of the method contains the target branch or if a member field of a class can help to cover the target branch. For each member field, we use MDR to identify the methods that modify the member field (the `write-read relation`). In addition, if a parameter of the target method affects the coverage of the target branch, we identify all the methods that write in the target method (the `read-write relation`). If the identified parameter is not a primitive type, we identify the methods' return as the same type object that can be passed as an argument to the target method (i.e., `accessed-data relation`).

- **Genetic Tester Component:** In our implementation, we use a similar GA to that used in previous work [3,4], but extend it to implement MDR [14].

1. **Individual representation:** We use an individual representation similar to some previous work [4,7] because it is easy to manipulate. Each individual consists of a set of statements of length N, which is set to 80. Each statement is a constructor, method call, field access, or array input.

2. **Fitness Function:** The fitness function uses branch distance (BD) and keeps track of how close an individual is to covering all reachable but not-yet-executed branches [3,7].

$$f(i) = \sum_{b_j \in B} BD(b_j, i) \quad \text{and} \quad BD(b_j, i) = \begin{cases} 0 & \text{if branch } j \text{ is covered} \\ k & \text{if branch } j \text{ is reached} \\ 1 & \text{otherwise} \end{cases}$$

The function $BD(b_j, i)$ shows how close an individual i is to cover the not-covered branch j. Here BD is all target branches and k is a normalizing function with value within $[0,1]$; we use the normalization function: $k = \frac{x}{x+1}$ [2], and x shows how far a predicate is from obtaining opposite value [7].

3. **Genetic Operations:** Our approach (GAMDR) implements common genetic operators: selection, crossover, mutation, and elitism, to manipulate and evolve successive populations. Following is a summary of these operators:

   (a) *Selection:* GAMDR implements tournament selection [11]. However, if two individuals have the same fitness values, the shortest individual is selected to prevent *bloat* [6].

   (b) *Crossover:* GAMDR implements a fixed single crossover point, where the two selected individuals are cut at the middle, to avoid generating long offspring [6].

---

[1] http://www.sable.mcgill.ca/.

(c) **Mutation:** After crossover, the individuals are subjected to mutation. Rather than just randomly changing statements of the chosen individuals, GAMDR uses MDR to direct the mutation operator towards relevant statements where changes may help to result in more fit individuals and increase exploration of the search space. Therefore, GAMDR randomly chooses a reached (but not covered) branch and analyzes its predicates. Then, GAMDR precisely identifies the relevant types of elements that are involved in execution of the target branch, e.g. member field, parameter method, or/and constant values. Consequently, GAMDR directs the mutation operations to explore those identified relevant statements (constructors, methods, and parameters). Finally, for a chosen individual with a length n, GAMDR randomly applies one of the following operations with probability $1/3$.

  – **Remove:** All irrelevant statements are removed; additionally a chosen statement from the identified relevant statements is removed from the individual with a probability r, where $r = 0.01$.
  – **Insert:** A random number r, where $1 \leq r \leq (N - n)$, of identified relevant statements are added at a random position in the chosen individual.
  – **Change:** Each identified relevant statement and parameter is changed in the chosen individual with probability r, where $r = 0.01$.

(d) **Elitism:** The best individuals are copied to the next new generation. The population size is set to 100, and elitism rate is set to 10 %.

4   Empirical Study

We compared the effectiveness of GAMDR in achieving branch coverage against three different approaches: a simple GA (without MDR enabled) [3,4], pure random testing (RT) [5], and EvoSuite [7]. We used seven popular Java projects as test subjects (Table 1). These projects are taken from the literature discussing cases where SBST faces problems in achieving high branch coverage.

We used identical configurations for GAMDR and the simple GA to ensure as fair a comparison as possible. We also used EvoSuite version 20130910 with the default configuration. To compare RT with GAMDR, we adopted the proposed approach by Ciupa et al. [5]; the length of test cases in RT was set to 200 [8]. We ran each approach 30 times with a time limit of 5 min with

Table 1. Details of the test subjects.

Test subject	#Classes	NCSS	#Branches
Commons Codec	41	3,269	1,373
Commons CLI	11	677	288
Conzilla	13	377	120
jdom2	40	3,196	978
lang3	55	9,182	5052
NanoXML	26	1,984	571
Joda-Time	57	9,152	2,207
Total	**243**	**27,837**	**10,589**

different random seeds, and used JaCoCoVersion 0.7.5[2] to measure coverage during test generation.

4.1 Effectiveness of GAMDR

Table 2 summarizes the average branch coverage percentages for the 30 experiments. In the table, the highlighted values with bold text indicates that a particular testing approach obtained the highest coverage (with Mann-Whitney-Wilcoxon test p-value < 0.05) for that test subject. For Commons Codec, GAMDR was significantly better than EvoSuite and the pure GA, but not RT.

Table 2. Branch coverage achieved at 5 min

Test subject	RT (%)	EvoSuite (%)	GA (%)	GAMDR (%)
Commons Codec	89.71	89.28	87.76	90.47
Commons CLI	95.96	95.67	91.97	95.81
Conzilla	70.05	82.79	73.78	**91.85**
Jdom2	**83.58**	81.22	80.02	83.03
lang3	88.48	78.64	86.98	**89.43**
NanoXML	62.87	61.34	62.51	**69.88**
Joda-Time	79.52	83.19	79.95	**85.10**

Table 2 shows that GAMDR outperforms other test approaches on Conzilla, NanoXML and Joda-Time subjects. One major reason is that these subjects contain classes which have constructors that call superclasses. These constructors require calling methods that are in a correct order and have valid arguments. For example, in the NanoXML subject, the constructor of the class CDATAReader requires a valid StdXMLReader object, which is a concrete implementation of the interface class IXMLReader. As a result, a valid sequence of method calls requires a correct order to create the desired objects: a valid StdXMLReader object must be created before a CDATAReader object. Despite the fact that the class CDATAReader contains only 4 public methods, our experiment revealed that RT, EvoSuite, and GA could only achieve 66 %, 68 %, and 71 % branch coverage of CDATAReader, respectively. This is because there is no guidance encoded in the fitness function identifying which constructors, methods, or parameters must be called to cover certain branches. In contrast, the static analysis used in GAMDR helps to identify all relevant methods based on the fields they write, and accessible constructors. For example, GAMDR identifies the StdXMLReader constructors and the method stringReader because they both return objects that can be used to replace the interface class type argument in the CDATAReader constructor, i.e., *accessed-data relation*. In addition, GAMDR identifies the CDATAReader

---

[2] http://eclemma.org/jacoco/.

constructor because it writes field `reader`, i.e., *write-read relation*. As a result, during the mutation phase, GAMDR tries to generate test data and method calls for these relevant methods and constructors instead of investing time on all constructors, methods and parameters. Our results show that GAMDR achieves 90 % branch coverage of the class `CDATAReader`, which is 23 %, 22 %, and 19 % higher than RT, EvoSuite, and GA, respectively.

The results also show GAMDR outperforms EvoSuite and GA on lang3, and improves some over RT, because lang3 contains classes that contain a large number of method calls. For example, the `ArrayUtils` class contains 229 different public methods to test, each of which takes primitive and/or array arguments. RT achieves 99 %, EvoSuites 68 %, and GA 88 % branch coverage of the class. We speculate the low branch coverage of the EvoSuite and GA are because the number of public methods decreases the probability of mutations of relevant methods and parameters to cover certain branches. GAMDR uses MDR to increase the probability of useful mutations, and achieves 98 % branch coverage.

The results indicate that MDR is indeed useful in helping to increase branch coverage by identifying relevant methods and parameters that need to be mutated in order to cover particular branches. The results also support the belief that the applicability of the search-based test data generation techniques are limited not only when the search space is large, but also when the search does not take into account data dependencies within the class under test (CUT) [11].

5   Conclusion

This paper has introduced and evaluated GAMDR, which applies a genetic algorithm (GA) to cover all target branches at the same time, and uses method dependence relations (MDR) for improving choice of mutations. Our empirical study shows that GAMDR achieves higher branch coverage than RT, EvoSuite, and a simple GA, for complex hard-to-cover programs.

References

1. Aburas, A., Groce, A.: An improved memetic algorithm with method dependence relations (mamdr). In: Quality Software (QSIC), pp. 11–20. IEEE (2014)
2. Arcuri, A.: It really does matter how you normalize the branch distance in search-based software testing. Softw. Test. Verification Reliab. **23**(2), 119–147 (2013)
3. Arcuri, A., Yao, X.: A memetic algorithm for test data generation of object-oriented software. In: Evolutionary Computation, pp. 2048–2055. IEEE (2007)
4. Baresi, L., Lanzi, P.L., Miraz, M.: Testful: an evolutionary test approach for Java. In: Software Testing, Verification and Validation (ICST), pp. 185–194. IEEE (2010)
5. Ciupa, I., Leitner, A., Oriol, M., Meyer, B.: Artoo. In: Software Engineering, ICSE 2008, pp. 71–80. IEEE (2008)
6. Fraser, G., Arcuri, A.: Handling test length bloat. Softw. Test. Verification Reliab. **23**(7), 553–582 (2013)
7. Fraser, G., Arcuri, A.: Whole test suite generation. IEEE Trans. Softw. Eng. **39**(2), 276–291 (2013)

8. Groce, A., Fern, A., Pinto, J., Bauer, T., Alipour, A., Erwig, M., Lopez, C.: Lightweight automated testing with adaptation-based programming. In: Software Reliability Engineering (ISSRE), pp. 161–170. IEEE (2012)
9. Harman, M., Hassoun, Y., Lakhotia, K., McMinn, P., Wegener, J.: The impact of input domain reduction on search-based test data generation. In: Proceedings of the ACM SIGSOFT Symposium, pp. 155–164. ACM (2007)
10. Harman, M., Islam, F., Xie, T., Wappler, S.: Automated test data generation for aspect-oriented programs. In: Proceedings of the Aspect-Oriented Software Development, pp. 185–196. ACM (2009)
11. McMinn, P.: Search-based software test data generation: a survey. Softw. Test. Verification Reliab. **14**(2), 105–156 (2004)
12. Ribeiro, J.C.B., Zenha-Rela, M.A., de Vega, F.F.: Test case evaluation and input domain reduction strategies for the evolutionary testing of object-oriented software. Inf. Softw. Technol. **51**, 1534–1548 (2009)
13. Sălcianu, A., Rinard, M.: Purity and side effect analysis for Java programs. In: Cousot, R. (ed.) VMCAI 2005. LNCS, vol. 3385, pp. 199–215. Springer, Heidelberg (2005)
14. Zhang, S., Saff, D., Bu, Y., Ernst, M.D.: Combined static and dynamic automated test generation. In: Proceedings of the 2011 International Symposium on Software Testing and Analysis, pp. 353–363. ACM (2011)

Preliminary Study of Multi-objective Features Selection for Evolving Software Product Lines

David Brevet[1,2], Takfarinas Saber[1], Goetz Botterweck[3],
and Anthony Ventresque[1(✉)]

[1] Lero, School of Computer Science, University College Dublin, Dublin, Ireland
`takfarinas.saber@ucdconnect.ie, anthony.ventresque@ucd.ie`
[2] University of Nantes, Nantes, France
`david.brevet1@etu.univ-nantes.fr`
[3] Lero@UL, University of Limerick, Limerick, Ireland
`goetz.botterweck@lero.ie`

Abstract. When dealing with software-intensive systems, it is often beneficial to consider families of similar systems together. A common task is then to identify the particular product that best fulfils a given set of desired product properties. *Software Product Lines Engineering* (SPLE) provides techniques to design, implement and evolve families of similar systems in a systematic fashion, with variability choices explicitly represented, e.g., as *Feature Models*. The problem of picking the 'best' product then becomes a question of optimising the *Feature Configuration*. When considering multiple properties at the same time, we have to deal with multi-objective optimisation, which is even more challenging. While change and evolution of software systems is the common case, to the best of our knowledge there has been no evaluation of the problem of *multi-objective optimisation of evolving Software Product Lines*. In this paper we present a benchmark of large scale evolving Feature Models and we study the behaviour of the state-of-the-art algorithm (SATIBEA). In particular, we show that we can improve both the execution time and the quality of SATIBEA by feeding it with the previous configurations: our solution converges nearly 10 times faster and gets an 113 % improvement after one generation of genetic algorithm.

Keywords: SPL · Multi-objective · Genetic algorithm · Evolution

1 Introduction

Software Product Lines (SPL) is a branch of Software Engineering that aims at designing software products based on a composition of pre-defined software artefacts, increasing the reusability and personalisation of software products [5]. Software architects, when they design new products or adapt existing products,

This work was supported by Science Foundation Ireland grants 10/CE/I1855 and 13/RC/2094.

F. Sarro and K. Deb (Eds.): SSBSE 2016, LNCS 9962, pp. 274–280, 2016.
DOI: 10.1007/978-3-319-47106-8_23

navigate a set of features in a Feature Model (FM). Each of these features represents an element of a software artefact that is of importance to some stakeholders. Through its structure and additional constraints, each FM describes all possible products as combinations of features. One of the issues with FMs is that they can be very large – for instance in our study we work with FMs composed of nearly 7,000 features and 350,000 constraints. *Optimising FMs*, i.e., *selecting the set of features* that could lead to potential real products, is then a difficult problem [3]. This problem is also called SPL configuration as it consists in configuring products from the FMs. It is even more challenging as this problem is typically a multi-objective one: software designers and architects make their decisions based on various perspectives [4,8], such as, cost, technical feasibility or reliability.

Another related problem that has not been studied yet is the *feature selection in a multi-objective context when the FMs evolve*. It is not a surprise to say that software requirements and artefacts evolve constantly. For instance, stakeholders and customers often change their opinions about how applications should work, or new coding paradigms are introduced. FMs reflect that, and for instance, we have seen in our study that a large FM (such as the one behind the Linux kernel) evolves regularly and substantially (every few months a new FM is released with up to 7 % difference from the previous one). In this context, it seems odd to generate random bootstrapping populations for the state-of-the-art genetic algorithms, such as, SATIBEA. It is tempting on the contrary to use the fact that FMs have evolved and that the SPL configurations generated previously, while not totally applicable, are close and can be adapted.

Our contributions in this paper are the following: (i) We propose a benchmark[1] for the analysis of evolving SPL; this data set has been generated following a study of the demographics and evolution of a large SPL (Linux kernel). This data set is important to provide a good evaluation of the different algorithms under different evolution scenarios; (ii) We propose *eSATIBEA* which is a modification of the state-of-the-art SATIBEA [4] for evolving SPL. eSATIBEA adapts previous solutions to new FMs to improve and speed-up the results of SATIBEA; (iii) We evaluate SATIBEA and eSATIBEA on the evolving SPL problem and show that eSATIBEA converges nearly 10 times faster and gets a 113 % improvement after one generation of genetic algorithm.

Seeding is not a novel idea as such (e.g., see papers by Fraser and Arcuri [2] and Alshahwan and Harman [1]) – but usually seeding is done by taking a few good/previous solutions that are inserted in the initial population. In this paper we take all the previous solutions that we adapt to create a starting population. We also work on a large scale and very constrained search space, which is not always the case in models for which seeding is known to work.

The rest of this paper is organised as follows: Sect. 2 describes the problem of configuring evolving SPLs; Sect. 3 presents our benchmark; Sect. 4 evaluates SATIBEA and eSATIBEA; Sect. 5 concludes this paper.

---

[1] Available here: http://hibernia.ucd.ie/EvolvingFMs/.

2   Problem Definition

Feature Models can easily be represented by a set of features and relations (constraints) between them. Figure 1 shows a simple FM with 10 features linked by several relations, such as, 'alternative' between features 'Screen' : 'Basic', 'Colour' and 'High Resolution'. These relations define constraints: for instance, a 'Screen' can only be of one of 3 types 'Basic', 'Colour' or 'High Resolution'.

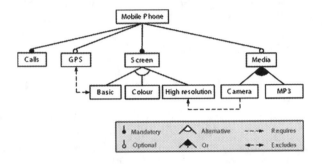

Fig. 1. Sample of a Feature Model

The objective of SPL engineering is to extract products from the FMs by selecting a subset of features $S \subseteq \mathcal{F}$ which satisfies the FM $\mathcal{F}$ – and the requirements of the stakeholder/customer. Often, the SPL configuration problem is described as a satisfiability problem (SAT) [7], i.e., a problem where we try to find an assignment to variables (here, features) in the $\{True, False\}$ space. Let $f_i \in \{True, False\}$ be a decision variable set to '$True$' if the feature $F_i \in \mathcal{F}$ is selected to be part of S and '$False$' otherwise. An FM is equivalent to a conjunction of disjunctive clauses, forming a conjunctive normal form (CNF). Finding a product in the SPL is then equivalent to giving a value in $\{True, False\}$ to every variable/feature. For instance, in Fig. 1 the FM would have the following clauses, among others: $(Basic \lor Colour \lor High\ resolution) \land (\neg Basic \lor \neg Colour) \land (\neg Basic \lor \neg High\ resolution) \land (\neg Colour \lor \neg High\ resolution)$, which describe the alternative between the three features. Now, software designers, when configuring a SPL, do not only look for possible products (satisfying the FM) but for products optimising some criteria – and there could be several of these criteria. This is why the problem of SPL configuration has been described as multi-objective. Here, following other classical approaches [4,8] we use 5 objectives: (i) number of selected features, (ii) number of selected features that were not used in the past, (iii) sum of known defects in the selected features, (iv) number of compatibility violations, and (v) cost of the selected features.

Evolution of the SPLs and FMs is known to be an important challenge for the domain, as they both represent long term investments [6]. For instance, in the next section we present a study of a large scale FM, the Linux kernel, and we show that every few months a new FM is released with up to 7 % modifications among the features (features added or removed). The FM/SPL evolution perspective has not been addressed in the multi-objective feature selection literature – as far as we know. This is likely because the problem is a large and complex optimisation problem and the repairs/adaptation of previous solutions to new FMs unlikely to succeed. In this paper though we prove that it is not the case and that it is possible to feed solutions of previous FMs into new FMs, with good results. What we work with is a mapping between two FMs. Let us assume an FM FM_1 evolved into another FM FM_2. Some of the features $f_i^1 \in FM_1$ are mapped on to features $f_i^2 \in FM_2$ – they are the same or considered the same, while some of the features $f_i^1 \in FM_1$ are not mapped onto any features in FM_2 (f_i^1 has been removed) and features $f_i^2 \in FM_2$ have no corresponding features in FM_1 (f_i^2 has been added). Obviously the same applied to constraints (removed from FM_1 or added to FM_2). The problem we address concerns adapting the solutions found previously for FM_1 to FM_2.

3   Towards a Benchmark for Feature-model Evolution

We studied the largest open source FM we found: the Linux kernel [9] containing 6,888 features and 343,944 constraints (in its version 2.6.28). We evaluated the demographics (features, constraints) and evolution of 21 versions of the kernel: from version 2.6.12 to version 2.6.32. We observed that on average there was only 4.6 % difference in terms of features between a version and the next: 21.22 % of removed features and 78.78 % of new (added) features. We also evaluated the size of the clauses/constraints in the problem, as we need to know how the constraints we add in the problem should look like. We found that a large proportion of the FMs' constraints have 6 features (39 %), 5 features (16 %), 18 features (14 %) or 19 features (14 %). From this study, we generated a synthetic benchmark of FM evolution based on the real evolution of the Linux kernel – hence a realistic benchmark but with more variability than in a real one, allowing us also to get several synthetic data sets for each evolution values. Our FM generator uses two parameters representing the percentage of feature modifications (added/removed) and the percentage of constraint modifications (added/removed). The higher those percentages are, the more different the new FM will be from the original one. Our FM generator uses the proportions we observed in the 20 FMs to generate new features/remove old ones, and to generate new constraints of a particular length. Values we use can be seen in our benchmark in Fig. 2: from 5 % of modified features and 1 % of modified constraints (FM 5_1) to 20 % of modified features and 10 % of modified constraints (FM 20_10). In our evaluations (see next section) we generate 10 synthetic FMs for each values of the parameters.

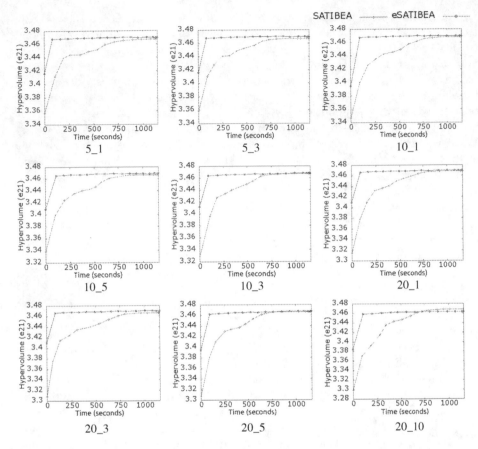

Fig. 2. Hypervolume of the solutions given by SATIBEA and eSATIBEA on evolved Linux kernels. We gave a label x_y to each evolution, 'x' representing the percentage of modified features and 'y' the percentage of modified constraints. We generated 10 evolved FMs for each combination and only show the average here.

4   Evaluation

This section evaluates two algorithms: SATIBEA, known in the literature as the best algorithm for multi-objective configuration of SPLs, and our contribution: eSATIBEA. We perform our evaluation on the benchmark described in the previous section and we compare the two algorithms using the hypervolume [11]. The hypervolume is a metric that indicates the space (in the n dimensions defined by the n objectives) dominated by the Pareto front of the solutions found by each algorithm. The bigger the hypervolume the better (i.e., more space is covered by the front of solutions).

The current state of the art in SPL configuration is the SATIBEA algorithm [4]. SATIBEA is the combination of a genetic algorithm (IBEA [10]) and a SAT solver. In particular, two steps are added to the genetic algorithm: 'smart mutation' and 'smart replacement', both applied with a certain probability, and both using the SAT solver to discover possible solutions to repair or replace infeasible solutions. We propose eSATIBEA, which aims at taking advantage of previous SPL configurations (when they exist) to feed in SATIBEA with previous solutions. Let's assume a FM FM_1 that evolves into another FM FM_2 over time (e.g., features and constraints added or removed). An SPL configuration was performed on FM_1 (e.g., using SATIBEA) and a set of solutions (S_1) was found. Now instead of randomly generating individuals for SATIBEA, we decide in eSATIBEA to adapt the set of solutions S_1 to the feature Model FM_2 and to give these solutions to SATIBEA. Our hope is obviously that these initial individuals will be of good quality, and anyway better than random solutions.

Figure 2 shows that both algorithms improve the hypervolume over time and eventually plateau after 1,200 s. However, eSATIBEA takes advantage of the relatively good initial population and gets a better hypervolume for most data sets. Furthermore, we see that eSATIBEA converges quickly (i.e., less than 100 s), whereas it takes SATIBEA more than 700 s to reach a similar hypervolume than eSATIBEA. We also notice that eSATIBEA achieves an improvement of over 113 % on average in comparison to SATIBEA at the end of the first generation of genetic algorithm (i.e., at 95 s on average). This percentage decreases over time until 1 % improvement on average. We see in Fig. 2 (20_10) that SATIBEA gets an hypervolume slightly better than eSATIBEA by the end of the execution – while, as for other evolved FMs, eSATIBEA converges faster. This probably shows the limitation of our approach: 20_10 is a very different FM than the original one and SATIBEA, generating an initial population adapted to the new FM, does a better exploration of the space – while eSATIBEA stays close to a FM that is now obsolete.

5   Conclusion

This paper has presented a new problem: the configuration of Software Product Lines when the Feature Models they are based on evolves. To study this problem, we have proposed a benchmark using a survey of the evolution of a large (nearly 7,000 features and 350,000 constraints) FM. We have compared SATIBEA, the leading algorithm in the literature, and our contribution eSATIBEA (which takes an adaptation of the previous solutions as initial population) in this evolving context. We have shown that eSATIBEA outperforms SATIBEA, in particular it converges nearly 10 times faster and achieves an improvement of 113 % after the first generation of genetic algorithm ($\simeq$ 100 s). The two directions we plan to follow in the future are: an adaptation of the seed given to SATIBEA in eSATIBEA, and an improvement of eSATIBEA to overcome the problem of the plateau phase.

References

1. Alshahwan, N., Harman, M.: Automated web application testing using search based software engineering. In: ASE, pp. 3–12 (2011)
2. Fraser, G., Arcuri, A.: The seed is strong: seeding strategies in search-based software testing. In: ICST, pp. 121–130 (2012)
3. Harman, M., Jia, Y., Krinke, J., Langdon, W.B., Petke, J., Zhang, Y.: Search based software engineering for software product line engineering: a survey and directions for future work. In: SPLC, pp. 5–18 (2014)
4. Henard, C., Papadakis, M., Harman, M., Le Traon, Y.: Combining multi-objective search and constraint solving for configuring large software product lines. In: ICSE, pp. 517–528 (2015)
5. Metzger, A., Pohl, K.: Software product line engineering, variability management: achievements and challenges. In: FSE, pp. 70–84 (2014)
6. Pleuss, A., Botterweck, G., Dhungana, D., Polzer, A., Kowalewski, S.: Model-driven support for product line evolution on feature level. JSS **85**(10), 2261–2274 (2012)
7. Pohl, R., Lauenroth, K., Pohl, K.: A performance comparison of contemporary algorithmic approaches for automated analysis operations on feature models. In: ASE, pp. 313–322 (2011)
8. Sayyad, A.S., Ingram, J., Menzies, T., Ammar, H.: Scalable product line configuration: a straw to break the camel's back. In: ASE, pp. 465–474 (2013)
9. She, S.: Feature Model Synthesis. Ph.d thesis, University of Waterloo (2013)
10. Zitzler, E., Künzli, S.: Indicator-based selection in multiobjective search. In: Yao, X., Burke, E.K., Lozano, J.A., Smith, J., Merelo-Guervós, J.J., Bullinaria, J.A., Rowe, J.E., Tiňo, P., Kabán, A., Schwefel, H.-P. (eds.) PPSN 2004. LNCS, vol. 3242, pp. 832–842. Springer, Heidelberg (2004)
11. Zitzler, E., Thiele, L.: Multiobjective optimization using evolutionary algorithms - a comparative case study. In: Eiben, A.E., Bäck, T., Schoenauer, M., Schwefel, H.-P. (eds.) PPSN 1998. LNCS, vol. 1498, pp. 292–301. Springer, Heidelberg (1998)

Interactive Code Smells Detection: An Initial Investigation

Mohamed Wiem Mkaouer[✉]

Department of Computer and Information Science,
University of Michigan, 4901 Evergreen Road,
Dearborn, MI 48128, USA
mmkaouer@umich.edu

Abstract. In this paper, we introduced a novel technique to generate more user-oriented detection rules by taking into account their feedback. Our techniques initially generate a set of detection rules that will be used to detect candidate code smells, these reported code smells will be exposed in an interactive fashion to the developer who will give his/her feedback by either approving or rejecting the identified code smell in the code fragment. This feedback will be fed to the GP as constraints and additional examples in order to converge towards more user-preferred detection rules. We initially investigated the detection of three types of code smells in four open source systems and reported that the interactive code smell detection achieves a precision of 89 % and recall on average when detecting infected classes. Results show that our approach can best imitate the user's decision while omitting the complexity of manual tuning the detection rules.

1 Introduction

Code smells have been known as bad programming behavior that can be introduced during the initial software design or during its maintenance. The existence of these smells is a strong indicator for poor software quality as the infected code tends to be more difficult to understand and to update. As a consequence, the risk of introducing errors while committing regular software updates becomes alarming.

There has been much work resulting in different techniques and tools for code smells detection [1–4]. These techniques deploy different detection strategies using various structural metrics due to the inconsistency in the definition of code smells and due to the subjectivity of the code smell interpretation by the software engineers [5]. In fact, the source code used measurements, i.e., metrics, may vary from one technique to another. Also, two detection strategies using the same rules may give different results based on various thresholds that can be used when interpreting metric values. One of the main limitations of these strategies is that they impose a pre-defined definition of what is seen as bad symptoms in the code although it should be subject to the developer's interpretation.

To cope with the above mentioned limitations, we propose a novel interactive code smells detection that dynamically adapts the developers' preference by deploying detection rules that have been tuned based on their feedback. This approach starts by

F. Sarro and K. Deb (Eds.): SSBSE 2016, LNCS 9962, pp. 281–287, 2016.
DOI: 10.1007/978-3-319-47106-8_24

using three state-of-art code smells detection techniques that each one generates a list of code smells along with their location in the code. One of the challenges is how to choose the most suitable detection technique for a given smell type. To this end, this approach starts by finding the overlapping code smells (type and location) among the detection techniques. Based on this analysis, the infected code fragments are ranked based on their frequency and suggested to the developer for each smell type. The developer can approve or reject each suggestion. This feedback is then used to evaluate the performance of the detection techniques using the accepted/rejected suggestions and rank them. In the next stage, this feedback is also used as a training set to refine the detection rules of the best-ranked detection technique. This approach was evaluated it on four open source systems.

2   Interactive Code Smells Detection

The general structure of this approach is sketched in Fig. 1. Our detection framework starts by generating, for an input software system, a list of detected code smells, for each detection strategy. Any detection strategy can be used as part of the initial detection stage as long as it is based on semi-automated or fully automated rules-based detection and its rules are defined using a set of structural metrics that can be easily computed using the code parsing and statistical analysis.

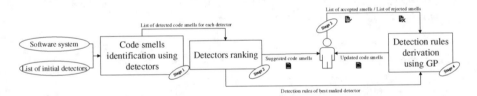

Fig. 1. The interactive Detection four main stages.

The generated lists, as outcomes of the first step, are firstly clustered per smell type. Each type is associated with a pool of possibly infected code fragments that are also classified by their originated detector. At the second stage, for each pool, the code fragments are sorted based on their occurrences among the classes of detectors, and so, for each smell type, a list of candidate code fragments to investigate is generated. In other terms, fragments are obviously sorted based on their overlap between detectors. More generally, any common feature among different strategies could be beneficial in search for more meaningful results that may achieve a tradeoff between these techniques [6].

The third stage suggests the top candidate fragments to analyze for each smell type. The developer can interactively confirm the existence of the smell in the fragment or report it as false positive. The developer does not need to evaluate the whole list of fragments, only with few evaluations, the ranking of detectors can still be effective, but the higher the number of evaluations is, per smell type, the more effective will be the generation of detection rules using the GP that is conducted after the interactive session with the developer.

The last step takes the developer's feedback along with the highest ranked detector's rules as input to the GP. A GP algorithm is a population-based evolutionary algorithm that uses natural selection to generate an optimal solution. GP encoding is optimized for trees structure, where the internal nodes are functions (operators) and the leaf nodes are terminal symbols. Both the function set and the terminal set must contain symbols that are appropriate for the target problem which matches, for instance, the detection rules representation. During the evolution, a training set is still applied to assess the learning process. The following pseudo-code highlights the adaptation of GP for the problem of detection rules generation.

Algorithm1. Rules generation using GP

Input: Software System (S)
Input: Detection rules (R)
Input: Set of Accepted (SA) and Rejected (SR) code smells
Output: Derived Detection rules
1: initial_population(P, Max_size)
2: P:= set_of(I)
3: I := rules(R, Smell_Type)
4: repeat
5:     for all I ∈ P do
6:         detected_smells := execute_rules(R,S)
7:         fitness(I) := compare(detected_smells, SA, SR)
8:     end for
9:     best_solution := best_fitness(I);
10:    P := generate_new_population(P)
11:    it:=it+1;
12: until it=max_it
13: return best_solution

---

3 Initial Evaluation Study

3.1 Research Questions

We defined two research questions to address in our experiments.

RQ1: To what extend can the interactive detection assist developers in the process of smells detection?

RQ2: Can the generated rules be generalized and used in the detection of code smell instances in software systems?

The answer to RQ1 is conducted through recording the number of accepted suggestions compared to the overall suggested fragments per smell type after the execution of all the stages of the interactive detection. A group of two Ph.D. students was asked to evaluate, manually, whether the suggested code fragments do contain the reported smell. Eventually, the number of meaningful suggestions per all suggestions constitutes the Manual Correctness (MC):

$$MC = \frac{|\text{accepted suggestion s}|}{|\text{all suggestion s}|}$$

To answer RQ2, a cross-fold validation has been conducted using the four open source systems used for in the experiment through four iterations. Precision and recall scores are calculated based on the ratio of the reported smells out of those suggested manually:

$$PR_{precision} = \frac{|\text{suggested smells} \cap \text{expected smells}|}{|\text{suggested smells}|} \in [0, 1]$$

$$RC_{recall} = \frac{|\text{suggested smells} \cap \text{expected smells}|}{|\text{expected smells}|} \in [0, 1]$$

3.2   Experimental Setting

We used a set of well-known open-source Java projects that were mainly chosen because they were the subject of several extensive studies in detection and comparison between code smells detection tools. We used two state of art code smell detectors namely InCode [7], Mäntylä et al. [5], as initial detectors for the first stage of the interactive detection. The choice of these techniques is based on the fact of their tree-based rules representation, Fig. 2 illustrates the example of the God Class detection rule based on [7]. The tree leaves are a composition of structural metrics and their ordinal values (Very_High, High, Medium, Low and Very_Low), the ordinal values are statistically interpreted using Box-Plot [8] in order to replace them with actual values extracted from the software system.

Fig. 2. Tree representation of the God Class rule in [11].

We applied our approach to four open-source Java projects: Xerces-J, JFreeChart, GanttProject, and JHotDraw. Table 1 provides some descriptive statistics about these four programs. We compared the performance of our approach with two deterministic detectors [5, 7] (previously used during the first stage) and one search-based detection rules generator [4].

Table 1. Statistics of the studied systems.

Systems	Release	# of classes/KLOC	# of flawed classes	Overlap % between detectors	# of interactive sessions with subjects	Average subjects' actions (accepted/rejected combined)
Xerces-J	v2.7.0	991/240	61	66 %	1	29
JHotDraw	v6.1	585/21	14	73 %	1	21
JFreeChart	v1.0.9	521/170	34	84 %	1	17
GanttProject	v1.10.2	245/41	19	89 %	1	12

During this study, we use the same parameter setting for all executions of the GP. The parameter setting is specified in Table 2.

Table 2. Parameter tuning for GP.

GP parameter	Values
Population size/Max Tree Depth	100/2
Selection/Survival/K	Roulette-Wheel/K-Tournament/2
Crossover/Crossover rate	Single-point/0.9
Mutation/Mutation rate	Sub-tree/0.1
Max iterations	1000/2500/5000

3.3   Results and Discussions

As an answer to RQ1, Fig. 3 reports the results of the empirical qualitative evaluation of the detection rules in terms of the MC ratio.

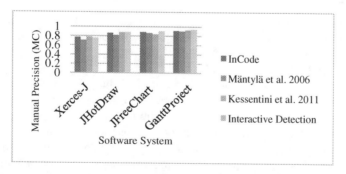

Fig. 3. Median of *MC* on all four software systems using different rules detection techniques.

Table 3. Median values of precision and recall for the detection of God Class, BLOB and Data Class in 4 systems over 30 runs.

Software	God Class		BLOB		Data Class	
	Precision (%)	Recall (%)	Precision (%)	Recall (%)	Precision (%)	Recall (%)
InCode	91	96	84	85	97	99
Mäntylä et al.	86	89	78	82	94	96
Kessentini et al.	88	97	82	96	89	97
Interactive detection	89	98	85	87	95	98

As reported in Fig. 3, the majority of the code smells detected our approach gained the satisfaction of the subjects. It is clear that the least performance of our approach in terms of median of accepted code smells among all reported ones over all the three smell types is with Xerces-J, which is the largest software used in our experiment, this can be explained by the fact that our approach may need a larger number of interactive sessions especially that the ratio of the number of interactions per number of flawed classes is relatively low compared to the other projects. For medium to small projects, the interactive detection performance was relatively acceptable.

In addition to the qualitative evaluation, we automatically evaluate our approach in terms of precision and recall to give more quantitative evaluation and answer RQ2. It is notable that we used the same training process for our approach as well as the By-Example approach of Kessentini et al. [4]. Since InCode [7], Mäntylä et al. [5] use pre-defined detection rules, no fold training was necessary for them and since they were deterministic approaches, no multiple runs were required as well. Then, we compare the proposed detected smells with some expected ones defined manually by the different groups for several code fragments extracted from the four systems. Table 3 summarizes our finding.

4   Conclusion and Future Work

We proposed, in this paper a novel interactive recommendation tool, for the problem of code smells detection rules' generation. The empirical study shows promising results as well as several further investigations to be conducted as part of the future work. Future work should also validate our approach with additional smells types, larger systems and especially a threshold that defines the maturity of the generated rules in order to draw conclusions about the general applicability of our methodology. We are planning on automating the whole smell management process through the combination of this approach as a first phase with the correction phase that has been the subject of a previous study [9].

References

1. Mäntylä, M., Vanhanen, J., Lassenius, C.: A taxonomy and an initial empirical study of bad smells in code. In: Proceedings of Conference Name, Conference Location, pp. 381–384 (2003)
2. Marinescu, R.: Detection strategies: metrics-based rules for detecting design flaws. In: Proceedings of Conference Name, Conference Location, pp. 350–359 (2004)
3. Moha, N., Gueheneuc, Y.-G., Duchien, L., Le Meur, A.-F.: DECOR: a method for the specification and detection of code and design smells. IEEE Trans. Softw. Eng. **36**(1), 20–36 (2010)
4. Kessentini, M., Kessentini, W., Sahraoui, H., Boukadoum, M., Ouni, A.: Design defects detection and correction by example. In: Proceedings of Conference Name, Conference Location, pp. 81–90, 22–24 June 2011
5. Mäntylä, M.V., Lassenius, C.: Subjective evaluation of software evolvability using code smells: an empirical study. Empirical Softw. Eng. **11**(3), 395–431 (2006)
6. Deb, K., Srinivasan, A.: Innovization: innovating design principles through optimization. In: Proceedings of the 8th Annual Conference on Genetic and Evolutionary Computation, Seattle, Washington, USA (2006)
7. Marinescu, R., Ganea, G., Verebi, I.: inCode: continuous quality assessment and improvement. In: Proceedings of Conference Name, Conference Location, pp. 274–275 (2010)
8. Williamson, D.F., Parker, R.A., Kendrick, J.S.: The box plot: a simple visual method to interpret data. Ann. Intern. Med. **110**(11), 916–921 (1989)
9. Mkaouer, M.W., Kessentini, M., Bechikh, S., Deb, K., Ó Cinnéide, M.: Recommendation system for software refactoring using innovization and interactive dynamic optimization. In: Proceedings of Conference Name, Conference Location, pp. 331–336 (2014)

Graduate Student Papers

Human Resource Allocation in Agile Software Projects Based on Task Similarities

Lucas Roque[✉], Allysson Allex Araújo, Altino Dantas, Raphael Saraiva,
and Jerffeson Souza

Optimization in Software Engineering Group, State University of Ceará,
Dr. Silas Munguba Avenue, 1700 - 60, Fortaleza 714-903, Brazil
{lucas.roque,raphael.saraiva}@aluno.uece.br,
{allysson.araujo,altino.dantas,jerffeson.souza}@uece.br
http://goes.uece.br

Abstract. The definition of which task should be assigned to each member of a team is a relevant issue on the software project management. This decision is complex because it involves a high number of variables, such as different levels of employee skills and several characteristics of each task. Thus, we propose a multi-objective approach aims at minimizing the time and cost of a software project through the allocation of suited and similar tasks to employees. In addition, we conducted a preliminary empirical study to investigate the performance of NSGA-II, MOCell and random search. Preliminary results suggest the approach is useful for allocating human resources in software projects.

Keywords: Human resource allocation · Multi-objective optimization · Tasks similarities

1 Introduction

Human resource[1] management is a key component to a software project [1]. The failure of software projects is often a result of inadequate planning and allocation of human resources [2]. A major problem faced by companies in developing or maintaining large and complex systems is determining which tasks should be assigned to each employee [3]. Without dealing with this problem, the efficiency of a software project cannot be achieved because employees may be involved in tasks in which their capabilities are not maximized [4].

Agile development employ iterative approaches where the software is developed and delivered to customers in increments called "releases" [5]. Given that (i) the productivity may vary significantly among developers [6] and (ii) the presence of tasks that are quite similar to each other [7], a good resource allocation which comprises these two aspects and helps to efficiently follow the release

---

[1] We consider as human resource the different types of professionals involved in the software project such as developers, analysts, external collaborators, etc. However, for the sake of simplicity, we will refer to these human resources as *employees*.

© Springer International Publishing AG 2016
F. Sarro and K. Deb (Eds.): SSBSE 2016, LNCS 9962, pp. 291–297, 2016.
DOI: 10.1007/978-3-319-47106-8_25

plan, takes on even more importance. Thus, we can mention the Resource Allocation for Software Release Planning (RASORP) problem that consists of finding
optimal assignment of resources to realize the releases' tasks [3].

Search-Based Software Engineering (SBSE) claims that complex problems of
Software Engineering may be reformulated as search problems [8]. In [3], the
combination of integer linear and genetic programming to generate operational
resource allocation plans was proposed. An Accelerated Simulated Annealing
based on individual-level and team-level constraints was evaluated in [4]. In [9],
it was exploited an ACO with an event-based scheduler as representation scheme.

However, one relevant limitation of current SBSE approaches to RASORP
is do not exploit the task's similarities during the human resource assignment.
We argue that allocating a group of similar tasks suited to employee skills may
collaborate to achieve an efficient and profitable release planning. Thus, we propose a multi-objective approach to RASORP aiming to minimize the time and
cost of the project by allocating suited and similar tasks.

2 Proposed Approach

As previously mentioned, agile methods are characterized by delivering releases
in an incremental and iterative way. Our approach is based on the Scrum method,
in which the development process follows a series of sprints cycles. Each sprint
cycle is a planning unit in which the work to be done is assessed, features are
selected, resources are allocated and the software is implemented. At the end of
a sprint, the completed functionality is delivered to stakeholders [10].

Consider $T_h = \{t_1, t_2, t_3, \cdots, t_N\}$ the set of tasks to be performed in a sprint
h and $E_h = \{e_1, e_2, e_3, \cdots, e_M\}$ the set of employees that represents the human
resources to the software project, where N and M are the total number of tasks
and employees, respectively. As representation to the solution, consider a vector
$S = \{x_1, x_2, x_3, \cdots, x_N\}$ with $x_i \in \{1, 2, 3, \cdots, M\}$, where $x_i = m$ indicates
that task t_i is assigned to employee e_m.

Each task t_n has a number of estimated hours represented by a vector
$TEH_t = \{teh_1, teh_2, teh_3, \cdots teh_N\}$ and a set of required skills depicted by a
matrix $TSM_{N \times Z}$, where tsm_{nz} indicates the value of skill z required by the
task t_n. On the other hand, each employee e_m is composed of:

- Hour value, $EHV_e \in [1, L]$, where L is the maximum amount paid per hour;
- Extra hour value, $EXV_e \in [L, K]$, where K is the maximum amount paid per
  extra hour;
- Standard workload, $ESW_e \in [1, H]$, where H is the total of standard hours;
- Maximum overtime, $EMO_e \in [0, G]$, where G is the maximum number of
  allowed overtime;
- Skills matrix $ESM_{M \times Z}$, where esm_{mz} indicates the level of skill z defined to
  the employee m.

The definition of these metrics was based on other works that also deals
with RASORP, such as [3] and [4]. It was necessary to adapt them considering

the context of agile development, such as defining the standard hours for each employee during the sprint. In practice, we may assume that ESM, TSM and TEH values are estimated by the requirements engineer, while financial values are provided by the company.

In addition, other four structures are defined: the first one is the similarity matrix SM_{NN}, where N is the number of tasks, which holds the level of similarity among tasks. The other three structures are vectors $ehvVec = \{q_1, q_2, \cdots, q_M\}$, $exvVec = \{k_1, k_2, \cdots, k_M\}$ and $eswVec = \{y_1, y_2, \cdots, y_M\}$, that respectively store the values of EHV, EXV and ESW from all employees.

As previously stated, our approach aims at allocating suited and similar tasks to employees. Therefore, the allocation of a task must be made considering the skills required for it and possessed by the employee. If the employee presents a level of skill higher than what is required by the task, it is expected that he/she will have less difficulty in performing it, otherwise the difficulty tends to be major. As can be seen, this fact directly affects the estimated time required to perform the task. Given a task t_n and an employee e_m, we may determine how effective would be this allocation through the function $EfcFactor(i, x_i)$.

$$EfcFactor(i, x_i) = \frac{\sum_{j=1}^{Z} ESM_{x_i, j} - TSM_{i,j} \times requiredSkill(TSM_{i,j})}{\sum_{j=1}^{Z} requiredSkill(TSM_{i,j})}$$

$$requiredSkill(TSM_{i,j}) = \begin{cases} 1, & if \ TSM_{i,j} > 0 \\ 0 & otherwise. \end{cases}$$

where $EfcFactor(i, x_i)$ returns the result of the sum average of the difference between the required skill levels and those possessed by the employee, by the the number of skills. The $requiredSkill(TSM_{i,j})$ determines whether a particular skill is required to complete the task, by checking if $TSM_{i,j} > 0$.

Another aspect that influences the tasks estimated time is the similarity between them, since similar tasks allocated to a single employee tend to be performed more efficiently. Our basis was one interdependence category, called *Similar_to*, from the requirements structural interdependencies, which describes situations where "one requirement is similar to or overlapping with another in terms of how it is expressed or in terms of a similar underlying idea of what the system should be able to perform" [7]. The function $SimFactor(i, S)$ expresses a similarity factor between all tasks assigned together regarding a task i.

$$SimFactor(i, S)$$
$$= \begin{cases} \dfrac{\sum_{j=1 | j \neq i}^{N} SM_{i,j} \times isCoupling(j, i, S)}{couplingNumber(i, S)}, & if \ couplingNumber(i, S) > 0 \\ 0 & otherwise. \end{cases}$$

$$couplingNumber(i, S) = \sum_{j=1 | j \neq i}^{N} \times isCoupling(j, i, S)$$

$$isCoupling(j, i, S) = \begin{cases} 1, & if\ x_j = x_i \\ 0 & \text{otherwise.} \end{cases}$$

where the function $couplingNumber(i, S)$ accounts if there are tasks allocated with the task i through the return of the function $isCoupling(j, i, S)$. If that is the case, the function $SimFactor(i, S)$ returns the average sum of the similarities among tasks, otherwise the value of $SimFactor(i, S)$ is 0.

To determine the total time consumed by the tasks in a possible solution, we propose the function $Time(S)$, based on the sum of all TEH values from the allocated tasks in the solution S, considering the impact imposed by $EfcFactor(i, x_i)$ and $SimFactor(i, S)$. Both factor functions behave similarly. If they return 0, they do not affect TEH value. If the result are higher than 0, the estimated time is decreased. However, if the result is smaller than 0, only function $EfcFactor(i, x_i)$ influences TEH value and, consequently, estimated time is increased. The function $Time(S)$ is given by:

$$Time(S) = \sum_{i=1}^{N} TEH_i \times (1 - \alpha \times EfcFactor(i, x_i)) \times (1 - \beta \times SimFactor(i, S))$$

where α and β represent the weights of the functions $EfcFactor(i, x_i)$ and $SimFactor(i, S)$ over the TEH_i value, respectively.

Differently from the $Time(S)$, where the TEH values of all tasks in the solution S are considered, function $EstimatedHours(e, S)$ is used to calculate the TEH value of the tasks assigned to each employee e_m. The function $EstimatedHours(e, S)$ is calculated by summing the amount of estimated time for each allocated task, considering the impact caused by $EfcFactor(i, x_i)$ and $SimFactor(i, S)$, similarly to the $Time(S)$.

$$EstimatedHours(e, S) = \sum_{i=1}^{N} TEH_i \times (1 - \alpha$$

$$\times EfcFactor(i, e)) \times (1 - \beta \times SimFactor(i, S)) \times isAllocated(e, S)$$

$$isAllocated(e, S) = \begin{cases} 1, & if\ e = x_i \\ 0 & \text{otherwise.} \end{cases}$$

where $isAllocated(e, S)$ determines if the task t_i is allocated to the employee e.

Given the total number of hours worked by an employee obtained by the function $EstimatedHours(e, S)$, we may account his/her cost to the project through the function $ValueHours(e, wH)$:

$$ValueHours(e, wH) = \begin{cases} ehvVec_e \times wH, & if\ wH \leq eswVec_e \\ (exvVec_e \times (wH - eswVec_e)) + \\ (ehvVec_e \times eswVec_e) & \text{otherwise.} \end{cases}$$

where, if it is estimated that the employee e will work only their standard workload represented by ESW, the amount of hours is multiplied by his/her hour value EHV. However, if he/she has to work more than their workload, the amount of extra hours is multiplied by the extra hour value EXV.

Furthermore, we propose the function $Cost(S)$ in order to obtain the total cost regarding all employees who received tasks in a solution S:

$$Cost(S) = \sum_{i=1}^{M} ValueHours(x_i, EstimatedHours(x_i, S)).$$

Finally, our multi-objective formulation consists of minimizing $Time(S)$ and $Cost(S)$, respecting two constraints. This model can be formalized as follows:

$$\begin{aligned}
& \text{minimize} && Time(S), \\
& \text{minimize} && Cost(S), \\
& \text{subject to:} && 1) \ estimatedHours(x_i, S) - eswVec_{x_i} \leq EMO_{x_i} \forall x_i \in S, \\
& && 2) \ ESM_{x_i,j} > 0 \ \forall \ TSM_{i,j} > 0
\end{aligned}$$

where the first constraint ensures that the amount of overtime worked by the employee cannot be greater than allowed, represented by EMO. The second constraint prevents a task that requires a specific skill to be allocated to an employee which does not has possesses this particular skill.

3   Preliminary Empirical Study

In order to evaluate the proposal, a preliminary empirical study was conducted using two real-world instances, both provided by the Invista Tech[2] company and available in this work's supporting page[3]. The first one, called *dataset-1*, is composed of 32 tasks, 5 employees and it is from a pre-order sales system. The second instance is called *dataset-2* and has 25 tasks, 3 employees and it is from a community management software. As stated in [8], it is always interesting to evaluate different search based algorithms, besides including the random search as sanity check. Hence, our experiments were performed considering the search techniques NSGA-II, MOCell and a random search. The main focus was verifying which algorithm reached the best performance and, consequently, investigating the feasibility of the search-based approach.

Both evolutionary algorithms' parameters were empirically obtained and configured with 256 individuals, 400 generations, 90 % crossover rate and 1 % mutation rate. It was defined a total of 102400 evaluations as stopping criteria. Regarding the measures to evaluate the outcome of the experimented methods, we used the Hypervolume (HV), Generational Distance (GD) and Spread (SP). To account for the stochastic nature of the meta-heuristics, each algorithm was executed 30 times with α and β fixed in 0.5. The results are available on-line, along with instances.

---

[2] http://invistatech.com.br/.
[3] http://goes.uece.br/lucasroque/rabs/en.

Table 1. Results from the Wilcoxon rank sum (WC) and Vargha-Delaney's $\hat{A}_{12}$ tests, comparing algorithms at line by column for each quality metric.

Algorithm	Metrics	Dataset-1				Dataset-2			
		MOCell		NSGA-II		MOCell		NSGA-II	
		WC	$\hat{A}_{12}$	WC	$\hat{A}_{12}$	WC	$\hat{A}_{12}$	WC	$\hat{A}_{12}$
NSGA-II	HV	3.40E-03	0.79	-	-	1.50E+01	0.71	-	-
	SP	6.30E-11	1.00	-	-	8.10E-11	1.00	-	-
	GD	7.40E-11	0.00	-	-	8.00E-09	0.05	-	-
Random	HV	7.70E-11	0.00	7.40E-11	0.00	8.50E-11	0.00	8.60E-11	0.00
	SP	2.90E-07	0.10	7.40E-11	0.00	1.40E-03	0.24	8.60E-11	0.00
	GD	7.90E-11	1.00	8.50E-11	1.00	8.60E-11	1.00	8.60E-11	1.00

Regarding the statistical analysis, it was firstly performed the Kruskal-Wallis test to ensure the statistical difference between more than two samples. To the pairwise comparison, we used the Wilcoxon rank sum test with the Bonferroni adjustment method considering a 95 % confidence level. In addition, we used the Vargha-Delaney's $\hat{A}_{12}$ test to measure the effect sizes. Table 1 show the results of these comparisons. Firstly both evolutionary techniques were compared and then random search is compared to them. As seen, significant statistical differences were achieved in all comparisons. Overall, the evolutionary techniques present similar performance to both real-world instances. Considering HV and GD values to dataset-1, NSGA-II outperforms MOCell in 79 % and 100 % of the time, respectively. Analyzing specifically the SP values, MOCell was superior for both instances. Despite of yielding better results in SP, the random search naturally lost in HV and GD when compared to the evolutionary techniques.

4 Conclusions

The human resources allocation represents a crucial component of software management. We proposed a multi-objective approach to the Resource Allocation for Software Release Planning. Regarding the preliminary results, we concluded that overall NSGA-II overwhelms MOCell and random search considering the real-world instances evaluated.

As future works, we intend to provide an automatic strategy to determine the similarity among tasks and consider multiples teams in the same sprint to the allocation process.

References

1. Sommerville, I.: Software Engineering, 9th edn. Addison-Wesley, New York (2010)
2. Tsai, H.-T., Moskowitz, H., Lee, L.-H.: Human resource selection for software development projects using Taguchis parameter design. Eur. J. Oper. Res. **151**(1), 167–180 (2003)

3. Ngo-The, A., Ruhe, G.: Optimized resource allocation for software release planning. IEEE Trans. Softw. Eng. **35**(1), 109–123 (2009)
4. Kang, D., Jung, J., Bae, D.-H.: Constraint-based human resource allocation in software projects. Softw. Pract. Exper. **41**(5), 551–577 (2011)
5. Fowler, M., Highsmith, J.: The agile manifesto. Softw. Develop. **9**(8), 28–35 (2001)
6. Acuna, S.T., Juristo, N., Moreno, A.M.: Emphasizing human capabilities in software development. IEEE Softw. **23**(2), 94–101 (2006)
7. Dahlstedt, Å.G., Persson, A.: Requirements interdependencies: state of the art and future challenges. In: Engineering and managing software requirements, pp. 95–116. Springer, Heidelberg (2005)
8. Harman, M., McMinn, P., Souza, J.T., Yoo, S.: Search based software engineering: techniques, taxonomy, tutorial. In: Meyer, B., Nordio, M. (eds.) LASER 2008-2010. LNCS, vol. 7007, pp. 1–59. Springer, Heidelberg (2012). doi:10.1007/978-3-642-25231-0_1
9. Chen, W.-N., Zhang, J.: Ant colony optimization for software project scheduling and staffing with an event-based scheduler. IEEE Trans. Softw. Eng. **39**(1), 1–17 (2013)
10. Schwaber, K.: Agile Project Management with Scrum. Microsoft Press, Redmond (2004)

Improving the Performance of Many-Objective Software Refactoring Technique Using Dimensionality Reduction

Troh Josselin Dea[✉]

University of Michigan-Dearborn, Dearborn, USA
deatroh@umich.edu

Abstract. Software quality Assessment involves the measurement of a large number of software attributes referred to as quality metrics. In most searched-based software engineering processes, an optimization algorithm is used to evaluate a certain number of maintenance operations by minimizing or maximizing these quality metrics. One such process is software refactoring. When the solution to the problem includes a large number of objectives, various difficulties arise, including the determination of the Pareto-optimal front, and the visualization of the solutions. However, in some refactoring problem, there may be redundancies among any two or more objectives. In this paper, we propose a new software refactoring approach named PCA-NSGA-II many-objective refactoring. This approach is based on the PCA-NSGA-II evolutionary multi-objective algorithm, and can overcome the curse of dimensionality by removing redundancies to retain conflicting objectives for further analysis.

1 Introduction

Real-world software refactoring involves the application of various software maintenance operations aiming at improving the structure of the system without altering it external behavior. When possible, it is desired to consider as many quality metrics as possible to evaluate the results of those maintenance operations. In order to address this concern, most automated software refactoring techniques utilizes multi-objective optimization approach using conflicting objectives. This approach ideally requires finding a multi-dimensional solution space, but comes with many difficulties. First, as the number of objectives increase, visualization of the solution is very difficult, if not impractical. Next, for the determination of a large-dimensional Pareto-optimal front, an exponentially large number of solutions is required, hence making the procedure computationally extensive. Finally, in refactoring, it is the engineer's role to make the final decision or choice of solution. This task is made tedious by the large dimensionality of the Pareto front.

In the context of the widely used evolutionary multi-objective optimization (EMO), it was shown that methodologies that show good performance for fewer objectives (two or three) are vulnerable to problems with relatively large number of objective [1, 2]. In [3], though the emphasis was placed on the performance evaluation of the refactoring methods, all three problems listed previously are made apparent in the proposed

© Springer International Publishing AG 2016
F. Sarro and K. Deb (Eds.): SSBSE 2016, LNCS 9962, pp. 298–303, 2016.
DOI: 10.1007/978-3-319-47106-8_26

solution – decision maker (DM) incorporation and visualization being the most obvious. The difficulties of finding multiple Pareto-optimal solutions in presence of large number of objectives, and the challenge that the decision maker faces to choose one of these solutions, have prompted researchers to incorporate the DM in the early stage of the search [4, 5]. These methodologies alleviate by using the DM preferences to reduce the dimensionality of the problem. There exist software refactoring solutions using EMO methodologies with a kind of dimensionality reduction, where the solution referred to as "knee" solution is obtained by sacrificing one objective in father of another [6, 7]. However, both dimensionality reduction methodologies are not without issues. First, there may be DM independent information in the problem that can be used to reduce the dimensionality of the Pareto-optimal front. Second, the need solution has been shown to be sensitive to parameter fluctuations. Thus for solving many-objective problems, the existing EMO may be improved by finding adequate methodologies for dimensionality reduction.

In this paper, we consider many-objective Refactoring problems where there may be DM-independent redundancies as the solution move towards the Pareto-optimal frontier. In such cases, methodologies exist that can efficiently reduce the dimensionality of the Pareto-optimal frontier. We investigate such problem by coupling the well-known Principal Component Analysis (PCA) with the Elitist Non-Dominated Genetic Algorithm (NSGA-II) – namely PCA-NSGA-II refactoring. This work is the first adaption of the PCA-NSGA-II algorithm to the problem of software refactoring [1].

2   Many-Objective SBSE Problem

The majority of existing works in search-based software engineering treats software engineering problems as single-objective problem [8]. However, in real-world software refactoring problem, in order to address all the quality factors of software, it is preferred to consider as many quality metrics as possible to measure the quality of maintenance operations. This leads naturally to a multi-objective optimization problem, where each quality metric considered represent an objective that need to be either minimized, or maximized. Many-Objective optimization is a term recently coined to address real-world optimization where the actual number of objective considered exceeds 3. The following equation shows a mathematical formulation of the many-objective optimization problem [9], and is useful to illustrate the difficulties addressed above.

$$\begin{cases} Min\ f(x) = [f_1(x), f_2(x), \ldots, f_M(x)]^T, M > 3 \\ \quad g_i(x) \geq 0 \qquad\qquad j = 1, \ldots, P; \\ \quad h_k(x) = 0 \qquad\qquad k = 1, \ldots, Q; \\ \quad x_i^L \leq x_i \leq x_i^U \qquad i = 1, \ldots, n. \end{cases}$$

Where M is the number of objective functions, and is strictly greater than 3, P is the number of inequality constraints, Q is the number of equality constraints, x_i^L and x_i^U corresponds to the lower and upper bonds of the decision variable x. A solution x satisfying the $(P + Q)$ constraints is said to be feasible, and the set of all such solutions defines the feasible search space denote Ω.

3 Many-Objective Software Refactoring Using PCA-NSGA-II

3.1   Software Refactoring

Refactoring is defined as the process of improving code after it has been written by changing its internal structure without changing the external behavior [10]. The basis of decision making for refactoring was highlighted in [10], and referred as code smells, or anti-patterns. Basically, the refactoring process seeks to remove from existing software system all occurrences of such smells. In this paper, we assume that code smells have already been detected, and focus on the correction phase, i.e., refactoring.

3.2   PCA-NSGA-II Methodology

The PCA-NSGA-II methodology was proposed by Deb et al. to tackle such problem by determining the lower-dimensional Pareto-optimal front [1]. It is a combination of PCA and the NSGA-II algorithm.

Although various redundancy handling methodologies have been used in conjunction with optimization algorithm to enhance performance [4], PCA is by far the most used dimensionality reduction techniques. PCA is a statistical analysis techniques used in multi-variate analysis, and reduces the dimensionality of a given data set when there is a large number of statistically interrelated variables. It retains as much variation of the original data set as possible. This is achieved by a transformation of the original variables to a new set of uncorrelated and ordered variable, referred to as principal components (PCs). The order of the PCs indicates which PC retains most of the variation of the original data set. PCA computation is posed as an eigenvalue-eigenvector problem, and is the basis of our proposed PCA-based dimensionality reduction algorithm.

The PCA algorithm start with an initial data set represented as a matrix $D = (D_1, D_2, \ldots, D_M)^T$, where D_i is the i-th measurement and T is the transpose operator. Each row of the matrix is a measurement while each column represents a sample (time or space) or an experimental trial. In the context of NSGA-II, a column will represent objective values for one generation. Before the PCA is performed, the data set must be standardized such that the centroid of the whole set is zero. This can be achieved by subtracting its mean from each measurement. Let the standardized matrix be $X = (X_1, X_2, \ldots, X_M)^T$. Since our target problem uses objectives of different nature (units), we will compute the PCs using the correlation matrix. In this case, the PCs are the eigenvectors of the correlation matrix. Given the covariance matrix V of the correlation matrix R is an M-Dimensional matrix defined as follows:

$$R_{ij} = \frac{V_{ij}}{\sqrt{V_{ii}.V_{jj}}}, \quad where \quad V_{ij} = \frac{X_i X_j^T}{M - 1}$$

Given the correlation matrix, the first principal component corresponds to the eigenvector associated with the largest eigenvalue, and so on. Each entry in the PC denotes the contribution of the corresponding variable to the hyperplane directed by this PC. A positive value denotes an increase in objective moving along the PC (axes) while a negative value denotes a decrease. Thus in terms of conflicts, variables corresponding to the most positive and most negative values are the most conflicting. These variables will be the best choice to consider for next step of the NSGA-II algorithm. When there is more than one PC, we will fix a threshold of variation base on the eigenvalues. For example, if the threshold is 90 %, we will select the first few eigenvectors such that the sum of percentage contribution of eigenvalues is 90 % of the total eigenvalues. Due to limitation of space, we refer the reader to the PC and objective selection discussed in [1].

Given the PCA-based conflicting objective selection, and the NSGA-II algorithm, the complete algorithm is given as follows:

Step 1: Set iteration counter $t = 0$ and an initial objective set $I_0 = \{I_1, I_2, \ldots, I_M\}$.

Step 2: Initialize random population for all objectives in I_t, run NSGA-II, and obtain a population P_t.

Step 3: Perform PCA analysis on P_t using I_t to choose a reduced set of objective I_{t+1} using a predefine threshold cut TC. The PCA steps are as follows: (a) Compute correlation matrix, (b) compute eigenvector, (c) choose non-redundant objectives.

Step 4: If $I_{t+1} = I_t$, stop and declare the obtained Pareto front. Else set $t = t + 1$ and go to step 2.

3.3   Adapting PCA-NSGA-II to Software Refactoring

The refactoring consists in finding the best refactoring solution among candidates within in a large search space. Each refactoring solution consists of a sequence of refactoring operations aimed at minimizing the number of code smells when applied to the target software system. Viewed as a many-objective optimization problem, the refactoring problem can be formulated as follows:

$$\begin{cases} Maximize\ F(x, S) = [f_1(x, S), f_2(x, S), \ldots, f_M(x, S)], \quad M > 3 \\ subject\ to\ x = (x_1, x_2, \ldots, x_n) \in X \end{cases}$$

Where X is the set of all refactoring sequences starting from S, x_i is the i-th refactoring operation, $f_k(x, S)$ is the k-th metric (or objective), and M is the number of objectives. In order to use the PCA-NSGA-II algorithm to solve the many-objective refactoring problem, we need to introduce some adaption step as noted by Harman [10]. These steps are as follows:

Solution Representation: For the refactoring problem, the solutions are refactoring sequences of N refactoring operations. These sequences are represented in the form of n-dimensional vectors x, where the position of each element indicate the order of application of the operation to the system. For each of these refactoring operations, we specify pre- and post-conditions to ensure the feasibility of their application [10].

PCA Step: After the NSGA-II algorithm is applied on a number N of solutions, we will form the $M \times N$ matrix of objective as explained in Sect. 3.2. Next, the correlation matrix of this objective matrix will be computed, and it principal components used to determine the conflicting objectives.

Solution Evaluation: Once the PCA step is performed and the conflicting objectives selected, further generated refactoring solutions will be executed on the system, and evaluated according to the selected objectives. The complete list of objectives used and corresponding definitions can be found in Sect. 4.3 of [6].

4 Evaluation

This work is still at the formulating stage, and has not been yet evaluated. The analysis will be conducted on a set of well-known open-source Java projects: Xerces-J, JFreeChart, GantProject, ApacheAnt, JHotDraw, and Rhino [6]. During our investigation our focus will be on answering the following research questions:

RQ1: How much improvement does PCA-NSGA-II add to the initial NSGA-II methodology? Knowing that NSGA-II's performance has been established in the context of refactoring, the answer to this question is important for further assessment.

RQ2: How does PCA-NSGA-II performance compare to existing many-objective refactoring methodologies – MOAE/D [6] and NSGA-III [3]? In answering this question, we will investigate the scalability of PCA-NSGA-II, and assess the maximum number of objectives that it can handle in the context of software refactoring.

5 Conclusion

In this paper, we presented a new software refactoring technique based on the PCA-NSGA-II algorithm. Our methodology seeks to tackle problem where there may be redundancies among objectives near the Pareto-optimal front. While this short version of the work does not contain actual evaluation, we highlight the methodology, and our target research question. In a longer version of the paper, a thorough investigation of the methodology will be conducted, and compared with existing many-objective refactoring techniques.

References

1. Deb, K., Saxena, D.K.: Searching for pareto-optimal solutions through dimensionality reduction for certain large-dimensional multi-objective optimization problems. In: IEEE Congress on Evolutionary Computation, July 2006

2. Saxena, D.K., Duro, J.A., Tiwari, A., Deb, K., Zhang, Q.: Objective reduction in many-objective optimization: linear and nonlinear algorithms. IEEE Trans. Evol. Comput. **17**(1), 77–99 (2013)
3. Mkaouer, M.W., Kessentini, M., Bechikh, S., Deb, K., Cinneide, M.O.: High dimensional search-based software engineering: finding tradeoffs among 15 objectives for automating software refactoring using NSGA-III. In: ACM Conference on GECCO, 2014 (2014)
4. Branke, J., Kaussler, T., Schmek, H.: Guidance in evolutionary multi-objective optimization. Adv. Eng. Softw. **32**, 499–507 (2001)
5. Jensen, M.T.: Guiding single-objective optimization using multi-objective methods. In: Raidl, G.R., Cagnoni, S., Cardalda, J.J., Corne, D.W., Gottlieb, J., Guillot, A., Hart, E., Johnson, C.G., Marchiori, E., Meyer, J.-A., Middendorf, M. (eds.) EvoIASP 2003, EvoWorkshops 2003, EvoSTIM 2003, EvoROB/EvoRobot 2003, EvoCOP 2003, EvoBIO 2003, and EvoMUSART 2003. LNCS, vol. 2611, pp. 268–279. Springer, Heidelberg (2003)
6. Mkaouer, M.W., Kessentini, M., Bechikh, S., Ó Cinnéide, M.: A robust multi-objective approach for software refactoring under uncertainty. In: Le Goues, C., Yoo, S. (eds.) SSBSE 2014. LNCS, vol. 8636, pp. 168–183. Springer, Heidelberg (2014)
7. Branke, J., Deb, K., Dierolf, H., Osswald, M.: Finding knees in multi-objective optimization. In: Yao, X., Burke, E.K., Lozano, J.A., Smith, J., Merelo-Guervós, J.J., Bullinaria, J.A., Rowe, J.E., Tiňo, P., Kabán, A., Schwefel, H.-P. (eds.) PPSN 2004. LNCS, vol. 3242, pp. 722–731. Springer, Heidelberg (2004)
8. Harman, M., Mansouri, S.A., Zhang, Y: Search-based software engineering: trends, techniques and applications. ACM Comput. Surv. **45**(1) (2012). Article 11
9. Deb, K.: Multiobjective Otpimization Using Evolutionary Algorithms. Wiley, New York (2001)
10. Fowler, M., et al.: Refactoring: Improving the design of existing programs (1999)

Field Report: Applying Monte Carlo Tree Search for Program Synthesis

Jinsuk Lim$^{(\boxtimes)}$ and Shin Yoo

Korea Advanced Institute of Science and Technology, 291 Daehak Ro,
Yuseong Gu, Daejeon, Republic of Korea
rhapsody_js@kaist.ac.kr

Abstract. Program synthesis aims to automatically generate an executable segment of code that satisfies a given set of criteria. Genetic programming has been widely studied for program synthesis. However, it has drawbacks such as code bloats and the difficulty in finer control over the growth of programs. This paper explores the possibility of applying Monte Carlo Tree Search (MCTS) technique to general purpose program synthesis. The exploratory study applies MCTS to synthesis of six small benchmarks using Java Bytecode instructions, and compares the results to those of genetic programming. The paper discusses the major challenges and outlines the future work.

1 Introduction

Program synthesis aims to automatically generate an executable segment of code that satisfies a given specification. A number of different approaches have been studied, including logical reasoning [11], similarity-based gradient descent [4], as well as the widely studied genetic programming [1,9]. While genetic programming has been used for many successful applications of program synthesis, such as coevolution of programs and tests [1] as well as automated patching [5], it has drawbacks such as code bloats [10] and parameter tuning [8].

This paper considers Monte Carlo Tree Search (MCTS) [7] for general purpose program synthesis. MCTS is a search heuristic that has achieved impressive results in a number of applications, most notably in computer Go [2]. It has a number of advantages over GP. First, it is more robust against bloats as it is a constructive algorithm. Second, it is mathematically well-established, with a provable guarantee for convergence. Moreover, it has fewer hyperparameters to tune, making it amenable to experimentations and analyses.

MCTS has been recently studied in the context of symbolic regression [12]. This paper extends the application area with an exploratory study of MCTS based synthesis of six small benchmark programs using Java Bytecode instructions. We report initial findings, which suggests that the performance of MCTS is comparable to that of genetic programming. The paper aims to serve as a launchpad for future research on applications of MCTS in SBSE with discussions of practical issues in MCTS based program synthesis.

© Springer International Publishing AG 2016
F. Sarro and K. Deb (Eds.): SSBSE 2016, LNCS 9962, pp. 304–310, 2016.
DOI: 10.1007/978-3-319-47106-8_27

2   MCTS for Program Synthesis

Although MCTS is typically applied to playing games [2], it has recently been applied [3] and evaluated [12] in the context of symbolic regression. In case of symbolic regression, MCTS iteratively builds a stack-based representation of an expression tree, in which consuming a subsequent symbol is equivalent to finding the next optimal move in a game state.[1]

This paper extends the same core idea to program synthesis by replacing expression trees with program trees. Both symbolic regression and program synthesis are based on the same intuition that sequences of nodes (symbols or instructions) can be interpreted as (expression or program) trees. However, unlike pure functions in symbolic regression, a general purpose program presents a few additional challenges, such as program control flow structure and typing.

2.1   Control Flow Structure

Since we rely on the stack representation of program trees, concatenation of an arbitrary number of program statements raises an issue. If each statement can be represented as a subtree in the program tree, these subtrees should be concatenated using a fixed-arity node type. Our solution is to introduce a binary node concat, whose semantic is equal to nop: it simply acts as a placeholder so that two subtrees can be concatenated. Concatenation of multiple lines require a successive use of concat nodes.

Similarly, branching instructions such as if are represented as tertiary nodes: they take three child subtrees, each representing the Boolean predicate, the true body, and the false body. When generating code from if subtrees, we insert goto instructions immediately following a comparison operator (e.g. icmplt), which points to the beginning of the else block, and immediately following the then block, which points to the instruction following the else block.

2.2   Typing

Use of typing system is either absolutely necessary, because the synthesis task or the actual instruction specifically requires statically typed elements, or strongly encouraged, because it greatly reduces the search space by restricting the set of instructions to consider at each phase of the search.

Our typing system consists of seven types: int, float, boolean, string, void, control, and conditional. The first five are natural consequences of choosing Java Bytecode as our code generation tool. The control is a special type reserved for instructions that affect control flow: if and concat. The conditional is used as the return type of comparison operators - icmplt ($<$) and icmple ($\leq$). In the expansion step, MCTS considers only those instructions that have compatible types as its next instruction, i.e., instructions whose

---

[1] A brief overview of MCTS, as well as details of the experimental results, is available from http://coinse.kaist.ac.kr/projects/mctsps.

return types are compatible with the type of the required arguments. The `true` or `false` body of the `if` instruction, as well as the (empty) program root, may start with instructions of any type.

3 Experimental Setup

3.1 Implementation

We implemented our MCTS based program synthesis tool using Java and Byte Code Engineering Library (BCEL)[2]. Not all of the instructions used by MCTS are Java bytecode. Some of them are lightweight Intermediate Representations (IRs) that provide shortcuts and type specific instructions. For example, instead of preparing appropriate method invocation of `System.out.println`, we provide `iprint` and `fprint` for integers and floats respectively. Others are directly from bytecode instructions (such as `iadd`, `fadd`, etc.). The IR program is translated into actual Java bytecode for fitness evaluation.

For comparison, we have also implemented a genetic programming based synthesis tool that generates Java bytecode instructions. Since no existing tool fits our exact purpose, we constructed a bytecode generation tool that takes node sequence as input and writes corresponding Java classfiles as output; the actual search has been driven by `pyevolve`[3], with all typing restrictions added.

3.2 Benchmarks

We evaluated our method on six benchmarks from Helmuth et al. [6], whose descriptions are given in Table 1. Each benchmark is given a distinct set of terminals and non-terminals which is sufficient to output a correct program. For the test cases, we follow the prescriptions outlined by Helmuth et al. [6].

Table 1. Subject Benchmarks from Helmuth et al. [6]

Name	Instructions	Expected Behaviour
ADD INTEGER AND FLOAT	iload_1 iadd isub imul idiv fload_2 fadd fsub fmul fdiv concat return iprint fprint f2i i2f	Given an integer (iload_1) and a float (fload_2), print their sum
COMPARE STRING LENGTHS	sload_1 sload_2 sload_3 true false nop breturn strlen if icmplt icmple concat	Given three strings s_1, s_2 and s_3, return true if $len(s_1) < len(s_2) < len(s_3)$ and false otherwise.
GRADE	iload_1 iload_2 iload_3 iload_4 iload_5 sload_1 sload_2 sload_3 sload_4 sload_5 sprint return if icmplt icmple concat	Given four distinct integer thresholds for achieving A, B, C, and D in descending order, and the fifth represents the student's score, print the letter grade.
MEDIAN	iload_1 iload_2 iload_3 nop iprint return if icmplt icmple concat	Given three integers, print their median.
SMALL OR LARGE	iload_1 iload_2 iload_3 sload_4 sload_5 nop iprint sprint return if icmplt icmple concat	Given an integer i, print "small" if $i < 1000$ and "large" if $i \leq 2000$.
SMALLEST	iload_1 iload_2 iload_3 iload_4 nop iprint return if icmplt icmple concat	Given four integers, print the smallest of them

---

[2] http://commons.apache.org/bcel/.
[3] http://pyevolve.sourceforge.net.

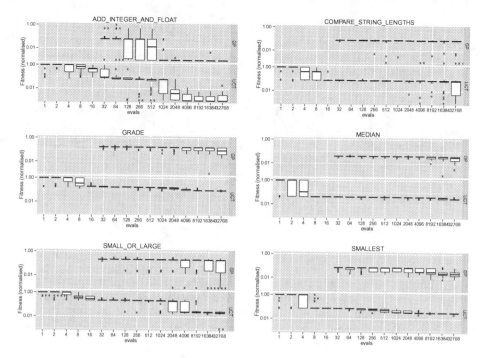

Fig. 1. Boxplots of test data fitness for UCT and GP across different number of evaluation budgets

3.3 Configurations

The variant of MCTS we implemented, Upper Confidence Bounds on Trees (UCT) [7], has two hyperparameters: exploration constant e_c and maximum program length l_p. In particular, l_p has to be large enough for a candidate program to be able to encode the correct behavior. We set l_p to be 100 and e_c to be 10 in our experiments. GP is configured with population size 32, rank selection, mutation rate 0.1, crossover rate 0.9 and maximum tree depth 7.[4]

Both UCT and GP were run for 30 times to cater for the stochastic nature of each algorithm. Each run was given a maximum of $2^{15} = 32,768$ evaluations. Experiments have been run on machines with Core i7 6700 with 8 GB RAM running Ubuntu 14.04, Java version 1.7.0_80, and Python runtime version 2.7.11.

3.4 Fitness Function

Each benchmark either prints or returns an output. Our fitness function considers three aspects of a candidate program: whether it is executable, whether it prints the correct output, and whether it returns the correct output. The

---

[4] GP should generate programs of lengths similar to l_p. As most non-terminals have one or two leaves, maximum depth of 7 achieves this.

fitness of a program P with respect to a test suite T is defined as follows for minimisation:

$$f(P,T) = \begin{cases} 1.0 & \text{if } P \text{ is non-executable} \\ w \cdot f_p(P,T) + (1-w) \cdot f_r(P,T) & \text{otherwise } (w = 0.5) \end{cases}$$

where f_p and f_r measures fitness for printed and returned output respectively. For each output type, we adopt a widely-used distance measure between two instances: absolute distance for int, float, and character, Levenshtein distance for strings, and NAND for boolean. Both f_p and f_r return the worst fitness when something is printed or returned when it should not be.

4   Results

Results for the six benchmarks are shown in Fig. 1[5]. Both UCT and GP show clear trends of improvement as the number of evaluations increase. Both perform well on the relatively easy benchmarks, Add Integer And Float, Small Or Large and Compare String Lengths: several runs produce correct programs. Grade, Median and Smallest are harder because correct solutions require non-trivial control flow structures. Both algorithms fail to output correct programs, although the fitnesses continue to improve.

5   Discussion and Future Work

Both UCT and GP shows inferior performance compared to those reported in Helmuth et al. [6]. This may be due to much smaller budget, but it may also be relevant that Helmuth et al. use a language specifically designed for GP.

We observe that typing is critical. A vast majority of samples by MCTS is non-executable when types are not considered. However, implementing a full type system on top of a tree search can make the algorithm bulky. We plan to investigate the feasibility of implementing a type system as a skewed sampling probability distribution.

Second, being a constructive algorithm, MCTS is prone to early suboptimal commitment. This tendency is shown in difficult benchmarks such as Median and Smallest: the fitness hardly improves past a certain number of evaluations. It appears that MCTS commits to an instruction that yields moderate rewards and keeps exploiting it, when in fact its rewards are suboptimal. Tuning the exploration constant and favoring longer samples may improve this behaviour.

The choice of code generation layer can have a significant impact on performance. While Java bytecode achieves good expressiveness with a relatively small set of instructions, the low level nature of the instructions introduces challenges such as having to deal with explicit jumps to implement branching. We plan to compare different levels of abstractions for program synthesis.

---

[5] Detailed statistics, as well as the output program instructions, are available from http://coinse.kaist.ac.kr/projects/mctsps.

Finally, it should be noted that MCTS is only concerned with a sequence of choices (i.e. selection of nodes); there may be alternatives ways to translate this into programs other than the stack-based representation of trees. We plan to investigate other forms of program construction.

6   Conclusion

This paper presents an early exploration on how to apply Monte Carlo Tree Search for general purpose program synthesis. Java bytecode based implementations of MCTS shows comparable performance to genetic programming. There are many challenges that are specific to different aspects of program synthesis, such as control flow structure, typing, and the choice of code generation layer.

Acknowledgments. Authors would like to thank David White and Kee-eung Kim for many thoughtful discussions about Monte Carlo Tree Search. This research has been supported by Undergraduate Research Program (URP) at KAIST.

References

1. Arcuri, A., Yao, X.: Co-evolutionary automatic programming for software development. Inf. Sci. **259**, 412–432 (2014)
2. Browne, C.B., Powley, E., Whitchouse, D., Lucas, S.M., Cowling, P.I., Rohlfshagen, P., Tavener, S., Perez, D., Samothrakis, S., Colton, S.: A survey of monte carlo tree search methods. IEEE Trans. Comput. Intell. AI Games **4**(1), 1–43 (2012)
3. Cazenave, T.: Monte Carlo expression discovery. Int. J. Artif. Intell. Tools **22**(1) (2013)
4. Desai, A., Gulwani, S., Hingorani, V., Jain, N., Karkare, A., Marron, M., Sailesh, R., Roy, S.: Program synthesis using natural language. In: Proceedings of the 38th International Conference on Software Engineering, ICSE 2016, pp. 345–356. ACM, New York (2016)
5. Forrest, S., Nguyen, T., Weimer, W., Le Goues, C.: A genetic programming approach to automated software repair. In: Proceedings of the 11th Annual Conference on Genetic and Evolutionary Computation, pp. 947–954 (2009)
6. Helmuth, T., Spector, L.: General program synthesis benchmark suite. In: Proceedings of the 2015 Annual Conference on Genetic and Evolutionary Computation, GECCO 2015, pp. 1039–1046. ACM, New York (2015)
7. Kocsis, L., Szepesvári, C.: Bandit based Monte-Carlo planning. In: Fürnkranz, J., Scheffer, T., Spiliopoulou, M. (eds.) ECML 2006. LNCS (LNAI), vol. 4212, pp. 282–293. Springer, Heidelberg (2006)
8. de Lima, E.B., Pappa, G.L., de Almeida, J.M., Gonçalves, M.A., Meira, W.: Tuning genetic programming parameters with factorial designs. In: IEEE Congress on Evolutionary Computation, pp. 1–8, July 2010
9. Orlov, M., Sipper, M.: Flight of the finch through the java wilderness. IEEE Trans. Evol. Comput. **15**(2), 166–182 (2011)
10. Poli, R., Langdon, W.B., McPhee, N.F.: A field guide to genetic programming. Published via http://lulu.com (2008). (With contributions by J.R. Koza)

11. Srivastava, S., Gulwani, S., Foster, J.S.: From program verification to program synthesis. SIGPLAN Not. **45**(1), 313–326 (2010)
12. White, D.R., Yoo, S., Singer, J.: The programming game: evaluating MCTS as an alternative to GP for symbolic regression. In: Proceedings of the Companion Publication of the 2015 on Genetic and Evolutionary Computation Conference, GECCO Companion 2015, pp. 1521–1522. ACM, New York (2015)

Dynamic Bugs Prioritization in Open Source Repositories with Evolutionary Techniques

Vanessa Veloso$^{(\boxtimes)}$, Thiago Oliveira, Altino Dantas, and Jerffeson Souza

Optimization in Software Engineering Group, State University of Ceara,
Doutor Silas Munguba Avenue, 1700, Fortaleza 60.714-903, Brazil
{vanessa.aragao,thiago.pinheiro}@aluno.uece.br,
{altino.dantas,jerffeson.souza}@uece.br

Abstract. The bugs prioritization in open source repositories is considered an important and complex task. Mainly because, a lot of information about bugs changes over time and affects the prioritization process. Based on this dynamic characteristic, this work proposes a model to prioritize bugs as dynamic optimization problem. A preliminary empirical study was conduced comparing two dynamic evolutionary approaches and a static one. The achieved results demonstrated that a dynamic approach outperforms the static one in all evaluated scenarios.

Keywords: Bugs prioritization · SBSE · Evolutionary dynamic optimization

1 Introduction

The Search Based Software Engineering (SBSE) is an area focused in solving software engineering complex problems applying search algorithms [1]. These problems have been addressed statically, without considering several changes that take place over time in a real-world environment. However, a dynamic problem should be solved by an optimization algorithm able to find a good solution for each new state of the problem. For this purpose, the Evolutionary Dynamic Optimization (EDO) arises, applying approaches based on evolutionary algorithms, in order to solve this type of problem [2]. The usage of evolutionary algorithms in dynamic context is interesting because they are based on biological evolution of individuals, similarly, subject to the environmental changes.

Often, works related the prioritization in SBSE have been accomplished in the requirements engineering [3] and test [4]. However, recently a static approach for bugs prioritization in open source repository was proposed by Dreyton *et al.* [5]. Their approach recommends to the developer a set of prioritized bugs which should be fixed earlier. Such mechanism benefits the software maintenance process, once prioritizing a lot of bugs manually may be a tedious task [6]. However, the previous proposed model needs be reformulated to dynamic context, given which information about bugs changes over time and the optimization algorithm must be able to react the change, tracking the global optimum.

© Springer International Publishing AG 2016
F. Sarro and K. Deb (Eds.): SSBSE 2016, LNCS 9962, pp. 311–316, 2016.
DOI: 10.1007/978-3-319-47106-8_28

Therefore, our paper proposes a novel model to bugs prioritization problem in open source bug repository, using techniques of the Evolutionary Dynamic Optimization, to a bugs prioritization more suitable to real-world environment.

2   Proposed Model for Dynamic Bugs Prioritization

The model proposed in this work was based on the previous mentioned work [5] and uses same principles to evaluate candidate solutions. However, we reformulated the problem as dynamic optimization problem aims at accomplishing the changes on bug's features (votes, priority and severity).

Thus, consider $B = \{b_1, b_2, b_3, ..., b_N\}$ the set of bugs in the repository, where N is the total number of bugs. A solution is a vector $P = \{p_1, p_2, p_3, ..., p_M\}$ with ordered bugs, where M is the number of bugs in P and $p_j \in B$. Thus, our formulation to bugs prioritization in dynamic environment is:

$$maximize(\alpha \times relevance(P,t) + \beta \times importance(P,t) - \gamma \times severity(P,t)). \quad (1)$$

The function $relevance(P,t)$ measures how relevant is a solution through votes number of each bug presents in P at moment t. This is obtained by:

$$relevance(P,t) = \sum_{i=1}^{N} votes_i(t) \times isIn(P,b_i), \quad (2)$$

where $votes_i(t)$ is the number of votes received by a bug b_i until at time t. The function $isIn(P, b_i)$ indicates whether a bug b_i is in P, i.e., it returns 1 if $b_i \in P$, 0 otherwise.

The function $importance(P,t)$ aims to anticipating the resolution of bugs with high priority value at a given time t. The function is given by:

$$importance(P,t) = \sum_{i=1}^{N} priority_i(t) \times (M - pos(P,b_i)) \times isIn(P,b_i), \quad (3)$$

where $priority_i(t)$ indicates the priority value of each bug b_i in P at time t. The function $pos(P, b_i)$ returns the position of the bug b_i in P. The value of the function increases as bugs with high priority are allocated at initial P positions.

The function $severity(P,t)$ intends early resolution of the bugs most severe at a given time t, as the function follows:

$$severity(P,t) = \sum_{i=1}^{N} severity_i(t) \times pos(P,b_i) \times isIn(P,b_i), \quad (4)$$

where $severity_i(t)$ indicates the severity value to each bug b_i in P at moment t.

The variables α, β and γ configure weight of objectives. Thus, the proposed model aims the prioritization bugs in open source repository considering votes, priority and severity values assigned to the bugs by repository users.

3   Evolutionary Dynamic Optimization Approaches

EDO approaches consists of evolutionary algorithm adapted to react to changes, tracking the movement of the optimal solution. In this work, two approaches were implemented with Genetic Algorithm (GA) and compared with a GA-Static. The Hypermutation (HP) [7], introduces diversity in the GA population by increasing mutation rate after the change happen, then decreasing it over the generations. Such approach allows to explore new search space area looking for good solutions related to the changes. On the other hand, the Genetic Propagate (GP) used by [8] is a mechanism in which the most adapted individual from a GA execution is used on the next, propagating genetic material over time.

4   Preliminary Experiment

An preliminary empirical study was conducted to analyze the performance of the three GA versions in the dynamic environment of bug repositories.

The settings of the GA-Static, GA-HyperMut and GA-GProp algorithms were 100 individuals per population, 100 % crossover rate, 5 % of mutation rate, 1 % of elitism and roulette wheel selection method. These parameters were empirically obtained by preliminary tests. In the GA-HyperMut the HP rate was varied from 30 %, 60 % and 90 % falling Gaussian way to 5 %. Regarding the GA-GProp, the GP also varies from 30 %, 60 % and 90 %.

The experiment was conducted with a total of 15 scenarios artificially generated by a simulator that modified a dataset composed of real data. This information was extracted from Kate Editor repository[1]. Each scenario represents a problem's instance containing 546 bugs and 1638 features likely to change.

The priority of a bug can be Very Low: 0.2, Low: 0.4, Normal: 0.6, High: 0.8 and Very High: 1.0. While the severity can be Wish-list: 0.1, Minor: 0.25, Average: 0.4, Crash: 0.55, Major: 0.70, Severe: 0.85 and Critical: 1.0. And the votes were normalized in a range between 0 and 1.

The three approaches were evaluated varying level and period of change. Where the change level corresponds to low (30 %), medium (60 %) and high (90 %) of modified features in each period. The change period (ρ) is a fixed time interval of 30, 60 or 90 seconds between each moment of change. Besides, specifically for dynamic approaches, the HP and GP rates were used at 30 %, 60 % and 90 %.

Each algorithm was performed by 30 runs, using the same weight in the fitness function. Due to the high number of possibilities in the environment only five moments of change were simulated and analysed.

Thus, experiments were performed to answer the following research question:

RQ: Is a dynamic approach more efficient than a static one solving the bugs prioritization problem in open source repositories?

---

[1] https://bugs.kde.org/

4.1 Results and Analysis

Considering a Cartesian Plane, where the y-axis is the fitness function value and the x-axis shows each one of the five moments of change, the metric AREA expresses the average of area formed with the best fitness values found before each five moments of changes, for all 30 runs. This calculation measures the algorithms' performance, to discover the best rate of HP and GP in each scenario. In the results, a high value of AREA indicates the best rate configuration.

Table 1 presents AREA values from GA-Static considering the three level of changes and period variations (ρ).

In general, despite the level of change, GA-Static is best for high ρ values. This is natural because the evolutionary mechanism has more time to evolve.

Table 2 shows the results of AREA obtained by GA-HyperMut varying the level of change, change period (ρ) and HP rate.

As it can be seen, when period $\rho = 30$ with low level of changes, the average was 957,639 for an HP set with a rate of 30 %, 904,999 and 898,094 respectively for 60 % and 90 %, indicating that the highest value obtained was with a 30 % rate. Looking at data from period $\rho = 60$ and medium level of changes, similarly, the average was 1,861,379 for HP with a rate of 30 %, 1,800,652 and 1,762,999 respectively for 60 % and 90 %. In summary, independent of the period of changes and level of changes, the GA-HyperMut algorithm with an HP rate of 30 % obtained the best results, however, it was always worse than results from GA-Static in each level of change and ρ variation.

Table 3 shows AREA results from GA-GProp with all level of changes and variations on period of changes ρ.

Based on the data above, we can notice that when $\rho = 30$ and level of changes was set as low, the fitness area average was 1,079,329 with a rate of 30 % GP, 1,067,504 with a rate of 60 % GP and 1,078,151 with a rate of 90 % GP, that

Table 1. Averages of AREA produced by GA-Static with each level of changes and period variations (ρ).

ρ	30	60	90
low	1012778	2006125	**3032840**
medium	1005407	2029532	**3026390**
high	1029091	2062091	**3104904**

Table 2. Averages of AREA produced by GA-HyperMut with each level of change, period variations (ρ) and HP rate.

ρ	30			60			90		
Rate	30 %	60 %	90 %	30 %	60 %	90 %	30 %	60 %	90 %
low	**957639**	904999	898094	**2063173**	2004010	2003525	**3176014**	3167268	3120031
medium	**877134**	821474	803961	**1861379**	1800652	1762999	**2875910**	2824359	2772308
high	**858282**	791873	766338	**1756232**	1659839	1610556	**2677564**	2544452	2479569

Table 3. Averages of AREA produced by GA-Gprop with each level of changes, period variations (ρ) and GP rate.

ρ	30			60			90		
Rate	30 %	60 %	90 %	30 %	60 %	90 %	30 %	60 %	90 %
low	**1079329**	1067504	1078151	2190891	2201917	**2211585**	3354821	3377404	**3387037**
medium	**1046152**	1045530	1042046	**2129243**	2117994	2113143	3182264	3197500	**3217737**
high	1041479	**1044387**	1041001	**2091892**	2080868	2081610	3128231	**3154354**	3145899

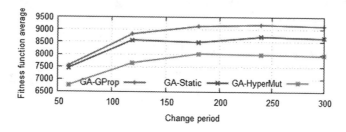

Fig. 1. Performance of the GA-HyperMut, GA-GProp and GA-Static algorithms obtained by average of the best fitness value found before each change in a scenario with level = medium, $\rho = 60$, HP = 0.6 and GP = 0.6.

means, 30 % of rate was the best configuration. Observing results related to medium level of changes, the best rate configurations were 30 % for $\rho = 30$, 30 % for $\rho = 60$ and 90 % for $\rho = 90$. Differently of GA-HyperMut, GA-GProp does not have a configuration that outperforms all of the others. However, a rate of 30 % achieved the best results in 4 of 9 possible cases, followed by 90 % rate with 3 and 60 % with 2.

In order to present the behavior of the approaches in a specific scenario, one with medium level of changes and $\rho = 60$ second was chose. According to previous Tables 3 and 2, in this scenario, an HP and GP rate of 30 % was obtained as the best results. Thus, these configurations from both AG-GProp and AG-HyperMut were selected to compare with GA-Static results. Figure 1 presents the comparison of the three algorithms through the average of best value of fitness obtained by 30 runs at each moment before of change. Such average is a adaptation of metric used in [7].

The graphic demonstrates that, in described scenario, GA-Static outperforms the GA-HyperMut, this is likely due the characteristic of hyper-mutation which starts with a high mutation rate and the ρ value could not be enough to the rate stabilisation. However, the GA-GProp overcomes GA-Static and GA-HyperMut. Given the analyses of AREA metric and the specific scenario shown at Fig. 1, we answered the RQ, concluding that the dynamic approach, named AG-GProp, outperforms the other ones. Due to space concerns, other results, instances and source code are available in supporting page of this work[2].

---

[2] http://goes.uece.br/vanessaveloso/dobp

5   Conclusions

The open source repositories are a natural dynamic environment, and, prioritizing the bugs is a complex task. Thus, knowing the characteristics of bugs may change, we have proposed a dynamic modelling to the bugs prioritization problem and applied three evolutionary techniques to solve it.

Through a preliminary empirical study we could notice that the static approach GA-Static outperformed a dynamic strategy (GA-HyperMut) based on Hyper-mutation principles. However, the dynamic evolutionary approach, GA-Gprop, based on Genetic Propagation strategy obtained the best performance.

As future work we intend to use other performance measures as best-error-before-change proposed by [9], to measure the the difference between the optimum value and the value of the best individual achieved before change; to implement other dynamic techniques and to compare them by statistical tests.

References

1. Harman, M.: The current state and future of search based software engineering. In: Future of Software Engineering, pp. 342–357. IEEE C. Society (2007)
2. Nguyen, T.T., Yang, S., Branke, J.: Evolutionary dynamic optimization: a survey of the state of the art. SEC **6**, 1–24 (2012)
3. Tonella, P., Susi, A., Palma, F.: Interactive requirements prioritization using a genetic algorithm. IST **55**(1), 173–187 (2013)
4. Wang, X., Jiang, X., Shi, H.: Prioritization of test scenarios using hybrid genetic algorithm based on uml activity diagram. In: Proceedings of the 6th IEEE ICSESS 2015, Beijing, China, 23–25 September 2015, pp. 854–857. IEEE (2015)
5. Dreyton, D., Araújo, A.A., Dantas, A., Freitas, Á., Souza, J.: Search-based bug report prioritization for kate editor bugs repository. In: Barros, M., Labiche, Y. (eds.) SSBSE 2015. LNCS, vol. 9275, pp. 295–300. Springer, Heidelberg (2015)
6. Kanwal, J., Maqbool, O.: Managing open bug repositories through bug report prioritization using SVMs. In Proceedings of the International Conference on Open-Source Systems and Technologies, Lahore, Pakistan, (2010)
7. Cobb, H.G.: An investigation into the use of hypermutation as an adaptive operator in genetic algorithms having continuous, time-dependent nonstationary environments. Technical report, DTIC Document (1990)
8. Basílio-Neto, A.D.: Planejamento de release baseado em otimização interativa através da formalização das preferências do tomador de decisão. Master thesis, Universidade Estadual do Ceará, Fortaleza (2016)
9. Trojanowski, K., Michalewicz, Z.: Searching for optima in non-stationary environments. In: Proceedings of the Congress on Evolutionary Computation, CEC 1999, vol. 3. IEEE (1999)

Author Index

Aburas, Ali   267
Adham, Manal   250
Aitken, Jonathan M.   238
Almenar, Francisco   218
Araújo, Allysson Allex   143, 291
Arcuri, Andrea   3

Botterweck, Goetz   274
Brevet, David   274
Bruce, Bobby R.   238
Busari, Saheed   250

Cabutto, Alessandro   159
Camilo-Junior, Celso G.   112
Ceccato, Mariano   159
Chen, Jianfeng   96
Cohen, Myra B.   128

Dantas, Altino   143, 291, 311
De Lucia, Andrea   64
De Roover, Coen   192
Dea, Troh Josselin   298
Di Nucci, Dario   64
Drake, John H.   244, 250
Dreyton, Duany   143

Eljuse, Basil   80
Esparcia-Alcázar, Anna I.   218

Falcarin, Paolo   159
Fraser, Gordon   3
Frezghi, Yosief Weldezghi   159

Gargantini, Angelo   49
Gay, Gregory   231
Geng, Jingyao   34
Grano, Giovanni   64
Groce, Alex   267
Guo, Junxia   34

Harman, Mark   18, 224

Jia, Yue   18, 224

Kapfhammer, Gregory M.   259
Krinke, Jens   18, 250

Langdon, William B.   224
Le Goues, Claire   112
Lee, Seongmin   211
Li, Zheng   34
Lim, Jinsuk   304
Liu, Yong   176

Martínez, Mirella   218
McMinn, Phil   259
Menzies, Tim   96
Mkaouer, Mohamed Wiem   281
Molderez, Tim   192

Nair, Vivek   96

Oliveira, Thiago   311
Oliveira, Vinicius Paulo L.   112
Oliveto, Rocco   64

Paixao, Matheus   250
Petke, Justyna   49, 224, 238

Radavelli, Marco   49
Ragkhitwetsagul, Chaiyong   250
Roque, Lucas   291
Rueda, Urko   218

Saber, Takfarinas   274
Saraiva, Raphael   143, 291
Scalabrino, Simone   64
Shang, Ying   176
Sohn, Jeongju   211
Souza, Eduardo F.D.   112
Souza, Jerffeson   143, 291, 311
Staicu, Cristian-Alexandru   159

Thianniwet, Thammasak   128
Turner, Andrew J.   244

Vavassori, Paolo   49
Veloso, Vanessa   311
Ventresque, Anthony   274

Walkinshaw, Neil   80
Wang, Weiwei   176

White, David R.   224, 244
Wu, Fan   18

Yoo, Shin   211, 304

Zhao, Ruilian   34, 176

Printed in the United States
By Bookmasters